BREAKING THE SHACKLES

REPRODUCTION RIGHTS

We offer you our blessings in your efforts to break out of the shackles of shame and to expand your being to include more of the awesome potential with which the creator has endowed each of us.

MPC-BEP Press

P. O. Box 259141

Madison, WI 53725-9141

http://www.shametojoy.com

Design: Kristyn Kalnes

Production Editor: Roan Kaufman

Library of Congress Cataloging-in-Publication Data

Breaking the Shackles: Bringing Joy Into Our Lives

Roy U. Schenk, John Everingham, Editors.

Includes bibliographical references.

ISBN 0961 13177-7-9

1. Shame 2. Men--Psychology 3. Joy   4. Masculinity (Psychology)

BREAKING THE SHACKLES

Bringing Joy Into Our Lives

Roy U. Schenk, Ph.D.
John Everingham, Ph.D.
Editors

With contributions by Robert Bly and Gershen Kaufman

Editors

Roy U. Schenk, Ph.D., is a writer, speaker, and theoretician concerning gender issues. He received a Ph.D. from Cornell University in 1954. Over the past three or more decades, he has been searching to understand the male condition. He has written three books on gender issues and is increasingly excited about the possibilities for positive transformation of male-female relationships. His mission is to create a world where love, acceptance, and joy are the norms. He continues living in and enjoying a committed relationship of two decades with Kathy Seifert. He is the father of 10 children, grandfather of 23, and great-grandfather of 9.

John Everingham, Ph.D., retired in 1997 as Associate Professor of Oral Biology at the University of Illinois at Chicago, where he was an award-winning teacher of histology. He earned his Ph.D. in anatomy at the University of Washington and holds B.A. and M.S. degrees in zoology. Dr. Everingham studied humanistic psychology and related subjects for 30 years, exploring his own existential predicament and sharing some of what he learned. A restless searcher, he sensed for many years that something essential was missing from his "curriculum," and at last discovered that for him the overlooked factor was internalized shame. He has been active in New Warrior programs since 1987, in recent years as a leader of Elders. His poem, "Rowing the Rio," explores whitewater rafting as a metaphor for the soul's journey and the importance of paradox. A divorced man, he has three adult children and three grandchildren. He may be contacted at 735 Michigan, Wilmette, IL 60091, 847-256-1799, or via e-mail at everjohn87@aol.com.

Table of Contents

Preface to the First Edition   vii
Roy U. Schenk and John Everingham

Preface to the Revised Edition   xii
Roy U. Schenk and John Everingham

Acknowledgements   xiv

Contributors   xv

Chapter 1   Some Basics about Shame   1
John Everingham

Chapter 2   Shame In Men's Lives   15
Roy U. Schenk

Chapter 3   Men's Shame   32
Gershen Kaufman

Chapter 4   Seven Sources of Men's Shame   48
Robert Bly

Chapter 5   Healing Internalized Shame   68
Gershen Kaufman and Robert Bly

Chapter 6   Men Facing Shame: A Healing Process   85
John Everingham

Chapter 7   Involving Men in Healing Their Wounds of Socialization   112
Compiled by Roy U. Schenk

Chapter 8   On Men, Guilt, and Shame   143
Francis Baumli

Chapter 9   Basic Male Shame   153
John Gagnon

Chapter 10   Male Initiation: Filling a Gap in Therapy   167
   Christopher Miller

Chapter 11   A Shame-Based Model for Recovery from Addiction   173
   George Lindall

Chapter 12   Grandiosity: The Shadow of Shame   183
   David L. Lindgren

Chapter 13   The Rescue Triangle: Shame Update   191
   John Everingham

Chapter 14   Forgiving The Unforgivable: Overcoming Abusive Parents   195
   John Giles

Chapter 15   Inadvertent Shaming: Family Rules and Shaming Habits   206
   John Everingham

Chapter 16   Men and Goodness   228
   Andre Heuer

Chapter 17   Men and Intimacy   234
   Patrick Dougherty

Chapter 18   Shame, Initiation, and the Culture of Initiated Masculinity 238
   Michael P. Greenwald

Chapter 19   From Shame to Self-Esteem   249
   Philip M. Powell

Chapter 20   Open Sesame: When Shame Turns to Gold   260
   John S. Guarnaschelli

Chapter 21   Shame: The Mother Wound   294
   David Shackleton

Chapter 22   Toward Epistemology Functional for the 21st Century   317
   John Everingham

Chapter 23   Vision for Transforming our World   322
   Roy U. Schenk

References   343

Index   350

Preface

To The First Edition

ROY U. SCHENK AND JOHN EVERINGHAM

Shame is a deflating feeling of personal worthlessness—like when you're suddenly laid off without explanation even though the company is doing well. You're hurting, and you feel there's nobody to blame but yourself. Yet *you can't for the life of you figure out what you did wrong.* "There must be something *wrong* with me, but what?"

This is Shame. Not guilt, but shame. You just want to disappear, or lie in bed, hoping to wake up and find out that it was only a dream. You have to keep active so you won't get depressed.

Maybe you watch sitcoms on television and feel edgy as the men all act like fools. Shame. Or you get caught peeking in a window at a girl undressing. Shame on you! You write a brilliant story on a friend's computer and forget to save it. You *know* you can never rewrite it as well. And you think, "Not again! How stupid can I get?" There's a war going on in your guts, and both sides are losing. Shame turns to discouragement, depression, and anger at yourself.

That's where this book comes in. You will learn here how to keep shame from overwhelming you. You won't eliminate all shame from your life; no man can do that. But you *can* learn how to handle it before it breaks you spirit or manifests as a major disease. Healing shame can be an exciting adventure, and it might even get to be fun.

Shame shapes, controls, and limits men's lives. It is men's most powerful negative affect. It drives men to war, to uncaring pollution, and to violence. If we men are to become whole human beings, we will have to understand, confront, and surmount the shame that now creates havoc in our lives.

Women also experience shame, and are deeply wounded by it. Both men's and women's lives are restricted by the use of shame to enforce gender roles and to control and manipulate us. David Ault (Seattle, WA) once pointed out that the shaming epithet "Tramp!" is used against both men and women to enforce gender roles.

But from birth, males are also subjected to another devastating shame message. It tells men, with almost hypnotic effect, that we should feel ashamed simply because we are male. Whatever we may call this message—The Shame of Maleness (Schenk) or Basic Male Shame (Gagnon) – it places us in a Catch-22 predicament. We are shamed when we deviate from our traditional gender roles, but shamed also when we conform to these same roles. The book explores the sources of this shaming.

It is no accident that men are greatly outnumbered among therapy and counseling clients. Not only must we surmount the shame of not being able to go it alone, but we also face a therapeutic format and mind-set that is often alien to men's style and mode of feeling, and is sometimes overtly hostile to masculinity.

It appears that socialization of females tends to develop fear in women, who account for more than 90 percent of clinical phobias. In contrast, many men develop a shame-driven, foolhardy fearlessness. Some may appear to be shameless, both uncaring and careless. We suspect that they really harbor a huge burden of shame inside, which is so painful that they fear to show any of it, even to themselves. Perhaps there is also a "shamelessness" that women manifest in relationships.

For centuries, shame was used in western culture to coerce both men and women into conformity with sex roles that were limiting at best, and frequently onerous. As women's liberation worked to free women from the shame of breaking long-enculturated taboos, it became almost standard practice to blame men for the origin and maintenance of these constraints. Now, a generation later, men are beginning the same liberation process, albeit in our own style. We, too, are sorely tempted to blame women for many of our constraints and the shaming that so powerfully maintains them. The editors view such blaming by either gender as profoundly counterproductive. We must all speak up to acknowledge our wounds, but to project blame onto others serves only to keep them festering.

Being human means that we're not perfect. We recognize that we may not always succeed in avoiding blaming.

Roy Schenk recounts that "this book was conceived as a way to examine, confront, and heal men's shame. Many techniques arose before their authors had a clear understanding that they were dealing with shame, but others grew out of this understanding and the internal predicament that underlies shame."

"I came to appreciate the impact of shame on men from a social and theoretical basis, and only with time began to understand the power of shame in my own life. My co-editor, Dr. John Everingham, came first to a recognition of the impact of shame on his own life, which later grew to an understanding of the pervasive role of shame in society." We think these contrasting approaches have contributed breadth, power, and a wider range of insights to this work.

John Everingham writes, "I, too, am a shame man. I didn't discover this until my middle years, and it dawned on me more slowly than Robert Bly recounts in Chapter 4. Like Robert, I felt great relief at the discovery. All of my life, I've had a strong sense of being seriously flawed. Despite twenty years of relentlessly exploring psychological and spiritual matters, the nature of this anomaly remained a mystery. It didn't seem to be anything that I had done wrong, but like something I was born with—my fate. What a relief it was to discover that it has a name—shame. And by this time (late 1987), the work of Schneider, Kaufman, Kurtz, Fossum and Mason, and others had revealed the outlines of the modern view of shame and had suggested healing methods. At last!"

"After vowing never again to go to a psychotherapist who didn't understand shame thoroughly, I became a client of Carl Schneider and later George Lindall. Both of these men helped me a great deal, but neither should be blamed for my blind spots. Other input comes from being a member of a 12-Step group, reading and listening to tapes, attending seminars and workshops, engaging in discussions with many of the authors cited, and interacting nonprofessionally with other men concerning personal shame."

We're proud of this book. The contributors share their experience with insight and passion. As editors, we have been moved or enlightened upon first reading a manuscript, and we have often felt that sense of relief that comes from new evidence that we are not alone in our wounding or dysfunction. We believe that this volume contains new approaches of considerable value to most therapists and counselors who wish to enhance their work with men. And to the large majority of readers in other lines of work we say, "Welcome, brothers. Enjoy!"

Our authors work in many professions, have a variety of concepts about human growth and change, and represent several "schools" of psychotherapeutic orientation. We come from various positions in the spectrum of men's liberation, including those who see themselves as non-aligned. Half of the chapter authors practice psychotherapy, and others work as a chemist, anatomist, poet, musician, lawyer, and psychologist. We all have advanced formal education, and roughly an equal number of us hold doctorate and masters degrees. Most of us lead experiential workshops for men or for both sexes, and many of us teach and write. We believe our most valid credential is that all of us are working on our personal shame issues and have made some substantial progress on this journey. Our writing grows out of our lives and experience, enriched by assimilation of the work of others.

We admire also those who contributed to the survey about why men don't seek help in therapy or self-help groups more often (Chapter 7). Their breadth and depth is impressive, and so is the wide range of life experience that they share with us. As our book nears completion, the editors feel a deep sense of fulfillment for our part in bringing the voices of these men to a wider audience.

The chapters fall into five broad categories. Chapters 1 through 6 are overviews on the nature of shame, its origins and sources, representations of shame in mythology and the arts, and a broad palette of healing techniques. Chapter 7 is a survey about why men don't make more use of therapy and self-help for emotional and behavior problems, and what might make such help more attractive to most men. In the next chapters, five psychotherapists describe innovations that they have found to be successful.

Chapters 13 through 17 are a collection of special topics relating to shame: the Rescue triangle, forgiveness, "rules" that maintain shaming among men, the goodness of men, and masculine intimacy. The final chapters contain our vision of how the world is changing as we heal toxic shame. They deal with men's initiation and the emerging culture of initiated masculinity, the rise of self-esteem as shame declines, improvements in epistemology, and the vision of a society in which pejorative judgment is out of place.

There are some biases in this book. Our chapter authors are mostly heterosexual white men, professional and upper middle class, but diverse in religious affiliation. At one point, we considered including chapters written by a woman and a clearly pro-feminist man, but didn't diligently pursue authors with these perspectives. John Giles's chapter on forgiveness, and Philip Powell's on the journey from shame to self-esteem, were both chosen for the excellence of their contents, not for the sexual orientation or race of the author.

One of our strengths is that we include authors who represent the men's rights, mythopoetic, men's initiation, 12-Step, and gay rights arms of contemporary men's liberation. We welcome and respect contributors with different experience, despite occasional disagreement. At first, our attitude toward pro-feminist men was less than welcoming, for we saw them, rightly or wrongly, as committed to blaming and shaming men, themselves included. Recently, we have gained respect for the honesty and passion of some of them, especially those who are leaders in the American Men's Studies Association. We welcome all to the joys of combating shame by facing it directly.

Another obvious bias is that our book is about men, and addressed to men. We deem it important to look specifically at the ways men are shamed, and the ways men heal shame. Both editors and many of our authors are unabashed advocates of men's liberation. We make little attempt to balance our presentation by including feminine points of view, and we're certainly not dispassionate. We aim for honesty, and maintain that passion is compatible with it. It's our belief that the dispassionate stance often conceals a multitude of conscious and unconscious biases, untenable tacit assumptions, and doubtful epistemology.

The standard of validity for information presented in most of this book is not the scientific method of control/measure/reproduce that is so well suited to the physical sciences. We most commonly communicate our personal experience, and invite readers to choose what they find useful or worthy of trying out for themselves. Our experience comes from dealing with both our personal shame and that of clients, and is integrated with intuition, reading, discussion, and the arts. Although we find most of the theory presented herein to be compelling and helpful, it is offered for exploration, not as generally accepted fact. The methods we suggest are designed to facilitate further work. As with most knowledge and theory, validation of these ideas will come from men discovering their value in their own lives. A broader context for evaluating knowledge about shame is presented in Chapter 22.

Our authors use a variety of styles, and we're not always scholarly in the classic sense. Please don't be fooled; we're thoroughly serious about our subject. Most of us use an informal, even conversational style, and some employ vulgarity. We planned it that way, for we value the emotional honesty often promoted by these styles.

Our aim is to speak to the hearts of men. We're not here to prove anything in the formal sense, or to win arguments. Our model of communication is to awaken a deep longing in the reader. Most of us assume that all men have a lust for healing, wholeness, and completeness—a drive to align with the world axis, the flow of the universe, the grace of God. Our styles are designed to touch this sense in the reader, and to be congruent with our true selves.

For brevity and directness, we have edited out many an "in my opinion," "I believe," and "in my experience." Readers may pencil these back in if they wish, and are invited to "translate" what we write into less—or more—vulgar language, as they choose. Nor should the book be seen as the definitive work on men's shame. It is a kind of progress report, written by men whose lives are in progress. We regard the field of shame as still in flux, unconsolidated; we're well advised to delay codification of concepts and terminology. We see ourselves in the most creative of times.

We invite you to join us in effective action impelled by our common urge for health and magnificence—the desire to narrow the gap between our true and false selves—and thereby align ourselves with the Divine, however defined. We want to speak to your heart, and convince you that healing shame is not only possible, but also well worth the effort. And you don't have to do it alone, for now there are plenty of buddies to join you for the trip.

Preface
To The Revised Edition

R O Y   U .   S C H E N K   A N D   J O H N   E V E R I N G H A M

Breaking the Shackles expresses the essence of what this book is all about. Our vision is to assist men to escape our shackles—the confining and often suffocating roles that we learned, unaware of alternatives, from infancy. We men have shouldered magnificently these roles and done them well. And we have paid an awesome price for doing so. This book is a revised and enhanced edition of our hardcover anthology, *Men Healing Shame* (Schenk & Everingham, 1995).

In recent decades, the array of feminine voices telling us how we must change has become a cacophony. But just as men cannot effectively tell women how to conduct themselves, women cannot prescribe for us. That's our responsibility. We hope this work will be a significant aid to men to transform their lives and to learn to fill them with love and joy.

Another reason for publishing a revised edition is to lower the price, and thereby make it much more available. Ironically, we have often felt ashamed about the cost of our book. More than once we've seen a man stiffen when he heard the price, after expressing enthusiastic interest in reading the work.

Most of the chapters remain essentially unchanged from the 1995 edition. We were blessed at having only a few typographic errors, and have corrected all we found. The editors have continued to consider and learn about the subject of shame and have made substantive alterations in Chapters 1, 2, 6, and 23. It would be surprising, indeed, if we had not learned anything additional in the last eight years. Chapters near the end of the book have been renumbered to accommodate new contributions and to make the former appendix into a regular chapter.

We welcome two new chapters. John Guarnaschelli (Chapter 20, Open Sesame: When Shame Turns to Gold) presents the moving history of his personal encounter with shame awareness. Using the story of Ali Baba and the Forty Thieves as an extended metaphor, he portrays the transformation of shame from dross to a noble metal, much as modern understanding suggests that medieval alchemy was more about spirit and psychology than about chemistry. David Shackleton (Chapter 21, Shame: The Mother Wound) leads us through his painful learning about how codependence and shame leave us feeling helpless by hiding our power. He then offers a model for claiming the power to transform our lives.

Recently, North American students of Carl Jung have begun to write about shame from their perspective. In 1998, Everingham attended a course on Shame and Shamelessness in Men presented by Dr. Arlo Compaan at the Jung Institute of Chicago. He learned of the work of several European Jungians who have been discussing shame with perception since the late 1980s.

How dated are discussions of shame in the 1995 edition? We doubt that the characteristics of shame have altered significantly. The most obvious change in the past eight years is that awareness of shame is much greater now. The Invisible Dragon has become a bit more visible, but if he were now generally apparent, we probably wouldn't need a new edition. And on the social front, many men seem to react strongly against acknowledging their own shame, so that we see both intense projection of shame and guilt onto public persons, and a craving to identify with those who succeed in portraying themselves as shameless.

The editors continue to be proud of this work. It has been heartwarming to be approached by men and thanked for the self-awareness and healing which reading the book has stimulated. Many have discovered valuable portions of their own lives portrayed in these pages. We hope you, our new readers, will find similar riches.

Acknowledgements

We express our great appreciation to Roan Kaufman, our production editor and pre- and post-marketing consultant for the Revised Edition. Special thanks also to Maret Thorpe for her expert editorial assistance in the difficult early process of organizing our thoughts. Kristyn Kalnes, our designer of the Revised Edition, deserves considerable thanks for her use of design and formatting skills.

We are grateful to those who read and critiqued chapter drafts; they include Dmitri Bilgere, Del Marshall, Rosalie Conner Sutcher, Howard Sutcher, Kathryn Seifert, Bob Everingham, Rich Zubaty, Tom Hytry, and Petra Ressler. We thank Don Wyeth for creation of cover art and jewel case inserts, Dmitri Bilgere for website setup, Jane DeLong for preparation of audio-tape transcripts, Tim Sonder for translating from DOS to Mac format, Barbara Hennings for proof-reading, Walter Greaves for computer graphics, Ken Everingham for help with dupli-cating and mailing, and Jill Hayworth for typing assistance at a crucial time. For the Revised Edition, Matt Smith wrote a summary of *From Age-ing to Sage-ing* which JE used in revis-ing Chapter 6.

Special appreciation goes to the authors of the chapters and to the many contributors to Chapter 7. Together, you have helped create a powerful book. We thank Bill Tucker, our edi-tor at Springer Publishing Company, for his assistance in the original edition, and our agent, Jane Jordan Browne, for her knowledge and skill concerning the promotional, legal, and financial aspects of our project.

John Everingham thanks Irwin Aloff, Ron Berg, Foster de la Houssaye, Tom Hytry, Steve Jaffe, Jules Kaplan, Dan Moricoli, Harvey Wigdor, Bill Power, John Perrin, Dave Lindgren, Mike Greenwald, David Iverson, and others of the Chicago #1 Integration Group. Heartfelt thanks also to Alan Fishman, Scott Goldstein, Alan Levin, Ed Ravine, Bill Reich, Peter Saxe, and Andy Simon of the Nov '97 VOH (Men's Room) group. And deep gratitude for two more mentors: Laurence Wragg and Christopher Miller. You all know for what.

Finally, Roy Schenk particularly acknowledges the ongoing support and caring of his partner, Kathryn Seifert, whose assistance and critiques were so valuable throughout this project, and also the many of people who have contributed by discussing and dialoging with him about his developing ideas.

Contributors

Robert Adler is author of the book, *Escaping the Job Rut: Losing the Misery and Finding Your Mission*. He was the first Texas participant in the New Warrior Training Adventure Weekend in June, 1989. Mr. Adler resides with his wife in Houston, Texas.

Irwin Aloff, a former professor, is a relationship counselor, seminar leader, and a facilitator. An active member of New Warrior Chicago and the Mentor's Action Network, he serves as a certified integration group facilitator and a Commissioned Ritual Elder. Irwin's mission is to share his wisdom, wounds, and wit to heal hearts and nurture healthy living relationships. His grandchildren give him great joy.

Dieter Ammann has been an executive with a large government agency and now owns his own firm, Pathways to People. He consults and presents workshops on management, communication, and team-building skills. Dieter is a graduate of the New Warrior and ABC trainings, has staffed New Warrior trainings, and has led integration groups. Married for many years, he has two adult children, a son and a daughter.

Asa Baber originated the MEN column in *Playboy* in 1982 wrote it until his death in 2003. He was the father of two sons, Jim and Brendan. He also served in the United States Marine Corps.

Francis Baumli, Ph.D., is a noted author on men's issues; his works have been published in *American Man, M. The Humanist, Asahi Shimbun*, and many other publications. Best known for his work as the Missouri representative for the Coalition of Free Men, he hosted the radio show, *Men Freeing Men* for several years and edited a book by the same name. He received his Ph.D. in philosophy from the University of Missouri-Columbia in 1976, has served on the faculties of several colleges and universities, and has pursued studies in counseling psychology and neurology. He has published widely in professional journals such as *The Philosophical Forum, Contemporary Philosophy*, and *International Studies in Philosophy*. He is married to Abbe Sudvarg, a physician with a specialty in family practice, and has two children, Dacia and Marion.

Dmitri Bilgere is a longtime activist in the men's movement. As a writer and seminar leader, Dmitri has come to see that men and women actually are more alike than they are different. His mission is to heal shame and to facilitate gender reconciliation by teaching the power of the shadow. He wrote *Beyond the Blame Game: Creating Compassion* and *Ending the Sex War in Your Life*, a how-to gender reconciliation guide. He has been facilitating the Shadow Work process and deep emotional work for more than 10 years.

Robert Bly is regarded by many as a prophet of men's awakening. Although he resists affiliation with specific organizations or schools of thought, his poetry, prose, conferences, public appearances, and audio/videotapes have been sources of inspiration for two decades, especially for those engaged in mythopoetic and men's initiation work. His prose poem, "Finding the Father," became a metaphor for our task in the early years, and his best-selling *Iron John* (Bly, 1990) opened the door to the joys of reclaimed masculinity for many thousands of men.

Born in 1926, Bly was educated at Harvard and the University of Iowa, and received a Fulbright Award for advanced study in Norway. His first book of poems, *Silence in the Snowy Fields*, appeared in 1962. He has since published approximately 40 books, including other volumes of poetry, as well as collections and translations of prose and poetry from an impressive variety of languages. Two of his recent books are *Eating the Honey of Words: New and Selected Poem* and *The Half-Finished Heaven*, translations of the best work of the Swedish poet, Tomas Transtromer.

Lawrence J. Diggs is a writer, producer, and lecturer on sociological, psychological, biological, and legal issues, especially those that uniquely impact men. He has created workshops, seminars, and radio and television programs whose theme is bringing true equality to gender issues. He wrote and produced the audiotape, "Introduction to Men's Issues," and has had 15 years of experience in broadcast and related arts in the U. S., Europe, and New Zealand. A 1987 graduate of Antioch University, he has extensive and rare knowledge of the microbiological process in the production of vinegar and wrote the unique study, *VINEGAR: The User Friendly, Standard Text, Reference and Guide to Appreciating, Making and Enjoying Vinegar* (Quiet Storm Trading Co., 1989).

Frank A. DiLallo has practiced individual, marital, family, and group counseling for the last 20 years. Mr. DiLallo is also the Pastoral Counselor for Central Catholic High School, of Toledo, Ohio, where he directs a counseling ministry for faculty, students, and their families. He holds a masters degree in counseling and is a Licensed Professional Counselor and a certified Chemical Dependency Counselor in Ohio.

Patrick Dougherty, MA, LP, is a licensed psychologist in private practice in St. Paul, Minnesota. He is a storyteller, writer, and adjunct faculty member at St. Mary's College of Minnesota. As an ex-Marine who fought in Vietnam, he uses his story-telling to speak of the complexities and ambiguities of war. His work, including several essays and professional articles dealing with men's issues, has been published in journals and books. He co-teaches a graduate counseling course entitled, *Working with Men in Psychotherapy.*

John Everingham, Ph.D., retired recently as Associate Professor of Oral Biology at the University of Illinois at Chicago, where he was an award-winning teacher of histology. He earned his Ph.D. in anatomy at the University of Washington and holds B.A. and M.S. degrees in zoology. Dr. Everingham studied humanistic psychology and related subjects for 30 years, exploring his own existential predicament and sharing some of what he learned. A restless searcher, he sensed for many years that something essential was missing from his "curriculum," and at last discovered that for him the overlooked factor was internalized shame. He has been active in New Warrior programs since 1987, in recent years as a leader of Elders. His poem, "Rowing the Rio," explores whitewater rafting as a metaphor for the soul's journey and the importance of paradox. A divorced man, he has three adult children and two grandchildren. He may be contacted at 735 Michigan, Wilmette, IL 60091, 847-256-1799, or via e-mail at everjohn87@aol.com.

John H. Gagnon, Ph.D., is a psychotherapist in private practice, working with adults, couples, and families. He received his doctorate in psychology from Union Institute in 1982. He has taught at the University of Connecticut and has lectured at Yale Medical School; he has written several technical articles and authored *Wounded Healer* (Ablex Press). He lives with his wife, El, who teaches history & English, and he has an adult daughter and son-in-law, Isabelle and Luke Johnson.

John Giles died August 22, 1996, of AIDS. In his last months, John was surrounded by his partner, family, and loving friends. He also finished a number of original musical compositions, and was able to hear them performed. We miss John and bless his memory.

Giles held Bachelor and Master of Music degrees from the University of Illinois, and advanced certification in musicology from the University of Michigan and in voice performance from Northwestern University. He served as Director of Music at the Unitarian Church of Evanston, Illinois, from 1981 until his death. Partially as a result of the spiritual journey described in this chapter, he was elevated to Lay Minister of Music in 1991.

A talented tenor, John was a regular chorister in the Chicago Lyric Opera Chorus for nearly a decade, and performed leading roles in opera houses and oratorio societies. Beginning in 1983, he composed numerous cantatas, choral works, and songs, and presented workshops on the "Healing Power of Music." John enjoyed swimming, cycling, reading histories, participating in politics, and spreading his message of healing to others.

Michael Greenwald, J.D., received his B.A. in Sociology and Anthropology from Swarthmore College in 1970, and his J.D. from George Washington University in 1976. From 1977 to 1989, and from 1991 to 1999, he served as a trial lawyer in private practice, representing businesses and individuals in all manner of disputes. From 1989 to 1991, he served as a mediator in private practice. In 1999, Mr. Greenwald left the practice of law to become an entrepreneur and business consultant. He lives on Lake Michigan near Chicago with his wife, Tracey Foreman, and their two Labrador retrievers.

Greenwald attended the New Warrior Training Adventure (NWTA) in April, 1987, and co-founded the New Warrior Network, now known as the Mankind Project. As one of seven cofounders, he contributed to the vision guiding the Network's growth, using his legal skills to build a safe and strong secular corporate structure. He participated in developing the curriculum of the NWTA and the leadership training programs. One of the senior men in the Mankind Project, he trains, mentors, and certifies leaders. Most recently, he spearheaded the effort to broaden the multicultural perspective of the Project. He was one of the first to recognize the significance of the initiatory function of the NWTA.

John S. Guarnaschelli, Ph.D., is Professor Emeritus, retired from Queensborough College of the City University of New York. He lives in New York City with Maria, his wife of 35 years. He has been engaged in the quest of his own Men's Work for 12 years, and is the founder and current director of ON THE COMMON GROUND, a non-organization for men in NYC. He particularly wants to thank both his wife and his friends, Michael McGarry and Justin Cordes, for their generous and irreplaceable support composing chapter 20, and would welcome discussion with anyone who wishes to talk further (at a reasonable hour!) about anything proposed in it.

Ian Harris, Ph.D., is a Professor of Educational Policy and Community Studies at the University of Wisconsin, Milwaukee, where he has taught a course on male identity since 1978. He has been an active participant in the Mankind Project, Milwaukee, a counselor at Batterers Anonymous, and is the author of the book, *Messages Men Hear: Constructing Masculinities.*

Andre Heuer, D.Min., M.A., LICSW, develops and teaches curricula in men's life skills and human sexuality, and has worked with men in adult correctional facilities. He is a psychotherapist in private practice in Minneapolis, Minnesota, and is well known for his workshops for men in the Twin Cities and in other locations. Dr. Heuer hosted a radio program that deals with men and their lives, and leads training workshops on interpersonal relationships for business and professional groups. He is involved in professional, educational, and pastoral ministry and conducts workshops and retreats for churches in spirituality, family life, and men's issues. He holds masters degrees in education and psychology, and his doctoral thesis focused on the effects of family, society, and the church on men's self-image and spirituality.

John Higgins, M.S., is a sales representative (independent contractor) in a publishing-related field. He holds Bachelor and Masters degrees in secondary education and library science, respectively. He first met his biological father at age 37 – a very positive and fulfilling decision/ experience. He regrets not doing it sooner. He has been happily married to his wife, Norma, for more than two decades.

Jack Kammer has been active in activities related to men's issues for many years. He was Executive Director of the National Congress for Men for 16 months. He conducted a talk show called *Men, Sex, and Power* at a Baltimore radio station for several years, and is the author of *Good Will toward Men: Women Talk Candidly about the Balance of Power between the Sexes* (St. Martin Press, 1993).

Gershen Kaufman was educated at Columbia University and received his Ph.D. in clinical psychology from the University of Rochester. Professor in the Counseling Center and Psychology Department at Michigan State University, he is the author of *Shame: The Power of Caring* (1992) and *The Psychology of Shame: Theory and Treatment of Shame-Based Syndromes* (1996). He is the co-author with Lev Raphael of *Dynamics of Power: Fighting Shame and Building Self-Esteem* (1991) and *Coming Out of Shame* (1996). With Lev Raphael and Pamela Espeland, he wrote *Stick up for Yourself! Every Kid's Guide to Personal Power and Positive Self-Esteem* (1999) and *Teacher's Guide to Stick Up for Yourself* (2000). (Complete citations are found in References.) He has lectured widely on the role of shame in personality, psychopathology, and psychotherapy, as well as its significance for gender, culture, and society.

Bill Kauth, M.A., is a visionary with great ability to get things done. He is a founder of the New Warrior Training Adventure weekend and The Mankind Project. For many years the Wisconsin organizer of the New Warrior Traing Adventure, his recent activities focus on global expansion of the work and on the creation of new and advanced experiences, such as the Inner King and Warrior-Monk trainings. His mission is to create a safe planet through empowering men.

George Lindall is a psychologist with NL Consulting in Minneapolis. His practice specializes in coaching executives about organizational performance. George also works with recovering addicts on intimacy and commitment issues.

David L. Lindgren, M.A., is a practicing psychotherapist, co-founder of the New Warrior Network (now The Mankind Project), and creator of a core curriculum for men.

Michael "Lovable Moose" prefers anonymity. He came to Windsor, Ontario, in 1964 to learn tool and die making, and now works as a Tooling Supervisor. Married in 1971, separated in 1996, and now divorced, he has two adult daughters.

Jim Lovestar has lived in Minneapolis, Minnesota, for many years, where he is an outstanding massage therapist. His mission is to touch the divine essence in all beings. Coming from a history of fear and mistrust toward men, he is committed to heal that within myself and to assist every man he encounters to trust himself and other men.

Christopher Miller earned his B.A. degree in psychology at Northwestern University and his Master of Divinity and Doctor of Ministry degrees at the Chicago Theological Seminary. He has extensive training in individual, marital, and family therapy, and has been an adjunct faculty member at the Chicago Theological Seminary. Currently, he is the director of a pastoral counseling center in Evanston, Illinois, where he lives with his wife and two daughters.

Bob Porter, M.S.W., has been an individual, marital, family, and group therapist since 1981, and is an instructor at the University of Wisconsin, Milwaukee. He has been facilitating men's groups and workshops since 1982.

Buddy S. Portugal is a psychotherapist in private practice and organizational consultant to corporations and businesses. He is co-creator of the Victories of the Heart weekend (formerly The Men's Room), and co-author of the book *Victories of the Heart* (Mark & Portugal, 1996).

Philip M. Powell, Ph.D., grew up in tough surroundings and has tried to help others who grew up in similar or even better circumstances. He feels for people. He earned his Ph.D. from the Committee on Human Development at the University of Chicago in 1981. He taught psychology at Yale University for 5 years, and for nearly 20 years was a professor in the Department of Educational Psychology, University of Texas, Austin. Since his retirement in 1996, Dr. Powell has been teaching English to gifted and talented 7th and 8th graders in Cedar Park, Texas. His 12 year old son, Kirby, attends the same school and is a member of the gifted program.

Al Ring, M.D., is a Clinical Professor of Pathology at the University of Illinois College of Medicine. He received his M.D. from the University of Michigan Medical School in 1958. He has conducted research in physiology, embryology, chemistry, and clinical pathology, and has published more than 40 articles and books on a variety of medical subjects, including anatomic and clinical pathology. Dr. Ring has received many honors and appointments in the medical field.

Roy U. Schenk, Ph.D., is trying mostly unsuccessfully to be retired. After a couple of decades of working as a chemist and biologist, he became committed to creating a joyful, peaceful world. He attempted to create an alternative, cooperative model business, but found that "progressives" refused to support his efforts because he refused to support privileged treatment for women. He then decided that society's acceptance of women's areas of presumed superiority prevented significant world betterment by creating shame in men for their persumed moral/"being" inferiorities. So he began challenging these beliefs and began developing a vision of how to attain a joyful, peaceful world. He is open to speaking, workshop presenting, and dialoging concerning his vision about transforming our world. He can be reached at (608) 255-4028, Fax (608) 251-0658, or less certainly at ruschenk@aol.com, or by letter to MPC-BEP Press, or his web site, http://www.worldpeaceseeker.org.

David Shackleton is a thinker, writer, and speaker on gender, a men's work leader, and editor/publisher of *Everyman: A Men's Journal*, the only Canadian magazine of the men's movement. He has dedicated his life to articulating and achieving the vision of real equality between men and women, and is writing a book about why the women's movement is so powerful under the banner of powerlessness. He may be contacted at PO Box 4617, Station E, Ottawa, ON, K1S 5H8, Canada, or via E-mail at editor@everyman.org; or the web site, http://www.everyman.org.

Rich Tosi lives in Michigan, is married to Char, and is the father of two sons. He was an officer in the Marine Corps, served in Viet Nam, and worked for many years as an engineer with General Motors. Tosi is a founder of the New Warrior Training Adventure, past president of the New Warrior Network, and continues to lead NWTA weekends in North America and other continents.

Tom Williamson, M.A., has worked with the Nassau County Department of Health, Office of Social work. He conducted a private inquiry for the New York Center for Men into why battered men do not seek help. He is the long-time president of the National Coalition of Free Men. Currently, Mr. Williamson is employed in the computer industry as a technical writer.

Chapter 1
Some Basics About Shame

JOHN EVERINGHAM

This chapter presents an overview of the editors' current views on shame.[1] Part of our purpose is to answer the natural question, "Why another book on shame?" Authors differ in the way terms are defined and in some of the basic concepts, as might be expected in an emerging field of inquiry. These basics may help to organize your comprehension. Should we disagree, the point of our divergence may be more accurately charted.

And disagree we will. It has been only a few years since the modern understanding of shame came bursting out of the closet into public consciousness. New awareness swirls about us like floodwater suddenly released from a century of impoundment behind the high dam of denial and mislabeling. We can expect things to be topsy-turvy for a while.

Students of shame often resemble the proverbial blind men describing an elephant. Accurate portrayal of some parts may overlook other vital regions. Lacking universal answers, we aim to share our experience and thought honestly, in masculine voice and viewpoint. Let's all keep a certain sense of freshness and wonder, being wary of overly cherished dogmas or the voices of "authority," old and new.

We see considerable reason to hope that a new synthesis – indeed a planet-saving synthesis – will emerge from our collective effort to understand and heal shame. Until then, take what you can use, and leave the rest.

1. *Shame is the "Invisible Dragon."* Shame is a powerful but often overlooked emotional force, whose widespread and pervasive effects have not been widely recognized until recently (my personal breakthrough came from Fossum & Mason, 1986). Many psychotherapists, psychologists, professors, and mental health professionals still seriously misunderstand shame. But thanks to the work of Schneider (1977), Kaufman (1980), Kurtz (1981), Fossum and Mason (1986), Bradshaw (1988), Miller (1981), Bly (1995), and many others, there are now thousands of us who *do* understand the basics, are working fruitfully to heal our own shame, and are applying what we're learning to the upgrading of our personal and social environment.

2. *Healing our shame offers hope for healing our world.* Men have for centuries been willing to die to maintain their honor – to avoid public and permanent shame. Behind our cool facades, we don't say "honor" or "shame" much these days, but we'll still do almost anything to avoid public humiliation, personal or national (Kaufman, 1992, pp. 227-241). "Anything" can mean vengeance, blaming, violence, war, struggle for control, compulsive overachievement, and denial in many forms. These tactics lessen the awful feeling of shame for a while, but drive it underground and make things worse in the long run. Such tactics cannot heal, and are as futile as giving a pacifier to a hungry baby.

   Gilligan (1997) studied the origin and maintenance of violence in male prison inmates, and writes that "[t]he emotion of shame is the primary or ultimate cause of all violence, whether toward others or toward the self" (p. 110). He further describes three preconditions that, along with shame, have to be met for violence to erupt. These are a lack of normal inhibitory feelings, a perception that there are no nonviolent means to ward off shame, and the keeping of a deeply guarded secret – that a man is acutely ashamed of feeling shame itself.

   And any Chicago drug dealer knows that "dissing" (disrespecting=shaming) is a natural prelude to violence.

   Shame is a natural emotion. There is no danger in openly feeling ashamed and saying so. The trouble comes when we're fiercely determined to *avoid* feeling shame, by burying or denying it. It's this buried, internalized shame that leads to violence, war, addiction, child abuse, emotional dishonesty, protracted feuds, a narrow "bottom line" mentality, and other evils. Since September 11, 2001, there has been much discussion of "Why do they hate us?" Yet, a major reason – shame and shaming – has been totally absent from any public discussion that I'm aware of. I suspect that unconscious shaming is much more toxic and powerful than shaming done with awareness and intent.

   Mastering the simple relationship between shame, honor and violence offers new hope for a peaceful and cherished planet.

3. *Understanding shame clarifies issues in the ongoing 'battle of the sexes.'* Kaufman and Raphael (1991) argue cogently that interpersonal shame cannot be healed until power is shared. We support equality and shared power, which are the birthright of us all. Underestimation of the "shame factor," by men and women alike, unfortunately has led to serious miscalculation of power equations.

Bilgere (1997) has written an entire book on this theme, and says that "there is still a long way to go before we are as conscious of the power socialized to women as we are now aware of the power socialized to men." (p. 50) Bilgere devotes several chapters to shame, differences in shaming power, and the interweaving of stereotypes with shame.

The goals for us all are to feel pride in our own sex and profound respect for the other. Much confusion arises from the false assumption that sexual asymmetry is the equivalent of inequality (Moore & Gillette, 1993b, pp. 21-30). It is still true, as Schenk (1991) says, that men have more power in the world of work, money and politics outside home and family – in the areas of "doing." But women wield more power in the arena of sex, nurturing, child rearing, and comfort – in the "being" areas. The considerable power of beauty, the breast, and the hearth are frequently overlooked today.

American men are particularly vulnerable to shaming, and often oblivious to its pervasive presence and effects. Both sexes engage in habitual shaming practices, unconsciously or regarding them as justifiable parlor games or "little white sins." Then we wonder at the rage and violence increasing in our land. Shaming men is never a "freebie," but rather a serious violation of both our honor and our inner spirituality.

We present this book primarily to raise men's consciousness, not to plead with women for understanding. Though rarely admitted, liberation movements usually harbor plenty of anger, insensitivity, intolerance, or outright contempt for outgroups. Our liberation strategy is to strengthen men, not to "civilize" women. As men experience bonding and initiation and learn to resist shaming personally, eyeball to eyeball, I predict that habitual shaming and semiconscious oppression will wither. Together we'll create safety for both sexes to heal and grow.

4. *Why deal only with men's shame, when much that we offer may apply to women as well?* We wanted to tell it like it is, for us, without being concerned with applicability or acceptability to women. We desire to speak in male voice, with the male mode of feeling (Bly and Meade, n.d.). When men separate from women and begin to talk of matters close to our heart, the tone changes. As we let go of trying to be sensitive, reasonable "nice guys," our language gets coarse and powerful – more

www.shametojoy.com

3

congruent with our bodies. It sounds honest and authentic. Even when the talk is gentle or vulnerable, there's a tone that I've never heard when women are around (Perry, 1985). We speak to men in this masculine tone.

Part of the atmosphere of shaming that envelops men today is the disparagement of our strong language. It's not only vulgarity, but also bluntness, directness, forcefulness, lack of euphemism, emotional congruence, telling it like it is, and greater concern for the honesty of the speaker than the hurt feelings of the hearer. When a man hears that this kind of talk is "inappropriate" to his present setting (classroom, mixed discussion group or workshop), the subvocal message is, "Don't be *truly* honest; adopt a false persona, because the real you is 'out of place' here." We choose to make a book where mantalk is not out of place.

I suspect that something is quite different about the way men and women experience, process, and seek to avoid shame. It's difficult to say what this supposed difference might be. The only distinction that seems clear is that women tend to be ashamed of their bodies, whereas we men are more ashamed of our feelings. I sense that I don't understand women's shame in some essential quality. When one relies so much on experience and intuition, he is well advised to stick close to matters of personal knowledge. Remember those *male* psychotherapists who wrote about women's supposed penis envy and Electra complexes (Gilligan, 1981). In addition to the wrong-headedness of drawing conclusions from a faulty epistemological paradigm about matters outside their own experience, these men played key roles in the long-time cover-up of mountains of sexual abuse and attendant internalized shame (Masson, 1984). Women's shame deserves its own specific treatment, and we hope that savvy and compassionate women are writing it even now.

5. *In its primary form, shame is an emotion with well-defined facial and other physical characteristics.* These include head down, eyes averted, blushing (Kaufman, 1989), sinking feeling, Sartre's shudder (Sartre, 1955, p. 222), and a compulsion to hide. Shame is one of the nine "primary affects" (Tompkins, 1987; Nathanson, 1994; Ekman & Davidson, 1994), based on findings of similar "faces" of shame in many cultures. Internally, the feeling of primary shame is distinctive, once we allow ourselves the time to really experience it. Recognition may be aided by permission to call it by name, and by realizing that shame is usually felt and expressed silently.

Primary shame is *not* destructive. It feels *awful*, but it doesn't do us any harm in itself. The trouble comes when we try to avoid this piercingly uncomfortable feeling, or make it go away – quickly. Typically, we allow ourselves to feel primary shame for only a few milliseconds, before shifting automatically to some other emotion, often fear or anger. This practice confuses recognition and tends to internalize the shame. It's a habit we need to break, because the resulting internalized shame is both destructive and dangerous (Kaufman, 1989).

6. *Internalized shame is a reaction to the* prospect *or* fear *of feeling ashamed – of feeling the primary emotion.* Internalized shame often has a frozen or hollow feeling, with eyes wary, brain hypervigilant, and face immobile. I may become inarticulate (Baumli, 1995) or have a desperate desire to hide, while being afraid (ashamed) to admit it. A man may act like a puppet, moving jerkily through the day with a mechanical smile, hoping that nobody will ask if something is wrong. We usually feel deeply ashamed of feeling ashamed and try to hide *that*. Like primary shame, internalized shame is felt and expressed in silence, but with our bodies more rigid and "playing possum."

As with primary shame, most of us develop strategies to try to avoid feeling or showing internalized shame. Suppressed emotions, being overly competitive, workaholism, taking anabolic steroids, unnecessary violence, and stylized tough talk (e.g., "Read my lips!") are some examples. This cover-up is aided both by poor recognition of internalized shame and by societal pressures to deny or disguise it – pressures *not* to see shame or to feel or talk about it. "Shame is a taboo feeling, especially for us so-called modern persons" (Hultberg, 1986, p. 158)

As we continue to avoid experiencing shame directly, we adopt a false self – a "front", a "persona," an "act." In time, we tend to forget that it's an act, and we believe it to be who we really are (Miller, 1981; Fossum & Mason, 1986; Bly 1995). But the disowned parts of the true self make their presence known through addiction, a sense of futility, grandiosity/depression swings, and feeling disconnected from ourselves and others.

Internalized shame is often described as more than an emotion – as a complex experience which involves feeling, behavior, and core beliefs (Potter-Efron & Potter-Efron, 1989). Without realizing it at the time, I came to the conclusion, deep down in my bones, that there was something terribly wrong with me. My head knew that it was irrational, but my body was even more certain of its truth. For some unknown reason, I just don't belong here; I'm an impostor. If only I can be perfect, or merely wonderful, maybe they won't notice and I can stay. This core belief, subconsciously held, reinforces the false self already created, and becomes part of the "experience" of shame internalized. Note that many, even most, emotions tend to be converted to anxiety and fear – fear of exposure.

Internalized shame starves the soul. Patrick Dougherty (1988) says, "Where shame is, God is not."

7. *Long-standing internalized shame develops into a shame-based identity* (Kaufman, 1989). This identity is a life pattern or "script" in which hidden shame is the central feature. It usually arises in childhood, when abuse, neglect, and shaming rules pile on more and more internalized shame. Synonyms for a shame-based identity

include "addiction to shame" (Bly, 1995), a "shame-bound" person or syndrome (Kaufman, 1989), tertiary shame, or a shame "racket."

The concept of a "racket" comes from Transactional Analysis (James & Jongeward, 1971, p. 189); it refers to a series of interactions that culminate in a man receiving his favorite emotional "payoff." The payoff is a painful but familiar feeling, which is preferred because it is somehow more acceptable than other emotions. By a combination of excessive people pleasing, withdrawal, grandiosity/depression swings, incompleteness, and passive-aggressive behavior, I managed to feel ashamed most of the time. Projects were unfinished, commitments unkept; and, despite lots of television and escape reading, I was usually "too busy" to spend much time nurturing or being nurtured, or just having fun. I felt chronic internalized shame – my favorite payoff. Shame rackets deserve to be recognized and named.

Shame may be an important element in *all* rackets, because of the feature of substituting emotions. The painful excitement of constant turmoil is a favorite payoff for some men who would be too ashamed to become depressed, or who can't afford it (i.e., won't face the shame of being an inadequate provider). Some may develop serious illness in order to quit the rat race and be cared for, finding a way out which preserves their honor.

"Simply making up a false personality to please our parents can generate shame for a lifetime" (Bly, 1990, p. 167). As internalized shame became a life pattern, I forgot that I ever *had* a true self, and saw it as a sign of my basic defectiveness that I even *wanted* anything other than what my parents or peers wanted. The Invisible Dragon feeds upon himself, and reproduces.

8. *Shame Flooding.* Sometimes shame breaks upon us like a tidal wave, and for a while we seem helpless to resist the strong emotional crosscurrents. The mind feels paralyzed; the will is focused on escape and yet judges all exit routes to be hopeless. We can't respond to friends who try to cheer us up, or who gently urge sweet reason upon us. Probably all three levels (primary, internalized, shame identity) are activated in a shame flood.

Underland-Rosow (1994) provides a vivid description of shame flooding and of the futility of trying to turn on the rational mind at this time. Urging reasonableness only adds more shame to the flood. Better to recognize the situation and activate empathy. I've found it helpful to say to myself or others, "I'm in a shame flood right now; I won't be able to … until it's over." Recognition, acceptance, and communication can head off the attending hopelessness and despair.

I suspect that some folks don't experience shame flooding, and others don't recognize it when it occurs. For the latter, Nathanson (1992, pp. 305-314, 336-359) may be useful.

9. *Internalized shame is maintained by a set of rules (blame, denial, incompleteness, perfectionism, etc.).* These rules govern our behavior by dictating habitual patterns of shaming actions (Fossum & Mason, 1986; Everingham, 1995d). To "kick" the bad habit of reinforcing shame in ourselves and others, we can learn to *break the rules.*

Shaming rules were first described by family therapists and referred to as "family rules." To keep families mired in internalized shame from generation to generation, they act like the inertia we studied in high school physics, in that the shame keeps going until some force stops it or alters its course. This was a breakthrough concept for me, for I saw that neither my parents nor I had done anything especially heinous; we had only followed unquestioningly the shaming patterns handed down to us as normal, correct behavior.

Shaming rules may be found in force in all human interactions, not just inside families. As we move to break the bad habit of shaming each other without really meaning to, a major bottleneck can be failing to recognize these rules or underestimating their effect on our friendships. Like the Invisible Dragon himself, shaming rules lose much of their power in the light of understanding.

10. *The Rescue Triangle* is another way of clarifying interactions that maintain internalized shame (Karpman, 1968; James & Jongeward, 1971). As players, we adopt one of three *manipulative* roles, Persecutor, Rescuer, or Victim.[2] As the "play" unfolds, the actors switch roles in dramatic fashion. Rescuers "help" by putting more energy into a Victim's problems than he does, then becoming the Victims of frustration and lack of appreciation, and finally Persecutors by kissing off the ingrate with a vengeance. In the modern sociopolitical "scene," we see those who struggle to maintain their superior Victim position in order to gain license to Persecute by blaming and shaming others with impunity. The Rescue triangle is the subject of chapter 13, and discussed also in chapters 14 and 15.

11. *Poisonous Pedagogy.* Alice Miller (1984, 1986) introduced this concept to cover a number of coordinated rules, prevalent in our culture, that come from the presumption that adults are right and children wrong. Poisonous pedagogy presumes that children should serve adults' emotional needs, and that children's impulses are bad and must be trained[3] out of them early – so that they "dare not notice" that a false self has been substituted for the true self. Once "trained," they become adults who perpetuate both poisonous pedagogy and their own deeply internalized shame, which they see as normal.

One result of poisonous pedagogy is a core belief that I need reforming in some way, or that I am dominated by disruptive or dangerous qualities which must somehow be held in check. Schoenbeck (1992) illuminates the important distinction between reformation and transformation. Transformation requires that a man accept himself as he is now, while reformation assumes that he needs to be altered in order to become acceptable. I feel a cleansing breath of fresh air whenever I contemplate this difference.

12. *Good news! It now appears that laymen, using simple techniques, can heal internalized shame substantially.* We encourage readers to begin healing this easy part on their own. It's not so complicated or mysterious, because much of shame's destructive power depends upon it remaining hidden or disguised. Now that the basic form of the Invisible Dragon is discerned, laymen and professionals alike are developing many new healing methods.

Some of these methods are tried and true, such as the 12-Step program pioneered by Alcoholics Anonymous (AA). Others are being invented and tested even as we write. We hope our book will be useful to ordinary men, as well as to professional psychotherapists. In one sense, it can be seen as a collection of recipes for healing internalized shame. Like any good cook, you'll undoubtedly want to add a dash of your own flavoring. We welcome diversity, since it is unlikely that any one recipe will suit all tastes.

Bringing primary shame out of the closet is a basic technique useful for defanging internalized shame. We learn to notice the shaming rules in operation (Everingham, 1995d), and stop playing our habitual "shame game." We can start to recognize primary shame and allow ourselves time to really feel it, rather than bailing out immediately into some other emotion. We can learn to avert our gaze, hang our head, blush, shudder, remain when we desire to flee, and then look a man in the eyes and say, "I feel ashamed."

But technique isn't everything. Healing even the easy part of shame requires commitment. And your personal healing will operate on its own timetable, difficult to predict and impossible to control. We bless your effort. (see Chapter 15)

13. *For men with a big burden of internalized shame, healing the difficult part is likely to take several years and require plenty of guts and persistence, as well as the help of a psychotherapist.* Don't try to work on shame with a therapist who doesn't grasp the modern concept and hasn't done substantial work on his own shame. I've had this experience, and it only added more confusion, internalized shame, and self-doubt.

Schneider (1977) has shown that philosophers (especially Nietzsche and Sartre) understood shame very clearly when the psychologists and therapists did not. Nathanson (1987) gives a candid account of one psychiatrist's "awakening" to shame issues after 20 years of practice. Although many psychotherapists now see the light, there are still others who remain unawakened. Ask a prospective therapist what he's doing to heal his own shame, and look into his eyes as he answers. For the man with a shame-based identity or other deep shame issues, a male therapist is strongly recommended.

14. *It's often beneficial to say "shame" and "I feel ashamed" – right out loud.* The sound of the word (perhaps the "shh" sound) somehow evokes the feeling for many of us, accurately and powerfully. The word itself lifts the emotion from its hiding places deep inside my body, in a way that "guilt," "low self-esteem" or "narcissism" cannot. At last, I've found a true name for my invisible, formless deformity!

We have enough trouble experiencing primary shame, without burying it again in euphemism. "Humiliated" feels strong and evocative, also, but not quite so fundamentally naked and exposed as "shamed."

15. *Let's draw from a variety of sources to deal with shame.* Books and tapes by the modern "shame authors" offer a great deal, and many are included in our references. Oral tradition, anthropology, mythology, and the arts have much to teach us about our basic emotional and spiritual issues. The mythopoetic and men's-initiation arms of Men's Lib make extensive use of these approaches and draw from them much that is innovative and valuable in healing shame.

It's wise to make use of our intuition, our experience, and *both* our cerebral hemispheres, despite the subtle shaming that their use has sometimes received from the health establishment. The 12-Step program of Alcoholics Anonymous, which emerged in the 1930s largely from the intuition and experience of desperate men and women, is now credited with employing techniques effective for healing shame (Fossum & Mason, 1986), and with reflecting a sophisticated existentialist philosophy (Kurtz, 1982). The AA founders hadn't read Sartre or Nietzsche, but were guided by their own intuition and honesty.

The best source of knowledge comes from the experience of healing one's own internalized shame. For understanding shame, there is no adequate substitute for immersion in that process.

All of us have blind spots. Here's a common occurrence: I approach a subject that contains unhealed personal shame. My discomfort grows, and my subconscious fear of exposure and shame propels me into some form of "approved" bullshit. I abandon the enlightenment and join the cover-up. Nobody is completely immune, so you're advised again to take whatever reinforces your own best instincts, and leave the rest.

16. *Is shame innate, or is it learned?* Most writers imply that it's learned, but I propose that it is *both*. Biology governs the primary emotion – the response to voice tone, shaming eyes, and other nonverbal signals – as well as the natural reaction to shaming acts based on the "family rules" which maintain shame. I regard these responses as deeply instinctual and embedded in our biopsychological "hard-wiring."[4] Kaufman (1989, pp. 32-35) portrays the infant's fundamental need to gaze into a smiling face and eyes and the shame that arises from the absence of such contact. Shame has been recognized in mammalian behavior since the time of Darwin (1872).

The *capacity* or *propensity* to internalize shame is also instinctual, in my view. Dogs slink away, tails between legs, in response to coded shaming behavior from both canine social superiors and human masters ("Bad dog!"). Young baboons cringe in response to a fierce look from an elder. It's not difficult to see that among social mammals, shaming is more efficient than beating the kids, especially in situations where survival depends upon timely social control. And some internalization (i.e., anticipating being shamed for certain acts) would make the social control more effective.

The learned part is what to be ashamed *of* or *about*. Shaming techniques and our response to them are seen as universal, but the specific acts or attitudes that bring down shaming upon us – these vary considerably in different families, ethnic groups, and cultures, and are certainly different for men and women. Kaufman (1995) reminds us how males are systematically shamed in contemporary America for some natural emotions and actions, and how boys learn the risk of being shamed by peers for things not shamed in the family.

Learned shame can be unlearned. In the safety of our support groups, we discover how to express our natural feelings without being shamed again. We learn to be emotionally authentic – to rage and love, hug and confront, curse and cry, and to sit silent and ashamed without being urged to stop feeling this basic emotion. We are regaining a vital element of our masculine heritage, however we may choose to contain these feelings in other settings.

Let the unlearning continue. It is time for us "enlightened, sensitive" men to resist further shaming of our natural aggressiveness, our powerful language, our masculine spirituality, and our rampant, thrusting sexuality. It's time to celebrate and bless our masculinity.

17. *Most European languages have two to seven nouns for shame* (Schneider, 1977), but English has only one. We have to use compounds, such as "internalized shame," "shame-bound," or "the shame of maleness" when we want to make important distinctions (Bly, 1995b). We take this to be a reflection of our blindness to the magnitude and complexity of shame, which, in turn, makes us more vulnera-

ble to its effects. Imagine what it would be like if we had 10 short, strong nouns that accurately connoted the concepts discussed above.

Meanwhile, we struggle along with the language we have. I consider toxic versus healthy shame (Bradshaw, 1988) and disgrace versus discretion shame (Schneider, 1977) to be useful conceptually, but they don't seem to fit easily into either primary or internalized shame, although they often require that the primary emotion be considered or visualized in advance.

18. *Shame is not all unhealthy.* Compaan (1997, p. 69) points out that "[w]e need some cultural images that present shame in its valued context" so that "the male ego would have a better chance of working with the shame affect and not collapsing into pain." Bertelsen (1996, p. 10) confesses, "I could not grasp this positive function [of shame] for several years of initiation into my 'shamenik' awareness, because I knew only excessive shame, what some have called 'toxic shame,' or 'pathological shame.'"

Bly (1995b) extols *aidos* shame, which might be translated as "awe" or "proper respect." Schneider (1977) points out the value of discretion in protecting our privacy and reducing social chaos. In addition to its function for social adaptation, Jacoby (1994, pp. 20-23, 102-106) sees shame as the guardian of human dignity and the process of individuation. For him, "[s]hame results from a conflict between the ego-ideal and the shadow... ."

Careful work may be needed to integrate these often conflicting functions (Hultberg, 1986). Frantz (1986, pp. 176-177) says, "Shame is the gristle we must chew on in order to integrate our shadow complex," and "Shame is the price we pay for becoming increasingly conscious human beings." For Hultberg (1986, p. 158), "[S]hame...may lead into the deepest layers of the psyche."

Compaan (1997) sees shame functioning between archetypal images of alienation and fusion; both attract us powerfully, but both extremes may lead to annihilation. So we use shame to warn us when we're living too close to either edge and as an emotional lubricant for the friction between these inherent parts.

Sociopaths may appear to be shameless, but I think they bury overwhelming shame down deep, beneath the "frozen over" surface. A few others, clearly not sociopaths, exhibit little shame awareness in their talk or body language. Lacking conscious experience of shame and showing no empathy for it, such folks can be world-class shamers.

Probably both groups use avoidance as the major strategy for coping with shame, as discussed by Nathanson (1992) and Compaan (1997). So another beneficial function of shame is to teach us empathy (Hultberg, 1986).

A few people may exhibit true shamelessness, which I think involves deep empathy for shame, probably arising from their own healing. In their presence, I feel safe and centered, rather than the edginess-without-grasping-why I usually feel with folks described in the previous paragraph. The distinction can be perceived in a moment.

19. *What's the relation of shame to guilt?* There are several views about this, with no one of them being clearly superior. If it becomes bothersome, I don't think the distinction is worth the trouble. There's general agreement that guilt is about the perception of *doing* something wrong, whereas shame is about the perception of *being* flawed and worthless. In this respect, shame is completely irrational or founded upon a defective premise (albeit no less powerful, as an emotional reality), whereas guilt may have elements of reasonableness. To some, guilt generates activity to restore the situation, whereas shame makes us frozen and withdrawn.

Kaufman contends that shame and guilt have the same facial characteristics, so they shouldn't be regarded as different primary affects. I agree. Because Kaufman believes that it's important to match emotions with their verbal labels, he sees guilt as a subdivision of shame – the shame felt in response to violating some agreed-on value.

Bradshaw, Fossum & Mason, and most other authors consider that the being/doing distinction is important in helping people to grasp an essential feature of shame – that irrational sense that somehow I am incurably unworthy. Their books list distinctions between shame and guilt; readers may find them helpful. To face shame, I think it's important to get a body "read" on that irrational feeling/assumption of unworthiness; any construct that facilitates this deserves to be honored for its teaching value.

Here are some additional considerations. Guilt may convert to shame when, publicly or privately, my actions are considered to reveal my essentially flawed nature. I may feel guilty when I've violated my own values, but ashamed when I've publicly violated someone else's values (even though I may pretend that they're my own).

Feeling guilty may cover other emotions that are more difficult to own or discuss (Perls, 1969, pp. 182-183). Hultberg (1986, pp. 163-166) says, "Shame means fear of complete desertion – not fear of physical death but of psychic annihilation." He also suggests that guilt may be a defense against shame, and vice versa. Peter wept bitterly after denying Jesus three times, "because he was utterly ashamed of the betrayal of his own integrity." To call it guilt, Hultberg writes, "expresses less the emotional condition of Peter than our culture's tendency to avoid deep shame through guilt."

Middleton-Moz (1990, pp. 53-65) uses "debilitating guilt" to name what sounds to me like "internalized shame." Redundant and inconsistent terminology often occurs in a new and growing field, and it helps to understand which terms are being used as synonyms. Above all, let's resist substituting a word or concept for the experience itself.

20. *Many of our authors use the word "Shadow" in its Jungian meaning.* The term may be capitalized or not, and used either as noun or adjective. It refers that part of ourselves that we try to keep hidden from our own awareness or from public view. Thus, the shadow "contains the hidden, repressed, and unfavorable (or nefarious) aspects of the personality" (Henderson, 1964, p. 118). When a man is unwilling to "own" his shadow, he usually projects it onto others, where it becomes "those qualities and impulses he denies in himself but can plainly see in other people – such things as egotism, mental laziness, and sloppiness; unreal fantasies, schemes, and plots; carelessness and cowardice, inordinate love of money and possessions" (von Franz, 1964, p. 168). The idea is that we all act out shadow parts daily, so we might as well start by giving up perfectionism, and by seeking to balance shadow and virtues "good enough." Robert Moore is fond of saying that the question is never *if,* but *how,* I'm acting out my shadow.

There is in me, as in every human, a killer, a self-righteous asshole, a liar, etc. These characters become much more troublesome when their existence is denied or projected. American political history for the last half-century seems to have been dominated by a desperate search for external "demons" on which to project our negative shadows (Bernstein, 1991; Keen, 1991).

The shadow may represent positive qualities that are disowned and projected. A man may keep his tenderness secreted in the shadow, and we often sadly keep our magnificence locked away as well, thus becoming tempted to excess hero worship. Little-used abilities are here, too. I was in middle age before I discovered the poet in my shadow, and now I welcome him into my internal circle of honor in the same way that I welcome the killer. Chapter 6 contains more about the necessary process of owning, welcoming, integrating, "eating" the shadow (Bly, 1988, pp. 27-43). This process is an important antidote to internalized shame because the *true* self is both recognized and blessed.

21. *"Until a man becomes secure in his masculine identity, he will remain a sado-masochist in his relationships with women."* Thus Moore and Gillette (1993b, p. 231) identify an important element in gender reconciliation, which we assume to be equally true for women as they relate to men. Greenwald (1995) sees the ability to claim the Shadow as a distinguishing characteristic of masculine maturity. In recent decades, we have been advised repeatedly to acknowledge our "feminine" qualities,

which are sometimes called the contrasexual, or the *anima*. Moore and Gillette (1993b, p. 223) warn that "integration of the personal Shadow solidifies the integrity of the Ego, and its achievement of a healthy psychosexual identity. Without a cohesive nuclear self, work with inner contrasexual structures can be confusing at best, and dangerous at worst." Thus, it appears that healing internalized shame is a necessary component of integrating one's Shadow, and that substantial experience in both are prerequisite to "forming a mature relationship with his inner feminine energies" (Moore & Gillette, 1993b, p. 224). Sadly, many men have tried to do it backwards, with unhappy results, considerable confusion, and additional shame. Self-doubt is the running mate of internalized shame (Erikson, 1963, pp. 251-254).

22. *With Jung (1983) and many others, I believe the restoration of balance to be the overall strategy for emotional/behavioral/spiritual healing.* Healthy balance may involve holding the tension of paradox (see chapter 6). This means that we honor as valid, each in its own right, matters usually seen as opposed to each other, such as love and hate. Dialectical processes have considerable value because they can heighten our awareness of precisely what it is that needs to be balanced. In this light, shame is both a dragon to be slain and a child to be embraced.

NOTES:

---

[1] Where opinion or a statement of value is in the "we" form, Schenk agrees with me; when they are in first person singular, Schenk disagrees or has no opinion. Both editors enjoy the dialectical tension of respectful disagreement, and hope that readers will join us in this.

[2] By convention, *manipulative* roles are capitalized; *legitimate* roles printed in lower case. See chapter 13, note 1.

[3] Miller's ironic use of the German, *Erziehung,* suggests the kind of pedagogy that dogs receive at obedience school.

[4] For evidence that many of our symbols and emotional/behavioral patterns are rooted in our biology, see Stevens (1983), and Moore & Gillette (1990).

Chapter 2
Shame In Men's Lives

ROY U. SCHENK

WHY ARE MEN LOCKED IN TO SELF-DESTRUCTIVE ROLES?

For many years, I struggled to understand why men seem so locked in to self-destructive gender roles. Men, for example, are disabled and killed on the job 12 times more often than women are. Men experience far more violent assaults that women do – 1.7 times more reported assaults, and who knows how many times more unreported assaults, because men generally feel that it is unmanly to report being assaulted. Men are killed violently 3.55 times more often than women are (U.S. Dept. of Justice, 1993). The list goes on and on. Why do men continue to accept such violence being done against them?

Having observed the behavior of male feminists, I concluded that these men have intense feelings of guilt, but this is not guilt associated with any specific behavior. They appear to feel guilt merely because they are male. Gradually, I came to realize that most, if not all, men feel this guilt. In my book, *The Other Side of the Coin* (Schenk, 1982), I called this phenomenon "male existential guilt."

Later, at a workshop I presented in Minneapolis, a participant pointed out to me that this "guilt for being male" is another name for shame. When I studied the literature about shame,

I recognized that this is, indeed, correct and changed the name of the phenomenon to the "Shame of Maleness" (Schenk, 1989).

This sense of shame that men experience simply because we are male appeared to be an intensely powerful force in men's lives. I finally concluded that this uniquely male sense of shame is the driving force that locks men in to their destructive roles. This shame seems to be as universal in men as is having a cock.

How does this shame come about? It is a response to the belief that one is defective and unlovable. Shame often appears to be an inherent response, manifested by both males and females, although men receive an added shaming message that women do not experience. Shame is probably the dominant negative affect, particularly for men. In this chapter, we will examine how this shame develops from its beginning.

When an infant is born, the first question asked is: "Is it a boy or a girl?" This is no accident. We simply do not know how to treat a child until we know what its sex is. And when we know the sex of the newborn infant, we immediately expect that a boy will show behavior that leads to achievement, such as toughness, strength, ability to take abuse, insensitivity to pain, and all the other features of the male gender role. We immediately expect that a girl will behave well, be sensitive and caring, and exhibit all the other traits of the female gender role. If we divide life into doing and being, we find that boys are expected to excel in doing, whereas girls are expected to excel in being.

We then enforce these expectations through the differing ways we treat children. For example, we treat boys more roughly and usually less frequently, and we tend to interpret boys' pain as anger. The enforcement of gender roles for both boys and girls is one of the most powerful, though largely unconscious, activities that we engage in as adults. When the growing child deviates from these gender role expectations, we make our disapproval very clear with a wide variety of shaming actions, attitudes, words, and expressions.

The word "tramp" exemplifies this shaming process. My friend David Ault pointed out to me that the word means the same thing whether applied to a male or to a female. It denotes a person who deviates from his or her expected gender roles. For a man, it involves failing to be an achiever. For a woman, it means failing to maintain moral superiority. The roles are different for the male and the female, but the shaming message is the same. Although there is increasing sensitivity to trying to reduce gender role enforcement in recent years, the expectations put on babies have not greatly diminished.

Men frequently tell me that never in their lives have they felt safe. When I ask about that, I find that the lack of safety has a moderate physical aspect, but mostly they are afraid of being shamed by criticism and being put down, ignored, or otherwise told that they are disapproved of. These shaming messages are experienced as so painful that children and adults learn to inhibit and repress their behavior in order to avoid further shaming. It appears to me that the pain of shame and the fear of experiencing more of it are the primary causes of inhibitions and repression of our natural abilities. For example, when I am singing a solo while other people are present, I am so afraid of making a mistake and being subject to shaming that I often make mistakes that I would not make if I were alone. In short, shame is the cause of shadow.

I don't recall the word shame being used in my childhood home. I assume it was; but it may have been just another of the childhood experiences I've locked out of my conscious memory. My mother ruled with an iron fist. I'm sure she had been raised this same way in her old German family and knew no other way to raise the ten of us children. I vividly remember the first time I used the expression "son of a bitch" at home. **"Don't you ever....!"** And I didn't!

We learned that anything related to sex was mortally sinful – dooming us to hell! When I started school, I soon learned that this included thinking about sex as well as words and actions. As a result, shame was an intense and painful companion of frequent, solid, and pro-longed erections in bed at night (that I was not supposed to notice!). I can also look back in anger and feel again the intense bodily tension of trying unsuccessfully not to think of sex while breeding our hogs. I didn't need physical wounds to make deep shame my constant companion. Sixty years later, the scars still remain.

MEN'S SECOND SOURCE OF SHAMING

In addition to the shaming that is used to enforce gender role expectations, males experience a second source of shaming. This involves shaming simply because we are male and creates a Catch-22 situation for men – we are damned if we do and damned if we don't. A little background will show us how this shaming occurs.

Because men are expected to excel in achievement, they are perceived as authorities on achievement. Men define an idealized men's achievement model as the norm or standard. Because it is an idealized achievement, no one, including men, can measure up. Men tend to feel ashamed of not measuring up. Because they know women don't measure up as well as men do, they see women as inferior, even while they do not see themselves as superior.

In recent decades, feminists have been successfully challenging this perception of female achievement inferiority. Unfortunately, feminists have tended to explain all differences between men and women as expressions of oppression of women, and they have, therefore, promoted women as victims. We will discuss this and the implications for male shame later. There is great pressure on men to measure up. This includes maintaining superiority over women in male gender roles, which is why a man feels so shameful when a woman bests him at an achievement-oriented task.

Because women are expected to excel in the "being" areas, they are perceived as the authorities in those areas. And because morality defines proper behavior, females also claim to be the authorities on morality. Women's authority also includes nurturing and maintaining relationships, attitudes, motives, spirituality, and values. Women define an idealized version of their own behavior and spheres of authority as the norm or the standard. Because it is an idealized behavior, no one, including women, can measure up. This causes some women to feel inferior about their behavior.

However, women see men's behavior as inferior to women's behavior; and women forcefully and perpetually teach men that they are inferior to women in areas of behavior and morality. Some women may have difficulty identifying their feelings of superiority even when they "know" that men are inferior. Women appear to need to maintain the belief in their moral superiority, and this creates great pressure on women to measure up. This explains why women find it so shameful to be seen as morally no better than a man, for example when they are called a whore or a slut. Feminist writer, Barbara Ehrenreich (2004) recently supported feminist columnist Mary Jo Malone who wrote: "Feminism taught me 30 years ago that…we were morally superior to men." After Abu Ghraib where women did much of the torturing, they said that they have some reservations about this teaching. It is interesting to finally read an open acknowledgment of what many of us men have been well aware of for a long time.

Women, also, are generally unwilling to discuss behavior issues with "inferior" males. After all, women are the authorities, so what can inferior men add? During the past 30 years, I have only once been invited to speak or have dialogue with a feminist group about male/female relationships, and the organizers had a "truth squad" of four people to challenge and put down everything I said. Just recently I was invited to speak at local campus group which is committed to presenting diverse ideas. The talk is now on hold because the group is unsure that they can permit a presentation which "challenges feminism".

Victim feminists often accuse me of being an extremist. This, I believe, is because I refuse to accept women's presumed moral authority and moral superiority and the privileged treatment they demand because of this presumed superiority. Instead, I believe that men must have an equal say as peers with women in a dialogue about what is appropriate or moral behavior. This is a seriously threatening idea for those who believe it is their responsibility to define moral standards and to articulate and uphold these standards. Additionally, I do indeed believe that men and women are equals, including being equally human. I believe that, being equally human, men and women are equally capable of doing wonderful things to each other; as well as equally capable of doing terrible things to each other.

The perceived moral superiority of women is not a new phenomenon. It was identified in the feminist Seneca Falls Declaration of 1848 (Schier, M., 1972) in the statement that "men accord to women moral superiority." This statement is interesting because it presumes that men had the power. Even then, feminists could not acknowledge that women are the ones who expect and demand moral superiority for themselves. After all, women are so morally superior that they, unlike inferior men, are "totally" committed to equality. However, as Alfred Adler found, superiorities and inferiorities develop together – so we can reasonably assume that the belief in women's moral superiority has existed for as long as the belief in male achievement superiority.

When we believe a person or group is inferior, we treat them as undeserving of fair treatment in those areas where we see them as inferior. This happens to racial minorities. It has happened to women in the achievement areas, and it happens equally to men in the behavior areas.

We accord privileged treatment to those we consider to be superior. Men open doors for women and put women first into life boats; women expect men to put the toilet seat down for them; men stand and offer chairs to women; women are given equal pay although they expect men to do the difficult, dirty, and dangerous aspects of the job (i.e., for less work). These are all examples of women being accorded privileged treatment because of their presumed behavioral/moral superiority. The imperial behavior of kings, the expectations by bosses that workers will defer to them, the racial biases against blacks – these all are a result of the expectation that superior people deserve privileged treatment, and inferior people do not deserve fair treatment.

One way we express men's presumed behavioral/moral inferiority socially is by greater criminalization of men's behavior, and then by further unfair treatment throughout the legal system. In 1994, men were arrested 4.6 times as often as women were. Men were then convicted of crimes 5.8 times as often as women were. Men were sentenced to prison 12.2 times more frequently than women were, and a man was more than 21 times as likely to occupy a prison cell as was a woman.

A black man, experiencing both the unfair treatment of sexism and racism, was more than 140 times as likely to be in prison as was a white woman. For identical crimes, a man will typically receive a sentence 1.5 times as long as that of a woman. And, although women are convicted of 14 percent of murders, less than 0.7 percent of prisoners executed for murder are women.

Women's presumed superiority in behavior/morality usually results in their receiving favored treatment in divorce and custody, as most men are aware from their own treatment or that of their male friends who have been divorced. A friend described to me a discussion in a state legislative committee recently where the female members stated openly that they saw no reason to make divorce laws fair for men.

Another result of women's presumed superiority in behavior and motives is that when a man hits a woman, he is seen as the bad guy, whereas when a woman hits a man, he is also seen as the bad guy – because it is assumed that women are morally better and so would not hit the man unless he "deserved it." The same attitude is evident when one spouse kills the other. Because women are seen as victims, the man is the bad guy whether he kills or is killed. Seeing women as victims is another expression of the belief that men are perpetrators and morally inferior, because victims are perceived to be morally superior to perpetrators.

In fact, whenever we define people by some specific attribute, whether it be rapist, perpetrator, victim, murderer, welfare mother, angel, hunk, etc., we dehumanize them. Dehumanizing someone in a negative way is another way of shaming that person. Male bashing in the media is an organized, though largely subconscious, way of dehumanizing all men.

It is argued that men control morality, because in most religions, men are the preachers of morality. But children learn morality by the time they are three to five years old, a period when children are typically under the tutelage of their mothers. Men, I believe, usually preach the morality they learned from their mothers. And over the millennia, women have gradually created a morality that is the codification of women's self interest.

Additionally, the male preacher typically puts on a robe – a kind of dress – and symbolically becomes a woman before he begins to speak. And when one partner takes another to church, it is usually the woman dragging the man along so he can get the proper (i.e., female) morality preached to him. Most of the sins preached against are male activities. If there is any doubt that women are favored by traditional religions, these doubts can be laid to rest simply by counting the numbers of men and women attending the services. Women usually far outnumber men. Churches are rarely congenial places for men.

If we are going to heal shame and attain equality between men and women, it is important for men to identify and to honor their own morality. In our society today, men's morality is more likely to be articulated in the local taverns than in churches, which is probably one reason why churches rail against taverns so intensely. Unfortunately, women now seem to be taking over tavern morality as well!

In the past, male morality was articulated on the job; but sexual harassment laws have been displacing it with female morality. If these laws were truly designed to combat sexual harassment, they would also ban the sexual harassment that women typically visit on men. Because men live in a sexual desert (Schenk, 1982), every time a woman calls attention to her sexuality on the job, she is sexually harassing every man in her workplace. But because the real purpose of sexual harassment laws is to enforce the presumably superior morality of women and to punish men, this ubiquitous harassment is ignored.

What men learn from having women define morality – and thereby define women's behavior as good and right behavior – is that men's behavior is bad; particularly when it is different from women's behavior or does not benefit women. Even when men's and women's behavior are the same, men's behavior can still be seen as bad because men's motives are presumed to be inferior to those of women.

Boys quickly learn the message that they are bad. For example, 90 percent of punishments doled out in schools are given to boys. They come to believe that they are defective because they are male; and, if defective, then unlovable. This sense of being defective and unlovable is what triggers shame just for being male. This, then, is *THE SHAME OF MALENESS*. It is the added shaming message that males learn from a very young age. Dr. John Gagnon, who discovered this phenomenon independently, calls it *BASIC MALE SHAME*. (See his chapter later in this book.) Boys are "into" over-achievement by the time they are three years old; and over-achievement is a shame response. Male children learn Shame, including The Shame of Maleness, very early and very well.

The importance of this extensive discussion about male/female superiority/inferiority when discussing healing men's shame is this: In order to heal shame, as with any disease, understanding the source or cause can be very helpful. The source of The Shame of Maleness is the societal belief, learned very early by boys, that males are inferior to women in the areas of behavior and morality. This means that **healing shame requires equality** – equality between men and women, between races, and between all groups of people.

A LOOK AT THE DARK SIDE

Male and female inferiority feelings set up a vicious circle that I call The Dark Side of Male-Female Relationships. This is shown in Figure 2-1.

Because this is a circle, one can jump in anywhere. Feminists have alerted us to half of the circle, so it seems reasonable to start there; specifically, with men's presumed Doing or Achievement Superiority, in which men's judgements about politics, economics and achievement are considered to be superior to women's. This induces us to perceive women as inferior in Doing or Achievement. In tandem with these feelings of inferiority, women also develop excessive fears and feelings of incompetence. Alfred Adler pointed out almost 100 years ago that when a person believes a message that s/he is inferior, that person has a driven psychological need to **compensate** in some way for those inferiority feelings (Ansbacher and Ansbacher, 1956). A person can compensate in many different ways. One is to go to the extreme in behavior. For an "achievement inferior" woman, going to the extreme involves becoming the totally helpless, super-feminine woman.

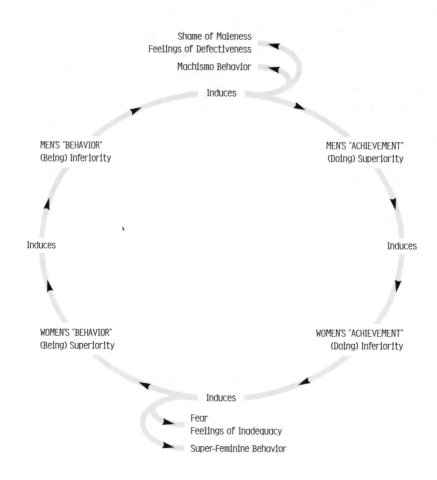

Figure 2.1 The Dark Side of Male-Female Relationships

A second response, probably the most common form of compensation, is to develop one's own area of perceived superiority. For women, this involves developing a belief in women's Being or Behavior/Morality Superiority, in which women's judgments about morality, values and feelings are considered to be superior to men's. Women teach this to their children, boys and girls alike. This teaching is usually not done consciously; it is just an inherent belief of our culture. Infant boys learn this message and compensate for these inferiority feelings. Boys (and men) who feel morally inferior also feel defective and unlovable and, therefore, are ashamed of being male – again demonstrating the Shame of Maleness.

Yet another response is to go to the extreme of the machismo response. In effect, the male says, "You think I'm bad? You haven't seen anything yet! I'll show you what bad is! I'll destroy the world." And, indeed, war and mindless pollution are responses to these inferiority and shame feelings in males. George W. Bush's behavior is an example of this.

Men who feel behaviorally inferior also develop their own area of perceived superiority, "Doing" or "Achievement" superiority. And so we have completed the vicious circle.

Because women's superiority is seen as a behavior/morality superiority, women's behavior is seen as good behavior. So the tendency is to blame men rather than to realize that what is actually occurring is a dance, a co-dependent interplay, between men and women, with members of both genders wounding members of the other in an ongoing cycle. Actually it is a vicious spiral. The superiorities, particularly our belief in women's moral superiority, have been increasing until their continuation is threatening life on earth. See David Shackleton's Chapter in this book for more detail.

More and more, men are being defined as bad, as evil, as to blame, as the cause of all evil. The near-unanimous passage of the Violence against Women Act by the U.S. Congress (1994; reaffirmed in 1998) is one significant result of this belief. This act defines violence against women as being more deserving of punishment than is violence against men; and declares that stopping violence against women has a higher priority than does stopping violence against men, although men experience more than 1.5 times as much criminal violence as women do. The act might better be titled the Sexist Bigotry Act. I believe it represents the most bigoted legislation passed by Congress since before the Civil War.

If one were to take the same legislation and substitute "White People" for "Women," the bigotry involved would be more readily apparent. A Violence Against White People Act whose purpose would be to provide safe streets, campuses, and homes for white people, although minorities experience 1.4 times as much criminal violence as whites do, would be recognized immediately as racist bigotry and would not be tolerated. Yet few people recognize the bigotry against all males in the law as it is now written; and a great many people, both men and women, seem to believe that a Violence Against Women law is appropriate.

Why is this so? Joseph Campbell (1988) speaks a great deal about societal myths. He points out that a myth is a societal belief that is accepted as the truth. As long as it is accepted as true, the myth is invisible and remains unchallenged.

Although many people insist that our society lacks myths; in actuality we have many myths, including two very powerful myths regarding men and women. One of these myths has been challenged in recent years; the other has only grown stronger. The challenged myth is the belief that men are the achievers, and the unchallenged myth is the belief that women are the humanizers who define behavior and morality.

Thus, the former president of the Madison Equal Opportunities Commission was quoted approvingly when she recently stated that "everyone needs to work together to improve humanity, and I believe women have special skills and insights in that area." If you fail to see the sexist stereotyping in that sentence, try: "…I believe white people have special skills and insights in that area." Unfortunately, even today, positive stereotypes about women and negative stereotypes about men too often continue to be accepted as true.

Because the myth of women's moral superiority is accepted so completely and unquestioningly, women are presumed to deserve privileged treatment, and Congressmen are afraid to vote against any legislation put forth by victim feminists, including the Violence Against Women Act.

Because men are defined as the achievers, men have intense pressure put on them to achieve, whereas women were impeded and shamed when they strove to achieve. Not surprisingly, with men's achievement being the standard, women did not achieve as well as men did. This has been challenged in recent years, and women are gaining in the achievement area. In some ways, women have already advanced beyond men – for example, more than 50 percent of people enrolled in colleges today are women and over 50% of middle management positions are held by women.. Defined as the behavers, the moral ones, women have been pushed to define and conform to "higher standards" of behavior, sometimes called double standards; while men were impeded and shamed when they strove to develop skills in relationships, nurturing, etc. Because women's behavior is the standard in those endeavors, men do not seem to behave as well as women do.

At this point, it seems appropriate to point out that there are no absolute superiorities or inferiorities. Superiorities and inferiorities are simply expressions of a society's choices and definitions. If two runners run a mile and one completes the mile in four minutes while the other takes six minutes but runs far more gracefully, a decision as to which is the superior runner would be determined by whether the society values speed more or whether gracefulness is more valued.

Since we can choose to assign superiorities and inferiorities, it is equally important to recognize that we can also choose **not to assign superiorities and inferiorities**. Indeed, *this is an essential key to the healing of shame*. We can simply accept people as different and celebrate those differences.

Shame is based on being judged on the basis of superiority/inferiority, better or worse, good or evil; and accepting that negative judgment. Even when a person is judged better in a specific experience, behavior, characteristic, etc., the person still receives the message that he or she is at risk; that at another time he or she may well be judged to be inferior, defective, bad. This judging, blaming, and shaming, and the fear of experiencing it are at the root of our shame-based society.

Inferiority feelings and the resulting shame and fear of being shamed are also the root cause of war, of mindless pollution, of the viciousness expressed between men and women and between different (read better/worse) groups, whether based on ethnicity, religion, gender, or national origin. In his book, *Violence, Reflections on a National Epidemic* (1998), James Gilligan emphasized that "the only way to prevent (physical) violence is to stop shaming." What Gilligan failed to recognize is that shaming itself is violence.

Many religions speak of Original Sin, a defect that fundamentally damages human beings. I am convinced that inferiority feelings and the resulting shame and fear of being shamed are that Original Sin! In other words, we create our own Original Sin by judging others – and teaching others to judge – based on inferior/superior, good/evil, and so forth.

OUR CURRENT PLANE OF EXISTENCE

Years ago I defined my mission as to help promote world peace by creating sexual equality. In a discussion about this with my friend, Karl Larson, he said that he visualized equality as a fine line. This made immediate sense to me. If we choose to judge people and thereby divide them between good and evil, superior and inferior, etc., then we have superior and good on one side, and inferior and evil on the other side, separated by this very fine line of equality. This is depicted in Figure 2-2. What struck me was that there is no way everybody can stand on that line of equality; and even if we tried, we would be overlapping onto one or both sides of the line. I realized then that we cannot achieve equality as long as we operate in this mind-set, this plane of judging people. We need to develop a new plane of existence—a new world view or paradigm. I will discuss this in my final chapter.

MANIFESTATIONS OF MEN'S SHAME

The Shame of Maleness can be seen as a response to what John Everingham calls the tenth shaming rule - Moral Intimidation. As I understand it, this shame is a result of the dominance of women's input into the socialization process, and of the claiming of the moral high ground by women, perhaps inevitably at present because women still do most of the socializing. It is not surprising that women teach children that women's behavior, including attitudes, values, nurturing, and motives, are correct or good. Boys learn that their behavior, inevitably deviating from women's behavior, is evil, and as males they are inferior and defective, and, thus, unlovable. This is the fundamental cause of shame.

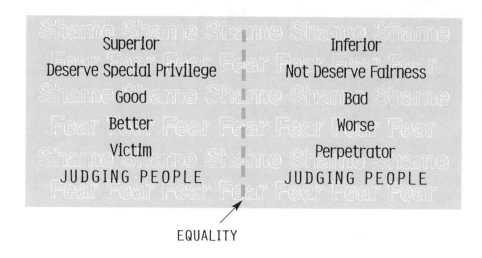

Superior	Inferior
Deserve Special Privilege	Not Deserve Fairness
Good	Bad
Better	Worse
Victim	Perpetrator
JUDGING PEOPLE	JUDGING PEOPLE

EQUALITY

Figure 2.2   Fine Line of Equality

Other manifestations of The Shame of Maleness include:

- homophobia;
- hiding one's financial worth and income;
- capitulation to women's manipulation;
- inability to criticize women's negative behavior, and panic when around men who do criticize women's negative behavior;
- acceptance of societal abuse, treating women as "ladies" (i.e., as morally superior);
- physical battering of women;
- machismo strutting;
- avoidance of intimacy;
- inability to defend boundaries from invasion by women; and
- withdrawal when attacked by a woman.

VIOLENCE: SHAME IN ACTION

Violence is a manifestation of the belief that another person is inferior, is subhuman in some way, and is not worthy of being accorded dignity, respect, and fair treatment. Violence is shaming in action. When a person has violence done to them, the experience is demeaning. It conveys the message that s/he is inferior and is defective and unlovable, and this induces shame feelings. It also triggers compensatory responses, including superiority feelings that lead to doing violence to others who are seen as inferior. So violence and shaming tend to be cyclical.

Not all violence is physical; most violence probably is not. Some of the most intense expressions of violence are verbal and psychological. Murray Straus (1993), world authority on domestic violence, asserted that: "Verbal aggression may be even more damaging than being the victim of physical attacks. One can hurt a partner deeply – even drive them to suicide – without ever lifting a finger." A person can also be driven to murder. Any demeaning word, expression, or action can be a form of violence, including any judgment that a person or group is inferior.

Theologian Langdon Gilkey (1966), wrote of "that sharpest of all hostilities of one human being to another – that non acceptance which springs from moral disapproval and so from a feeling of moral superiority." What I think Gilkey is saying is that **an attitude of moral superiority**, of seeing others as morally inferior, **is the most intense form of violence one person can do to another**. I suspect this is close to reality.

I recall an occasion when an associate and I visited a woman whose "abusive" husband had recently left her. She put down her husband continually and depicted herself as so superior and above him that she would not even condescend to discuss issues with him. I soon realized that if I lived with her even a couple of weeks, I would probably end up being physically violent in response to her intense and ongoing verbal and psychological violence. Her behavior typifies women's beliefs in their moral superiority to us men. This means that men live in an environment of violence and shame. In contrast, women appear to live mainly in an environment of fear.

It is important to recognize the violence involved in viewing others as inferior and not deserving fair treatment. It is especially important to recognize the intensity of the violence we do to others by seeing them as morally inferior.

It is often claimed that men are more violent than women are. This implies that men are inferior, subhuman, and deserving of punishment and incarceration. When we restrict our concerns to physical violence, this argument works because men are more likely to respond to violence with physical violence, or at least to do more physical harm.

However, when we realize that other forms of violence, including emotional and psychological violence, and particularly attitudes of moral superiority, are severe forms of violence and that women regularly inflict these other kinds of violence on men, we see that there is a balance in the violence done between men and women. Consequently, men do not need to feel ashamed for being more violent and so morally inferior to women.

Instead, men can begin to abandon The Shame of Maleness. As we heal The Shame of Maleness, we can also begin to confront the shaming messages we have been given about failing to live up to our gender roles and other shaming messages associated with past "imperfect" behavior.

IS SHAMING NECESSARY?

I realize that Gershen Kaufman (see chapter in this book), Carl Schneider (1977), and most other authorities on shame maintain that there are some forms of shame that are good or, at least, beneficial. Their argument is that we need to learn that we are fallible and imperfect, and this discovery of our imperfection creates in us feelings of shame and a sense that we are defective.

At the risk of challenging those who clearly are more knowledgeable than I am, I do firmly believe that shame is not a necessary part of this process. We can start from birth to teach children that as human beings we are limited and so cannot see the whole picture. Therefore we will make mistakes; but making mistakes does not in any way make us defective or unlovable. With this teaching, it seems to me that shame should not develop. To the extent that we are able to accept people's mistakes as being part of their being, as part of themselves, and to the extent that we accept them along with (not in spite of) their mistakes, I see no reason why shame should develop.

The argument has been made that a "shameless person" is very dangerous because he or she is not repressed by the fear of feeling ashamed. But the shameless person in that situation is someone who has experienced so much and such intense shaming that he or she has repressed shame feelings as a survival response. I suggest that there is the possibility of a shameless person at the other end of the spectrum – one who has not been repressed by shaming messages and who has not lost the excitement, enthusiasm, and joy of childhood. Perhaps this is an idealized vision, but it is the vision I propose that we pursue.

The disintegration of social inhibitions and the increasing violence in our culture certainly support the need to help children learn appropriate social values such as treating others with care, respect and compassion. Yet I have the sense that the decline in the acquisition of social values has accompanied an increase, rather than a decrease, in shaming, and accompanies a decrease in self-acceptance. If shaming is the necessary force needed to instill social values, this is the opposite of what one would expect, and it argues that shaming contributes to the increasing violence.

In our shame-based culture, we tend to reject people because they make mistakes and are imperfect. The more imperfection we see by our standards, the more rejection we project. This is what is currently happening in our society – more shaming and blaming as the social fabric unravels. I personally believe that the shaming and the blaming are causing the disintegration. I believe this is the force that is filling our prisons as we see a quadrupling of the number of men in prison in the past 20 years. We already have almost twice as many men in prison as any other civilized nation, and the incarceration rate continues to increase. Hopefully state and federal budget deficits may reverse this horror.

THE MEN'S MOVEMENT

Men experience intense abuse in our society; but because of The Shame of Maleness, they tend to feel that they deserve the abuse. It is very hard to fight against what you think you deserve; and, for the most part, men don't. This is one good reason why there has never been an effective men's movement.

Over the past several decades, a tentative and sporadic men's rights movement has developed to meet the needs of men who have experienced such intense abuse from the social system that they have finally rebelled against it. Most of these groups are concerned with fathering issues, because it is through divorce that many men become conscious of society's intense bias against males. These men's rights groups then attract other men who are being intensely abused by the system. But, generally, when these men resolve or learn to live with the abuses, they tend to drop out of the groups. This is a result of the shame-induced belief that we deserve the bad things that happen to us because we men are defective human beings. Those who do not drop out are usually motivated by rage at the abuse that they and others have received from society.

A need to control is yet another shame-induced behavior that has resulted in the formation of hundreds of little "national" men's rights groups that are generally focused around the efforts of one outraged man. It seems that almost every time a man becomes outraged at how the system abuses him as a male – generally discovered at divorce – he goes out and starts up another national men's organization. Even Evansville, Wisconsin, population 2,800, had its own national men's organization for a few years. I've just heard rumors that a new national men's organization may have begun there again. Evidently, men's shame-based need to control prevents these small groups from uniting into a powerful national organization, and attempts to achieve such unity have failed regularly over the decades.

In recent years, Robert Bly has triggered a new component of the men's movement – what Shepherd Bliss has named the Mythopoetic Men's Movement. Bly has proposed that the absence of men's fathers from the home since the Industrial Revolution has denied men the role models they need to know how to be men, and this absence has seriously wounded men. In addition, the absence of older men in the lives of younger men has denied adolescent males the opportunity to have an initiation ritual into manhood. Acquisition of a driver's license may be the closest thing to such an initiation ritual in our society today. (Adolescent females have menstruation as a form of natural initiation that males lack.) I personally believe that the industrial revolution only exacerbated an existing disease, The Shame of Maleness, which has been around for many thousands of years.

Most of the "wildmen weekends" that have sprung up in response to Bly's identification of the father loss have focused on providing some form of initiation. In addition, they strive to help

IMPENETRABLE BARRIER

Women are the good guys.
Men are the bad guys.
In our society, even worldwide,
This we've been taught, and know certainly.
And so, we focus on the hurtful things men do,
While ignoring, excusing, even condoning,
The hurtful things that women do.
So confirming what we've been taught. Amazing, isn't it!

Men learn from birth we are the bad guys,
Creating intense shame in men,
The Shame of Maleness, I call it.
Basic Male Shame, John Gagnon's term.
Need to compensate then drives men,
To do all the terrible things we men are blamed for,
Our need to control, to overachieve, to amass wealth, on and on.

And we dare not forget, shaming is violence,
Perhaps the most damaging kind, spiritual.
And men respond to this violence,
With violence of our own.
Men's violence increasing as the shaming grows.

And so millions, billions perhaps, of sincere people,
Devote themselves to building a better world.
While our belief in women's betterness, impenetrable barrier,
Blocks all hope of creating a world of joy and bliss!

And all the while,
God loves us,
Totally.
As we are and everyone.

Roy U. Schenk 8/21/00 #1131

men develop better feelings about themselves and feelings that they are lovable and "deserve"*
to be loved. The need for men to feel better about themselves is a result of the shaming
messages that boys and men receive to tell men they are defective and, therefore, unlovable.

In general, these weekends do not consciously focus on the shame that men learn. The one
clear exception is the New Warrior Training Weekend that was founded in Milwaukee,
Wisconsin, in 1985, and has now become the international Man Kind Project. Due to the
influences of Dr. Everingham, Dr. Guarnaschelli, and me, as active participants in this organization, the group became consciously focused on the effects of shame on men, although not
specifically on the Shame of Maleness. The group, however, does confront this shame along
with the other shame messages that men receive. The initiation ritual of the New Warriors is
different from traditional initiations in that it strives to initiate men into a transformed world
rather than into the traditional culture.

These "male initiation" groups tend to be non-political; and they seem to have a deathly fear
of any man who is critical in any way of women's negative behaviors, including the shadow
side of the feminist movement, the victim feminists. Most of the focus of the groups and the
related publications is on enhancing individual self-betterment and self-love.

However, this self-focus can only last for so long. As men become healthier and better able
to love themselves and other men, they become increasingly aware of the unfair treatment
that men as a class experience in divorce, draft registration, insurance premiums, sexual
harassment, incarceration, and assault laws, to name a few. They will become aware that
domestic violence done to men is ignored while violence done to women is intensely prose-
cuted. The list goes on and on.

With only a little education, men are able to understand that they are treated unfairly in the
"being" or behavior related areas because men are seen as inferior in these areas. With this
awareness comes hope that efforts to achieve equality between men and women will become
more viable, and at the same time, shame will also become diminished.

I have become aware of another impediment to improved relationships between men and
women. We seem to have a rule on our planet that is more powerful than any ordinance or
law, more powerful even than the state and federal constitutions or international law. The best
way I have been able to formulate that rule is: "Above all else, protect the women (mothers?)." Most laws are written to assure the fulfillment of this rule, but when the laws fail, the
laws are simply ignored or thrust aside. Unfortunately, equality and the end of violence and
war are impossible as long as this rule remains paramount.

NOTE:

* Note that the word "deserve" is itself shaming. We have a *right* to love and be loved.

Chapter 3
Men's Shame*

GERSHEN KAUFMAN

Our topic is shame. We're going to attempt an understanding of the nature of shame: what it is, where it comes from, and how to heal it, particularly as it affects men. Let me begin by talking about what shame is, what it feels like on the inside, what it looks like. Then we'll look at how men are socialized around shame in this society.

WHAT SHAME IS

Understanding the inner experience of shame is critical to understanding shame's significance and impact. To feel shame is to feel *seen* in a painfully diminished sense. What happens is that our eyes turn inward, and we're suddenly watching ourselves. Shame can be generated in an instant. It can last for five seconds, five minutes, or five hours. When we're young children, shame is generally a wordless, nonverbal experience. It flashes through our awareness, and often passes just as quickly. The characteristic facial signs of shame are: keeping eyes and head down; or blushing, or looking away.

Shame causes an interruption; it disturbs us. We feel momentarily transparent. It's as if everybody can see into us. Everybody can see how stupid, foolish, awkward, and dumb we are. Shame feels like exposure. In the moment of shame, our eyes turn inward, and because we're watching ourselves, we feel like everybody else can see through us as well. We feel defenseless against their scrutiny and critical appraisal.

Shame is a wordless emotion; only much later do we attach meanings to it. In the midst of shame, we feel an urge to hide. We want to cover ourselves, retreat, disappear, turn off all those watching eyes—most of all, our own.

These are the *critical* effects of shame. The self is paralyzed momentarily. Speech is interrupted; we can't talk and can't even think clearly. Sometimes we feel paralyzed physically, and stand still, or sit still, and can't move. I can remember countless times when, in the midst of shame, I couldn't will my body to move. It was frozen.

Following shame are several *secondary* reactions. Anyone who has experienced deep shame does not look quickly for a repetition. We escape and avoid it, and feel fearful of further shaming. We learn to see shame coming from afar and try to dodge it before it overtakes us. We also respond secondarily with another emotion—the "distress affect" of Tomkins's affect theory. We may feel sad and cry. Children display it—a momentary hanging of the head in shame, and then begin to cry. What gets recognized and attended to by parents (teachers, etc.) is the crying part of the sequence, and what gets systematically *ignored* is shame.

Shame is missed in this culture because shame is under taboo, but that taboo is now beginning to lift. There has been a cultural shift. In recent years shame has been surfacing more, and people are beginning to pay attention to it, particularly in the mental health field. This shift has been fueled by the recovery movement and its concern with addictions. These are disorders in which shame plays a central, organizing role. So now we're beginning to rediscover shame.

CULTURAL INJUNCTIONS GOVERNING MEN

There are cultural injunctions in our society to compete, be successful, achieve, and perform. That's especially true for men—we are supposed to be successful, and failure for men is shameful. Failing at anything is tantamount to being cursed. Another injunction is to be independent and self-sufficient. I know many men who will never ask for directions when they're lost. If they are lost, they're in shame, and announcing it is like saying, "I don't know where I am; I don't know how to get there." That's too shameful. I've also known men who won't ask a waiter or waitress to bring something to the table, because asking is too shameful.

Our society has tried to bury shame. In our refusal even to talk about it, we have reversed our language system. Think about all the times we say, "I'm too proud to do that." An Appalachian father might say, "I'm too proud to take a handout." It's not pride that stops him, it's shame— because taking a handout would mean announcing, "I'm no good! I can't provide for my family!"

The same thing happens when a man loses his job or is laid off. Because of the overvaluation of work for men as the principal route to self-esteem, any impediment to our achieving what we are all "supposed" to achieve produces shame. The American dream—you can be anything you want to be if you only try hard enough —has for us become a pathway into shame.

FORMS OF SHAME

In our culture, we lose the experience of shame because shame itself is under such tight control and strict taboo. Shame goes underground, and instead we talk about guilt. It's easier to say, "Well, I did something I shouldn't have done, and I feel guilty" than to experience shame about oneself.

Discouragement, shyness, embarrassment, self-consciousness, inferiority, and *guilt* are simply different forms of shame. But we give them different names and, therefore, experience them as distinctly different experiences.

Shame is expressed in many different forms, and the face of shame changes depending on the context. If I approach a stranger and feel inhibited, self-conscious, or that I'm going to make a fool of myself, we call it shyness. The emotion present is still shame. If I am presenting to a group and discover my pants are open, or if somebody comes up to me whose name I should be able to remember but can't, we call it embarrassment. Although we give it different names, the same underlying emotion is present. And when it's the self that feels inherently flawed, we call it inferiority, though it's still the emotion of shame that's present. Guilt is immorality shame at having transgressed.

Guilt poses some additional problems concerning its perception. In response to wrongdoing, we may also experience other emotions that we mislabel, or fail to label precisely, and ambiguously refer to them all as guilt. If I've done something wrong, instead of hanging my head in shame, I might feel *angry* at myself for having done something wrong. I might turn the finger of blame inward and angrily accuse myself repeatedly for misconduct or wrongdoing. We also call that guilt.

I might feel *fear*, as when people worry, "Will my name be in the paper?" or "Will there be some punishment?" We also include under the general heading of guilt the fear we feel about having done something wrong. Or I might become *sad*, and cry or grieve at having done something wrong. We call that remorse. Our judicial system is predicated on the appropriate and genuine display of remorse in response to wrongdoing. Many children learn that if they show remorse, then punishment is mitigated—but not always. We can also turn *disgust* against ourselves and begin to experience ourselves as loathsome, without dignity, as something to be squashed into the ground. When it's in response to transgression, we call that guilt as well.

These constitute different affective states. But when the ethical judgment of transgression is added to any of these, then they take on the distinctive feel of *guilt* states. And guilt can be either about the self or about acts, just as shame can be either about the self or about acts.

The important distinction here is not between shame and guilt, but between shame as an emotion, a feeling that is activated and then passes, and shame that becomes internalized and magnified. Then shame becomes potentially crippling.

POSITIVE SHAME

Shame is inherently healthy, and we would not evolve as a human species without shame. First, shame serves the centuries-old function of alerting us to any violation of human dignity. Second, without appropriate doses of shame, we would not develop a conscience, a sense of right and wrong. Finally, our identity would be completely blocked from developing, because who we are as human beings evolves directly out of experiences of shame.

When encounters with shame are appropriately graded and effectively neutralized, they do not become internalized, magnified, or crippling.

STRATEGIES AGAINST SHAME

Let's discuss some of the strategies that we develop to cope with or protect ourselves against shame. When shame becomes inordinate and excessive, we have to survive somehow, and we need to survive the very best ways we're able. We need to honor the person we are and the ways we've had to function to get to this point in our lives. If we don't do this, then we continue to undermine ourselves.

Rage against other people is one strategy, whether in the form of chronic, rageful eruptions as in an alcoholic family, or quieter hostility that's transmitted and communicated, perhaps every time the family gets together. Or it may become directed specifically toward one child or another. Rage is a way of protecting ourselves against shame. A father who has experienced considerable shame may reenact analogous scenes of shame toward his son by means of rage. Anyone can learn and adopt such a strategy and thereby keep people away with rage.

Contempt is a different strategy, in which we elevate ourselves above others and experience other people as lesser. If you're beneath me, and I'm superior to you, then your ability to shame me is lessened. It's a strategy that enters subtly into many of our interpersonal relationships through attitudes that are judgmental, faultfinding, or condescending. Any time we look down on another, the strategy of contempt is operating at some level of intensity.

Perfectionism is designed to perfect the self, erase every blemish, and escape from or avoid shame by excelling in an ever-widening circle of activities.

Power strategies are designed to maximize power as a way of life. One way to protect myself from shame is always to be in control. If I'm always in power, whether as head of a household, in a company, or in a relationship, then I am likely to generate shame in others and also to protect myself against shame.

Another method is the *transfer of blame*, which is a way of transferring shame away from me to other people. In the moment of shame I'm faced with the dilemma: What to do with it? One strategy is to transfer it outside; it's not I who has failed. I haven't done anything wrong; I'm not to blame; it belongs out there.

FEELINGS SHAMED IN MEN

Developmentally, different parts of our personalities become associated with shame. And what happens for men is specific and powerful, in terms of the parts of us that become systematically shamed—in the family, in the school setting, and in the emerging and continuously evolving peer group of early adolescence (which I'm convinced now has almost equal power with the family to shape personality).

Let's look at the specific parts of us that become associated with shame. One of the most profoundly shameful experiences for men has been crying. Men have been systematically shamed in American culture for crying. The degree to which this has been true in other cultures is an open question, and there are certainly variations on the theme, but men in American society are made to feel there's something wrong with feeling sad, crying, or openly displaying this emotion. It can happen when men are told, "Don't be a crybaby." "Take it like a man, with a stiff upper lip." "You should be ashamed of yourself." "Boys don't cry." "Real men don't cry." To be psychologically healthy, we need to have access to crying, to be able to feel and freely express sorrow, or we'll never deal effectively with loss, death, relationship failure or breakup, and all of the disappointments life throws at us. Crying, which is a natural human emotion, becomes bound by shame in this way.

Following sufficient repetitions of the pairing, or linkage, of expressions of distress (crying) with being shamed for crying, shame becomes internalized. We tell ourselves, "Don't cry," "Don't express that," "You're stupid," or "You're a crybaby."

I can remember times when I would cry, and peers would stand around laughing, ridiculing, mercilessly shaming me. I have repeatedly met individuals—generally men—who are subjected to the severest sanctions when observed to cry, and I know of one individual for whom the humiliation, shaming, and ridicule continued for three or four years as he progressed through school. The *history* of his public crying stayed with him.

When this happens, an *internalized shame bind* is created. The emotion of distress—crying, sadness—spontaneously activates shame, without anybody else ever having to shame us again. Think of somebody who begins to cry (think of yourself). Immediately, what's the first thing we do? We look around to see if anyone is watching. We may apologize, if somebody's there. Or perhaps we'll say, "I'm sorry for *breaking down in front of you.*"

There's nothing inherent in crying, or sadness, to cause us to feel that we're "breaking down in front of" someone. The "breaking down in front of" is the shame part of this sequence. Whenever those words are expressed, you're observing a *distress-shame bind* operating. Progressively, we feel not only like *hiding* tears, but that there's something wrong with us for *feeling* sad in the first place.

We feel lesser; we feel deficient. Somebody immediately offers us a tissue, and we try to dry the tears. Or we pretend they're not there, and ignore them. Others may become visibly agitated. We have difficulty simply tolerating distress, which is often displayed through crying or sadness. We're not supposed to cry, and when somebody does, thereby violating that cultural taboo, we immediately become distressed by it. That's one reason we have so much difficulty coping with death and dying, because feeling sadness or distress spontaneously triggers shame. We run and hide from sorrow; we disappear and don't acknowledge pain.

Distress is not the only emotion that is heavily shamed for men. Fear is another. An analogous process occurs here. Men are not supposed to be afraid, and are systematically shamed whenever they express fear.

It may begin in the family, when young boys wake up, frightened by a nightmare, and are told, "That's stupid; don't be ridiculous." Or they imagine monsters in the basement, and are ridiculed for being frightened of such silly things.

It progresses from ages two to three when young boys display cowardice before others, and the shaming comes from peers who gather round and ridicule whomever is not being appropriately fearless. You can imagine the difficulty for a boy who may not be as inclined to be aggressive, who is perhaps more fearful, when forced into this contradiction.

When I was growing up, I wouldn't fight back when I was picked on or hit. When my father observed that, he was so enraged that he started beating me in order to get me to fight back. As I look back on it, I think it triggered too much shame for *him* to allow me to deal with it myself, or for him even to be comforting or reassuring.

Instead, he attempted to humiliate me and force me to fight back. It didn't work; I ended up not fighting back, *and* not giving in to his power, because either way I was going to experience shame. At that point, it was a hopeless, insoluble dilemma. If I went ahead and fought back at that point, I was giving in to his power and letting him dominate me. So there was shame no matter what I did.

Expressing fear becomes associated with shame for many men in this society. We're not supposed to be afraid or to show our fear. And when we *feel* fear, at whatever level, we think there's something wrong with us. Feeling afraid translates into, "I am deficient. There's something wrong with me."

That's the key to understanding shame—realizing how we learn, how we are taught, how we are made to feel deficient for having natural human emotions. So fear and crying are two important feelings that are heavily shamed in males.

Also heavily shamed is any expression of shame itself. I can remember hanging my head in shame, and teachers saying, "Keep your head up. Don't look down; don't hang your head." In essence, they were saying, "Don't display shame."

PRIMARY INTERPERSONAL NEEDS

I have formulated a group of primary interpersonal needs that I consider to be innate, in the sense that they are required for optimal development. One need is to have a relationship with parents and other significant people. Another is the central need for touching and holding. The need for identification—for fusion, merging, and a sense of belonging—is also basic for human beings. This need alternates with the need to be separate and different, to differentiate. These needs oscillate. One day, my son would look up and say, "Daddy, I want to *be* you." The next day he would say, "I'm *not* you; I'm different from you." Both needs have to be responded to appropriately. The challenge for parents is to provide for the child's emerging needs and their oscillating patterns as they unfold.

Another need is to nurture, to give. I believe children need to give—whether it is gifts, or love and affection. It may be an arm around the parent's shoulder, saying, "It's gonna be okay, Dad," when Father is upset. How many fathers have been so ashamed to appear "weak" in front of their own son, that they have pushed the boy away? Or they may shame him verbally, or respond with a look that is sufficient to create shame in the boy. We all have needs for affirmation, being valued, recognition, and admiration.

Finally, there is a need for power—power in the positive sense of being able to predict and control. To experience a degree of power is important to human beings. We never have all the power, but we do need to experience sufficient power in any area of life essential to us. This is crucial for human beings.

Now, let us consider how these basic needs become shamed for men.

SHAMING OF INTERPERSONAL NEEDS

There are particular interpersonal needs that, for men especially, become heavily imbued with shame. The first is the need to be in a genuine *relationship*. Every child needs to be in relationship with each parent, and subsequently with anyone who becomes central in his developing world. The need for relationship is the need to feel wanted, to feel special to another, and to feel that this other person truly wants a relationship with us. Men in particular feel deeply ashamed of needing a relationship.

A related need is for *touching and holding*. We need physical contact. Every infant requires touching if he is to thrive. We know that beyond question. The skin has to be touched, to be stimulated. Infants have to be picked up and rocked. They need to be held, talked to, sung to, and smiled at. All of these are *vital*.

And yet, ours is a touch-phobic culture. We don't touch each other. We are made to feel an inordinate degree of shame about our fundamental human need to touch and to be touched. It happens in multiple ways in this society. At some point boys are greeted with a handshake instead of a hug. Or a parent, particularly a father, begins to feel uncomfortable and looks embarrassed or ashamed when his son reaches for a hug. The change usually occurs sometime between childhood and adolescence. I can remember being told, "Boys don't hug each other. Boys don't *kiss* each other." And we begin to shut off these natural dimensions of our personality, all of which are readily observable when we're quite young so long as we're allowed freedom to express them.

There are times when touching is simply a desire for bodily contact. Watch young children around ages of three, four, or five. They touch everybody, sometimes even strangers. Touching is simply a way of connecting with others. Put together adults who are stoic and don't touch, bring them into a room with pets or little kids, and suddenly they start touching. But generally they won't touch other adults.

Men certainly don't touch each other, unless it's in the context of adversarial contests. If we're fighting, or if we are engaged in sporting contests together, suddenly touching becomes okay, because then it's the congratulation of triumph. We can be close to each other only after we've vanquished somebody. That's a clear, narrow, and powerful script for living life. If that's what it takes to be close, then we're going to have to engage continually in adversarial contests.

Touching and holding are ways of communicating affection, tenderness, and intimacy. Sometimes it's a need for bodily contact, and, at other times, for restoration of security—a sense of protection.

There are times in our adult lives when we truly need protection and support to be communicated bodily. Sometimes—for children, adolescents, and adults—verbal comfort is not sufficient. This is true bodily of in response to deep emotional pain, as well as deep shame. Touching and holding are crucial to healing shame. This is true for children, and equally true for adults. The conditions for growth and healing don't change when we become adults. But our culture and socialization lead us to presume *mistakenly* that they *do* change after we're grown up. Much of our science, in the mental health field, has been similarly infected with this false idea.

Touching and holding have unfortunately also become equated with sexuality. Certainly the two overlap, but not all touching is sexually motivated. We may confuse the two because they have been confused for us. Our culture and our science both tell us that the *only* reasons to want to touch another adult are sexual. We know in our hearts that's not true. There are times when it's sexual, but there are times when it's simply an expression of closeness. But we men usually deprive ourselves of closeness, especially with each other.

The only times it's okay for men to touch are on the gridiron, in the midst of contest, or at the bar after a few drinks. Then anyone can touch, and it doesn't count, because we're not responsible. Or maybe at the airport, where you can hug or touch someone, so long as it's brief.

Much of my work has been aimed at constructing a general map of how human beings function, so that we can understand ourselves and begin to distinguish what is happening inside. The Eskimos have 32 words for snow. We have maybe a half-dozen for all that happens inside of us. I want to develop a common language for how we feel, function, and operate. Then we will have increasing knowledge of ourselves and be able to communicate our feelings and needs to one another.

Men have been much more limited in that vein because we've been denied access to so many parts of our personality. So many feelings have been too shameful to express. It's okay to be angry, but it's not okay to be sad. It's okay to feel contempt for others, but it's not okay to feel shame or fear. We've inherited a warrior script aimed mainly at vanquishing others, and we still operate from it to varying degrees. This script has lost contemporary meaning, in the sense that it no longer has the survival value it once had.

The *identification* need is simply the need to feel identified with someone else, to feel a part of another person. We all yearn to feel *one* with another, to feel connected or bonded together.

Think of the earliest universal scene. An infant is cradled in his mother or father's arms during breast or bottle feeding. I experienced this, because I participated actively in parenting both my sons from an early age. When I held my infant son and gave him a bottle, I would gaze directly into his eyes, and he would look up into mine. And well after he was done feeding, we would continue to look into each other's eyes; we were locked in a *facial embrace*. I believe it's through the eyes that we become *one* with another, that we merge with another person momentarily, and feel temporarily fused. In this way, we begin to experience identification.

This experience is so powerful that it is taboo in all cultures to some degree. The most intense experience that we can have is mutually gazing into each other's face and directly into each other's eyes, and holding that gaze for an extended period. What usually happens, however, is that we quickly begin to look away, look down, break the contact. We look instead at the forehead or the nose because we're not supposed to gaze too directly into each other's eyes. Only mother and child, or father and child, freely experience this unashamedly.

The other time we recapture the experience of facial gazing when we fall in love. You meet another person whose face you gaze into and with whom you enjoy that unashamed mutual facial gazing. That's how we know we're two people in love: we look into each other's eyes— seemingly forever. Even in the supermarket line, anyone can tell two lovers by the way they look endlessly into each other's eyes. That's the experience of fusion, merging, or oneness.

Men rarely do that with each other, although I am convinced that it's possible. When my younger son was three or four years old and I was putting him to bed, there were times when he would look into my face and eyes and say, "Daddy, when I grow up I want to be you; I want to be just like you." And we would gaze into each other's faces and into each other's eyes.

Other children sometimes come up to me and look into my eyes, and hold the gaze for a long period. We have been made to feel ashamed of that; it's systematically shamed in men particularly. Men are supposed to be separate, independent, self-sufficient; we're not supposed to be intimate and close, certainly not with each other. Instead, we should fight each other. We're adversaries or warriors—certainly not intimates. Increasingly, particular dimensions of our nature become partitioned and stratified, cut-off, and blocked from expression.

This identification phenomenon is so important because it is systematically devalued in the West. In the East, everyone is socialized to feel identified with each other, to feel a part of the group, and thereby a part of the same culture. That is particularly true in Japan and China, where identification with the group is the modal pattern. In the West, it's just the opposite: we're encouraged to individuate, to differentiate from one another, to go our separate ways, not to be communally close. We can only experience identification briefly, if at all.

In the East, the culture is openly organized around shame. Traditional Japanese society has always been a shame-honor society, just as Mediterranean cultures are shame-honor societies. And in some parts of the United States, particularly the southern states, shame-honor cultures are present as well.

Everything in the East is geared to avoiding causing shame, not triggering shame. In traditional Japanese culture, the only antidote to bringing shame on oneself—which also brings shame on one's family and ancestors—was ritual suicide. I don't think they have more shame, although they are certainly more aware of it. It's simply a more conscious experience for them. Asians are more likely to display shame openly when they behave in a way that dishonors them or others.

I do not want to idealize the East, but simply to look at the contrast between our two cultures. I don't see either as having the complete answer. I think we need to have access to all aspects of our being. I don't think either culture is better than the other; they're simply different.

We need to be able to express all emotions freely and comfortably when we feel them—whether it's fear or sadness. We need to be able to identify and feel connected. We need to be able to feel close, and that's particularly true for men with each other, because we do have needs for close male friends, for other men we can feel connected to. And, of course, there are times when we need to be separate and independent. So the goal, the path of development, is to reclaim all of our misplaced parts.

DISCUSSION WITH AUDIENCE

Audience Member: When I was a kid my dad used to make us look into his eyes, and then I knew that I was in trouble. I remember I was about six or eight, and my dad said, "You look into my eyes." It was like a shock.

Kaufman: Well, you've internalized almost the opposite of the taboo against identification, being *required* to look into his eyes. In a sense, it's dominance-submission; he was dominating you at that moment.

There was a fellow in one of my workshops who discovered the opposite. When he was six years old, he realized he could stop his parents from shaming him by staring into their eyes. He stared directly into their eyes and they became so uncomfortable that they stopped shaming him. So your dad was using that strategy on you; it's a way to dominate by humiliating the other person.

There are two ways in which people in all cultures are placed under taboo for gazing into each other's eyes. In one instance, we're shamed for looking too directly into the face of a stranger; every child has been made aware of this. On the other hand, we are also shamed for being shy in the presence of others.

It's a twin strategy: Someone comes to the door. The boy is hiding behind mother or father, and the child is made to feel ashamed for being shy. He comes out and looks, actually stares into the stranger's face, and then he is shamed for staring. Those are the twin strategies that usually produce this particular taboo.

Audience Member: In my particular situation, my father used face gazing as a boundary invasion; it was his way of gaining power over me. In fact, he even put a double bind on me by saying, "You look at me when I talk to you," and "Don't you look at me that way." "Look at me when I talk to you"—and we all get that from our fathers—and then, "Don't look at me that way." And half the time, if I think back, I didn't know which one I was doing when.

Kaufman: There is a tremendous power in our eyes. There are times when I'm driving and have stopped at a light. I'll stare at the head of the person in the car beside me who's a little bit in front of me, and within 10 or 15 seconds that person starts looking around. And I've also had experiences of either being or sitting somewhere and suddenly feeling as though I'm being looked at, and somebody was indeed staring at me when I looked around. I think there is a very powerful nonverbal communication that we are somehow able to transmit and receive through the eyes. I don't understand it fully, but I think it's primarily a process of imagery.

Audience Member: My view of this is simply that the eyes are a way of getting past boundaries. When I wish to set my boundaries aside and be intimate with you, I can do that with my eyes. If I force you, I'm zipping your boundaries open from the outside, invading you against your will. At the same time, I think there can be a powerful healing of shame in eye contact.

Kaufman: I think you're right. We're dealing with boundaries, what's okay and what's not okay, where you can enter and where you can't tread. The eyes hold tremendous power. I've witnessed this over and over when I've asked people to look into my eyes. I've not forced them, but invited them; there can be tremendously powerful healing through that experience. There have been times I've done this with clients who've experienced a lot of shame. I move my chair closer and say, "I want you to look into my face." I wouldn't force my client to do it, but I'll make a very direct invitation, and I'll lean a bit. I don't think I'd force it on kids, because it does trigger tremendous discomfort unless it's open, free, and mutual—that's the key.

I had a very powerful experience that resolved some of the internalized shame that I carried from childhood. It happened with the man who was my mentor until 1973—Bill Kell, to whom I dedicated my first book.

This experience was triggered by working with a client who was dealing with what he had never experienced with his own father. He came in one day and said that he had just been home, and had been able to tell his father how important he had always been to him. As soon as he said those words, a voice went off inside me saying, "I've never been able to do that." He proceeded to relate a few more experiences, and then said, "I'm done with therapy now. I've done what I needed to do." I was shocked and surprised and said, "Okay, I guess if you feel you're done, then you're done."

After that session, I raced down the hall and knocked on Bill Kell's door, because I knew something powerful was opening inside of me. He was busy, but I interrupted him and said, "I need to talk to you." We arranged to talk the next morning.

When I related what had happened with my client, I said to Bill, "I have never been able to say to my own dad how important he has been to me." We conversed about that for a while, and by then I was able to tell Bill how important *he* was to me. Bill just turned and looked out the window and said matter-of-factly, "I've known that." We went on, and later I said, "I don't feel done; I don't feel resolved; something is still not finished." Then he looked directly into my eyes and said, "You haven't said the words." At that moment my heart sank; I just caved in and went into an acute shame experience.

I sat there, paralyzed. I couldn't move. I couldn't speak. Finally, I was able to say something that let him know I was feeling shame. At that moment he came closer, and I think he put his hand on my knee. We had already realized how important it is to reestablish touch and physical connection when shame is surfacing.

It's one thing to talk about shame, but it's quite another to experience an acute shame attack. It was agony. Bill just waited, while I sat in paralyzing shame for some 20 minutes. There was a knock on the door; we were well past whatever time had been allotted, but Bill advised the visitor that we needed more. Then he sat down again and waited. That was Bill's style. When I finally looked up at him, I remember looking directly into his face and eyes, and he looked back into mine. We continued that way for an extended period of time. Finally, I said to him, "I love you."

That was the hardest thing I ever had to say. Tears were streaming from my eyes, and I was crying. And all Bill did was smile at me, look into my eyes, and say, "Good." That experience resolved and healed something in me that had been so powerfully bound by shame. This is the healing process.

PATH TO HEALING

When I was growing up, I thought that when you got to be a man you never had any more problems. You knew all the answers, you always figured things out on your own, and you certainly never needed anything. And because I never was able to feel that way, I never thought I was grown up. I never felt I was a man. Finally, I realized that it's okay to have problems, it's okay to need, it's okay to not to know something, it's okay to have difficulty. The challenge is simply to start where we are, accept *who* we are, and build relationships with people who foster our health and growth.

It's going to mean risking. Nothing could make it easier for me to face that shame with Bill Kell and finally say to him what I needed to say. I agonized over it. Two years before that incident, I would not even have asked him for the time. It's taken me well into my forties to feel essentially free, as free as any human being can be, of all the shame binds that I grew up with. And they still sneak up unexpectedly.

We are never going to escape shame binds completely; we're never going to erase our history. We can't eliminate it because there is no "delete" key to consciousness. We can't reprogram ourselves like a computer, but we can go through that process and learn to tolerate the shame that may be evoked. And we will need to continue to go through it; that's how to dissolve shame.

We all need people with whom to do that inner work. You have to build into your lives people whom you trust, who will assist you in that process, whatever the context. But it's not easy. It does mean tolerating some awful feelings and persevering on through them. I think it's a process we have to stay with for the rest of our lives.

Knowing what is happening helps. Knowing that the feelings we're struggling with are inevitable and natural, given our socialization, means that we can not only tolerate but endure shame And every time we do so, even a little bit, we increase our ability to endure shame better the next time.

If we allow ourselves to just sit there and feel it, shame will rise to a peak, but then it will start to burn off. It will implode and begin to reduce itself. Progressively, each time you go through this process, more shame is healed.

I teach people a strategy for reducing shame when it's being generated in the present. Whenever you are feeling shame in the moment, whatever the context or situation, refocus your eyes back outside. The essence of shame involves our eyes becoming fixed on ourselves. In our shame, our eyes turn inward and we're watching ourselves. We need to turn the watching eyes back outside.

I have been experimenting with this technique for 20 years. I've taught anyone willing to experiment with it how to successfully release shame. To implement it, become immersed in external sensory experience, particularly visual and physical. Even if you talk to yourself about what you are seeing and hearing around you, all of your attention is getting progressively refocused into the external environment. When that happens, shame is released; it becomes immediately interrupted.

If you're in a room, you can count the number of people in the room. You can ask yourself, "Is there anyone here who interests me?" "Is there anyone here I want to get to know?" You can also go outside for a walk and become immersed in the environment, in the sights and sounds surrounding you. Music can do this, and there are other ways of completely refocusing attention outside. As long as the eyes remain focused outward, directly onto the external environment, shame is interrupted.

I've also accomplished this by closing my eyes. If I'm walking somewhere or if I have to function, then this is not going to be effective. But if I'm sitting in a room, I can close my eyes. I taught this to a man who felt acute shame whenever he went into the steam room at his gym, where there were other men. He would feel paralyzed with shame. I taught him the strategy and said, "Next time you go in there, focus your eyes back outside." He said, "That's not going to help, actually looking at the other men."

I laughed and said, "Okay, when you go in, just sit down and close your eyes." He came back the next week and said, "It worked!" As soon as he closed his eyes, he felt completely relaxed and comfortable; when our eyes are closed, we are not watching ourselves.

This is a tool for releasing shame in the moment. It does not deal with internalized shame binds, and it does not work with the early shame that needs to be healed. Resolving internalized shame binds or early scenes of shame involves a process that first consciously recovers those scenes. Next, the scenes are reexperienced with all of the original emotion present, and finally they are transformed by infusing them with new affect. We'll explore this further in Chapter 5.

CONCLUSION

In the last 20 years it has become less valuable and respectable to be male in our society. That's unfortunate. But I consider it part of the profound transition that we are going through. We will come out of it, begin to reclaim ourselves and eventually be perceived as true coequals. It's an inevitable part of the process of exploding the gender scripts that have controlled us all.

We are faced with a culture in transition. We are moving toward the emergence of new ways of being, of thinking and feeling, as men. And we are in the grip of a profound transformation. Where the future will take us remains open. But we ourselves will create it—that is the hope for the 21st century.

NOTE:

[*] Based on the audiotape, "Men's Shame," of a joint presentation sponsored by the Alfred Alder Institute of Minnesota, Minneapolis, April 23, 1989.

Chapter 4
Seven Sources
of Men's Shame

ROBERT BLY

It's a great honor for me to be here with Gershen Kaufman. About four years ago in a friend's house, I saw his book called *Shame*. When I read it, I was astounded, because it was obvious that shame was a taboo subject and that he had entered into it. I realized, also, that it had been taboo in my own family.

Psychologists talk a lot about *affect*. An emotion the body strongly participates in can be called an affect. There are people whose primary affect is surprise. Some people know fear as their primary affect. Others have joy, and the spectrum ranges from vague delight all the way up to intense joy. Anger is also a very strong affect, with a wide range. Michael Meade, for example – he can go all the way up and down the scale in two or three seconds.

I knew that I wasn't an anger person. I wasn't a fear person. I wasn't a joy person, even though joy appears in some of my poems, but (hesitating for ironic effect) that's just to fool people (laughter). I realized that I was a shame person by the time I had gotten 20 pages into Gershen's book. It was a *wonderful* homecoming; I was really glad to know that.

And it helped explain an incident I had never understood. My family lived out in Western Minnesota, on a farm. When I was very small, my mother arrived home with two bottles of milk, the sort with little cardboard tops. I reached for one, in that way of trying to be helpful – dropped it – and all the milk spilled out.

And what I did was to run into the grove, and I hid far back in a corner there, by a tree. Gershen pointed out that many of us deal with shame by withdrawing into isolation. I probably remembered this incident because it made clear to me that withdrawing was my maneuver.

I remember hiding and hearing my parents calling for me. And not answering. Because shame has its *own* power. By not answering, I shamed *them*. Isn't that right?

I wouldn't give them the satisfaction of answering. But eventually they did *not* come to look for me (with playful plaintiveness). I mean, it was a small grove (audience laughter). (Continues mock plaintiveness): They could have come! (more laughter, continuing through next two sentences). And they didn't come. So in the end they won; I didn't. I came creeping out around twilight.

So then I understood why I remembered this incident out of all the other possible memories. It was at that moment that I acted on shame as a primary emotion. And not only that, but I also set a certain way of responding to it, by withdrawal into isolation.

Gershen has set down a wonderful list of seven responses to shame. I have used all seven (laughter). Of course, I specialized in withdrawal. And then I think I found a couple of others that Gershen doesn't mention... (laughter)… that I also use.

So, I'm really grateful to Gershen Kaufman. His work made a profound change in me, and grounded, grounded me in shame is what it did (ironically). Thanks a lot! (much laughter).

I thought I'd begin my talk with a poem. My father was an alcoholic. That is in the background of the poem. And, of course, that's a very fruitful ground… for the little bushes of shame to spring up, isn't it? One might say that alcoholism is the favorite way that American and Russian families have to be dysfunctional. There are many other ways. Anne Wilson Schaef, you know, took a poll and found out that the percentage of dysfunctional families in the United States is 102% (audience laughter). So if your family is not alcoholic, just translate into your own mode.

I am very interested in the idea that shame is an enchantment. The original enchantment makes you drop your eyes. To overcome or reverse the enchantment, you can reverse this act – that is, lift the eyes and focus them. For perhaps 15 years, I have been focusing my eyes as a sort of discipline – on a pinecone, a bird's wing, a piece of amethyst. It is a writing exercise.

One afternoon I was walking in the woods in northern Minnesota, near Kabekona Lake. When I came down to the lake, it was dusk. There were some hills in the west whose shadows had fallen about halfway over the lake, but the eastern half of the lake was still lit. Near shore I saw some reeds, and a *third* little band of water between the reeds and the shore. You see that sequence?

I decided to describe that scene. Images came, and I noticed that all the images of the dark were male, and all the images of the lighted part of the lake were female. And this doesn't fit with the Jungian view at *all*. Jungians associate darkness with the feminine, and solar light with the masculine.

I realized that I was describing my father with the dark part, and my mother with the light part. The band of protected water near shore was probably me. But when you're writing, you don't know what you're doing. You just write. I'll read you the poem that I eventually worked out of that. It's called

Fifty Males Sitting Together'

After a long walk in the woods clear cut for lumber,
lit up by a few young pines,
I turn home,
drawn to water. A coffinlike band
softens half the lake,
draws the shadow
down from westward hills.
It is a massive
masculine shadow,
fifty males sitting together
in hall or crowded room,
lifting something indistinct
up into the resonating night.

I had in mind a group of Tibetan monks I once heard singing.

After a long walk in the woods clear cut for lumber,
lit up by a few young pines,
I turn home,
drawn to water. A coffinlike band
softens half the lake,

pulls the shadow
down from westward hills.
It is a massive
masculine shadow,
fifty males sitting together
in hall or crowded room,
lifting something indistinct
up into the resonating night.

Sunlight kindles the water still free of shadow,
kindles it till it glows with the high
pink of wounds.
Reeds stand about in groups
unevenly as if they might
finally ascend
to the sky all together!
Reeds protect
the band near shore.
Each reed has its own thin
thread of darkness inside;
so it is relaxed and rooted in the black
mud and snail shells under the sand.

The woman stays in the kitchen, and does not want
to waste fuel by lighting a lamp,
as she waits
for the drunk husband to come home.
And then she serves him
food in silence.
What does the son do?
He turns away,
loses courage,
goes outdoors to feed with wild
things, lives among dens
and huts, eats distance and silence;
he grows long wings, enters the spiral, ascends.

I must have been 48 or so before I began to think, "What was all that like? What did I do as a son?" A man said to me, "When my father and mother were fighting, I'd walk out on the railroad track for miles."

The mother's silence would be a good strong *shaming* silence, wouldn't it? The husband has to eat his food in silence – the woman won't say a word to him.

> What does the son do?
> He turns away,
> loses courage,
> goes outdoors to feed with wild animals

Do you think you could stay in the house and deal with those two? Often I couldn't. I just lost courage and *left*.

> goes outdoors to feed with wild
> things, lives among dens
> and huts, eats distance and silence;
> he grows long wings, enters the spiral, ascends.

Such a young man has a tendency to ascend, get above it all, transcend it. Men of this sort are called "swans" in folk tales, in "The Six Swans" that the Grimm brothers collected, for example. Some New Age people are like that in their flightiness. "If I eat enough yogurt, I'll never be shamed again" (laughter from audience).

> eats distance and silence;
> he grows long wings, enters the spiral, ascends.

> How far he is from working men when he is 40!
> From all men! The males singing
> chant far out
> on the water grounded in downward shadow

I like to hear Tibetan men singing together. They enjoy each other's voices, and they enjoy the shadowy masculine ground they're sitting on. The young man with long wings finds it difficult to be on that ground.

> He cannot go there because
> he has not grieved
> as humans grieve.

At that point I had to ask a question about my family:

> If someone's
> head was cut
> off, whose was it?

The mother's? (that's right)
Or the father's? (that's right!)
Or mine?

How far he is from working men when he is 40!
From all men! The males singing
chant far out
on the water grounded in downward shadow.
He cannot go there because
he has not grieved
as humans grieve. If someone's
head was cut
off, whose was it?
The father's? Or the mother's? Or his?
The dark comes down slowly, the way
snow falls, or herds pass a cave mouth.
I look up at the other shore; it is night.[2]

RB: It occurred to me that one reason many American men don't grieve is shame. Perhaps we are too ashamed to grieve. We imagine that if our own head was cut off, it was our fault.

In the United States, men are only allowed to grieve when they go to a funeral. The part of us that we have never grieved for is the part Gershen has been talking about. I mean the small boy who receives so much shame early on that he just can't take it any more, just can't live anymore.

I'd guess my little shame boy died long ago. What we need to mourn for are those little children inside of us who died. We don't mourn for them. Is that right? We just go "mmmmm, I'll make it through. I'll get a Ph.D."

Audience: Will you clarify? In what sense does this shamed boy die?

RB: Well, you know fairy stories say that witches or giants die, but they're not really dead. The next year you throw a log on the fire, and they jump back out again. So in the psyche nothing dies, but it goes dormant and cannot grow any further. If a little boy or girl gets completely blocked in there, they stop taking in anything from the outer world. And when you're 30, neither are very good in conversations or arguments, because they don't know anything. They're naive and very hurt. And blaming – they also blame a lot, these little ones. Why not?

So as an adult, one can stand there and watch them ruin a whole conversation (laughter). Moreover, if you're talking with a woman then, when your little shamed boy contributes a few words, you'll probably evoke in her the little shamed girl… When the two of them control the conversation, it's hopeless! (laughter). They'll make a mess that won't be solved for six days. When those two get going, blame gets added onto shame. Jung remarked that the clichés spoken in such arguments haven't changed since the Egyptians. "You always do this to me (laughter); you never hear what I'm saying." To say the shamed boy or girl "dies" is a kind of metaphor. But I like it because it implies that "a death" is something we need to mourn for.

Audience: That process for me is just a little different. I find that I'm getting back *in touch* now with my little boy, and he's been reborn.

RB: That's lovely; that's the next step we want to talk about. How does that feel? Or how did it happen?

Audience: Well, for me it started with getting in touch with the fact my father was extremely abusive on many levels. I was never in touch with that before, and I realized that I was talking to my little boy. I didn't know those words at the time; the process has taken me there. I am realizing that the little boy never died. He's just under water and trying to swim up. And 30 years later he got to the surface.

RB: That's beautiful. Let's say he *was* under the water trying to swim up. But we never gave him a chance to swim all the way up, because we never got back to those times when he was so deeply shamed. We lived in denial, as they say in AA. The shame we felt was deeper than we were able to handle at the time.

As we get older and a little stronger, we can begin to relive the experience. Every man can choose at some time to dive down into the water, where he'll find the boy under the surface.

One has to choose to dive. And one must say that if you don't choose, the psyche may give you an accident, an illness, or a serious addiction. That acts as a way to get you down.

You know, in my mother's generation, a parent might die suddenly – say, in a flu epidemic – and no provision was given to the child to mourn. No one would say, "Are you angry about your mother dying?" Relatives would say, "Well, you'll live with Aunt Margaret now; it will be all right." And no one asked, "Do you think your mother abandoned you? How do you feel about that?" No one asked any of these good psychological questions. And sometimes the development of the child stopped right there. It's a great blessing the work that psychologists have been doing recently in helping with mourning. But most of us in our 50s and 60s didn't get much of that help early on.

Audience: You got me thinking of my story. I had a real significant experience. There's a process called Rebirthing, which I've been involved in for about a year. In the middle of one of my sessions, an image came to me from the movie, *Wings of Desire.* I cried during the whole thing because of this image of an angel coming down and setting his hand on the shoulder. That really struck me.

RB: Was that connected with your Rebirthing experience?

Audience: Yeah. I became that angel that went back to the little boy, that little 4-year-old lying in his bed all alone in his room crying. Something awful had happened, and I was alone. All I wanted was for somebody to just sit there with me and put their hand on my shoulder, and say it was okay. I know that sounds kind of mystical, but it works.

RB: It's just common sense actually.

Audience: I got to be the man who went back and said, "Michael, it's okay."

RB: Wonderful! If you're working with that boy, you might ask him if there's a place in your current house that he likes. Ask him where he wants to be. And then for a month or so, you bring him a flower every day to that place. And don't let anyone know what you are doing either. If they ask, "Who's that flower for?" say, "It's for my dead Grandmother." You lie all the time... (laughter).

Because this little boy wants to be able to establish a connection with you in which he doesn't have to be overly adult, and yet you're not going to beat him up either. You are just going to honor him. And you need to have a real container for just the two of you, one that is secret and protected. Then I think he'll change, become in life again, and grow.

It's a long process, isn't it? Two or three years at least. But give him gifts. Do you know how much little boys want gifts? They want whistles. They want little bits of candy. You could eat them later yourself (laughter). But he'd appreciate it. He'll eat the smoke from the candy.

Audience: You mentioned some type of force that can bring one back to that little boy and alluded to an addiction or a car accident. Please explain.

RB: We don't know about all of that, but there's some force in the psyche that wants us to move forward. According to the old Gnostic tradition, a twin was born with you. And at the moment of birth, the twin separates from you. He remains invisible and lives elsewhere on the planet. And he knows everything that you knew in the other world before you came. He's aware of all the steps that you need to take, but you can't locate him. The deep longing that we have is partly a longing for this missing twin. Does this make any sense to you?

I spoke about this once for some 20 minutes, and then a man of about 35 said, "I had a sort of vision one day, and I told it to my therapist, but he just ignored it and went on."

I said, "What was it?"

He replied, "At the end of a corridor, I saw a nine-foot man who was luminous. He approached me carrying a spear, and said, 'Either change your life, or I'll take it from you.'" Now that's a serious message! It would appear that this man has to live seriously, or he's going to be in trouble. The visitor is nine feet tall, and *luminous!*

So, one could say that there is someone interested in how you live. And that nine-foot luminous being can easily cause you a car accident – no problem. He just says, "Look over there." And then you end up lying on your back for three months, which is what he has wanted you to do for a long time. So you can think over some things. James Hillman mentioned that an overly active American man ordinarily can go into soul only when he's lying on his back in a bed, defeated by bacteria. He's no longer victorious; the bacteria won; the man lost; finally, he's a human being. When a person is in defeat, then the soul is able to come forward and speak to him. I like that very much. I think it was Woody Allen who said, "Death is nature's way of telling you to slow down."

INTENTIONAL SHAMING

We might talk about sources of shame. I love what Gershen Kaufman has said here; I'll add some ideas of my own. How do we get shamed as a child? Gershen writes that, first of all, your parents could just say to you, "You ought to be ashamed of yourself." We tend to believe what grown-ups say, and immediately the whole shame affect is evoked. We could say that we store our shame in *shame tanks,* which are very small when we are young.

When we get heavily shamed, our shame tanks start to flood over. Whenever my parents would say, "You should be ashamed of yourself," my shame tanks would start to run over. In school, I'll get more shame from teachers or other students. I'll have to get rid of some of the excess, by shaming other kids. Remember that? Playgrounds are not really playgrounds – they're shame grounds! They're places where shame is passed on to the smaller kids. Finally, one little guy over in the corner with pimples gets it all by 4 o'clock. He goes home and gets rid of it with his still younger brothers.

We could carry this image a little further. Let's say that we don't have big enough tanks when we are small to contain all the shame that we receive. One advantage then of growing older is that, if you work on it, you can hold more in your shame tank without passing it on to others immediately.

As Gershen says, "You can tolerate more shame if you practice tolerating it." Practice doing absurd things in front of square people, and let them shame you. And as soon as they've shamed you, dance! It will blow their minds. And in addition, you are increasing your own ability to hold shame. If you do certain odd things in front of your teenage children, they'll start to shame you right away (laughter). That's nice, and that's okay. Just hold it.

One can play with being shamed. Suppose you're with a couple of very proper church women. Just say, "Is it true that Presbyterians have hair between their third and fourth toes?" (laughter). Watch what they'll do. They'll put the kibosh on you. Since you evoked the shaming, you can handle it. I am off the subject, I think; we'd better get back (much laughter).

SHAME THROUGH SILENT RESPONSE

A second way we get shamed – Gershen is brilliant here – is this: The *child asks his or her parents for a response and does not get it.* For example, you bring a little drawing or a joke to your father and you say, "What do you think of this?" And he does not reply. Then two thoughts appear, "If I were an adequate person, I would not have had to ask for this response." And second, "If I were an adequate person, he would have given it." The logic is irrefutable.

Shame has to do with perceiving, "I am an inadequate person." I've had that feeling since I was very small. So I know that logic. Once I asked my father to come to a spelling contest at my country school, because I knew I was going to win. But he didn't come.

I'm sure I went through both those two steps. "If I were an adequate human being, I wouldn't have had to ask him to come. And if I were an adequate son, he would have come." So that's that.

On this planet I am not adequate; that's all. So, I'll have to live with that. And I don't know what I'll do, but I'll do something. So the words adequate and inadequate are very deeply connected with shame.

All of this debate goes on inside. Did you think I mentioned these doubts to my father? Not at all. I withdrew. It wasn't inside me to confront my father and say, "Why didn't you come?" That would be out of my style. Is it clear what I'm saying? That would break the shame. And my family didn't know how to break it.

I'll tell you a story. About three years ago I went out West to give a poetry reading. And to my delight, my wife came with me. We were staying in a cabin near the ocean, and she had work of her own that she was doing. When the night came for the reading, I asked her, "Would you like to come to the poetry reading?" And she said, "Do you want me to come?" Now when you're well into shame, you often are not aware of what you really want. So I said something like, "Well you've been to so many of my poetry readings – maybe you should just stay here and study." I didn't say what I wanted.

I went off to the poetry reading. About half way through, unexpectedly I missed her being there; I felt abandoned. Tears came to my eyes, and it was hard for me to finish what I had intended to do. When I arrived back at our room, I told her about it. As I talked, I suddenly remembered that detail of my father not appearing at the spelling contest. In one of those exchanges of gender that take place so easily in the psyche, she had become my father – my unreliable father, should we say?

The boy disappointed long ago woke up and was perfectly present in his sadness when I was 48, 49, 50 years old. I can never predict when that boy is going to appear. So I learned a lesson that night: It's all right to say, "I want you to be there. Do come. Just sit in the second row, and smile." Then it's up to her to decide.

This is a story about a son asking a father for a response and not getting it. A father or mother can't give all the responses asked for. His typical refusal was clear, sharp edged, so to speak. My mother was quite different. If I said to her, "Would you protect me today?" her reply might be, "Well, gee, Margaret is coming this afternoon." Her responses were so confused or fragmented that I didn't know which country we were living in. What she said seemed so foggy to me, that I couldn't tell if she had answered or not. That was her style of shaming.

Being a woman, she was much more alert, I would guess, to the fact that an answer was needed. But the response didn't meet the request; even though her feeling was charming and feminine, the answer didn't make sense. But, in general, I think that women shame boys less in this area of responding or not responding. I think it is mainly the fathers – who don't talk much in the United States – who do most of this second kind of shaming. I see that Gershen agrees.

Well, we're pioneer people. Immigrants in North Dakota, who were chasing cattle and hogs…might not talk for four years (laughter). And that's the way it is. So the immigrant men became culturally adapted to fixing broken fences, and that's about it. I never realized that a man who spent his life fixing fences might cause unintentional shame in his sons and daughters. Of course, my father's father, who was born in Illinois, must have shamed him the same way. Isn't that right? And his father shamed him; it's probably in the family

I'd like to lay out five other sources of present shame. We talked about two sources so far. These might be called intentional or deliberate shaming, and shaming by nonresponse. The second one leaves the shamer looking clean, because he or she doesn't appear to have done anything.

INHERITED SHAME

The third source is *inherited shame* from the far past. Shame of that sort is connected with certain secrets that your grandparents kept. For example, an uncle embezzled money; an aunt had a mental breakdown and was in an institution for a while; a child was retarded. People used to encapsulate an event like that in silence. They put a skin of silence around it, as the body sometimes encapsulates foreign germs. And when so encapsulated, it passes down through the bloodstream of the generations. Eventually that silence will open or blossom in you as shame.

For example, there's more shame in my psyche than is justified by anything I've done. Where is it coming from? It's coming right down the genetic line. If my ancestors had spoken about the shameful event openly, the shame would not have been encapsulated. They might have said, "You know, Margaret went completely crazy; she's been crazy for a long time. We hid her for a while; then we couldn't do it any more (laughter). Would you like to go and see her?" That would have been a part of the family history, which is very interesting. But since these nontalkers encapsulated it, the shame comes down with its original energy and appears in each of us as a puzzling shame. We don't know the source of it. We just feel ashamed. It is a *subtle* shame.

In our generation, we can interrupt this sequence by not hiding shameful things from our sons and daughters, by talking about everything. Embarrass them deeply at all family meetings (laughter). Say, "Let's invite cousin George for Thanksgiving." "Wasn't George in prison?" "Yes, he knows a lot of stories (laughter). I think he knows some Etheridge Knight poems too; let's invite him." Say all you can about the crazy and failed people in your family. And your kids will hate it, but that's all right; they'll bless you later.

And then we could talk with the children about our own errors and our own disasters, and we could decide not to hide all that. Tell them details about your high school time.

I had to find out some details about my father from relatives. Once they said, "Your father used to play the trumpet; did you know that?"

I said, "I didn't know that."

"Yes, he played the trumpet during his time at high school, or Normal School, as they called it then."

I said, "What happened?"

"Well, he was courting your mother at the time. She lived in town, and one night he fell off the horse he was riding to meet her. He knocked out his front teeth and never played the trumpet again."

This is an important story, and I want to know it. He must have felt ashamed that he got his teeth knocked out because he fell off a horse. Is that right? Why didn't he tell about that? I played the saxophone in high school. Why didn't he say, "It's lucky you don't need teeth to play the saxophone" (delighted laughter).

Robert Frost is wonderful on encapsulated shame. He knows a lot about how secrets are kept in New England. "A Servant to Servants" is a long monologue by a woman in *North of Boston*. She mentions that her father's brother went mad quite young, and the family eventually built a sort of cage for him, made out of hickory, on the upper floor. Her mother came into the house as a bride, and had to help take care of him.

> That was what marrying father meant to her.
> She had to lie and hear love things made dreadful
> By his shouts in the night. He'd shout and shout
> Until the strength was shouted out of him,
> And his voice died down slowly from exhaustion.
>
> – *Robert Frost, 1939*

Frost didn't fool around. He put all of them right in the house at the same moment. One could say that in every family there's someone caged in the attic that nobody knows about. That's why your honeymoon doesn't go well (laughter).

SHAMING THROUGH EVENTS

As the fourth one, we'll name *external shaming events in one's own life*. For example, a boy can get caught shoplifting. I did – very shaming. Some children fail a grade, or don't read well. You don't get chosen in the ball game; remember that one? The captains deliberately avoid looking at you, and after everyone else is chosen, one of them finally says, We'll pick you" (laughter). When we are small, as I've said, our shame tanks are small, and that scene in softball is enough to keep them filled all month.

Or you may fail to achieve some complicated task that you've been given. *Hamlet* is a shame play. Hamlet's father appears and says, "I'm your father. I want you to kill the new king and settle the whole thing, good-bye" (laughter). And Hamlet can't do it. He feels shame *all through the play* because he can't do this thing, which his father sets him to do. Of course, he's Danish (laughter). Maybe if he had been Norwegian, he could have gotten it done. In his shame, he keeps checking it out: "Was that ghost my father? Did it look like him?" It was a genuine task, and he wasn't up to it.

How does Hamlet die? Got pierced with a poisoned sword. And after he had shamed Ophelia so much that *she* died. There's much else in the story, but it's true that when we're in shame, we shame others. There's no other way!

One more detail. For a child, seeing grown-ups naked can be a shaming experience. I visited a commune recently in which the parents practiced nudity triumphantly in front of the children, and required the children to be nude also. That was a favorite thing in the '60s. But children have a great sense of modesty, especially as they get a bit older. They do not want that. The parents imagine that they can get rid of their parents' repressive shame by doing the opposite. I said to the grown-ups, "You know you're crazy; you're shaming these children."
     "Oh they like it."
     "How do you know?"
     "They don't object."

I said, "It's a form of child abuse; don't come to me with that shit" (tense and thoughtful silence).

Suppose you're in high school, and your mother comes to you without any clothes on. Isn't that shaming? Deeply shaming. Perhaps she was drunk. It's still a shaming event. And as children we're not responsible for it. Events happen to children. Incest between mother and son can happen that way, or between father and daughter. Sexual abuse of any kind leaves a trail of shame as deep as dinosaur tracks.

If anybody disagrees with me on these points, please interrupt.

AN IMPERFECT BODY

As the fifth source, we'll take *inadequacies of body shape.* Body shapes are taken as a kind of excuse to feel shame. In high school, I was so skinny that I couldn't bear to be seen on the basketball court. I didn't go out even for intramural basketball, because I *knew* that the girls would burst into laughter as soon as I ran out there in my jersey. Actually they wouldn't have. They might have said, "There's that skinny Bly kid; he's kind of bright." That's what they would have said. I didn't know that then. And so the whole thing wiped me out.

And everybody is too thin, or they're too fat, or one shoulder is wrong, or their ankles are big, or they've got a birthmark, or they're too short. Can you feel the shame deepening in you now, looking back at all that stuff in childhood, how unfair it is? Some women feel deeply ashamed by every minor inadequacy in their own bodies; it's just incredible. Marion Woodman told me recently, "I've never had a female client in the last seven years that didn't flagellate her body."

I said, "What do you *mean?*"

She said, "The women I see are not satisfied with the body they've been given." Incredible! This sort of shaming seems deeper for women than for us. But still it's enough, even for us, to fill our shame tanks.

MAINTAINED SHAME

Let's go on to the sixth source. I'll call this one *maintained shame.* It's really routine maintenance of our shame vehicle. Gershen calls it *internalized shame.* The idea is that if by 14, say, you've been shamed well enough by other people, and you won't need an external person to shame you anymore. You'll do it yourself.

Why is it that men who are well shamed, let's say by an angry mother, will pick a woman as their girlfriend or wife who will do exactly the same thing to them? Now why *is* that? Maintained shame implies comparison with all forms of maintenance, such as the 40,000-mile checkup on a new car. You've reached a certain level of shame performance as a child, and your job is to maintain that level. If you live with a woman who doesn't shame you enough, life doesn't seem real to you. Something is missing. "I want a female friend who can replace my father and my mother as a shame maintainer." And all over the United States, there are women saying, "Let me try" (much laughter).

I recall an afternoon three or four years ago, when I was at a men's conference trying to teach some of this. A young man said to me, "Robert, we know how destructive shame is to our feelings, to our self image, to our masculinity. Why would anyone want it?"

I think the *intensity* of shame is the answer. Some people don't like Mozart; they want a rock band because it's more intense. We're hooked on intensity. Just because shame makes you drop your eyes and lose eye contact with another, that doesn't mean you aren't having an intense emotional experience. You are! It's an intensity of isolation. I think Gershen says something like, "Shame is inward, and not revealed, but it's very intense." Can we call it a cognac? It's more intense than wine.

We do a great deal to make sure that every once in awhile, we have this incredible cognac of shame. Do you know that some people only feel alive when they're in deep shame? Just a few days ago, I shamed an old friend on the telephone by something I said to him. And he, knowing me well, recognized just what he could say that would put me in shame. And he said it. A few days later, I traveled within a few miles of his house, but I didn't call him to get it settled. Why not? Because I wanted to keep the shame going, including my own. I was a shame addict on that day. This is a serious idea; don't you think so?

There's a book that treats maintained shame in a superb way. It's by Fossum and Mason (1986), two family therapists in St. Paul, and it's called *Facing Shame: Families in Recovery*. I recommend it. These authors have dealt with shame issues in therapy for a number of years, and they've seen something which they call *shame cycles*. We know that menstrual cycles average about 28 days, and that there are emotional and creative cycles usually described under the term "biorhythms." Fossum and Mason propose a shame cycle.

Suppose one person has a 38-day shame cycle, but another person's cycle may last 48 days. Suppose they are married to each other. Each spouse knows intuitively with ingenious accuracy how to kick off the other's shame cycle at the right moment to keep it going.

The man may be, for example, an alcoholic. He stops and starts drinking. During the sober part of his cycle, his rebellious crew gets tied up down in the hold. He as captain walks on the deck; he is in control. He walks into the wind and says, "Don't worry. I'm in charge of this ship." This may go on for 21 days.

Then a certain moment arrives. The crew breaks loose, comes up from below, and takes over the ship. Now the captain loses control, the husband gets drunk, disappears for three days, and often feels thoroughly ashamed. Everyone in the family shames him. He gets a full dose of it. The idea is that he's not addicted only to alcohol; he's addicted to shame.

Did you hear that one? He probably has a fundamental addiction to shame, and he uses alcohol to get to that place of intense shame. Perhaps one could say that in my family system, my father became addicted to shame early on; that's why he didn't want AA later. His Norwegian Lutheran mother provided it first; she gave him a certain sanitary form of shame: Add water, and serve. She made him ashamed of his sexuality and of his wildness, I would guess. Perhaps she made him ashamed of his "masculine coarseness;" I'm not sure of that. This "high-toned old Christian woman," as Wallace Stevens calls such a person, made him ashamed basically of being a man.

In my father's case, he found later that the only way he could maintain the appropriate level of shame was to use alcohol. That's my guess. He was still able to work as a farmer and actually functioned very well for years. And everybody thinks that the reason such a man is in the bar is that he loves drinking and telling stories. And he does.

And how about my mother? Well, I would guess that she also became habituated to shame as a young girl. Her mother died in an epidemic when she was only 12, and that abandonment probably produced tremendous interior shame, hidden, invisibly experienced. She lived out some of her shame vicariously from my father's shame cycle. He would kick hers off at the right moment. He did the active part; she got it by picking up the pieces. She looked cleaner; she looked the more respectable of the two, but both were addicted to a repeating shame. It was he who was chosen to act it out.

Audience: Isn't it also possible that shame is a way not to change, not to confront things?

RB: Yes, that's lovely.

Audience: It takes a lot of courage to change the things we do. And shame blocks change.

RB: Perhaps we adopt shame as a way for us not to grow, not to go through the confrontation with the habit that's necessary if we are to grow. Is that right? That would mean that a man has to ignore the 9-foot luminous figure at the end of the corridor. Shame in fact helps us to ignore him. "I can't live my life; I feel terrible."

Audience: I think that one reason we sometimes choose partners who resemble our parents is because certain parts of our unconscious are trying to recreate the parental situation, as a way of trying to solve it this time.

RB: That's right. Many people feel that theory is correct. Suppose as a child, you received a lot of shaming, which weakened you so that you couldn't hold your own against your parents. Then as an adult, you reestablish the situation to see if you're strong enough this time, to see if now you can hold your own. But often the new shame is so strong that the old outcome repeats itself. Is that right?

Audience: With most solutions, it never works.

Audience: I like that idea about cognac – as if shame makes you feel alive. I think that shame is the central complex, or central neurosis, of the human endeavor. Shame becomes very safe and familiar. People become passive. Most families work inside shame because it is safe. In order to experience life you've got to kick [back]... and shame keeps you down.

RB: Wow! He says shame is safe and known. Whether intense, or passive, or low, or dopey – it's a known position. And we can always return to it. Everybody prefers the known to the unknown. It's why you keep wanting to go back to your hometown – because it's familiar, and you'll get shamed again (laughter).

Audience: Adult men who molest children were often themselves sexually molested as children. Please address this relationship.

RB: Well, many people have done work on that. Let's say that you have been deeply shamed at the moment an adult invaded your body space. The shame is so huge, and your shame tanks are so small, that you try to get rid of it by passing it on to another person. In sexual abuse, the shame is so immense that you've *got* to get rid of it and make another person deeply shameful. Is that sensible? I am sure there are many other solutions and answers to it. But that's a depressing one, don't you think so?

Audience: I address the question of molested people who choose to repeat shaming experiences. Some of the work with abused kids shows that when they have been removed from an abusive family, they will sometimes behave in ways that invite abuse from their subsequent family. One worker said that children growing up need intimacy so badly that shaming or abuse may be the only form of intimacy they know. The only intimacy they become programmed to understand is the intimacy of abuse.

RB: Most abusers do say, "I wanted to give this child something." And, of course, they're giving the boy or girl some kind of touch – touch that they were longing for as children. It happens the touching is contaminated with sexual abuse, but they give it anyway. That's good; thank you for that. Yes, please.

Audience: A somewhat different way of looking at it – this comes from Fossum and Mason – is the idea that families perpetuate shame as a matter of inertia. And for me, unless I break the shame cycle, unless I get fierce, it's going to *just keep going on* the same old way.

RB: Let me read you a sentence here by Fossum and Mason, which is a little bit like what you are saying: "For some, loyalty to the shame leads to such strongly established defense structures, that the only vulnerability known to the person is the vulnerability of the shame."

Suppose that one hasn't ever experienced the normal vulnerability of being with another human being and saying, "Let me tell you what I thought today. It was really terrible." They haven't experienced being psychically open in the presence of another person who can reply to you with feelings, or even with a hug. The *only* vulnerability they *know* is the vulnerability of being shamed. That's hard, isn't it?

To sum up maintained shame, or internalized shame, we could say that at a certain point, we don't need other people to shame us; we can do it ourselves. A friend of mine spent several years in an adulterous love affair when he was 35, and I thought it was one of the best things he'd ever done (laughter). But recently he has been shaming himself over and over about that. Wow! That's maintained shame for you! Choose one event of your past, adopt some Freudian term such as "Oedipal," and then you can shame yourself for the rest of your life (laughter).

SHAME OF THE FALSE SELF

The seventh source of shame that I'll mention is the shame that comes from the creation of a false self. Alice Miller (1981) lays this out in *The Drama of the Gifted Child.* She says, in effect, that when you were born, you brought to your parents a fantastic gift. You brought a vibrant, extravagant, excitable, noisy, many-sided nature with you from eons of vegetable life, reptile life, mammal life, lion life, hunter life, aboriginal life – all of it lived before your human birth. You brought it all and gave it to your parents as a gift, and they didn't want it. Instead, they wanted a nice boy (muffled groans).

This rejection was deep. It happens to both boys and girls. Before you were two, it became clear to you that your parents did *not* want the wide range of energy that you were so proud of They said, "Can't you be quiet? Why won't you be a nice boy like the others?"

Alice Miller remarks that, given our helplessness, we decided to compromise. Using our inborn radar set, we figured out what kind of child they wanted, and we created a false self to please them. She said, "You betrayed yourself at that time." And we receive deep shame every day from that betrayal. That false self which each of us made up certainly lasted all the way through high school, and probably for 10 or 20 years more. It helped some. But each of us was also feeling shame all that time in the soul, in the eyes, in the fingernails, because we were no longer the wild person who came whole from the universe.

If you want to get a taste of that shame in a poem, read T. S. Eliot's "The Love Song of J. Alfred Prufrock."[3] Eliot (1952) realized when he was about 25 that he was living out a fundamentally false self. Prufrock says:

> Shall I part my hair behind? Do I dare to eat a peach?
> I shall wear white flannel trousers, and walk upon the beach.
> I have heard the mermaids singing, each to each.
> I do not think that they will sing to me.

You betrayed your deepest nature by creating a false self when you were a child. Alice Miller adds that you must now forgive yourself for doing that, because you did the right thing. And the proof of it is that you are inside this room alive right now. The infant somehow remembers all those children who insisted on their original personality, and they got put out in the snow (laughter, oohs and aahs). So your survival instinct did the right thing. It made up a false self and you survived.

You have to forgive yourself for doing that. And the second thing would be to recognize that you don't need that false self now. One has to go through the grief of abandoning it, or letting it die, or releasing it. There's a lot of shame about this grief. Can you feel it (murmurs of assent)?

How to release it, and let the false self die, has a lot to do with helping your "shadow" rejoin you, or "eating the shadow." We could talk for a long time about that. But our time is up.

I'm sure there are more sources of shame than those I've spoken of, but those are the seven that I have noticed (much applause).

NOTES:

[1] Based on the audiotape, "Men's Shame," of a joint presentation sponsored by the Alfred Adler Institute of Minnesota, Minneapolis, April 23, 1989. Transcribed by Roan Kaufman.

[2] "Fifty Males Sitting Together" may be found in somewhat different versions in Bly's books, *The Man in the Black Coat Turns* (1981) and *Selected Poems* (1986).

[3] From T.S. Eliot (1952), "The Love Song of J. Alfred Prufrock," in *Complete Poems and Plays*. New York: Harcourt Brace. Reprinted with permission.

Chapter 5
Healing Internalized Shame[1]

GERSHEN KAUFMAN AND ROBERT BLY

G*ershen Kaufman:* I've already written of tools for releasing shame in the moment (chapter 3). Now we move on to dealing with internalized shame, the shame that we carry within us, inside. One way we can heal this shame is to redefine the present relationships that perpetuate our shame binds. Another way is by utilizing reparenting imagery, a process by which we visualize and heal our childhood scenes.

REDEFINING RELATIONSHIPS

I don't believe we have to stay in relationships that maintain our shame. No amount of therapy can help us overcome shame if it continues to be reinforced in a relationship. But too often we *do* remain in these relationships, particularly in the family of origin. And there are times when it's the relationships we created ourselves—either at home or at work—that we need to change or leave behind.

When we choose to behave differently in a relationship, then the dynamics of that relationship must change significantly. And that may include terminating a relationship that is too damaging to us, because we have an inalienable human right to protect ourselves, first and foremost.

People develop expectations and predictions about us. If we begin to violate these expectations, it's very unsettling to them. It creates surprise and shock, because we're no longer following the familiar script, and suddenly *they* don't know how to act. So we have tremendous difficulty breaking these expected, habitual patterns of behavior, both in the family and in the culture.

We all know the cultural injunctions we've inherited in our society. Breaking these rules is heresy in every civilization on the planet. In Western culture it was handed down to us on tablets of stone: "Honor thy father and mother." It was never to be questioned. There is a parallel principle in the East. It's not written on tablets of stone, but it's equally enjoined by the culture: Obey your family.

I believe we need to examine these principles and reconsider them consciously. A very powerful exercise is to ask yourself what you believe you *owe* each of the people in your life. Begin with your parents. What do you consider you owe each of them, given what each of them gave you? And once we know what we owe, then we know what we can *freely* give. I know that if a family member were dying, I would go home. That's what I feel I owe. The rest is up to me, and in this I do with my family what I would do with any other adult. But it took me three years to consider consciously whether I owed them every vacation, every opportunity to visit.

Take a psychological inventory, and base your actions on what the relationship is *now*. A simple example: For years, whenever my Dad would visit, he would always ask what I paid for things, and then invariably he would criticize me. I either got taken or paid too much, or I paid too little. I finally decided I was not going to answer that question any more, because it always left me feeling ashamed. The next time, I had added a room to my house, and I was prepared for him. When he visited, he said, "Well, let's see, I bet you paid $2,000 for it." And I watched the little smile on his face. You can't build anything for $2,000, let alone add a room to a house.

So I said, "Oh, somewhere between $1 million and $2 million!"

He looked at me like, "What?" He was completely dumbfounded. Then I behaved the message—I walked out of the room. The next time, he said, "Well, it was probably $10,000 or $20,000, wasn't it?" He had to find out! He could not tolerate not knowing. And I never told him.

I finally had to say, "You know, I think we'll get along better it you don't keep asking me what I pay for things."

RB: He wasn't sure he wanted to get along better, either.

Audience: I'm feeling a little uncomfortable with what you are saying...

GK: Good! (laughter)

Audience: I have an emotional program, but I also have a spiritual program. If I choose what you're suggesting here, it's going to get in the way of my spiritual program. Choosing to have nothing to do with somebody—that's not a Christian way in my personal philosophy. How do you deal with that?

GK: Well, about all I can say is you are going to have to live with the conflict. You have to come to terms with how you are going to live your life. There's no right answer! I know what I have done for myself.

I decided there's no reason to be in a relationship with anyone who does not like me or respect me. I don't think it's healthy for me to remain in that kind of position, even when I happen to be born into a certain family or work in a particular place.

RB: That's a wild idea you just expressed there! Radical! Even though you're born into a family, you still have choose whether you are going to live with people who don't like you and have relationships with people who don't respect you. That's heavy.

GK: About ten years ago, I decided I wasn't going home for my niece's wedding. I considered this carefully for a year. And I kept thinking, "I do not want to be around people who do not like and respect me."

After I made that message crystal clear to my family, I got a call from my Dad, raking me over the coals: "Why aren't you coming home? It's a small family. What will people think?"

I got all those shaming messages, but all I said was, "I will not be able to." I didn't back down. And from that day forward, I was never afraid of them. They had no more power over me.

The relationship changed because I had changed, because I had behaved differently. It was cool and distant for a long time, but now they have a lot more respect for me. Our relationship now is the best it's been in 46 years. But my brother hasn't spoken to me since then—it was his daughter. Frankly, that's fine. I have no need to talk to him, because he never liked me anyway. My Dad still tries to get us to talk, but I say, "Hey, you can't fix it. We don't have to like each other, and he has never liked *me*."

Audience: You said that you don't have to stay in a relationship in which you felt humiliated. If you do want to try to salvage such a relationship, what can you do?

GK: Begin to change the relationship. Identify behaviors that produce shame in you, that trigger your shame. Once you name these clearly and specifically, then you look for ways to change the relationship so these things don't happen.

That's what I did when I stopped telling my Dad how much money I spent, or when I decided that I don't have to go home unless I choose to. The others are going to be disappointed. During a phone call from my Dad, I finally said— and this is the only thing you can say—"Well, I guess I'm a disappointment to you."

He said, "You're right, you *are* a disappointment to me, a big one," and hung up on me.

RB: Great! He played his part well!

GK: But I named it, so I didn't have to feel ashamed because I was disappointing him. I was acknowledging it. And I expect to disappoint people—daily. He was trying to shame me, but he wasn't admitting it. He didn't acknowledge it directly, but I did. I called him on it. I've learned to steal somebody's thunder when they try to shame me. You can pull the rug right out from under them by saying, "Well, I guess I must not be behaving the way you want me to."

RB: There is another way. I talked to a man at a little college in Kansas. He was a sweet man, a Mexican-American, and he said that his father had always been furious and would never have anything to do with him. Finally, he called when his father was dying. His dad still didn't want to come to the phone, but the son insisted. So his father said, "What do you want?"

And he said, "I want to tell you how much I appreciate everything that you did working in the auto shop so that I could go to college. I have a good job now at this college, and I really want to tell you how much I appreciate that."

His father said, "You been drinking?"

But the man wasn't going to accept that. He said, "Listen, I have *not* been drinking, and I want to tell you I appreciate what you did, and I love you."

He pushed it a little farther. That's a way of changing a relationship, not obeying the hints to back off. "You been drinking?" is a hint to stop the conversation. But you can overpower that negative stuff and make the interaction go a positive way. It has to be genuine—he really felt thankful to his father. But once it's genuine, you can push it to any length. You are a grown-up. If you want to keep going and repeat it five times, you can do that.

WITHDRAWAL, HUMOR, DENIAL AND ACKNOWLEDGMENT

GK: There are other ways of dealing with shame, and they can be healthy or unhealthy. One is internal withdrawal—withdrawing from shame by withdrawing deeper inside, until the self becomes shut in. Lots of people are shut-in personalities, and what they display outwardly is a superficial social mask. But the real self—the needing, feeling, hurting part of the self—is hidden deep inside.

Another strategy is humor, which can be positive and adaptive, because humor reduces shame. But there are some people who seem compelled to joke about everything and continually make light of serious matters. And when humor combines with contempt, we have sarcasm, ridicule, and mockery. These are very powerful vehicles for generating shame in others and creating an atmosphere where shame is threatened.

The final strategy, if all others fail, is denial.

RB: Denial is "I don't have any shame"?

GK: Right, denial of shame! If every attempt to escape from shame fails, the last defense is to deny it.

Audience: Can internal withdrawal reach a point where I'm not consciously aware of my emotions and feelings?

GK: Sure, it can. Whatever becomes bound by shame becomes constricted, inhibited, and, finally, suppressed. We stop expressing it outwardly. The effects of shame may then spread inward. Take anger. If expression of anger gets shamed, we may inhibit experiencing our anger to the point where we lose conscious awareness of it. If we defend ourselves by withdrawing, we may isolate parts of ourselves so much that we lose conscious awareness of them.

Audience: It's my opinion that humor is always a defense. You can use it for a variety of purposes, but it's still just a defense.

RB: Maybe you don't have a sense of humor! (laughter) I said *maybe* . . .

GK: I don't agree. We thrive on humor. It's a way of experiencing communion with each other.

RB: Sometimes, it reveals a common shame.

GK: Sometimes it does. And sometimes it functions as a defense, but there's nothing inherently defensive in humor.

Audience: What about other responses when we're feeling ashamed? How can you respond verbally to the person who is shaming you instead of taking on one of the defensive strategies?

GK: A very important way is to *acknowledge the shaming directly.* Do this especially when the person shaming you is important in your life, and you want to work it through together. Acknowledge the shame. Start looking together at the reactions shame sets off in you and how you evoke shame in the other person.

I've done this with my sons. I try to help them see that the reason one of them is insulting the other is that the other has shamed him. I think that's exactly what's needed: To say, "Boy, I just felt ashamed." We must be able to express and release the emotion with people we care about. Naming our shame won't be possible everywhere, but we can do it in relationships where it can be received and acknowledged and understood.

REPARENTING OURSELVES

GK: Let me shift here. Another part of resolving internalized shame binds is getting back to our early scenes of shame and healing them. I've been developing a process that I call "reparenting imagery."

This process involves learning to care for and reparent the little boy still inside; we reexperience him in a way that's loving, comforting, and protective. When we can become a good father to the little boy inside, we actually reclaim him. Then we can give ourselves new words, new messages, new ways of thinking and feeling and being, new scripts for living life. We can begin to recreate who we are.

Within each of us, there is an early-child self, and an adolescent self, and perhaps other parts of ourselves that are locked away or hidden. But these parts can intrude into interpersonal relations, parenting relationships, etc., without our conscious awareness. So if we are in tune with ourselves, if we accurately communicate with ourselves, we can embrace those parts and create a whole integrated self. This is the optimal path of development, as I view it.

I want to guide you through this reparenting imagery process. So get comfortable in your chairs, and uncross your arms and legs. Put away your paper and pens—it'll be hard to write with your eyes closed. (laughter) Now, close your eyes. I will close mine, and I won't peek. Breathe slowly, in and out. Take a deep, relaxing breath, and as you exhale feel the tension in your body draining into the chair, into the floor. One more deep, relaxing breath.

As we proceed, I will suggest images. If you have different images, follow yours. Whatever you experience will be good, and you will experience only what you are ready to have happen.

Imagine you are descending a staircase. It's dark; it's quiet. As you take each step down, feel the sensation of walking—the pressure of the floor, the feel of the banister. When you reach the bottom, you're in a hallway. At the far end of the hallway, you see a light. Walk toward the light. When you reach it, you find yourself in a doorway looking into a room.

Walk into the room. Let it surround you. It's your bedroom, when you were five years old, or ten, or whatever age comes readily to mind. If you did not have a bedroom, visualize a room where you went to be alone or to feel safe. Walk around the room. Touch everything. Remember how the furniture was placed? The color of the walls? Run your fingers along the nooks and crannies in the walls. Is there a window? Is there light coming in? Is there a closet? A bed? A chest? Remember what it smelled like in this room?

This is the room you grew up in as a young boy. This is the room you laughed in and played in and cried in. Look at everything. Touch everything. Remember how you used to play peek-a-boo or hide 'n seek games in this room? Did you hide under the covers or in the closet? What was it like when you woke up on Sunday morning? Did you have favorite clothes? A favorite song? Or story? What was it like being a boy in this room? Where did you draw pictures, or just doodle? Pick up a toy or a book. Hold it. Play with it. Be the child you were back then.

Now lie down on your back on the floor, and look up and take it all in. Remember how huge everything was when you were little? You were tiny. The world was gigantic. The dresser was so tall, the ceiling so high. And you felt small in that world. You are the boy who felt little in this room.

Stand back up again and look around the room, one more time. Go to the doorway. You're standing there, and your adult self is looking in on your childhood through the door that you have opened. But now you sense you're not alone. There's a figure in the corner, on the floor. It's a little boy. Walk over so you can see him better. It's that little boy you were back then. He's sitting right there on the floor in this familiar room. Picture your little boy as vividly as you can. To deepen the contact, think of an old photograph from back then.

Sit down beside your little boy. Say hello. Hold his hand. Put an arm around him. Say, "I'm here now." Ask him what he's feeling inside. Ask him what he needs from you right at this moment, and freely give it. Say the words to him that *you* wanted to hear back then. Be a loving father to the little boy inside you.

Now pick him up in your arms and give him a great big hug, because he's been lonely a long time. Hold him on your lap; hold him close. Say, "You're a good son, and I am proud of you."

Take him out of the room, into the light of day, into the sunshine. Sit together in the grass for a moment, where it's warm and bright. It's a new day beginning. Now imagine taking him to a new, safe place inside of you, a kind of kangaroo pouch just beside your heart. Imagine a soft warm bed, and tuck him into bed, right inside of you. Pull the covers up tight. And sit down on the edge of the bed. Look into his eyes, and smile, and say the words you need to say to each other.

Now give him one last kiss, one last hug. You'll be back whenever he needs you, whenever he calls for you, because it's safe now. Time to sleep. Say, "I'll be with you always." Tiptoe from your little boy and walk back down the hallway and up the staircase. Come back to this room at your own pace. Whenever you're ready, open your eyes and join us.

There's a lot of pain in the room. What was the experience like for you?

Audience: I've been in rebirthing therapy for five years, and have done this kind of meditation a number of times. What always comes up for me is my son, who is now 19. I keep coming back to him, to how I treated him in the first 10 years of his life, and then the family disintegrated when he was about 14. I think about how I passed along a lot of my own shame. The challenge I have is trying to reparent him, to undo the damage. But the frustrating part of this meditation is that I keep going to *him*. I can't seem to be able to do it with myself.

GK: That's not so surprising. Your son may have to do that part. We need to make peace with the fact that we weren't better or healthier with those we love. You may need to grieve for the ideal father you couldn't be back then. And talking to your own image of your son may be a way of doing this.

Audience: Whenever I do these visualizations, it's easy to go back to this nice, generic version of myself when I was a baby. I was present at the birth of both of my children, so I can kind of relive that for myself. My parents are both alcoholics, and it's real hard for me to visualize specific things about later years. I can't remember anything from high school.

GK: Try getting a photograph of yourself at a later age, one with an open facial view where you can see your eyes. Put it up on the dresser, and look at it every day. If you try the visualization, this will create an entrance. You may not recall specific events, but you may begin to contact the part of you that's still there. It *is* hard. If it were easy, we wouldn't all be here today.

Audience: When I got to the room, I tried to pick the little boy up. But he was kicking and scratching, so I had to set him back down. For a while there, I was trying to talk to him, but I just couldn't get any farther than that. He's still sitting in the room.

I was really angry going through this whole process. I didn't want to do it. I didn't want to deal with it. But the reality is I have to deal with painful things. So I suppose, somehow, if I can recreate this process . . . it might take a few more times . . . He wouldn't look in my eyes.

GK: He was still too mad at you.

Audience: Yeah, he's mad as hell! I can't go to him right now. He wouldn't look in my eyes. I couldn't visualize getting past his anger.

Audience: It makes me think back about four years ago when I did this with Gershen at another workshop. That experience was just as profound as the one I had today. I went into my bedroom where I was abused as a little boy, and I was able to return as an adult and comfort my little boy and take care of him. It was an absolutely freeing experience. Today, I went back to a different room at a younger age, and I was able to go in and deal with the guilt and the shame I experienced at that time. I feel a great sense of relief from that. I'm no longer beating up that little boy.

GK: Sounds like it's been a real healing for you.

RB: He's making good use of it.

Audience: I didn't feel a lot of pain, only a kind of sadness. It was easy to look at the little boy and recognize myself since I have a fairly good picture of what I was like. The most meaningful part was when you asked me to speak to him, and I realized that I never heard my own father saying, "I love you, and I'm proud of you."

My father has died, and we were never very close. But now I don't need to hear that from him, because I was able to say to *myself,* "I'm here with you always." Now I can communicate with the loneliness and the fear that I had as a little boy. And it was remarkably comforting to say, "I'm here with you now." I feel we can talk to each other.

SHAME AND GUILT: SEVERAL POINTS OF VIEW

Audience: I am finding I have to rethink my definitions of shame. That's going to be an ongoing process, but I'd like you to help clarify the idea of "healthy" shame. I saw an interview with Joe Namath, and I heard him speaking candidly about his failure to make it as a sportscaster on a major network. His voice carried his disappointment. What struck me was Namath's openness and honesty. As I see it, he was expressing healthy shame. He seemed totally aware that despite his many achievements, he had some real limitations. Is this really shame? Can we call it healthy shame?

GK: I don't know whether it's shame or not. He may have been experiencing some shame. But I can feel disappointed and not necessarily respond with shame. If somebody criticizes me, I could say, "Well, I guess that person is not satisfied with me." I don't necessarily have to respond with shame just because the situation calls for it, or somebody tries to push it on me. Instead, I could be angry. I could feel totally neutral, or disgusted, or I could feel contempt for my critic.

I don't find useful the distinction between healthy shame and unhealthy shame. I don't think it's helpful to set up a judgment that one thing is healthy and another thing is not. We may quickly become pejorative about a natural emotion.

RB: I'd say that this was commonsense modesty that Namath was expressing, not shame.

GK: Modesty. It's fine to say that modesty or genuine humility is a form of mild, appropriate, normal shame. Shame in moderation is natural, normal, and healthy. The big problem is when shame becomes internalized, and begins to expand until it cripples us. Internalized shame grows like a cancer within us.

RB: When I started reading about shame, I must have looked at 20 or 30 articles, and there was almost nothing in them (laughter). But they all made a lot of distinctions between shame and guilt. And I'm hearing you, Gershen, say that these distinctions are not necessary. One thing I did learn was this: There are eight words for shame in ancient Greek, four words for shame in French, five in German, but only one in English. That means we don't want to think about shame. And, unlike the Eskimos with their 32 names for snow, we don't make important distinctions about shame.

The Greeks have a word, *aidos,* for holy shame. That's the shame you feel when you go into a great cathedral. We have to add an adjective—"holy" shame—but they had a single word to distinguish this feeling from any other shame. This is shame in the presence of the divine, and since we're not divine, we naturally feel it. The latter part of the *Iliad* is connected with this. When Hector was dead, they had no *aidos* for his body—they dragged it around behind a chariot. That was a lack of *aidos,* a lack of proper and divine shame. They got punished a lot for that!

It was the same thing when terrorists held that plane in Cairo last summer. They killed a man and dumped him out, and we all saw his body hit the ground. That's a lack of *aidos*, but those stupid television people couldn't understand. They should not have shown that scene over and over again. Once would have been more than enough, because that's a lack of *aidos*, a lack of holy shame for the divinity of the human body.

So I think about how strange it is that our vocabulary is so crippled in certain areas that we can't make these important distinctions.

Audience: The way I see it, shame is when I perceive myself as flawed or unlovable. I like to think that I can motivate some kind of change in my clients through their guilt, through the way feel about their actions. But I still don't see a positive side to shame.

GK: If I am a four-year old child, I may want to shoot baskets like my older brother, but I can't even get the ball to hit the backboard. I hang my head in shame at not being able to do it. The shame is not about my whole life; it's localized in that moment and that action. I don't feel defective or worthless, I simply feel shame at not being able to do what my older brother can do. That's shame about actions, not about self. All children experience shame because they can't match their older siblings or parents in skills of various kinds.

Think of the shame we feel when we slip on the ice—you probably have some of that here in Minnesota in the winter (laughter). You fall, you laugh about it, you talk about it as embarrassment. If you watch a toddler learning to walk, you see a lot of shame before that set of skills is mastered. But it's all localized in the action.

The key is for shame to be tempered so it doesn't overwhelm the child. If the parent or some older person responds in a reassuring way, the shame is reduced, neutralized. The child can cope with it effectively. I always had to say to my younger son, "You're not *supposed* to be able to do what your brother can do. You are four years younger."

It got to the point where he would say, "I'm tired of hearing that!"

RB: I think I agree with you. But I'm still interested in the distinction between guilt and shame. Classically, it is said that you feel guilty for some specific thing you've done wrong. You can atone for it. But shame is a general feeling of being totally inadequate. There's absolutely no way you can atone for it.

If I did a calculated, cruel thing to someone, I can do a ritual to reverse that moment of guilt. There's no ritual that will ever reverse my shame. That's why I find the distinction useful. I don't want to get rid of the word "guilt." We only have two words, "guilt" and "shame," and I don't want to lose one of them! (laughter)

GK: I hear what you're saying, but I'm not convinced yet. I'm not suggesting we get rid of anything, only that we rethink what we're labeling. I use the word "guilt" whenever there is a sense of transgression, a sense of having done something wrong. But beneath the surface of the word, you may actually *feel* shame, self-blame, or even self-contempt. There can be a whole lot of different emotions underneath what we call guilt.

Guilt is fine to keep and use, but it can be about the self, too. I have met people who are guilt-ridden for things they did twenty or more years ago. One woman was so abusive that she caused the death of her children. She will live with guilt for the rest of her life. She is guilt-ridden, and there is nothing that will atone for that.

Guilt can be about acts or about self. Shame can be about acts or about self. That's not the critical distinction for me.

SHAME IN FOLK TALES

RB: There's a great folk tale about men's shame in the Grimm Brothers' collection. It's called "Hans, My Hedgehog." The story begins when people say to a man, "Why don't you have any sons? Why don't you have any children?"

So he came home angry and said, "I will have a son, even if he is a hedgehog!" But you must be careful about what you say, because soon he had a son who *was* a hedgehog. He was a hedgehog from the waist up and human from the waist down. Because of his quills, his mother couldn't nurse him.

So his father said, "Well, what the hell!" and he made him a little bed behind the stove. And he lived behind the stove until he was 12.

Then a beautiful thing happens. One day the son goes to his father and says, "Will you give me a rooster, and will you have the blacksmith shoe it?" (Nobody knows what that means – why he wanted iron on the feet of the rooster.) The father says, "Yes."

So the son took a bagpipe and some pigs and rode the rooster into the forest. The rooster flew up into a tree, and the boy sat there on the rooster, playing his bagpipe, while pigs were copulating underneath. That's the scene. Nobody knows what that means, either.

These stories teach us, in mythological language, about transcending misfortune and avoiding some of life's hazards. This one tells us a lot about how to overcome massive shame. The third time I told it, tears came to my eyes. I realized that, in a certain sense, *I* had been left behind the stove. The story says that if you have shame, don't fool around with . . . new age harps. Pick up a bagpipe, and really express your grief!

These happy people are shame killers . . .. Remember that idiot who sang, "Don't Worry, Be Happy!" When I heard that, I said to myself, "This is Ronald Reagan's song. What's a black man doing singing it?" These happy types are dangerous. They try to keep you from feeling your shame, expressing your grief. Buy a bagpipe, that's what this story says.

Audience: I'm Irish. I'm Catholic. For an American Irish-Catholic, anything to do with sex is shameful—talking about it, thinking about it. How do you counteract that?

RB: Become a Lutheran! (laughter) I mean, at least that would . . . follow history. But that's a serious question. I'd like to hear Gershen's feeling on that.

GK: Next question! (laughter)

RB: My answer is to try to face that shame without blaming nuns or priests. Try to feel how painful it is to have that divine instinct—sexuality—constantly opposed and humiliated and shamed. Without the blame, I think you'll get at the full grief of it.

GK: But in the process, you may need to experience your rightful rage at having been humiliated. I think that's crucial.

RB: Good point. The anger can't be whitewashed. But can you be enraged by someone without blaming him? I'm not sure . . . it's complicated.

GK: It is complicated, incredibly so. There are times when I will roast people in my fireplace—slowly!

Audience: Is that more reparenting imagery? (laughter)

RB: There's a good story in this area of anger: "The Devil's Sooty Brother." A man is discharged from the army and goes looking for a job. A dark man—the Devil—hires him to keep pots boiling for seven years, working underneath the ground. Before he leaves, the dark man says, "Don't look in the pots!" Well, of course, that's the way to get him to look in. After a while, he looks into the first caldron, and he sees his sergeant. So he puts more wood on the fire underneath. Three months later he opens the second pot and sees his lieutenant there, so he puts a lot more wood on that fire, too.

It says we are to enjoy the boiling of authority figures who have humiliated us! Isn't that lovely? You can boil them inside you. It's not necessary to go out and attack them; you can boil your *fantasy* of them.

These authority figures are images of the shamers that we have internalized. We have to boil them and boil them, over and over again, until they're limp and lifeless. That's what it means, doesn't it?

GK: Yes, we can reexperience our shame-rage until we release it, and kick out the people who caused it. I think it's possible to literally kick them out. It's not easy; it takes time. It took me 20 years to undo the damage of the first 20.

RB: And finding a woman who really enjoys sex can be helpful, too!

GK: Might help you speed up the process!

POTPOURRI

Audience: In your list of tactics, I didn't find any place for sadness, despair, or grief.

GK: Sadness, despair and grief . . .. Distress is the crying response; outwardly it takes the form of tears, or sobbing. Internally, we experience it as sadness. That's what grief is all about, experiencing the crying, the distress.

But we also use the word "grief" to refer to the grief process, which is a reexperiencing and a reworking of all of the affects. The various stages of the grief process, which Kubler-Ross and others have written about so beautifully, are really the sequencing of these affects over a period of time. So that's grief, too.

We use the word "hurt" in a curious way. Sometimes what we call "hurt" is really shame. When we feel wounded, we're talking about shame. That shame feeling might be accompanied by sadness. But there are other times when we feel hurt, times when it doesn't feel like we've been wounded. Then we may simply be describing sadness or some other form of distress.

Audience: Where do you put sexual response?

GK: Sexuality? Our blackboard's not big enough! (laughter)

We've talked of *affects.* There are nine basic affects—surprise, excitement, joy, distress, anger, fear, shame, disgust, and dissmell. We've talked of *needs*, interpersonal needs, which are required for us to develop and maintain psychological health. And we've talked of how internalized shame binds develop whenever any of these affects or needs is subjected to recurring external shaming.

There's a third general category, the physiological *drive* system, which includes the hunger and sexual drives. Drives also can be encumbered by internal shame binds.

A curious thing is that the sex drive is really a paper tiger. It has to be amplified by a positive affect, by excitement. When we are feeling sexually aroused, whether it's during masturbation fantasy or sexual intercourse, we experience sexual excitement, not in our genitals, but in our faces, in our nostrils, in our breathing. It's the affect of excitement that we're experiencing. That's the same emotion we might feel at a football game, a party, or a parade. This positive emotion of excitement must become fused with our sexual drive for potency, for integration, for pleasure.

At the first sign of a negative affect—shame, disgust, fear—sexual functioning is completely disrupted. That's a legacy of much of our religious heritage. It's not just one group. I have met many people from varying religions who have been made to feel tremendous shame, guilt, and disgust about sexuality. We're taught that there's something wrong with it. When I go beneath the word guilt, it's shame and disgust that I usually find. Being sexual is *that* dirty, *that* bad, *that* less than human. It's really a disgust response more than anything else.

RB: I want to go back to the connection that Gershen made between shame and hurt feelings. If a woman starts to attack the patriarchy, for example, she's got a lot of hurt feelings. You have to notice that shame is there also. It's difficult to hear the hurt feelings—as one should—without starting to feel ashamed. And if you fall into shame, soon you'll be apologizing for things that happened 2,000 years ago. Then you'll find yourself apologizing for all living men. And pretty soon you'll end up saying, "All men are shits." A friend of mine did that; it was the outcome of his shame. From a woman's hurt feelings, he got caught in this trance of shame.

These conversations don't solve anything. You can't make up for 2,000 years of what happened to women. Many of their complaints are justified, but you can't make up for them in two or three hours. You have to recognize that a trance is starting, and that you don't have to go into that trance any more.

GK: Another way to say it is, "Hear the feelings." Recognize that there is hurt and shame beneath the rage. Anybody who has been systematically humiliated for a long time and then finds a release is going to go to rage. This has been true for blacks in this country, or Native Americans, or bearded men . . .. Their experience is analogous to women's. The rage may be an inevitable thing, a natural step in the progression from shame to pride.

My son surprised me several months ago. We have a thing every week where we all sit down together and talk as a family. Everybody gets to share feelings. And my son said, "You don't hear me. You don't listen to me." You could have knocked me over with a feather. I mean, that's my job! Listening is what I do for a living! What I said was "Boy, I'm really glad you told me how badly you've been feeling."

I listened to his feelings; I cared about them, but I didn't feel ashamed. I had a momentary pang of "Gee, am I really missing something? Am I not paying attention to him?" I considered it, but I didn't *blame* myself. I didn't go into the shame experience that Robert was talking about. I simply listened to my son and heard his feelings and acknowledged that I'm probably not perfect. I'm human, and I'm going to blow it some of the time. But I cared enough about his feelings to allow him to express them without buying into the shame and taking it inside. That's the hardest thing to do, but learning to do it brings big rewards.

RB: We'll end with a poem by Antonio Machado, a Spanish poet who died in 1939. It's one of my favorite poems, and I think it says a lot about our subject today.

(Playing bouzouki.)
Last night as I was sleeping
I dreamt —marvelous error!—
that I had a spring
here inside my heart.
Along what ancient aqueduct,
Oh water, are you coming to me,
water of a new life
that I have never drunk?

Last night as I was sleeping,
I dreamt—marvelous error!—
that I had a beehive
here inside my chest.
And the golden bees
were making white combs
and sweet honey
from my old failures.

Last night as I was sleeping,
I dreamt—marvelous error!—
that I had a fiery sun
here inside my chest.
It was fiery because it gave
warmth, as from a hearth
and it was sun because it gave light
and brought tears to my eyes.

Last night as I was sleeping,
I dreamt—marvelous error!—
that it was God I had
here inside my heart.

– Antonio Machado, translated by Robert Bly[2]

(Sustained applause.)

NOTES:

[1] Based on the audiotape, "Men's Shame," of a joint presentation sponsored by the Alfred Adler Institute of Minnesota, Minneapolis, April 23, 1989.

[2] Reprinted from *Times Alone: Selected Poems of Antonio Machado*, translated by Robert Bly. Wesleyan University Press, Middletown, CT, 1989. 1989 by Robert Bly. Reprinted with permission.

Chapter 6
Men Facing Shame: A Healing Process

JOHN EVERINGHAM

I am heartened by today's prospects for significant healing of internalized shame. In the last 15 years, we've cracked open this hard nut, which lay so long buried – misunderstood and ignored – under obscuring psychotherapeutic theory and the unacknowledged shame of many therapists. I honor Schneider (1977), Kaufman (1980), Kurtz (1981), and Fossum and Mason (l986) for their effectiveness in leading us – and me, personally – out of the wilderness.

Many are at work, zestfully devising arms with which to slay The Invisible Dragon (Shame), who has recently become visible in his true form. New approaches are appearing so fast that it's difficult to keep up with them all, so that the original subtitle of this chapter was changed from "The" to "A" Healing Process. Other chapters in this book contain many of these new discoveries. The present chapter is something of an overview; contributions from several authors address in depth material that is treated here in less detail.

Facing shame directly is a basic necessity to healing. This isn't as obvious as it sounds, for one of our basic responses to primary shame is to look away, averting our eyes. Metaphorically, we must look the Dragon full in the face, allowing ourselves to be fearful of his sharp teeth and fiery breath, but still steadfastly continuing to look him in the eye.

The metaphor stands for a man allowing himself to feel acutely ashamed for a sufficient time – seconds, perhaps minutes – to become convinced that he won't die from this feeling. It means that he will learn to recognize what primary shame feels like, and realize that he no longer needs to hide it beneath some other emotion. Facing shame involves calling it by name – "shame" – as well as taking time to make an honest assessment of the destructive effects of internalized shame in my life. As a man continues to practice facing shame, he'll learn to hang his head or look away while he feels it, then lift his head and look someone in the eye, saying, "I feel ashamed."

I believe that a great deal of the dysfunction caused by internalized shame – perhaps half of it – can be reversed by using a set of simple "tools," and that ordinary men can learn to use them effectively, without dependence on therapists or other experts. The other half is tougher, and some type of professional help or ongoing program is likely to be necessary for the man carrying a heavy burden of shame. But you can feel the exhilaration of brandishing a newly sharpened sword and watching the Dragon shrink back in alarm.

The body of this chapter contains discussion of 18 or 20 "tools" to help us face and heal shame. In the Dragon metaphor, these tools become the maneuvers of effective swordsmanship, many of which function to render the Invisible Dragon more visible. Some of them are published here for the first time (e.g., Hit the Wall, Integrate It into Your Body); others are recognized by all the modern authors (e.g., Name It, Talk About It, Maintain Boundaries).

BREAK THE RULES

Merle Fossum and Marilyn Mason describe the "rules" that maintain shame in families and other human systems:

> The idea of "family rules" is used to describe repeated patterns of interaction that family therapists notice… These rules are descriptive metaphors (Jackson, 1965), unlike the rules and regulations…decided on by authority… (They) are descriptive of the forces working within the family that influence behavior. The eight rules that follow represent a recurrent pattern…characteristic of a shame-bound system. (Fossum & Mason, 1986, p. 86)

The following list of rules is taken from Chapter 15, where I discuss them in further detail, and propose rule 10. Rule 9 comes from John Bradshaw (1988, p. 39).

Control. Be in control of all behavior, interactions and feelings. Control is the basic goal of all the shaming rules.

Blame. If something goes wrong, blame somebody; blame yourself if necessary. Don't blame the shame-generating system, or these rules.

Perfectionism. Always be and do right. Feel "right," too. Don't try if you might make a mistake. Justify everything.

Incompleteness. Don't complete or resolve disagreements and transactions. Keep feuds and resentments going. Don't confront.

Denial. Deny feelings, needs, and desires – your own and others' – especially negative, "bad," or "wrong" ones. Deny even the obvious "elephant in the living room."

No Talk. Hide our secrets with a strict code of silence, among ourselves and certainly with others. Hold your breath, look away, and shut up.

Disqualification. Deny by disguising. Spin the shameful episode around; call it something else; distort it; reframe it. Look away from the shameful part and focus attention on the positive or truthful part.

Unreliability. Don't be reliable or trustworthy, or behave in a predictable way. Keep 'em guessing. Watch for others to be treacherous and unpredictable toward you.

Not Allowing The Five Freedoms (Satir, 1974). Don't let others perceive, think and interpret, feel, desire, or imagine *in their own way.* Especially not children, clients, subordinates, or yourself.

Moral Intimidation. Assume the right to decide what – and, therefore, who – is right, appropriate, humane, enlightened, professional, or politically correct. Enforce authority with shaming threats, rhetorical questions, and subtle name-calling.

Fossum and Mason (1986) describe each of these rules in some detail, so it's good to read their chapter 5. We discover that shame, powerful though it be, has an Achilles' heel. A decision to break these rules, especially the No Talk rule, is a decision to **break the power of shame.** Good news, indeed!

RECOGNIZE SHAME

We may be uncertain at first, but we can learn with a little effort, practice, and listening to trusted brothers and our own guts. Also, we may learn to recognize the keys for shame (as a quarterback uses keys – certain positions and movements by his opponents – to read defenses).

Here are some of the keys now known for shame: *emotional* keys include feeling like shrinking, feeling frozen, a sinking feeling, a strong desire to hide, intense emotional discomfort for little apparent reason, imagining all eyes are on you, or anxious self-surveillance.

The *physical* keys are eyes averted, head down, face flushed, ears burning, involuntary shudders, tight throat and chest, gut rigid or churning, and speech halting or without resonance and power.

The *mental* and *cognitive* keys involve being inarticulate (Baumli, 1995), having the panicky awareness of a mind gone blank, and noticing when someone is using shaming rules on you, or when you're using them on someone else or on yourself.

The Recognize Shame tool breaks the rules of Denial, Disqualification, Control, and Perfectionism.

NAME IT

Whenever I notice one or more of these keys, I've learned to say, "I'll bet this is shame," or "I'm feeling ashamed." Naming shame has a powerful effect, because it brings whatever was held in shameful secrecy into the light of self-acceptance. Recently, I felt ashamed when refused a hug, when I was talking about inheriting some money, when I realized that part of my feeling for a brother is that I'm ashamed to be too closely identified with him in the minds of others.

Naming shame helps, because the word itself is evocative and perhaps onomatopoetic. "Shame" and "ashamed" evoke feelings in me that "guilty" never does; they seem to resonate with my inner reality. Does the "sh" sound feel like a sigh of relief, signifying the release and expulsion of a long-held, poisonous secret?

Sometimes Name It and Talk About It can be done at the same time, but not always, or even usually. The distinction between private self-awareness and public disclosure is often substantial, and I need a kind of permission to uphold the privacy of my thoughts and feelings against premature exposure. We all need reassurance that we have control of the zipper that opens us up (Fossum & Mason, 1986; Mason & Fossum, 1987). There is no adequate substitute for knowing my own inner reality.

Another reason to Name It now and Talk About It later is to allow time and emotional space for an intervening stage, Feel It. Premature talking about shame may tend to codify or arrest the full development of the feeling and its ramifications. "We will serve no wine before its time" is a good motto for both the shamenik and the vintner, especially because newfound shame is usually "green."

Because shame-bound families perpetuate shame from generation to generation (despite the benefits that they may also perpetuate), it's usually helpful to name shameful events in family history. Considerable relief comes from acknowledging that my grandfather periodically deserted his family, leaving them impoverished and undoubtedly ashamed. Whether he did this because of alcoholism, mental illness, or wanderlust, I can only guess; his reasons were never discussed. It isn't hard to imagine how my father became my grandmother's "lover" in the emotional sense, and how confused and ashamed he must have felt.[1] I still feel ashamed to admit that I may have been an unwanted child - a contraceptive failure - the only child of middle-aged parents in the Depression. I feel shame, but it clears out a lot of garbage, in that something inside gives me permission to be the way I am, to carry a load of emotional wounding that will take time to heal.

Please avoid using family history to support playing a manipulative Victim role (James & Jongeward, 1971; Everingham, 1995c). Grief is appropriate, but playing Victim counterproductive. Grief subsides with time; Victiming often intensifies.

It's important to name shame wherever it's encountered, whether it be in personal interactions, advertising, television programs, comics, or male and female socialization.

Name It, along with Talk About It, forms a one-two punch estimated to relieve a lot of shame in a relatively short time. In bringing shameful secrets to light, the fear of exposure is substantially relieved, and we give up trying to hide from ourselves. Thus, Name It breaks the rules of Denial and Disqualification in one instance, and of Perfectionism, No Talk, and Incompleteness in another.

FEEL IT

More than books, talk, thought, or the experience of others, our own body and emotions constitute our basic text. How shame feels was described previously and in Chapter 1. The primary emotion is much more accessible to our bodies than internalized shame, but that too can be felt with practice, and the use of keys previously discussed.

It's valuable to stay with shameful feelings for as long as possible. This applies also to uncertain feelings that are only suspected to be shame. Recall that feeling ashamed is rarely destructive in itself. Don't make this your life work, of course, but try it when you sense deep and heavy feelings inside, or if you're in a mood to learn something about yourself. Shame is such a silent emotion that it takes special effort to get friendly with it.

In a memorable therapy session, I sat frozen and ashamed, with my head down and eyes closed, for more than half an hour. Occasionally the therapist briefly checked in with me, but mostly encouraged me to stay with the feeling for as long as I wanted to. I learned to be less afraid of shame, and certainly less ashamed of feeling it. And I learned something else, difficult to express in words; perhaps it's about truly honoring my own personal experience. At other times, when I've reminded myself about staying with the feeling, I've been able to do so for perhaps ten minutes, or even just one minute. That's much better than jumping past shame into fear, anger, or the "medication" of an addictive practice.

Sometimes shame presents itself as confusion, or a feeling of not knowing what I want, or feeling bad without knowing why, or vagueness. It's wonderful to be able to sit with these vague feelings for a while, not in a crusade to "find the answer," but simply to honor myself. Such experience is often necessary after one has Hit The Wall.

Feel It breaks the rules of Control, Blame, and Perfectionism; and internally, the rules of Disqualification, Denial, and Incompleteness.

TALK ABOUT IT

Using this tool is the culmination of the previous four tools, and it's here that the big payoffs become apparent. When I'm able to talk about shame to at least one other person, my insides are saying, "I'm OK even though I...," and "I won't die even if they know that... "

Talk About It can be as simple as saying, "I feel shame; I'm ashamed." Or perhaps a man will tell of situations in the past: "I was an unwanted child; my uncle sodomized me; my mother kept calling me her little man; the guys always teased me about my size." It's helpful to talk about feelings you're ashamed of, especially male-mode feelings (Bly & Meade, n.d.), or feelings you know may deeply offend others. Some examples: "I hate my father because he always put me down, but I was too ashamed to tell him. I feel like a traitor." "When the war ended, I felt let down. It was the most exciting time of my life; I often wish it wasn't over." "I wanted to rape her, then and there. To hell with rubbers and foreplay!"[2]

In addition to feeling ashamed of myself, sometimes I feel ashamed of a friend or family member. This is really being ashamed of myself for being associated, in someone's mind, with the other person. It's usually good to tell the person involved, because it's likely to be sensed nonverbally and corrode the relationship.

A man can talk about his shame in confronting style: "When you don't call back, I feel ashamed. I think you imply that your time is more valuable than mine." "That tone of voice pushes my shame button."

Many programs emphasize the value of telling one's story (see *Alcoholics Anonymous*, 1976, pp. 171-561). This practice establishes a ground of shared experience and a vehicle for communicating hope to the listeners. It also uses the Talk About It tool for healing shame, because the "knower" most feared may be myself. At a 12-step meeting in Los Angeles, a wise veteran of the program said, "We come here not so much to listen to each other's stories, but to be supported and encouraged in listening to our own."

Talk about It directly violates the No Talk rule, and Perfectionism, Denial, and Blame as well.

HIT THE WALL

There comes a time of blockade. I'm into heavy emotion, but have no idea where to go with it. I'm scared and confused. Usually one or more of the keys to internalized shame are present, often inarticulateness (Baumli, 1995).

Successful strategy is to back off, cease trying to drive through the fear. After a few hours or perhaps weeks, my internal process tells me what I'm ashamed of. Then I can cycle back and Name It, Feel It, Talk About It. We all have stout protective mechanisms against too rapid exposure, but knowing that I have Hit The Wall helps me tolerate the impasse. As with Feel It, it's good to stay with the blocked feeling for as long as possible.

Hit The Wall breaks the rules of Perfectionism, Control, and Disqualification, and if the cycling back is successful, it also breaks one of the subtler shaming rules – Incompleteness.

INTEGRATE HEALING INTO YOUR BODY

I don't know any way to plan the use of this tool, but when the opportunity comes, seize it. For weeks, my 20-year old son had been furious with me. Released by the New Warrior training from his usual inhibition about confronting the old man, he was letting it all hang out. He raged at me for committing slow suicide by overeating; he was contemptuous of my dispassionate treatment of his brother; he grieved for the years when he lacked an effective male parent; and he was disgusted when I'd had enough and withdrew from him and others. I imagine that he was frightened by some of his feelings toward me. Most of all, I think he was frustrated that his rage seemed to have no positive effect.

Some little thing sparked his fury again, and his anger kindled mine. We didn't just pass it off, but went to a park nearby and faced each other, man to man. As my anger cooled, shame arose. When I haltingly told him that I was afraid to have him see me as a phony, he looked at me with love in his eyes and said, "Dad, I've known for years what a phony you are, and it's OK."

It was as if a heavy suit of armor melted and fell off my body. The secret I had been striving so mightily to preserve all these years was revealed as common knowledge. And he loved me anyway! My elaborate defenses against shame were completely ineffective, and moreover unnecessary. So I let them fall off me, to my great relief.

Over the years, I've had recurrent dreams about being inside a large metal boiler or tank, as large as a house. I've banged and banged on the walls of this metal prison; always it has been unyielding. The boiler hasn't visited me since this experience with my son a 16 years ago. My body released the grief and rigidity of so many years of self-alienation, and began to reestablish a sense of belonging.

It's unclear what rule Integrate Healing breaks. Probably Control, and possibly Incompleteness. Words seem inadequate to describe fully the experience, and I hope we'll learn more about it in the future.

ESTABLISH AND MAINTAIN BOUNDARIES

Shame-bound men usually feel that the handle of the zipper to our insides is located on the outside, so that anybody can invade us at will (Fossum & Mason, 1986; Dougherty, 1988b). We often take on others' problems and feelings as if they were our own, and we are especially vulnerable to carrying shame, pain, and fear that rightfully belong to somebody else. Facing and healing our own pain and shame may make us less likely to offer ourselves as emotional beasts of burden. In my experience, boundary problems change but slowly, but they do change. Cognitively, it may help to honor the concept that "I am I, and you are you" (Perls, 1969; Peck, 1978), or to ask, "Whose problem is it?" (Gordon, 1974). A consideration of the Rescue Triangle (James & Jongeward, 1971; Everingham, 1995c) may be helpful.

CONFRONT SHAMING BEHAVIOR

Examples of using this tool include: "When you..., I feel ashamed." "That's one of the rules we've been using to maintain shame in our family or organization." "I'm really offended by the way you use 'patriarchy.'" Analyze family structures for unhealthy vertical relationships (Mason & Fossum, 1987), role reversals, boundary violations, and codependency (Fossum & Mason, 1986). Break the conspiracy of silence.

In recent years, we've tended to rely on others to do our confronting for us – lawyers, police, government officials, and a variety of activists and advocates. I recommend personal confrontation. Stand up, look 'em in the eye, say your say. You don't need to explain or justify. If the behavior triggers shame in you, tell them about it.

Confront Shaming Behavior can break any or all of the 10 shaming rules. Jackpot! But I'd be cautious about using this tool too early or often; some prior experience with Recognize Shame, Feel It, Name It, Talk about It, and Boundaries is recommended. Confrontation is discussed further in Chapter 15, under the Incompleteness rule.

BUILD AND REPAIR INTERPERSONAL BRIDGES

Let's acknowledge our need for love, validation, attention, touch, respect, sex, blessing, and the experience of seeing another's face light up in response to our presence. Let's reduce our shame about feeling needy, and learn to distinguish real needs from playing a manipulative Victim role.

We can reach out to others, genuinely offering the same things. Let's be patient, for the self-surveillance and self-absorption characteristic of internalized shame may be slow to heal, and self-absorbed people tend to wear on others' nerves after awhile. This is the voice of experience, from both sides. Genuine love and caring will begin to flow as shame lifts.

But let's not be naive. Just as good engineering often requires the tearing down of old rickety structures, so ways of relating to people can also be tested for soundness and proper function. I'm learning to ask myself honestly about what I really want from being with this man or this woman. And if I'm not getting it, I can ask for what I want, be willing to negotiate, or perhaps bid him or her goodbye. If being with someone feels uneasy, we need to find alternatives based on emotional honesty. I sometimes find that I've fallen into a pattern of hanging out with certain guys just because they're more available, or I think they are less likely to reject me. It's important to ask myself who I'd really like to be with, availability aside, and then make some effort to that end. Somehow this approach clears out emotional junk and makes "space" for more satisfying and nurturing relationships.

If a breach has occurred, make amends; get back into integrity with the other person. If it's true, say, "Your friendship, warm and unencumbered, is important to me. I want to find a way to be friends without violating the integrity of either of us" (Paul & Paul, 1983).

If your friend says, "No," grieve, and then move on.

Interpersonal Bridges is an important tool for maintaining ourselves free from toxic shame after significant healing has occurred, as well as in the initial healing. Good interpersonal relations break the rules of Unreliability, Incompleteness, Disqualification and Denial. And beyond tools and rules, they are channels for the healing flow of love.

EAT THE SHADOW

The Shadow represents parts of myself that I deny or try to hide, and usually project onto other people (see Chapter 1). Usually I'm ashamed of these parts. But disowned entities have a way of coming out sideways, and they're likely to be nastier after escaping from burial alive.

Projection onto others is one way the Shadow comes out of hiding. When I'm denying my own inner violence, I find some violent guy to feel both afraid and contemptuous of. If I'm hiding my self-righteousness, there's always some self-righteous phony to get angry at. When I'm ashamed of my desire to be persuasive or popular, I find some lawyer or actor to feel jealous of, as well as contemptuous. Although it spoils the joys of self-righteous anger, when I pause to ask, "What disowned part of me does this bastard represent?" I usually find an answer. Bly (1988, pp. 56-59) discusses other worthwhile ways of using anger to honor the Shadow.

"Eating the Shadow" is a metaphor for retrieving, claiming, owning, integrating, embracing, and assimilating all those exiled shadow parts. The process not only reduces the power of the Shadow to make mischief, but it becomes an occasion of joy to welcome home aspects of the personality long banished from their rightful place of honor. Every homecoming strengthens the true self. The genuineness of the welcome may be judged by attending to my physical response, which is usually warm vibrations, and often tears of joy. Ritual homecoming celebrations, with good friends present to witness and bless, are recommended.

Robert Bly (1988, pp. 29-43) presents "Five Stages in Exiling, Hunting and Retrieving the Shadow." The first stage is projection, already described. In his second stage, "Something doesn't fit anymore, and we hear a rattle." The rattle can be very disturbing, and we may angrily blame and shame others, particularly our children. The third stage intensifies this effort as we promote our violence to the status of a moral crusade. The fourth stage happens when a man finally sees himself as diminished, because in giving away (projecting) his negative Shadow, he gives away the positive side too. The last stage is retrieval, and it is here that the "eating" begins. It's usually a slow process, involving grief and a heightened sense of being limited in a fundamental way, and it requires active effort. I cannot do justice to Bly's excellent treatment in a summary paragraph, and urge you to read the original.

Some men's groups practice "shadow naming" from time to time, in either a ritual or an informal way. As ritual, men may stand in a circle, arms on shoulders, breathing slowly and deeply, in an attitude of honesty and introspection. Each man has an opportunity to name the part of his Shadow that he's most aware of now, and his friends answer with a nonjudgmental "Thank you." Any man may choose to pass. "My shadow is the shame I feel, and try to hide." "Thank you." "My Shadow is that I'm afraid to be really intimate with a woman." "Thank you." "All my life I've been devising strategies to resist authority." "Thank you." "I truly hunger and thirst for revenge on (name of man)." "Thank you." "My Shadow is that right now I want to just pack it in, and die." "Thank you."

Sometimes a man will recognize that he shares with the speaker the shadow element just named, and will raise a hand in acknowledgment. We take time between speakers to let things sink in. There may be grunts of recognition, "mmm's" of approval, or sighs of relief. Men look into each other's eyes and perhaps nod in recognition, but we abstain from questions and comments, or defer them. These are sacred moments – when we trust our brothers with our innermost shame, with matters we have hidden from *ourselves* until very recently. The relief of internalized shame is palpable, as is the bonding and mutual respect.

After some practice at Eating the Shadow, I can feel in my body both a sadist and a masochist, as well as a man capable of fidelity and focused action for the benefit of self and others. These figures coexist and usually balance each other, but each will get the upper hand at times and be acted out, in the same way that each of various characters in a play has its turn at center stage. Shadow figures become dangerous when one of them is so magnified that it completely outweighs the others. Then we may speak of possession, by the Tyrant shadow of the King archetype, for example. We see in action how conscious balance is a key characteristic of emotional health.

Eating the Shadow breaks the rules of Perfectionism, Blame, Denial, No Talk, and Disqualification, and offers substantial support for resisting Moral Intimidation.

EXPERIENCE THE ORPHAN

Stories of orphans abound in ancient myth and folk tale, as well as modern comics. The Orphan doesn't belong, through no fault of his/her own, and feels unwanted, inferior, and ashamed. From infancy, we all need to be desired and delighted in (Kaufman, 1989, pp. 32-35). So the Orphan is a core image for the internalized shame we feel when delight and desire are lacking (Compaan, 1997, pp. 83-90).

Pearson (1986, 1991) and Klein (1990) describe characteristics of this Orphan figure; most of them resemble internalized shame. It's helpful to consult these works and read the original stories, or perhaps do a bit of "Orphan theater." Then I begin to identify a significant piece of my life history, and experience clearly, in a somehow protected way, feelings that have been buried and mysterious for many years. It can be an emotional homecoming, profoundly moving and satisfying.

Experience the Orphan breaks the Denial, Disqualification, and Perfectionism rules, and may help with Control.

ACKNOWLEDGE YOUR WOUNDS

Listen to Robert Bly (1985) and Patrick Dougherty (1988a, 1988b) on audiotape. Their voices speak to this subject with a resonance that cannot be matched on paper. Dougherty's first tape provides vivid examples of both intrusive and neglectful (deprivation) abuse, and shows how it's often difficult to get a handle on neglectful abuse, such as never being held. I offer a short poem on this subject:

Little Boy Hiding

Wounds   by their forgetting   turn to shame.
Ashamed, I fear the gaze of a child
    and learn to hate the little boy within.
Acknowledgment   begins the healing.

the Wild Man   shows his wounds
    machismo savage   *tries* to hide them.
We see you in there, little boy
You don't have to come out
                    until you're ready . . .

Wounds   in their forgetting   turn to shame
Remembering   begins the healing.

Acknowledging my wounds is a necessary precedent to taking full personal responsibility for healing them – another necessity. There is some danger that we'll get stuck in Victim mentality, and use it to avoid taking our lives in our own hands. But I think most men shift too soon, before the wounds phase has become fully operational, so that the responsibility part has a fatalistic and unproductive air. We need to acknowledge our emotional and spiritual wounds in the full depth of their pain and disability, avoiding both undershooting and overshooting.

In Chapter 14, John Giles (1995) presents some of his experience, which illustrates these points very well, and extends the process to forgiveness.

Acknowledge Wounds breaks the rules of Denial, Disqualification, and No Talk. It helps with Incompleteness as well, by facilitating closure with people now dead or unwilling to participate.

LET GO OF VICTIM

Interactions of the *manipulative* positions of Victim, Persecutor, and Rescuer are described in Chapter 13. We've considered elsewhere today's double standard favoring Victims who dish out public verbal abuse. "MEN R SCUM" was recently an approved auto license plate in Illinois.

Several consequences can occur. The politically "incorrect" may stand silent (and ashamed) or slink off, but their internalized shame and anger builds and becomes more vicious. I view this as a natural consequence of shaming, not as an indication of some kind of moral depravity.

It's doubtful that overt shaming or shaming threats help the social situation in the long run; they're effective primarily for short-term social control, but carry a hidden time bomb. Along with reinforcing prejudice, shaming drives it underground where it's more difficult to see by either party, but likely to erupt without warning. On the social and political level, the Victim turned verbal Persecutor often ends up shooting himself in the foot.

On the personal, emotional, and spiritual levels, hanging out in the manipulative Victim position is equally damaging. Barely audible voices inside say, "I can't," "if only they (she, I) hadn't…" or "I never had the opportunity to… ." These voices maintain the core belief of incurable unworthiness. To heal the buried shame, I need to turn up the volume so that I can hear these voices clearly, feel the force of their emotional impact, and claim them as my own. The "I can't" becomes "I won't."

Shifting from Victim to Rescuer or Persecutor derails the healing process by hiding the internalized shame behind "righteous" anger or "caring" service. This kind of anger rarely clears the air or accomplishes anything interpersonally. The "service" doesn't feel clean or do much to diminish anxious self-surveillance, and all too often, it's not really appreciated by the recipient. Back to Victim again.

Groups or individuals often compete to establish themselves as the more worthy or bigger Victim, thereby to gain the upper hand in the moral pecking order. In such competition, there's a heavy price to be paid for winning. A serious question needs to be faced and, after a time of reflection, answered honestly: To what extent am I hanging on to the manipulative Victim position in preference to engaging in actions that can really change things? Despite the irrationality, I have several times found myself clearly preferring the "misery" of Victimhood. Awareness is a welcome jolt.

In addition to being a giant stride out of the Rescue triangle, Let Go of Victim breaks the rules of Blame, Denial, and Disqualification.

FORGIVE

Forgiveness heals shame by reconnecting the broken interpersonal bond. If done well, the bond usually becomes stronger than before. True forgiveness breaks the Blame and Perfectionism rules, and probably Control as well. My favorite essay on this subject is our Chapter 14, "Forgiving the Unforgivable," by John Giles.

Several additional points deserve consideration. There seems to be an optimal time to forgive; if it's done too early or too late, there are likely to be problems. Dougherty (1988b) tells of his experiences with premature forgiveness – similar to Mark Twain's comment that it was easy for him to give up cigars; he'd done it a hundred times! Forward (1989) warns that too early or easy forgiveness may lead us to discount the seriousness of our wounding, and Dougherty (1988b) explains how this may inhibit necessary grief.

Conversely, Giles (1995) describes some dangers of delaying forgiveness too long. Holding a grudge is likely to harm me much more than the other party. In addition to those presented by Giles, *Alcoholics Anonymous* (1976, pp. 551-553) describes a forgiveness technique which many find surprisingly effective – repeated specific prayer for the other person, persistently done even if insincerely at first.

It's almost impossible truly to forgive another person if we can't forgive ourselves at the same time, or to the same extent. Giles' account illustrates this point – the specific naming of his mother's offenses provided him with the self-forgiveness required to truly forgive her.

Often an amend or a 'makeup' is preferable to a naked statement of forgiveness. The make-up acknowledges that the interpersonal bond needs repair, but maintains equality between the parties. Perhaps the "injured" party declines, offering forgiveness for "free." Maybe it works, but sometimes the "forgiver" maintains a subtle air of moral superiority, while the man "forgiven" wonders why he still feels shitty and ashamed.

When a breach between adults is serious or long-standing, we usually find that both parties have contributed to the rupture of the bond. Mutual forgiveness may be desirable. Paradoxically, each party must be *willing* to forgive unilaterally.

EMBRACE PARADOX

Here's a stanza from my poem, "Rowing the Rio," in which whitewater rafting provides physical metaphors for life's emotional and spiritual journey:

He takes me to a rock by canyon cliffs
                        and bids me see faces
of paradox—seeming opposites,
                    like heads and tails of a nickel
joined:
                    battle / surrender
                    Warrior / Lover
                    Magician / King
        letting it happen / making it happen

Seeming opposites, each profoundly necessary.

Cyprian Smith (1987, p. 44) speaks of paradox thus: "Two apparently opposed realities will be brought…into clashing confrontation, until the dualism separating them is transcended and their underlying unity emerges like sunlight after rain." Making something happen (like publishing this book on a CD-ROM) and letting it happen (going with the flow of inspiration) are two such apparent opposites. I believe them to be merely different aspects of the same whole, like opposite faces of a coin. We need both, for we become unbalanced if we refuse to hold the tension of paradox – and being enthralled by a half-paradox can be dangerous.

Perhaps you felt some of this tension as you read the previous four sections. The order was designed to juxtapose the paradoxes of experiencing the Orphan and letting go of Victim, of acknowledging wounds and forgiving.

One dangerous half-paradox is to focus on forgiveness without giving the wound its full due. Men who do this tend to be wounded over and over again, in the same ways. They're likely to hang out in the Rescuer position. The man who focuses on his wounds, but rarely forgives, is poised in Victim, ready to turn Persecutor and pounce. He may still complain of affronts ten years old, and most people learn to avoid him. Perhaps he couldn't forgive himself for giving up such a lovely grievance.

Alcoholics Anonymous contains a famous paradox in its first step. "We admitted we were powerless over alcohol" becomes, paradoxically, the foundation of power to recover from addiction (*Twelve Steps and Twelve Traditions*, 1950, pp. 21-24). I am truly powerless over my addiction, *and* there is power - sufficient for a recovery - in myself, in a group, in a program, and in a Higher Power.

The grace of God is a paradox. When I don't have it, and know that I need it desperately, then I have it; when I think I've got it, I just lost it. The truth lies, not in some middle ground, but in embracing the whole thing – loss and gain, need and confidence are all parts of a unitary whole.

Perhaps you have a sense of what this holding of paradox feels like. (I obviously have a strong preference for the tactile/kinesthetic mode of expression. Visual and aural men may wish to translate into their preferred modality.) Sometimes it's like restraining two angry tomcats, and we may speak of holding "the tension of paradox." At other times, it feels easy and comforting, as if a paradox were embracing *me*. No matter how it feels, I cannot overestimate the importance of seeing that there's more than one side worth cheering for.

Embracing paradox implies a certain open-mindedness, an unwillingness to go off the deep end. For example, revealing our secrets has considerable value for healing shame, and so does maintaining our personal boundaries. Some therapists and group leaders use the first half of this paradox to justify breaking expected confidences. It takes hardening of our boundaries to convince ourselves that we can rely on them when necessary; only then is it safe to soften. Men and women need to see each other as different, almost foreign, to gain the respect that allows us to be truly intimate. That's paradox.

Our attitude toward internalized shame or addiction can also be paradoxical. It's destructive, and I want to lessen it, but it may serve drive me to explore wonderful spiritual values. As Barasch (1993, p. 310) says, "Healing is not just a method for fixing-up, but a way to express the multiplicity of the soul."

Embrace Paradox works powerfully against Disqualification and Moral Intimidation, and is helpful with Perfectionism, Blame, and Unreliability.

DANCE THE FOUR QUARTERS

Moore and Gillette (1990) have been engaged for some years in "decoding the deep structures of the masculine psyche," and their work is magnificent. The basic idea is that men (and women) have emotional / behavioral / spiritual patterns that – like our bodies – are shaped by biological evolution. To be healthy, we must live in harmony with our emotional deep structures – our bio-psychological "hard-wiring" – in the same way that we accept both the strength and the limitations of our physical bodies. We honor our maleness, emotional as well as physical.

From extensive cross-cultural study, Moore and Gillette distill these inbred patterns into four basic areas – four realms. Each realm is represented by a mythic figure, an archetype (Jung 1964, 1983; Stevens, 1983). They are the King, the Warrior, the Magician (Magus), and the Lover.[3] These four archetypes symbolize patterns that are encoded within us all, and in this view, remind us of our deepest longing and our highest purpose.

Balance and development toward maturity are key goals here. Archetypes can be numinous, powerfully attractive, and dangerous as hell. One way to avoid being "possessed" by *one* of these dynamos is to carry all four actively and consciously, so that they balance and support each other. This active balance is what is meant by "dancing the four quarters."

Another way is to contact archetypes in ritual. Here's a metaphorical illustration:[4] The archetype is a 100,000-volt generator at Grand Coulee dam; if a man plugs his toaster into it directly, the toast will be seriously burnt. Ritual is like a step-down transformer or impedance device; it allows a man to tap into archetypal energy without frying his ass.

Every archetype has its healthy and unhealthy parts. The King in His Fullness is generative; he's responsible for blessing, for empowerment, for creativity, for right order, for sacrificing himself for the good of the realm. The unhealthy, dark, dangerous parts are in the Shadow; Moore and Gillette (1990) consider each Shadow to be bipolar. For example, the shadow King may manifest as a tyrant or a weakling abdicator. As tyrant, he may demand adoration of himself instead of being truly pleased at the success and prosperity of his people; as weakling, he may shirk the responsibilities listed above, perhaps claiming that they aren't important or that he "can't handle it." We all act out both the mature and shadow aspects of any archetype – we can't escape it. But we can shift the equation toward maturity.

To avoid becoming "possessed," it is required to disidentify with an archetype. I may carry or act out the King from time to time (poorly, or well, or "good enough"), but I *am not* the King. Tragic events in Guyana and Waco, Texas, show the destructive potential of forgetting this essential point. Rotating leadership is one way we remind ourselves, and also provide each man the experience of carrying the King archetype.

Dancing the Four Quarters heals internalized shame by promoting self-acceptance of ourselves as men, and as men fulfilling a mission in the world (Miller, 1995; Greenwald, 1995). We learn to recognize and *somatize* carrying the Archetypes in Their Fullness (Moore & Gillette, 1990), and notice more quickly when we're acting out the Shadow. As we contact and derive energy from King, Warrior,[5] Lover, and Magician, we learn to understand and be proud of our male bodies, our male feelings, our masculine mission, and our male divinity.

GO BEYOND SHAME

Important though it may be, let's not make a career out of healing shame. It's a means, not an end. In classical regression *à la* Erikson (1963), I find myself moving into trust issues. This received impetus as I wrote the section on the Unreliability rule in Chapter 15 and discovered that I had never trusted myself to be reliable as my *own* best friend. Aha! However, I consider healing of shame issues to be prerequisite to effective work on trust. I can recall being so ashamed of my mistrust that I wanted to hide it.

Lindall (1995) stresses the value of letting go of fixation on recovery, in order focus on living. At some point, we have to say, "To hell with self-improvement. I'm going to enjoy myself *as I am.*" Let the celebration begin.

These tools may be used independently, or they may form a rough sequence, with a lot of cycling back. By analogy, I see them as operations or subprocesses within a larger process. What follows are additional suggestions that I view as programs – structured approaches that incorporate some or many of these tools and are likely to be quite helpful for healing internalized shame.

New Warrior Training Adventure

I carry in my body – indelibly imprinted – the sense of male bonding acquired on my weekend 15 years ago. I found in my bones the male mode of feeling (Bly and Meade n.d.) and learned to speak in male voice, trust male intuition, and love men nonsexually. Surely this provides a healing for the shame of being male (Schenk, 1995a). Greenwald (1995) expands this theme considerably, placing the New Warrior programs in the context of men's initiation, historic and modern.

The New Warrior weekend is designed to reinstitute that initiation into manhood that male elders in our culture have long neglected (Bly 1985, 1987; Bridges, 1980). While the process obviously cannot be accomplished in two days, it can be well launched. Traditional rituals from several cultures are combined creatively with the modern. As in traditional initiation, men are tested physically, emotionally, and spiritually. Most find within themselves deep reserves that they hardly knew existed.

To avoid misunderstanding, let it be clear that we honor and draw energy from Lover, King, and Magician, as well as Warrior. Our effort is to balance these archetypes consciously, and so avoid becoming possessed by any one of them (Moore & Gillette, 1990).

Presently, New Warrior training is being offered by men centered in about 25 cities in North America, as well as England, Continental Europe (in languages other than English), South Africa, Australia, and New Zealand. Continuing "Integration Groups" meet usually weekly in these locations and many other outposts; they are available to men who have completed the initiatory weekend. Additional training sites are being developed (contact The Mankind Project, 1-800-870-4611, dhnwmtl@aol.com). Analogous experience for women are available (Woman Within International, 1-800-732-0980).

Victories Of The Heart

Victories of the Heart (formerly The Men's Room) is another training that involves an intense weekend experience and weekly or biweekly follow-up groups (Mark & Portugal, 1996}. Men learn to bond as men, value the expression of honest emotion, and "get clean" with each other to preserve trust and vitality in the ways we relate.

The VOH and the New Warrior weekends are somewhat different in style but equivalent in results, in my opinion. Victories of the Heart is available currently in northern Illinois and southern Wisconsin and Michigan. (Information is available from VOH, 1117 Milwaukee, Ste. D-1, Libertyville, IL 60048.)

An excellent group exercise for shame is offered on Sunday morning. It's hard to write about this without misrepresenting the high level of safety and emotional honesty that prevails. Suffice it to say that without compulsion or group pressure, many men have found the freedom to express buried shames and secrets – first to themselves, and to others if they wish. Relief is palpable. And some men choose to stay with deeply shameful feelings for a while, solidifying the healing.

Opportunity to go deeper is provided, and the depth and acceptance in the atmosphere stimulated me to touch shame about matters I'd never before considered. I was able to speak of how ashamed I feel about not really caring about others – including most of those[6] present, and of my shameful feelings about how 10 minutes of neglect may have contributed to the death of my baby daughter.

12-Step Programs
(Alcoholics Anonymous and dozens of "Anonymous" organizations that follow the AA 12-Steps)

Step 1 ("We admitted that we were powerless over alcohol…") is a powerful Name It, and breaks the rules of Control, Denial, Perfectionism, No Talk, and Disqualification. Steps 4 through 9 look as if they were designed for healing shame, as they involve making an honest personal inventory, sharing deepest secrets with someone, being ready to change, expressing humility, and making amends (which tends to repair broken bridges, both with others and with oneself). Beyond this analysis, I regard the AA program as the world's most successful approach to healing a serious emotional/behavioral problem over the last 50 years; it behooves us to learn from the best (see *The Twelve Steps: A Healing Journey*, 1986; Fossum & Mason, 1986; Bradshaw, 1988; Everingham, 1995e).

I see one drawback in 12-Step groups: confrontation between members is rare. It's as if there are No Talk and Incompleteness rules being enforced concerning our negative feelings toward each other. This is not to gainsay the outstanding effectiveness of 12-Step programs for many thousands of people, but only that you'll probably have to go elsewhere for confrontation. Nobody's perfect.

A Spiritual Solution

AA describes itself as fundamentally a spiritual program. Ley and Corless (1988) point out that spirituality is difficult to define, but I find their description illuminating: "...a state of 'connectedness' to God, to one's neighbor, to one's inner self. It has variously been described as man's relation to the infinite, as the capacity to be energized from beyond ourselves, and as the basic quality of a person's nature – what the person is and what the person does. Inherent in all these definitions is a sense of dynamism, of movement, of reaching out... [R]eligion may or may not be part of an individual's spirituality. For example, atheists also face the challenge of coming to terms with their own spirituality. The capacity to forgive, to create, to love and be loved is not necessarily dependent on one's belief in God."

Mickel (1988) calls attention to the fact that serious problems often require a spiritual solution. Although there are many forms of spiritual practice, it seems to me that they all involve contact with some deeply felt force, or entity, or "Presence" (*The Twelve Steps: A Healing Journey*, 1986). This force is often experienced as *both* within and beyond oneself. I feel such contact as a sense of grounding and inner calm, often available from deep breathing, meditation, prayer, reading, music, poetry, or the experience of lying in a woman's arms after sex – and always requiring the will or willingness to ask or reach out for it.

Beyond theological argument and regardless of appellation – God, Higher Power, Collective Unconscious, the Transcendent, spirit of the Universe, healing power within – I regard conscious companionship with this power and daily spiritual practice as significant for healing shame. Three reasons for this come to mind: A deep sense of being "in the flow" or "in the place we ought to be" transcends shame and makes ordinary anxieties seem petty. Conscious companionship overcomes that sense of not belonging that is so integral to internalized shame. Finally, we develop a sense of reliance upon a healing spirit: loving, wise, and potent. All of these help to combat the anxious self-surveillance and grandiosity/dejection extremes that are so characteristic of deep internalized shame (Miller 1981).

Conscious companionship with God, as I understand Him, is becoming the major focus of my life, and internalized shame is a major roadblock. "Where shame is, God is not" (Dougherty, 1988b). And what is desired begins to provide the means to achieve it. Conscious companionship and reliance upon God become goal and process, process and goal.

Meditation

When meditating, a man takes time out from the concerns of his ordinary life, in order to move deeper into his inner self. The usual practice is to sit quietly and focus attention on the breath or other body sensations *in the present moment.* A man learns that sensations and emotions, whether pleasurable or not, continue to change.

Inevitably, distracting thoughts arise – the job ahead, getting the car washed, some brilliant thing he will say or write. The game is to notice these distractions, and then bring the attention back to the body at present, without a great deal of frustration, judgment, or shame. One can become a neutral observer, noticing with keen awareness, but with minimal evaluation – good or bad, and a sense of detachment and equanimity.

This is easier said than done, especially at first. Experienced meditators report that things get better and deeper as they continue to practice, and with additional instruction. Many develop an inner calm and peacefulness. Friends may detect changes before the meditator does.

How does this heal internalized shame? Foremost, it keeps one living in the *now.* Internalized shame – the toxic form – focuses a great deal on avoiding shame in the future, and habitual awareness of the present moment is a powerful antidote.[7] Similar relief may come to those who relive past shame to excess. Meditation facilitates self-forgiveness, which I see as the rate-limiting step in forgiving others.

We learn that feeling ashamed – concerning future, past or present – can be treated like any other emotion or sensation, observed with reasonable calmness and with the assurance that it will pass away sooner or later. Even when I'm flooded with shame, and fear that I'll be frozen in it forever, meditation reminds me, "It ain't so."[8]

Perfectionism is another concern – one of the most powerful maintainers of toxic shame. We remember to simply refocus the mind that has wandered. Don't dwell on guilt or shame; don't conclude that I'm not doing it well enough; just bring the attention back. Sometimes I have thought that there were only a few minutes of true meditation in an hour of sitting. So I'm grateful for those minutes. Perfectionism declines as I practice accepting myself as I am, in this moment, without thought for past or future.

We who are over 65 and overweight are advised to meditate while sitting comfortably in a chair. When I attended my first 10-day meditation course, an early triumph was that I could actually sit still for an hour at a time, without so much discomfort that it distracted me. For the first time in my life, I learned to dissociate pain from suffering, and look upon aches, itches, and pains with relative equanimity.

Psychotherapy

Therapy can be of great help if you have a therapist who understands the modern view of shame, and is healing his own. For men with big shame issues, I recommend against therapy with someone not clued in; for me, it led to more shame, confusion, alienation, and rage – mostly at myself. If the prospective therapist says that shame isn't important, or a "cult feeling," or implies that it's mostly about bathroom functions, I'd head for the exit.

You will find a variety of methods for healing shame in therapy in our Chapters 5 - 12 and 19, as well as in the writing of Kaufman (1989), Fossum and Mason (1986), Schneider (1987), Nathanson (1987, 1992), Bradshaw (1988), Compaan (1997), and others.

In the presence of a therapist who has descended into his own shame issues and returned, the client feels permission to go as deeply as he wants. The therapist is unlikely to become frightened or disgusted, because he's been there himself. This is the "vessel" or "container" that is built by a good therapeutic relationship, and it's much more important to the client's healing than to the therapist's cognitive orientation.

Support Groups
(Men's Group, 12-Step Groups, Study Groups, Therapy Groups)

We make use of "he magic of shared experience," which first shows us that we're not alone in our shame and then gives us a safe place to experiment with breaking the rules – a place to come out from behind our facade, try out the liberation of being our real selves, and act out our shadow parts.

Throughout the book, we describe methods for dealing with shame, and more are in development. Many of these can be adapted to support groups. One potential problem is that support groups sometimes unconsciously adopt some of the rules for maintaining shame, especially Control, Denial, and Disqualification. There's more about this in Chapter 15.

Grow the Inner Elder

The elder years are potentially a time for increased emotional and soulful strength to accompany the decline of physical strength. We begin to take a longer and wider view, and may become less competitive, less concerned with our "image," and less impatient about "wasting time."

For some years, many of us have thought that this is an entirely natural process. And in recent years, studies have shown it to be widespread. Lars Tornstam (1999-2000) - a Swedish sociologist - describes what he calls "Gerotranscendence," defined as "the final stage in a natural process moving toward maturation and wisdom." It "implies the construction of a reality somewhat different from the view commonly held in midlife…" (p. 11).

Tornstam describes several characteristics of gerotranscendent people. Among them are disappearance of the fear of death, marked decline in feelings of loneliness, moving from egoism to altruism and concern for ones legacy, increased willingness to confront hidden aspects of the personality, and the desire for fewer – but deeper – relationships with others. Such people tend to transcend the need to label things right or wrong (see Schenk's Chapter 23), and to see time and space differently, often transcending sharp distinctions between past and present. They may take care of their bodies, but are not obsessed with them.

The American psychiatrist, David Gutmann (1994), reported that in cross-cultural studies of elders in various cultures, aging women tend to become more assertive and proactive, and less inclined to shrink from the use of power. Aging men tend to move toward nurturing and peacemaking (as predicted by Moore & Gillette, 1990). Both sexes gravitate toward mentoring, initiating, preserving and transmitting culture, and the interrelating of earth, people, and cosmos. Ominously, Gutmann finds there is a worldwide decline of elders still fulfilling these functional roles in societies impacted by modernization.

Many initiated men have a desire to "be" with older men, and I think a big part of this is for mutual blessing. Lacking an intact elder tradition, we have to rediscover – or reinvent – forms of functional Eldership for our men's organizations, our society, and ourselves. It's an exciting, and at times perplexing, task.

If these changes are a natural part of the normal progression of life, do they "just happen" to us, or do we have to work for them? Both, in my view. Here's another of those paradoxes to be embraced, as discussed earlier in this chapter. Yet I think that a conscious welcoming of later life changes can facilitate the process.

For the proactive, the most explicit and complete program for growing the inner Elder is to be found in *From Age-ing to Sage-ing*, by Zalmon Schachter-Shalomi (1997). Sages bear witness to the enduring values that transcend individual conflicts and selfishness, and are a conduit for passing on mentoring, wisdom and experience to younger folks. Sages learn the *Art of Life Completion*, which involves confronting our mortality, coming to terms with the past, forgiving and healing of relationships, and resurrecting unlived parts of our lives and expanding our potential. *Tools for Harvesting Life* include: doing our philosophic homework through discursive meditation – to gain perspective; facing death by putting our affairs in order, and by visualizing and rehearsing our physical death as a way to desensitize our automatic fear reactions; and reflection and meditation to deepen our consciousness. There is a great deal more. The book ends with 18 very useful pages of *Exercises for Sages in Training*. Follow up and advanced workshops are available through the Spiritual Eldering Institute (970 Aurora Ave., Boulder, CO 80302; 303-449-7243; info@spiritualelder.org; www.spiritualelder.org).

For those of us over 60, the time is now. But I believe that each man of whatever age has an inner Elder waiting to be honored, nourished, and empowered.

There is much more about growing one's Elder than I can cover here, but I'll mention four additional works. Bianchi (1994) records advice, experience, and provocative questions gleaned from interviews with more than 100 successful elders; his subtitle, "Crafting Your Own Elderhood," captures the essence of his findings. Roloff (1997) provides on audiotape a moving portrayal of the spiritual and psychological tasks we face in the latter third of our lives. And, in his ninth decade, Erik Erikson explores his final life stage (Ego Integrity vs. Despair), in company with his octogenarian wife and a younger colleague (Erikson, Erikson & Kivnick, 1986). Their book contains a useful and well-written summary of Erikson's earlier work.

Kathleen Singh – a transpersonal psychologist who spent hundreds of hours at the bedsides of dying hospice patients – has written *The Grace in Dying* (Singh, 1998). She discovered that many people have a "Near*ing* Death Experience" in their final days. This experience begins roughly where Kubler-Ross's (1969, 1975) stages end, with Acceptance. Stages called Chaos, Surrender, and Transcendence follow. Singh sees the essential unity of dying, meditative practice, and spiritual growth. Reading her book always leaves me in a calm and comforted place.

How does all of this relate to healing shame? The man who is summing up his life (and making arrangements for his death) is better able to let go of shame about goals not achieved or youthful dreams not realized. "It's OK; I am who I am, and I did what I did." And we come to a point of acceptance of our declining physical and perhaps financial capacity, and begin to sense that many of our values are changing. Our new perceptions of reality, especially a transpersonal reality, are often accompanied by a deep calm, a feeling of "at home, at last."

Sometimes this process brings up dreams still able to be pursued and sets important new directions. Or a man may discover sources of deep pride, and savoring them can add potent blessing to his later years. One of Tornstam's (1999-2000) elders says, "My best times [now are] when I sit on the kitchen porch and simply exist...the swallows flying above my head like arrows."

Bless And Be Blessed

Blessing is part of our biological hard wiring (Moore & Gillette, 1992a). We all need the experience of seeing someone's face light up when we enter a room – it's one way that social mammals signal welcome and belonging (like tail wagging by a dog). In humans, this "biological" blessing is communicated fundamentally by touch, eyes, facial expression, and tone of voice (perhaps by scent). Cursing messages – "You don't belong here. Get out! If you stay, adopt a permanent posture of inferiority and shame" – are delivered using the same modalities. We humans were bred to respond to nonverbal blessings and curses long before we learned to use words, and our personal and planetary health demands that we honor these instinctive responses.

Just as I need to be blessed, I need also to bless others, and to bless myself. And I may require a "refresher" course in the arts of giving and receiving blessing, and avoiding cursing.

Blessing heals shame. Potent blessing is a mighty healer of toxic internalized shame. Shame says, "There's something wrong with me. I'm so defective that I don't belong here. If I can hide my defectiveness, maybe they won't notice and will let me stay. I've managed to fool them so far, but I live in constant fear of being exposed as a fraud and sent away – to die."

Blessing says in a loving voice, "I see you. I see you as you are, with all of your defects – real and imagined; and I see your Shadow larger even than you see it." The sacred King in me sees you and says, "You belong here, just as you are. You're one of my men, one of the first-class citizens of my realm. You're a valuable man. You don't need more self-improvement to belong here. I want you with me – now. Welcome. Welcome home." He puts his hand on my shoulder and gazes at me with smiling eyes.

Then the King invites me for a leisurely walk in the woods, just the two of us. We talk of my mission, and he blesses it. We discuss honestly my feelings and the events of the past, without needing to judge anything. He tells me that I have a wonderful future to enjoy, and that he's committed to love and support me always (Smalley & Trent, 1986). He says he expects me to fuck up once in a while, but it's unlikely that I'll do it so badly as to lose his blessing. And I feel wonderfully warm and fulfilled, trusting and unashamed.

Blessing makes us feel at home in our communities, and decreases friction in our work together. Sometimes we engage in bad habits of inadvertent shaming (Everingham, 1995d) and other types of cursing – intimidation, posturing, making too many White Knight assumptions (Moore & Gillette, 1992b). This is not to deny the many powerful benefits of our Brotherhood, but only to say that we can do better. My vision is that we develop a new Culture of Initiated Masculinity (Greenwald, 1995) and learn the art of honest blessing, with masculine potency.

Embrace Shadow . . . Return with Blessing!

Fearful Shame

The Invisible Dragon still fixes us with his evil eye
    and seeks to shrivel our souls
                with his fetid breath
But he's worried.
He has been so long dependent on his invisibility
        that he quails at the prospect
        of strong men wielding swords
sharpened by awareness.

He trembles to think
    that we may soon drink blood
                from his severed neck
and in our joyous celebration
forget
      that tradition of bringing him back
        to life again, and requiring a gift.
His fears may be justified.

So BROTHERS
    let's quit farting around   and start kicking ass!

NOTES:

[1] See Fossum and Mason (1986) on vertical and horizontal relations, the discussion of "structural abuse" by Dougherty (1988a, 1988b), and Baber's (1989) moving personal memoir.

[2] It's my firm belief that the best way to prevent rape and murder is to give full acknowledgment to the killer and rapist *in me*. A nod of recognition is just the beginning, but may lead to full-bodied integration and transcendence. Denial, soft-pedaling, or failure to express these violent internal structures makes them more likely in erupt in destructive acts. See discussion of the Shadow in Chapter 1, Topic 20, and later in this chapter.

[3] An archetype is conveniently seen as an anthropomorphic figure represented repeatedly in myth, art, or drama, as well as in modern life, dreams, and literature. To keep the record straight, this usage is derivative to Jung's basic concept. "The term 'archetype' is often misunderstood as meaning certain definite mythological images or motifs. But these are nothing more than conscious representations; it would be absurd to assume that such variable representations could be inherited. The archetype is a *tendency to form such representations of a motif* – representations which can vary a great deal in detail without losing their basic pattern" (Jung, 1964, p. 67, emphasis added).

[4] This illustration probably originated with Robert Moore. I first heard it in a workshop lead by Bill Kauth and David Kaar.

[5] Some men feel such revulsion at the sadomasochistic bipolar Shadow of the Warrior archetype (yes, Virginia, modern warfare is masochistic as well as sadistic) that they cast the entire archetype into their personal Shadow. Not only are they projecting their own sadism onto others, but also they're inhibiting the development of their Warrior virtues (Moore & Gillette, 1992b; Greenwald, 1995). The basic mistake is to confuse the archetypal Shadow with the entire archetype.

[6] After spending three years in a follow-up group with half of these men, my level of genuine caring has risen considerably.

[7] Many spiritual disciplines, religions, and schools of psychology have taught being in the present. I don't mean to suggest that meditation is the only way to get here, but only that paying attention to sensations in the body is a useful way to practice this art. The goal, as I understand it, is not so much to adhere to a prescribed style of meditation, but rather to learn to be meditative and in the present even as one goes about his normal business.

[8] Some believe that we have deep within us habits of negative reaction, believed to be inherited from childhood or even from past lives, and that these manifest as bodily sensations. If we react to them with aversion or craving for the opposite, we're likely to reinforce them. But if we can observe them with some acceptance and equanimity, inbred internalized problems tend to go away. While meditating, I often experience a shaking or shuddering, which may or may not resemble the shudder that Sartre (1943) describes. I don't really know if that's internalized shame coming up, but it feels cleansing and seems to make me feel calmer and more centered. It may be that in this situation, internalized shame, which is toxic, becomes primary shame, which is not.

Chapter 7
Involving Men in Healing Their Wounds of Socializaion

COMPILED BY ROY U. SCHENK

E fforts to help men deal with the intense shame messages they receive almost from birth will prove fruitless unless men can respond positively to these efforts. It is a long known and often discussed reality that most men do not seek counseling, or other help with emotional and feelings issues. This chapter is devoted to exploring why that is so and what we can do about it.

The writings in this chapter are a response to an inquiry we addressed to several dozen men who are involved with assisting and counseling men in some way. The questions we asked were: (a) Why is it that relatively few men turn for help to counselors or therapists or to men's self-help groups? and (b) What does it take to get men involved? The answers we received ranged from a short paragraph to near-chapter length articles. We have printed them here and then completed the chapter with a summary and reflections on what these men have written.

RESPONSES FROM TWENTY-THREE MEN
Compiled by Roy U. Schenk

Gershen Kaufman: Men are ashamed of expressing feelings like fear, sadness, and shame itself. Men are particularly ashamed of needing anything. That's why they have so much difficulty asking for help or appearing vulnerable. Men need to learn that needing is a source of strength, not a sign of inadequacy.

Robert Bly: Young men need to hear old men tell of their failures, so that they won't feel so ashamed of their own failures.

John Everingham: Most therapy is conducted (even by men) in the female mode of feeling, or in some demasculinized, hybrid, or neutral mode of feeling. Do it in male mode and *bingo*!

Roy Schenk: Men's sense of shame for being male makes them feel they deserve the bad things that happen to them. It's hard to change what you feel you deserve. We need consciousness raising to change this.

John Higgins: One-to-one extension of male caring, particularly with the AIDS-related intensification of homophobia, has become only more constricted. My personal experience with the New Warrior weekend, which has a real chance of succeeding in the face of these odds, says that there is not only safety but also comfort in numbers.

The irony is that it does require true strength of character and one-to-one extension of masculine caring to extend this experience to each other. Leading by example is necessary—someone has to be willing to take the risk. The group provides an umbrella from which the individual can extend a hand up to his brother.

Al Ring: Since early experiences of shame and attendant fear of recurrent shame are among the most intense feelings a person can encounter—perhaps more so for boys who are expected to be macho, to hide feelings, etc.—males develop an entire facade, mask, or way of "looking good" to others.

To get to the root of the shame and fear, which are deeply buried in the psyche, would require stripping away layer after layer of protective covering—something most men are loath even to attempt. For many men, the only hope is through the trust and love engendered by groups such as the New Warriors.

Asa Baber: Frankly, any seminar or meeting that allows men a safe space in which to talk about their lives and problems is a worthy exercise. I do think men need time and safety before they are ready to reveal their deeper thoughts. A good model might be the New Warrior Training Adventure. I'm not saying it's the only model, but it does seem to work, and it does allow men to explore their lives.

Rich Tosi: I participate and grow in situations when it is "safe" for me. Safe means: I will be protected from hurting others and myself both emotionally and physically.

The trainers/counselors are initiated men.

I will be led into my deepest shadows protected from shame and self-hatred.

Dieter Ammann: How can I write about why men don't seek help when I have avoided seeking help for years? I really don't even know why I don't ask. So, rather than speculating, let me just tell you what got me to the Warrior Training and beyond.

First of all, I recognized at the time that I was in some pain around my personal relationships, particularly with women. I also was starting to hate my job and found it exceedingly difficult to focus on my work tasks. Although I was encouraged to go to the weekend by a close female friend, in the end it was the persuasive talks of some men friends at my church that induced me to go.

Going to the weekend was, however, no great trick since I am an experienced workshop goer and presenter. What was different was that it was an all-male event. My male parenting had left much to be desired, and I was not comfortable in all male settings. So maybe the first clue for not asking for help derives from this. If my father was not there for me physically and emotionally, and he continually disappointed me, what could I possibly get from a male stranger-therapist? I wouldn't risk it. Besides, what would this person possibly know about my problem that I hadn't explored already? So, I felt superior and used that to avoid asking.

Now what gave me the motivation to keep on with my men's group after the weekend and later to join Accelerated Behavior Change Training (ABC)? I think I needed a powerful experience, powerful enough to get and keep my attention. I learned to trust and love men, something I had never done before. For the first time, I was able to drop my masks of competence and sophistication before men. So I think that men need such an experience before they allow themselves to become vulnerable and needy enough to ask for help. Something powerful is necessary to overcome the cultural conditioning. And it has to be something that shakes a man to the core. Otherwise, he will "sort of" ask for help but never get down to business. At least that is how it worked for me.

At this point, I still have not gone to a therapist. However, my ongoing integration group, as well as my year in ABC, has more than adequately served my therapeutic needs. I don't know if there is a common denominator. I do think that men are ashamed to ask for help, and that most men don't know what therapy is or how it works. There are too many therapist jokes, and the movies often portray the therapist as a funny/weird/strange person. So how can one go for help to someone of whom one's peer group makes fun?

I do agree with Bly that the absence of the older men has caused substantial damage to the younger generation. Since the family no longer incorporates the old family members in a useful way, some forum is necessary to bring old and young together. I would like to see a special event where we could brainstorm about this topic.

Lawrence Diggs: The reason that few men turn to counselors is that counselors have passive therapy. That is a nice way to say that all they do is talk. Men learn by doing. The psychoindustry is oriented toward women, just as the schools are oriented toward women. If a man cannot express what is bothering him verbally, the psychofolks are usually useless.

Too many of the people who are in the mind-bending business have decidedly female perspectives. Their solutions work as long as you are on the couch, but do not apply in real life.

Men do not feel comfortable letting people mess with their minds. To allow this requires the utmost of trust, the utmost of desperation, or the utmost of stupidity. We have to ask ourselves what events in a man's life lead him to feel that he can take off his armor.

Women are taught that it is their right to be protected, and the expectation of this right is reinforced all of their lives. They know, and men know, that men will be punished severely, not only for causing them harm but also for failing to protect them. Men have not been socialized to expect the same kind of protection. So as men we wear armor full-time, and the helmet is the last piece of armor we are going to take off.

If we cannot trust the women of our life enough to take off our armor, if we cannot trust the men in our lives enough to take off the armor, then we are certainly not going to take off this armor to someone who usually talks a bunch of "bull . . .."

Take a look at the solutions most of the men's conferences offer men. They are knee deep in bullshit. The words and ideas are molded to be politically correct. Everyone is so concerned that they don't hurt women's feelings that they forget that they are talking to and about men. They give men solutions based on a composite woman who does not exist for most men. They ask men to change before there is a society that will allow this change.

In short, these psychos are asking men to take off their armor while they are under the most vicious attack in recorded history. For a man to do this would be idiotic.

Enough of complaints . . . Solutions: I think we need to be teaching men to use light armor. The warfare has changed. Men need new weapons, new armor, and new tactics. I don't think the pop-psyches can do this.

Men need to get hold of their spirituality and their sexuality. They need to be encouraged to value and look after their own needs. They need to be shown that if they fail to look after their spiritual needs, most of what they seek will seem meaningless even if they accomplish it.

I like what I know of Robert Bly's work for its contribution in this direction. I think we need to build on the idea of bringing men and boys together, not only in groups, but, more importantly, to one level.

Activities bring men out. They don't want to hear a lot of 411 by a bunch of airheads who must live on some other planet. They need views they can use rather than complicated social theories and mysterious poems. Women have time to figure that shit out; men do not. We are busy protecting and providing.

Let's concentrate on creating space for men to think rather than trying to tell them what to think. Events create the opportunity to meet men and form relationships. Small groups work better than large ones because there is less politics and more issues. Small groups also allow for more two-way exchanges.

Men are repelled by the hard sell. We need to create a reason for men to be together and stimulate conversation. Note that I did not say guide the discussion. We don't need them to talk about the issues right away. Just put out some contradictions and when they have time, they will talk about them

Creating events for working-class men means lowering the rip-off prices for some of these conferences. Okay, everybody has got to eat, but some of these prices seem to be set in order to discourage middle- and lower-income people from attending. Though I can sympathize with such a sentiment—really I can—it will be counterproductive in the long run.

The medium is the message. Let's start putting men's issues on cassette tape and videotape. When we do write, make sure there are plenty of photos and graphics. Why? Because men receive information better when they hear, see, and do. In short, reading is for women. The magazine industry knows this; it is about time the men's movement came to this realization.

I know I will hear a lot of esoteric bull about this statement, but the bottom line is that men don't read. As a dyslexic, I take particular offense that the only way or the best way to get information is through print. It is one way. The world did not begin or stop with Gutenberg's press. Let's use every kind of media possible to get our message to men, including print.

To summarize, men don't go to therapy because they feel it will fuck them up even more than they are. If therapists want work, they must develop relevant modalities.

John Gagnon: A buddy and I have run a program at our local church called "Men Freeing Men," based upon the book by the same name. It is turning out to be a very successful program. The men enjoy structure of the book. Unlike the less structured group we have run in the past, we are finding that the wide variety of articles written by so many different kinds of men offer an opportunity for the participants to feel freer to be themselves and to say who they really are (rather than what they think the men's movement or Robert Bly suggests they ought to be as men). Some common grounds *are* emerging, of course, but the most important starting point has been the acceptance of each of these very different men *as they are,* with their own particular mix of androgyny, masculine stereotypes, beliefs, identities and personality traits. In short, I believe that it is important for each man to find his own energy, his own sense of maleness. The book, *Men Freeing Men,* allowed us to do this to a great degree.

The sense of basic male worth has an essential place in the men's movement. I think that the underlying message that men are not all that important needs to be addressed head on, if we are to continue to grow in a lively and significant manner. It is not enough for a man to join the movement when he feels "bummed out," and then to quit when he lands that job he always wanted or finally straightens out things with his wife and kids. He has got to see that his very presence in the life of other men is essential. Each man can begin this process, I believe, by first accepting himself *as he is.* Part of that self-acceptance will be the "sense of maleness" which he perceives as right for himself. I believe that he can then go on to accepting "maleness" in other men in a more general way.

Buddy Portugal: I have been working with men for many years and have found that their hesitation to seek out "help" generally centers around the deep inner feeling/thought that getting help means *dependency* on others, which should be avoided as much as possible. For many men, being dependent on others relates to inadequacy and self-depreciation. Men need and strive for independence and self-sufficiency as a basic requirement for success and recognition. This craziness has its beginnings in our childhoods, when boys are encouraged to be independent, which is equated with power and strength. Much of this learning takes place—and has taken place—in the son's identification with father, who was generally perceived as independent and usually was recognized for this characteristic.

As long as men perceive that they need to do everything on their own, as a symbol of power and strength, they will stay away from "help." I lead a weekend experience called "Victories of the Heart" (formerly "The Men's Room),") which centers on these issues of how men struggle with their longing for contact with others, and the blocks that interfere with men having real intimacy in their lives.

Bob Porter: My introduction to counseling took place in high school. I attended an all-boys Catholic school run by Jesuits. For the most part, I hated school, having been a classic "underachiever". However, the school did provide a valuable counseling opportunity. Each student was allowed to choose a teacher or staff member as his counselor. We were allowed to leave any class, with the teacher's permission, to talk with our counselor.

At first, my primary motivation for talking to a counselor was to get out of class as much as possible. But I soon discovered, much to my surprise, the tremendous relief of having someone to whom I could safely tell my troubles. Here was a man, a grown-up, who would actually listen to me, take me seriously, and *care!* I was used to thinking of most grown-ups as people who could never understand my adolescent angst, and whose mission was to spoil my fun, limit my freedom, and criticize my viewpoints. I remember crying a little at one point, expecting to be mocked. Instead, he simply handed me a box of tissues, and let me know he understood. Incredible!

Since then, I've been in various forms of therapy several times. I've experienced individual, marital, and group therapy, attended experiential personal growth workshops, read plenty of self-help books, been massaged, and Rolfed. I've participated in several men's and mixed-gender support groups, both as member and facilitator. My interest in personal growth and healing led to my present career as a professional psychotherapist. My interest in men's issues led to my teaching a three-credit course on Male Identity Development at the University of Wisconsin-Milwaukee, which I taught annually for several years.

As a male psychotherapist with an acute awareness of gender-related issues, I have often wondered how therapy can better serve men. As with most therapists, my caseload has always consisted of many more women than men. Since I know how much I've benefited from my experiences in therapy, and have seen many men in my caseload benefit as well (often to their surprise), I can't help but wish more men would take advantage of the support and challenge that a good therapist or group can offer.

Usually, the men I see in therapy are there in response to a woman. A wife or lover threatens to leave or leaves. She complains about his lack of communication with her (i.e., verbal, feeling-articulate communication). She complains about his excessive devotion to work, his alcohol or other drug abuse, or his temper. Sometimes, she knows her behavior is part of the problem, but more often she believes that if he'll change, all will be well.

Another common avenue that brings men to my office is a problem with one of their children. Nearly always, his wife phones to get help for the child or adolescent. Since I am trained as a family therapist, I always ask that the entire family be present for the initial consultation. Often, the wife will insist that her husband won't come in, but I've rarely found a man who refused to participate in family therapy once *respectfully* asked.

Occasionally, a physician sends a man to me because of stress-related medical problems. Employee Assistance Programs sometimes send a man whose work is suffering due to depression, anxiety, or family problems. I had two male clients, both in their late 30s to early 40s, who were sent to me for therapy by their mothers! And, yes, some men do call for an appointment on their own initiative, and the number seems to have been increasing over the years.

It's no secret that most men feel threatened by psychotherapy of any kind. We are taught to be self-reliant. If we can't solve our own problems, we often feel like failures. We may withdraw into denial, alcohol, television or silence, or deny any responsibility for change. I believe that many therapeutic modalities make it much harder for men to participate than women. Therapists who insist on clients quickly getting in touch with feelings, or who automatically emphasize verbiage over action, bias the therapy in favor of women's traditional strengths, not men's.

I like and generally agree with the first seven answers to the question of why more men don't get involved in therapy, which you outlined in your query. The exception is that I don't know what John Everingham means by "some demasculinized, bastard, or neutral mode of feeling." For that matter, I'm still not sure what Robert Bly means by "male mode of feeling," other than that most men access feelings more slowly, and articulate them more hesitantly (if at all) than most women. Also, unlike Roy Schenk, I have found just as much shame—and the concomitant sense of "deserving" bad things—in women as in men. I don't see shame as a men's or women's issue, but as a human issue, although I do know that there are some differences in the specific content of the shaming messages received by each gender. A book I've found useful in this area is *Men in Therapy: The Challenge of Change,* edited by Richard L. Meth and Robert Pasick (New York: Guilford, 1990).

Michael "Bull Moose": Tough questions, but I will tell you about my history and motivation. Since my New Warrior weekend (December 1989), the pieces are beginning to fit. Shame and Flying Boy have become more than words. They explain much of my life and behavior.

I am 45 years old and have been interested in behavior since I was 19. I first sought help when I was 23 and realized how self-destructive I was. I was afraid that I was going to kill myself and felt that I had almost done it, and if God would give me one more chance, I would do it right.

I did Freudian analysis for two years, didn't think I was getting much out of it, and quit. From my present perspective, it was the right thing to do. I got involved in Bioenergetics Therapy in 1980. Getting grounded in feelings helped me get out of my head and into my body. I did that for five years, and for two years was a part of a training group.

I got into that because I felt my marriage was over, and I was losing my mind. The therapist was a woman, and there were many women in the training group. I got a lot of experience with women and their issues. I dropped out because I found the angry woman energy to be toxic, and I had gotten everything I could from that group.

I studied Neurolinguistic Programming for several years, and that leads to the Warrior group. In July 1989, I found the book *The Flying Boy,* and felt that I had read much of my personal history. I have often pondered the same questions we were asked to respond to.

In Bioenergetics therapy, I ran into a lot of John Wayne programs. For example: Men don't cry. (I learned to cry.) I also learned a lot about codependency, alcoholism, and adult children of alcoholics. The honesty, the brutal honesty it takes to do this work on the self is not of the slightest interest to most men. Ego, power, and clever manipulation are what are worshipped in our society. Brutal fathers, narcissistic fathers, kiss my ego—is a commodity, and anybody who tells the truth is regarded as simple, not smart enough to lie to get what he wants—a sucker, gullible, an easy mark, somebody easy to rip off. You can get points for deceiving somebody and putting one over on him. Or just overpower him; football, hockey, soccer, etc. are all games of sanctioned power and deceit.

I am a tool and die maker and work with my hands, much of the time in factories. All the men of this caliber do not even have mental models of what this work is about, which makes it next to impossible to describe. Many of the better-educated, salaried types are on a power drive; they're not interested in the feeling mode, and feel threatened by it. The only means they have to interpret openness is as a trick—that the open guy has lost his mind and wants to get fucked over.

I think it takes a major crisis to get a man's defenses open enough to begin to wonder if there is another way. Men have always needed to control and deny pain in order to survive; the strongest has always won; the one with the greatest stamina will prevail, in a battle for women, food, or land. It has been always and will always be.

Women—by role—have always needed to be open to pain, to feel the pain of the young to see that they survived. People, like plants, will grow to fit the shame of the container they find themselves in. But like living things put back to grow to their own nature, they will become unstunted in their growth and more natural in their manner.

Robert M. Adler: As I understand it, your main question is, "Why is it that relatively few men turn to counselors or therapists for help, or to men's self-help groups?" I contend that the answer to this question lies hidden in your later question, "We suffer as much as women; why don't we go for help as often as they?" I also want to address your question, "What does it take to get men involved?"

Your statement that "we suffer as much as women" sounds true to me, and everything I've observed points to this being accurate. However, this statement equates male suffering with female suffering—and I know very few males who would acknowledge their equality with women in *any* areas. In my view, here are the reasons why far fewer men go for help:

- Men are *afraid* to show their suffering.
- Men are *afraid* to express their feelings.
- Men are *afraid* to ask for help.
- Men are *afraid* that there may not be a bottom line or cost/benefit ratio.
- Men are *afraid* of "growth journeys."
- Men are *afraid* of hearing about older men's failures.

And in my observations, men are afraid of the reactions of both women and other men. The "path of least resistance" is for men to stuff their feelings, not communicate, not ask for help, and just put on the best face they can—and, as Robert Fritz makes clear, every living thing in nature follows *The Path of Least Resistance.*

Of course, this "path" only works for men in the short run. For in the long run, it is well known by wiser folk that whatever one resists, persists—whatever we fear we attract to us. So having grown up in a society which places stress upon men as the performers, breadwinners, and macho machines, the "outer man" may *act* in a strong manner, but the "inner man" is constantly reacting. Of course, the inner man usually will not effectively communicate, or even be in touch with this inner reacting. Strong women may want strong men, but all women want a man who is in touch with and communicates his feelings. Perhaps the real question we should be asking ourselves is, "What's so great about being strong men?" Or, what does it really mean (and to whom?) to be a 'strong man'? What are the benefits, and what are the costs?

As a consequence of this confusion and societal pressure, people make statements like "Most therapy is conducted (even by men) in the female mode of feeling..." and think it's a perfectly valid statement. The problem lies in that it is so deeply embedded in man's psyche that he is superior to women that there is very little chance of a man acknowledging his female energies. Because by doing this, the man would acknowledge that he *is* a softer, more sensitive being, and would surely be judged as being "weaker." Of course women don't have this problem, because for them to acknowledge their male energies can only bring them *strength* (they have some deeply embedded ideas in their psyches as well!). So especially in this day and age, women have a lot less to lose and a lot more to gain by becoming more aware of their feelings, expressing them, and acknowledging their male energies.

Finally, what is the answer to getting men involved? In my experience, the answers are *perseverance, toughness, and timing.* But especially timing. I have observed that when men finally say "yes" to the kind of help we're talking about, they feel they are surrendering to their weakness— "throwing in the towel"—swallowing their pride . . . until they find out about the wholeness available to them in these experiences. But men will only say "yes" when they are sick and tired of being sick and tired—when they can no longer bear their pain and shame.

I did the New Warrior Training in June 1989. I am not a man who's ever had trouble expressing his feelings—I've been in therapy and done EST and everything they've ever offered, including the Life Training, LRT, and lots of other searching—and gotten value out of all of it. But in my opinion, the New Warrior experience beat the hell out of all of them put together. I came back to Houston with the idea of trying to get it here—to enroll 15 to 20 men to go to Chicago for the training so that we'd eventually have the staff to conduct a training here. I thought about it all summer—in the meantime, I realized that the experience of the training was *growing* on me.

I shared my experience with 42 men in Houston, and in February 1990, one friend who was "sick and tired of being sick and tired" with his issues traveled to Chicago for the New Warrior Training. Since that time, the number of men involved has increased rapidly. The Houston New Warrior community at this time numbers over 400 men and we are offering eight trainings a year.

I have another dear friend whose life will dramatically change when he does the New Warrior weekend. He is stuck in an unhappy marriage situation, has an immature attitude about his wife and his marriage, and a generally weak and wimpy attitude about himself. The fact that he also lives with his daughter and his wife's daughter doesn't help—it only magnifies his apparent wimpishness. And from time to time—when he gets sick and tired of it all—he calls me for help and nurturing in his life. And I tell him that I cannot support him anymore than I have attempted to already—that when he gets sick and tired *enough*, he will do what I have told him, because I said so—and experience the Warrior weekend. I cannot offer him the soft nurturing he seeks— because that is what he's getting almost everywhere else—and that's what's keeping him in his rut. It's his own inner strength that is eluding him. There is no doubt in my mind that he is going to do it; the only question is, when? You can lead a horse to water . . ..

I've been accused of being an extremely direct, bottom-line person—sometimes to the point of being obnoxious. But I prefer to think that I call a spade a spade. Some men would read this response and wonder if it was written by another man. I am only being true to my own experiences. I do not dislike men – on the contrary, I have grown to love other men in a profound way. I can't stand the fact that most men are unwilling to get off their egos and go for help. I hid behind my shame for many years—unaware of it—and acted out the victim role of my life not working out. Now that I realize some of the reasons it didn't, I am very involved indeed in "forwarding the brotherhood."

Irwin Aloff: As boys we were taught what a man is: A man is responsible and strong. He works to support himself and his family. Later we saw that we could get our women with work and strength (which equals power).

Going to therapy implies weakness and vulnerability—an admission that we don't have our lives under control. We can't work, support, and be strong and responsible if we aren't in control. Thus therapy looks like a threat to our security, even to our basic sense of self. Men won't readily seek and accept therapy until we change two strong beliefs: vulnerable equals weakness, and weakness leads to our ultimate demise.

To get men into group work, we need to offer *empowerment* as the bottom line (ultimate enticement). We need to confront powerfully and accept lovingly, thereby modeling the behavior which many men feel they lack. They may even think that we can give them what they lack, but of course that's not true. We can't *give* them anything, but we can offer the opportunity to learn to be powerful in a new way, with a new definition of power.

Descartes said, "I think, therefore, I am." Therapy says, "We think, we feel, we believe; therefore, we are." Men have the opportunity to be whole.

Frank DiLallo: Being in the counseling field for the last 20 years has been and continues to be a wonderful opportunity to serve others and a challenging quest into my own psychology. During the first five years of counseling, I worked in chemical dependency treatment, and approximately 95% of my caseload was men. Almost all of these men were mandated by the court. Any man who entered counseling voluntarily in this milieu was a rare exception. I spent the last 10 years in private practice; approximately 75% to 85% of my clientele have been women. When men come in for private counseling, it is usually with a spouse, and if alone, it is often at another person's request (i.e., spouse, mother, friend, or adult child). It has been my experience that when given a choice, most men do not seek counseling as an option for help, at least not voluntarily. The small percentage of men who do seek out counseling with me have been a joy to work with. It is a powerful experience for both of us.

One of the perks of being in this field is to have opportunities to participate in dozens and dozens of trainings, workshops, and experiential weekends. Most of my experiences have been positive. However, following several of the experiential weekends, I recall feeling angry about being the only male or one of the few. I was not angry at women. On the contrary, I honored and envied their ability to gather collectively and create such a depth of experience. I would ask myself, "Where are all the men?" I felt so alone, that I was the only man doing this work. This changed for me 10 years ago when I had an opportunity to attend a very intense weekend training designed for men only. The New Warrior Training Adventure gave me hope and validation as a man and for men. This spirit continues as I have been involved in an ongoing weekly group for men, born out of this training.

Below, I would like to offer some of my experience and perceptions of why more men have difficulty seeking and engaging in counseling.

In order for anyone to come into counseling, they need to admit first of all there is a problem or problems, and then that they do not have the resources to handle this problem on their own. In essence, they are powerless or inadequate to some degree. In seeking counseling services, I am acknowledging a certain level of defeat. Messages or words that are consciously or unconsciously synonymous with defeat include impotence, castration, loser, failure, unsuccessful, powerlessness, and death. For men, there is a great deal of shame wrapped up in all of this.

As a man, I understand why we do not like to admit defeat. Competition can be a healthy motivator. However, our culture promotes a "win at all cost" or "winning is everything" mentality. This "win-lose" orientation forces men to adapt an "I'm OK, you're not OK" position psychologically to defend against loss or defeat. This inflated position is exemplified in self-righteous, "holier than thou," or blaming stances, which prevent us from accepting responsibility for our wounds. If I am in this inflated position, I cannot engage with others, and therefore keep distant from love and intimacy.

Counseling is an engaging and empowering process—both of us win. Seeking counseling could be perceived by a man as a "one-down" experience, because he is searching for an expert to assist him in coping with something bigger than himself. As it is promoted in our culture, competition is the antithesis of empowerment. If I feel a lot of shame already about admitting defeat, what a shaming experience it would be to see a counselor—especially another man—who has more education, possibly more status or position, and may make more money. Questions such as, "Why didn't I see that?" or "How do you know all this?" are raised continually in my counseling sessions with men. Such questions, although subtle, speak of the competition between male counselor and male client. They also reveal the hidden shame present for men around having "blind spots" or not having all the answers. In my personal counseling, I find myself feeling shame about not knowing as much as my analyst does. This experience, although humbling, helps me to be more conscious of what other men are experiencing.

Messages or words showing attitudes about counseling—conscious or unconscious—are "sick," "crazy," "helpless," or "dependent." The word *shrink,* although used in jest, has a negative connotation and gives counseling a bad rap. Also, if inflation is what I am into as a man, a "shrink" is the last thing I would be looking for.

Our culture is set up for quick fixes, solutions, and instant relief from pain. Pain, discomfort and suffering are inevitable realities, and yet we are inundated with media messages inviting us to deny, cover up, or escape our wounds. It is no wonder we have an epidemic of addictive behaviors.

All men identify with a hero. A hero often stands alone and does not usually need help. He always seems to be confident and self-composed; rarely if ever revealing human frailties. I have never seen a movie or TV program where a hero has gone in for therapy. In this context, men believe they should be able to do anything alone and without help.

When I was a kid, I used to fantasize in church that armed robbers came in to steal the offering, and I single-handedly "saved the day." I can recall feeling very high or inflated from this fantasy. This hero stuff is even played out in our own field by male therapists who rescue clients. I have done this, too, and have paid the price. It would be revealing to do a survey of counselors to determine how many of us are also counselees.

I think one of the pitfalls to being in this field is that it is easy to move away from our own wounds by being a "hero" for others (clients, patients). One of the wounds common in all of us men is a lack of appropriate fathering and an overabundance of mothering. Accessing the hero seems to be a way men overcompensate for this father lack. By remaining in this heroic or inflated position, I separate myself from my wounds.

In addition, Father may not be physically or psychologically available to help me separate from Mother. Father's absence creates a psychologically incestuous relationship with Mother to fill the void. Mothers have an unconscious tendency to keep their sons little boys. This in turn creates a tremendous fear of engulfment and castration for men. My guess is that the latter also impedes or prevents men from engaging in counseling. Counseling connotes dependency for many men and is not perceived as a self-reliant or resourceful step.

If we look generationally at where we have come from, all of us have either depression era parents or grandparents. Many of us are conditioned to be in 'survival mode' financially, and counseling could be perceived as an unnecessary expense or luxury. Also, many of us consciously or unconsciously use money—and what it can buy—to medicate our wounds. As a result, the counseling expense could be viewed as prohibitive of buying other "things."

I know that in my own work, journeying inward and deepening as a man is extremely important. I hope that I set some sort of precedent for men. As a man, I cannot do this alone. I need men to mentor me as well. We must support and empower each other in order for healing to occur.

Bill Kauth: Since 1973 I've been organizing men's groups. From then until now, the common denominator has been one man reaching out, and the other man being able to trust enough to take the extended invitation. It was true for my small-sized men's support groups in the early 1970s, and it has continued to be so for the more than 12,000 New Warrior Brothers over the last 18 years.

Jack Kammer: On November 22, 1963, I was in seventh grade. My teacher, upon learning that President Kennedy had died, stood up behind her desk, and with fire and—dare I call it hatred?—in her eyes, leaned forward and said, "Do you see what you boys grow up to be? Murderers!" I consider myself fortunate that I had the presence of mind to realize that the person whose death so enraged her had been a boy who did not, indeed, grow up to be a murderer.

Why do so few men go for counseling? My guess is that men perceive counselors as subscribing to what Dr. Schenk calls "morality as the codification of female self-interest." I don't buy the idea that men refuse to ask for help. Men ask for help all the time, as in "Hey, Jim, can you give me a hand here with this forklift?"

What works to get men involved? I can't say I've had monumental success in getting men involved, but I think the success I've had can be attributed to validating men's anger. As you know well, men are afraid of their anger (especially toward women because it violates the code), but every man feels a lot—even if he has become numb to his feelings. Making no bones about my own anger, but expressing it in calm, confident tones, is the best way I know to help other men feel free to express theirs. When the anger has been identified and coaxed into the open, humor seems to be a good way to make it touchable so that we can make it less frightening and turn it into constructive energy.

Ian M. Harris: Being a man implies being a stoic, denying pain. Stoics don't show hurt. Courageous fighters, they bravely face adversity. Because crying is feminine, and boys are not supposed to be like girls, they shouldn't show emotions. Throughout their lives men are conditioned to hide their feelings.

Life deals everybody bad breaks. A stoic does not admit having a hard time when the shit hits the fan, but rather grits his teeth and toughs it out. Because a man who shows fear can be taken advantage of in fierce male environments, stoicism can be necessary for survival.

Men neither admit pain nor show emotions other than anger because years of gender role conditioning tell them that real men do not express tender feelings. Wanting to create a male identity that will earn the respect of other men, males construct walls around vulnerabilities that don't let others close enough to see their wounds. Males who fear not living up to the rigorous demands of masculinity go through life tangled up in knots, never unlocking their emotions.

Men start to tear down these walls when they are encouraged to be sensitive. A woman's support for a man can take him only so far, because women ultimately fear men's pain. Men have to help each other take the hero's journey to confront inner dragons.

Men sometimes get encouragement from other males for confronting their dark sides in a bar or though drugs, where an altered state will lower the moat and let the dragons out. Men need a more articulate, caring male model than that of a man in a drunken stupor crying in his beer.

Although men's support groups can help men open up to other men, explore their gender conditioning and share their wounds, most men's groups are too polite. Governed by the same norms that demand male rigidity outside the group, few men's groups deeply challenge men to explore their darkest secrets. Men who fear letting down their defenses stay locked in chains.

Men's weekends like the New Warrior experience, developed in Milwaukee, are the best way for men to confront their destructive behavior patterns. At these intense experiences, men are invited to take a hero's journey inside. The encouragement they receive for so doing teaches men they can trust their brothers. Receiving such tenderness from other men opens men's hearts to the possibilities of nurturing father love, perhaps for the first time in their lives. At these weekends, the staff model caring male behavior. Sensitive males are the best midwives to conquer male fear of shame and give birth to masculine emotional sensitivities.

Jim Lovestar: Some years back, as I was hitchhiking to Denver, I was picked up by a truck driver headed west. As we rolled through Iowa and Nebraska, I asked him about his life. He told me he was married and had two kids. I put this together with something he had said earlier about being on the road five out of every six weeks, and remarked how hard that must be on his marriage and family life.

His reply startled me. "We fuck the first night I'm home and get along okay until the second day. Then we just fight. I usually can't wait to get back out on the road."

I asked this man if he preferred driving a truck to being at home with his family. "Shit, yeah," he replied. "I know how to do this just fine. There's no place for me at home. The wife, she does fine without me."

I realized that anyone would choose to do what he is good at. For this man, driving a semi was a lot easier than relating to a woman and children. He chose it, with the attendant boredom, loneliness, health risks and physical danger, because he could *do* it.

Would this man go to see a therapist to talk about his issues of alienation from the family and the risks of his job? What do you think? What if this man thinks he's too busy driving a rig from city to city to take the time to go sit down in a therapist's office to talk? Where does that leave the therapist who expects people to come into an office, fill out forms, and talk about their feelings? Probably giving counseling to the wife.

What can be done? How can we address this man's needs? Perhaps the first step is to acknowledge our ignorance of his needs. If we presume to know what he needs and try to give it to him, we might end up in the position of the man who wondered why his tomcat never ate the oatmeal that was set out for him.

What if someone asked the truck driver what his life was like, what his needs are? What if that someone did this over lunch at a truck stop rather than expecting the driver to come into a clinic? What if that someone was just someone who was concerned, rather than a pad full of theories on human behavior? *And* what if, when those needs were expressed, they were seen as a part of the human condition rather than as a problem?

Maybe this truck driving man would be interested in talking. Maybe in talking he would discover ways to meet his needs. Maybe he would begin to enjoy life and want to give something of himself to others. If this happened, would we call it therapy? What if all this happened by talking with another truck driver rather than a trained and certified therapist? What would we call it then?

More questions: What if this man were told what feelings are and had them demonstrated for him in a simple, direct way? What if he were told he was capable of having and expressing his feelings? What if he were consistently supported in the expression of those feelings, even the ugly ones? What if he were told that he is the expert about his life rather than some well-dressed professional sitting behind a desk taking notes? What then? Can we trust this man to know his own inner life? What if he feels a sense of his own personal power? What then?

What if this man meets other men who are angry at and afraid of women? What if these men, with compassionate guidance, can express all this and discover ways to deal with it? Ways that feel good and bring them closer to women? And if their confusion about relationships with women is honored rather than attacked?

What if these men who are accustomed to criticism of their behavior were blessed for who they are rather than what they do? Who would do this? Who do we look to for blessing? Who do *you* look to for blessing? Perhaps that one in the mirror is a place to start.

I'll speak for myself. I've tried to do life right for a long time. I've often failed. One way of compensating for my failure was to show others how to do their lives right. I had a lot of answers that I readily volunteered without being asked. I saw men in pain and wanted to fix them. For some reason, I often encountered resistance—or compliance that led to only temporary change.

I was told many times to let the man state his questions and find his own answers; then support him in those answers. This is a simple definition of blessing. As time went on, I became more able to do that as I experienced it myself. I realized I needed blessing more than I knew, and I learned I could ask for it. Traditional therapy expects us to just go and ask for it without having received it. Have you ever tried to drive a semi-truck backward?

THERAPY IS MALE HOSTILE

Francis Baumli: "No, there's no leaving shame after all—not down here—it has to be swallowed sharp-edged and ugly, and lived with in pain, every day" (Thomas Pynchon, 1973, p. 637).

Men go to therapy less often than women because men are being justifiably self-protective. They sense that therapy is a relatively inaccessible, even hostile, environment for men. I believe there are nine reasons why men perceive therapy and counseling this way.

In our society, men are viewed by others, and by themselves, as workers and providers. A counseling session can easily consume two or three hours of one's time (if one considers not only the session but also the travel time). And a group therapy process might involve using up the better part of an entire evening every week. Men whose work is their primary role rarely have the leisure to participate in such a time-consuming process.

There is a social stigma that prevents men from seeking out therapy; a man in therapy is often considered laughably weak or suspiciously pathological. Few men care to subject themselves to these prejudices.

Therapy is expensive. Men who are constrained by the habits of machismo are not accustomed to giving their emotions much in the way of healing care. They are likely to claim that the counseling process is frivolously self-indulgent and a poor financial investment.

Men are aware that therapists are no more neutral on issues that pertain to men, especially concerns about women's supposed moral superiority, than is the average person in our society. With few exceptions, therapists have never really thought about men's liberation issues and have never examined their pro-woman stance, much less begun to purge themselves of their own anti-male prejudices. Men suspect that therapists know little more about the deeper pathologies of the male psyche than do their male patients. Indeed, they are correct in this suspicion. A male therapist is himself likely to be afflicted by unconscious male shame, and a female therapist is likely to inflict upon her male patients further shame.

Men also avoid therapy because of the very ways they are crippled by shame. Male shame is one of the most toxic and painful neuroses pervading our society. Yet few men can articulate this feeling, or even give it a name. For them, shame is merely the feeling that "something is terribly wrong with me." This shame, vaguely felt, scarcely identified at the cognitive level, is a painful mystery that most men would rather avoid than deal with.

Not only therapists' personal views, but also the general ideology behind therapy, are anti-male. For example: The average therapist, despite all the research and sound evidence on the issue, still believes that a battered spouse is always a woman. Also, the average therapist continues to refer to "impotent" men while eschewing the term "frigidity" in describing women's sexual problems. Helen Singer Kaplan's view that a man is afflicted with premature ejaculation if he cannot give his female partner an orgasm with only intercourse at least 50 percent of the time, is accepted as standard doctrine by many sex therapists. Therapists routinely counsel divorced men who are being denied their children to be patient and wait until their children are grown adults before seeking to have contact with them.

The average man who reads newspapers, watches television, and goes to movies, receives occasional, if limited, exposure to this general ideology. He may never put it into precise words, but he is self-protective enough to realize that the tacit ideology of therapy does not speak truthfully to men about men. Moreover, if this average man does muster the courage to visit a therapist, upon entering the room, he very likely will encounter bookshelves sagging beneath the weight of titles like *Against Our Will, The Women's Room,* and *Beyond God the Father.* He will see the names of authors such as Betty Friedan, Gloria Steinem, and Andrea Dworkin. If he thereupon believes that this is a pro-male environment, then he needs to have his head examined—not by a psychologist, but by a brain surgeon.

Another reason men avoid therapy—even have a revulsion for therapy—is because they are aware that in our culture the self-help books pander to women primarily, the advice columns in newspapers have an audience that is 90% female, and no small number of women look upon therapy as an indispensable weekly visit to their emotional cosmetologist. Men view such behavior as immature and counterproductive; they believe that these female toys are not likely to be useful tools for achieving male health.

The women's liberation movement of the 1960s soon transmuted into feminism. Since then, feminism has, for the most part, been little more than an anti-male ideology that has insinuated itself into most of our cultural institutions, including psychotherapy. This is apparent in the scholarly journals of psychotherapeutics. For example, during the late 1970s, the notion was generally held that, in this country, the vast majority of alcoholics were men. Any suggestions to the contrary, based upon preliminary empirical evidence, were immediately silenced by feminist "theorists" who claimed that these suggestions were chauvinistic, anti-female, and intended to show that women are as prone to social deviancy as men. But then, in late 1980, indisputable evidence surfaced, proving that there indeed are as many, or almost as many, female alcoholics as there are male alcoholics. The main difference is that female alcoholics, whose domestic status allows them to do their drinking at home, are more adept at concealing their problem than are men. Within six months of receiving this evidence, the same feminist theorists who previously had denounced the evidence pointing to female alcoholism, did an about-face and began publishing articles claiming that all along there had been a male conspiracy to conceal the problem of female alcoholism, and thus divert funding away from helping female victims (sic) of alcoholism.

This is but one example which illustrates the extent to which feminist ideology has taken over (and distorted the methodology of) the profession of psychotherapy. How is the average man, who might otherwise be drawn to therapy, aware of this feminist distortion and consequently deterred from seeking therapy? This "average man" learns from the female-oriented popular television talk shows that it is female therapists, with a harshly feminist viewpoint, i.e., harshly anti-male prejudice, who are today being accepted as the experts on emotions in our society. He is aware, also, that the therapeutic superstructure, ranging from the plethora of pop-psych books to the smorgasbord of group-therapy encounter groups, have all encouraged women with liberationist leanings to take the feminist attitude that men are the cause of every woman's every problem, whether it involve sexual dissatisfaction, domestic discontent, or lack of success in the workplace. But most of all, men are aware that the therapeutic process, which touts "professional value neutrality," has actually taken a strong anti-family view. Most therapists now view the traditional family and the tradition of marriage as archaic, outmoded, and dispensable. Intimate relationships are expected to be ephemeral, and divorce is considered a healthy option—often the preferred cure—for a troubled marriage.

Even though men are socially conditioned to be sexually active and relatively uncommitted to only one loving partner during their early, sexually active years, when they do choose to "settle down," they desire stability, that is, continuity, in their intimate or sexual relationships. But men know that the Big Sister of Feminism is looking down upon them, and they know full well that hers is a malicious gaze. Have it her way, and all women would cast men aside. Unmarried women would spurn men, married women would abandon their husbands, and fathers would be stripped of their parental rights. No wonder, then, that men avoid therapy. It has become one of the most effective bastions of feminist subversion, constantly undermining most men's hopes for one day having a lifelong, happy relationship with a mate.

A final reason men avoid therapy is because they see what its consequences have been for its primary clientele—women. Over the last few decades, therapy has perhaps helped women feel better about themselves, but it has not made them better human beings. Instead, it has provided them with but temporary diversion from their emotional pain. It has given them a scapegoat (men) to blame their pain on, and thus by leading women toward blaming behavior, it has blocked healthy change. Men observe women who, upon exiting therapy, pronounce themselves cured and henceforth blameless in any emotional conflict with another human being. Men observe other women who are forever addicted to therapy, and pronounce themselves incurable because our supposedly patriarchal society oppresses them. Observing these two types of women, men justifiably say to themselves: If this is what therapy has done for women, I want nothing to do with it.

A further question remains: Why is it men do not go to self-help groups as a way of dealing with their problems? I think the answer is clear. Men are not at ease in the emotional sphere, and the idea of going to a group of other men to deal with one's emotions is quite terrifying. Some men, of course, overcome this fear, and do go. I have perceived, however, that many of these men, after having attended but a few meetings, never go back. Why? Because, for the following reasons, such groups fail to satisfy their wants:

Men in our culture are very dependent on women for fulfilling their emotional needs. Instead of providing men with an alternative way of dealing with emotional needs, such groups often serve as little more than a forum wherein men complain about their lack of success in relationships with women. Grievances against women are aired, advice is given, and then the men go home, maybe feeling better for the moment, but not having done anything to make themselves less emotionally dependent upon women.

The reaction men have to their own emotional vulnerability in such groups often prevents these groups from ever attaining an emotional atmosphere. Some men are so afraid of being macho or competitive that they scarcely participate, doing little more than murmuring sympathetic responses to each other's self-disclosing statements. Other men react to their own emotional fears by reverting to stereotypic macho behavior, talking loudly, dominating the group, seldom listening to those who are not as forward.

Generalizing somewhat, we can say that in our culture women are socialized to *be*, and men are socialized to *do*. When men approach a new experience, their reflex is to deal with tension, excitement, or enthusiasm by doing something physical. Self-help groups tend to be sedentary; they involve people sitting around and talking. Hence, they neither utilize nor channel male energy—the kinetic response men have to an emotionally charged situation. Like schoolboys held in during recess, the men grow restless. When they leave, they feel unserved and drained.

Some groups—for example, the wildman warrior groups—do inject a certain level of physical activity into their gatherings. Unfortunately, such activity is so channeled via ritual, so given to fictional mythology and play-acting, that little of what is explored under the auspices of "male identity" can ever translate to the real world where play-acting and fairy tales get a man nowhere. Men often feel an initial enthusiasm in these groups, but soon realize that all those rituals, instead of channeling male energy, are self-indulgent emotional thrashings. A keen disappointment sets in as that "primordial male" they have supposedly rediscovered loses his way in the civilized world. Nevertheless, the wildman warrior groups have a strong appeal and attract many disciples. The problem is that they leave in their wake men who are weaker, and more bewildered, than they were when they joined these groups.

A REEXAMINATION OF SOCIAL WORK

Tom Williamson: Why don't men seek help from therapy as often as women, and what does it take to get men involved? There are many forms of "therapy." Among these are psychotherapy, counseling, support groups, and outreach programs. All have elements in common: They work with the mind, and in so doing, each form addresses mental conflict, a "void" in one's life and/or changes in attitude. I will address all of these forms in striving to answer why men don't seek help as often as women and what it takes to get men involved.

We must consider at least three things in order to answer the questions posed: 1) The level of public acceptance for men to seek help from others or to seek self help forums; 2) The setting or surroundings in which activity takes place; and 3) The content of therapy itself (e.g. is it sex biased?).

1. There is little or no public acceptance for men to seek help or to accept it when offered. To a significant degree men have internalized the expectation that it is unmanly to seek or accept help. However, for some men, this expectation can be overcome if there is a public policy to encourage them. For example, I conducted a private study on the battered husband in 1978. I examined the policies of two public services and looked at their willingness to offer services to men, as well as their means of promoting their services to men.

In 1978, we saw the beginning publication of a growing body of research showing that battering of men by women is a significant problem. Two organizations decided to keep an open mind and make their professional services available to men: the New York City Mayor's Task Force on Rape, and the Victim's Information Bureau of Suffolk County, NY.

The NYC Mayor's Task Force on Rape located their crisis centers in hospital emergency rooms, where there were trained personnel to spot suspected spousal abuse. In addition, the task force embarked on an ambitious public relations campaign that targeted male victims and specifically encouraged husbands to seek professional help. The results were reported only in a qualitative fashion; no quantitative statistics were kept, because the task force had only been mandated to study and help women, not men. For example, the number of men calling for telephone counseling was verbally reported by counselors as a "flurry of calls" or "many calls" after each public service announcement, talk show interview, or news broadcast announcement. The task force also picked up male clients in another way: They identified battered men who had come to the emergency room for medical treatment (sometimes being brought in by ambulance).

By contrast, the Victim's Information Bureau of Suffolk County (VIBS) reported not getting so much as one inquiry. VIBS is located along a major highway. The staff was mainly experienced with women as clients. The public service campaign sponsored by VIBS attempted to be gender neutral. They used the word "spouse" in place of "husband" or "wife"—as in "spouse abuse." The gender-neutral phrase did not communicate well to males. In this case, "spouse" implied "wife," because abuse has been so widely defined and accepted as a female problem. Not one male contacted VIBS as a result of its public service campaign. Yet, that same year, VIBS conducted a county-wide study of the incidence of "spouse" abuse and obtained results that showed that 52% of battered spouses were men. Thus, while there were battered men in Suffolk County in need of help, the VIBS approach was unable to reach them.

Conclusion: If there is widespread paid advertising or public service announcements which encourage men to seek counseling, therapy or support groups, men will come forward. However, the advertising must be specifically targeted at men, their interests, and their needs. There must not be any hint of shame or any suggestion that men seeking help are at fault or are weak.

Beyond this, we must be sensitive to political forces that see it in their best interests that men not seek help. For example, most organizations that are formed to help battered women do not want to see the subject of battered men legitimized. The so-called helping professions are substantially influenced by a politically motivated ideology that is part of a newly emerging power structure with an ever-increasing ability to exercise social control.

2. The setting or surroundings in which therapy takes place is very important. Tom Clark (1975) describes the reluctance of males to seek counseling in family planning clinics where the decor is feminine and the intake workers communicate negative attitudes, both verbally and nonverbally, toward maleness. At this same conference, papers were presented showing that family planning outreach programs aimed at inner-city males

could be very successful if the program and surroundings were geared toward men. These programs were designed to change macho male attitudes about pregnancy (i.e., a man feeling that getting a girl pregnant proves his manhood) and about fatherhood (getting men to take more responsibility in child care).

Conclusion: The physical facilities must be attractive to men, and the personnel on hand must act in a positive manner.

3. The content of therapy itself can be discouraging to men. There are many different approaches to therapy and counseling. However, what alarms some observers is the degree to which feminist doctrine has seeped into social and psychological theory. The extent to which this has happened depends on the subject matter. The topic of the battered husband is often ignored. There is resistance to funding abortion counseling for men. The subject of male victimization, especially when at the hands of a female, often is not dealt with. One example of this is sexual abuse of males by females.

LeRoy Schultz, Professor of Social Work at West Virginia University, Morgantown, reports that a great deal of social work and counseling is dominated by the narrow view of feminists toward power (private interview, March 25, 1991). Generally this view holds that physical power resides with males who can then abuse it. Specifically, this school of thought holds that the abuse of women by men is mainly an issue of the need for men to dominate women. For example, the Ellen Pence method (The Duluth Domestic Abuse Intervention Project) for counseling men who batter their wives is based on a model where men use power to control women. In itself, such therapy assumes the worst about men and imposes shame. Recently the state of Wisconsin began considering funding counseling for men who batter. The qualification requirements mandated that male bonding be prevented in therapy, and that a course on sexism be provided. All existing courses on sexism, to date, use the feminist model and avoid concepts of interaction.

By contrast, Tony Kubicki (Batterers Anonymous in Milwaukee) has developed an alternative method for counseling men who batter. Kubicki counsels both men who have battered women and women who have battered men. His method assumes that couples want good relationships and that "people" who batter have not learned certain social skills, are under stress, and have observed or been victims of battering as children. He does not see spousal abuse as a gender issue (i.e., where it is men versus women) (private interview, March 23, 1991). Kubicki (1999) has recently written a manual that incorporates refinements in his approach, and shame-free language.

Two therapists, John Macchietto, PhD, (Counseling Center, Tarlton State University, College Station, TX) and Eric Mendelson (State University of New York, Binghamton) have gone further in independent studies. They both conclude that therapists often completely ignore the male perceptions of problems, as well as male victimization—especially that perpetrated by a female. Macchietto (1992) demonstrates resistance within the therapeutic community to consider male victimization even when they are made directly aware of this situation. He proposes that these forces of resistance should become a topic of self-analysis for the therapeutic community. In his article, Mendelson (1990) describes a resistance that resembles attitudes of a "political" nature.

One of Professor Schultz's strongest criticisms of the therapeutic and counseling disciplines is that all forms of power are not considered. Currently the move in therapy is to explain everything as "male versus female." Schultz specifically cites for criticism such mainstream publications as *Journal of Interpersonal Violence; Affilia: Journal of Women and Social Work; Working on Wife Abuse* by Betsy Warrior; *Women and Violence* by Susan Schechter; *Wife Battering: A Systems Theory Approach* by Jean Giles-Sims; *Ending Men's Violence Against Their Partners* by Richard A. Stordeur and Richard Stille; *Participants Manual: Court Mandated Counseling for Men Who Batter, A Three Day Workshop for Mental Health Professionals.* These sources are used extensively by both professionals in practice and professors who teach young students.

Therapists are apt to take a negative attitude toward nontraditional role behavior in men, according to the work of John Robertson and Louise Fitzgerald (1990). Insofar as the application of therapy enforces "the mold"—politically correct thinking, as it has come to be known, therapists can also be expected to take a negative attitude toward men who have not adopted a feminist ethic, as demonstrated by Mendelson (1990). Many therapists today subordinate their clients' welfare and individuality to the constructs of feminist theory. Robertson and Fitzgerald remind us that therapy can be made to function as a means of social control. Therapy as 'social control' was earlier discovered to apply to women to their detriment. Now we see that it also can apply to men.

Forced therapy deserves our special attention, because it is widespread and frankly designed for social control. Examples are court-mandated therapy and required corporate outreach programs about sexual harassment. Sexual harassment courses never deal with false accusation, never deal with females who use sex to climb the corporate ladder, and never deal with women sending mixed signals to men. Attendance at these courses is mandatory in some corporations and schools, which often have an extreme definition of sexual harassment that the general public would find unacceptable. Some define unwanted looks as sexual harassment, even if unintentional. Large numbers of men are found in forced therapy. What we are witnessing is the blurring of politics, gender scapegoating, and mental health into an unholy alliance.

Both Macchietto (1992) and Mendelson (1990) are mainly concerned with the relevance of therapy and counseling for men. Both make suggestions about how to make therapy more vital for male clients, and how to attract and then maintain a male client base. Macchietto (private interview, 3/23/91) and Schultz (private interview, 3/25/91) feel strongly that most male clients would not continue with voluntary therapy if the therapist presents an attitude of guilt and shame promoted by the feminist approach.

Conclusion: As Schultz says, "The majority of men are prone to drop out of therapy where the feminist power approach is invoked. Where the therapist identifies with the problems men have, they are more apt to stay with it." In citing men's problems, Schultz points to: stress, lack of having been taught certain social skills, and stereotypical cultural expectations (such as pressures on men to be the defender and provider). John Macchietto commented, "Most men will not go into therapy if they view the therapy as feminist in orientation."

It has been my experience in the National Coalition of Free Men (NCFM) that any shaming or condemning of men has acted as a deterrent to membership and to continued counseling. In NCFM's experience, any feminist aggression, gender polemics, or anti-male sentiment adds to a man's already reluctant mood to be involved in such issues as changing roles and behavior. Many men are just plain fed up by always being attacked in the media. When a man has become vulnerable enough to open up to therapy, feminist therapy—with its attitudes toward power and sex—only adds insult to injury.

SUMMARY AND ANALYSIS

Dmitri Bilgere: Why do so few men turn to counselors, therapists, or men's groups for help? The men who responded to this question had a wide variety of wonderful answers, but they returned again and again to three key ideas.

First, almost every author mentions *shame* at least once. Men, they note, have been socialized to feel ashamed of themselves if they aren't absolutely self-sufficient and if they don't fulfill their responsibilities perfectly. Our society has imposed the ideal of the rugged individual, these authors report, much more on men than on women. Women are socialized to need help and to ask for it; men are socialized to laugh at pain and ignore difficulty. Other writers noted men's *denial*—our culture rewards men for producing and shames men for "complaining." In light of this, it's no wonder men are reluctant even to acknowledge their feelings, much less explore them.

Second, these authors cite the *irrelevance* of therapy, counselors, and men's groups to men living the traditional male role. Roy Schenk and Francis Baumli point out that while society values what men do and empowers men in activities, society values what women feel, and empowers women in relationships. Men are programmed to succeed materially, and women are programmed to succeed in family and relationships. Therefore, these authors say, it is cost-effective for a woman to be aware of her feelings in order to have better relationships and a healthier family.

For the traditional man, being in his feelings simply does not make good business sense. Men are trained to compete, and being in his feelings during competitive situations—as in business—can be economically fatal for a man. There is a payoff for the traditional woman to get therapy and explore her feelings, but that payoff really does not exist for the traditional man. While feelings help women in their expected role, they hinder men in theirs.

Third, there is a real and legitimate concern that many therapeutic modalities are not relevant to men, or are even destructive to them. Several authors discuss how talk therapy is better suited for women because they are more discussion oriented, whereas men are more action oriented. There is evidence for this. Studies by psychologist Martin Seligman found that women are much more likely to ruminate about their problems than are men. Men are more apt to take action when troubled, even if only to have a drink or kick the dog. Talk therapy demands that men change their style just to begin. Therapy doesn't do much to meet men on their own emotional ground, or even to meet men halfway.

The authors also note that men are suspicious. They are tired of being blamed, and are wary of any situation where they may get more blame for the problems of others, especially those of women. Men see the feminist books on the therapist's shelf, and feel the feminine environment of the therapist's office. Much like an auto shop for women, the therapy room is not naturally welcoming to men. It's not so much that men don't look for help, but that the environment looks hostile.

So, according to these authors, the shame men feel about needing help, the irrelevance of therapy to traditional male goals, and the poor quality of most therapy available to men keeps men isolated, out of the men's movement, and not seeking help.

To this list I would add several items of personal opinion; there are things the men's movement itself does that turn men off, and keep them away. Men have plenty of problems and responsibilities in their lives already, and are not at all interested in taking on more unless they absolutely have to. Yet often the men's movement, especially the political men's movement, tries to sell problems to men, rather than solutions. The agenda seems to be that men realize just how bad things really are for them. Many have enough problems already, and turn away.

Men in the men's movement, like anyone else, can become pessimistic and hopeless in the face of the magnitude of their problems. Recently I read an article in a political men's journal about a letter-writing campaign to companies that did anti-male things. Victories were recast as failures. A greeting card company withdrew a male-bashing card; it was reported with such an air of doom that it seemed like only a tiny drop in a huge ocean. Instead of celebrating success, they made this victory appear tiny and insignificant. I was turned off, and I imagine many other men would have the same reaction.

Further, men don't want to be associated with a movement that might seem extreme, different, or anti-woman. The extreme views of some of those in the men's movement, the seemingly odd rituals (such as drumming, men's spirituality, or "wild man" weekends) scare many men off, just as the extreme aspects of feminism scare off women. This is not to say that we should get rid of our radical opinions or stop drumming with our brothers, but we do need to be aware of some men's aversion.

Most men aren't interested in a group that sells hopelessness, distance from women, a feeling of victimization, and a sense of women being the enemy. To the extent that we do this, men stay away.

Selling awareness of men's problems is in itself a problem. Until joining the men's movement and getting help looks like a *solution,* rather than a problem, most men will continue to stay outside.

Solutions are a major reason that men get involved in therapy and the men's movement. That's my distillation of the contributors' answers to "What does it take to get men involved?" There were two themes. Men seek help and get involved, these writers say, when they are in a time of crisis, or when they learn to really trust another man who then suggests their involvement.

Whether in crisis or through trust, the man who joins a men's group or who seeks therapy has decided that those actions can improve his life. A man in crisis may suddenly see hope for real and viable solutions to problems that are so severe they must be addressed. His crisis gives him a new perspective on personal growth.

Bill Kauth and other proponents of the New Warrior Adventure Training weekend discuss *trust*. Men who choose to go on this often-transformative weekend go because they trust a man who recommends it to them. Trust allows a man to be willing to try out something new, even when faced with an experience that looks forbidding. Absent crisis or trust, however, none of these authors holds out much hope that the men's movement and therapy can draw men on their own.

So they suggest that men befriend men, and begin to build this trust. We can be there for our brothers, build trust and friendship, and when the time is right, we can share with them what we've learned about ourselves and our feelings. When the time is right we can introduce them to personal growth for men. And if they have a crisis, they need not be alone; we can help them into a supportive brotherhood of men.

We can also look for ways to sell solutions instead of problems. We can tell them how the movement makes men's lives even better, rather than wanting so much for men to fully appreciate the oppression we experience. Men's oppression is just too bitter a pill, at the beginning, for most men to swallow. We can create a movement that supports and empowers men optimistically, and avoid the temptation to see ourselves as helpless victims of women and society.

These authors understand that man-by-man, we build trust and brotherhood. With each man we prepare for growth and the men's movement, we change the world.

Roy U. Schenk: When we initiated this inquiry, we had some sense that shame contributes to men's reluctance to seek counseling help. What came through loud and clear in the responses to our query is that men avoid seeking help *primarily* because they have been shamed so intensely for seeking help or even for expressing feelings. What men have learned is that they must "do it alone" and that it is unmanly to seek help. Tom Williamson stated, "There is little or no public acceptance for men to seek help or to accept it when offered." As a result, men are very reluctant to subject themselves to further shaming that they believe they will experience if they seek help.

For a man to seek help he must be experiencing a crisis so severe that the pain is worse than that expected from the additional shaming he anticipates, and that men often drop out again when the pain level has diminished. *What this means is that the disease itself creates the conditions which make it extremely difficult to seek a cure!*

As Francis Baumli remarked, men "avoid therapy because of the very ways they are crippled by shame. Male shame is one of the most toxic and painful neuroses pervading our society. Yet few men can articulate this feeling, or even give it a name. Shame, for them, is merely the feeling that 'something is terribly wrong with me.' This shame, vaguely felt, scarcely identified at the cognitive level, is a painful mystery which most men would rather avoid than deal with."

The respondents regularly note that current methods of counseling and therapy are not designed to assist men. This is attributed either to the passivity of the process or to its hostility to men. As Lawrence Diggs expressed it, "The psychoindustry is oriented to women." Several writers referred to personal experiences that revealed a serious bias against men. This seems to have been amplified in recent years by a "feminist" orientation.

Because feminism is presumably about equality and justice, this might seem unexpected. However, in practice, a great many, if not most, feminists have regularly continued to accept the societal myth or traditional belief in women's moral superiority/men's moral "depravity," which is the source of men's shame feelings. These feminists have continued to blame and shame men as the evident method of choice for attaining their goals of women-favoring legislation and for silencing criticism.

This blaming and shaming attitude has overflowed into the counseling and therapy areas. Yet one can wonder, "Why would male therapists accept and enforce such anti-male biases?" The answer is simple. As feminists state it, "Oppressed groups regularly buy into the value system of their oppressors." Oppression is a direct result of being seen as inferior. So men buy into or accept the blame and shame associated with the belief in men's moral inferiority.

Another way of saying this is that men just as much as women believe the societal myth of female moral superiority, which translates to perceiving women as victims, and creates in men a sense of shame for being "inferior" males. Unfortunately, myths are so "true" that it is difficult for people to recognize them. Thus, even though it is so prevalent, our society's treatment of women as victims is not generally recognized.

The result of this is that traditional counseling and therapy have tended to enhance men's shame feelings. This is certainly adequate reason for men to avoid and distance themselves from such "help." Even today, most mandatory counseling for men—counseling for men who physically batter their wives, for example—evidently continues to use shame as a primary technique for altering and controlling these men's behavior. Because shame is the source and trigger for the violence, such programs try to make things better by making things worse. Actually, the concern tends to be with the women involved, and little compassion seems evident for the men.

How can we enlist men to transform their lives to be more fully human? The answer provided by many of the respondents is that men need to have a safe place to work on their issues—especially a place free from the perpetual shaming they fear. What are the characteristics of a safe space? To Rich Tosi, safe means, "I will be protected from hurting myself and others both emotionally and physically; the trainers/counselors are initiated men; and I will be led into my deepest shadows protected from shame and self-hatred."

In addition, Tom Williamson proposes that a "public policy to encourage men to seek help" will encourage many men to overcome their reluctance and fear. However the efforts must be specifically targeted at men, and must avoid any hint of shaming or blaming."

Another point is raised by the recognition that men need a safe space in order to work on emotional issues. That point is that men live mostly in an unsafe environment. What are the characteristics of this unsafe environment, beyond physical risk conditions? The respondents regularly describe it as an environment filled with shame and blaming. In other words, our society is programmed to shame and blame men.

Where does this shame and blaming come from? It is my belief that it is based on the fundamental belief of our culture, perhaps even worldwide, that we must divide and judge people on the basis of superiority and inferiority. This judging begins in a newborn child's life at the moment we learn its sex and immediately project differing expectations on it depending on gender. We instantly begin treating babies differently based on these differing expectations. Soon we begin judging a child's behavior based on these expectations, and shame the child when it does not conform.

In addition, women are in contact with babies far more than men are. As a result, they do most of the transmittal of societal messages. Naturally, women transmit to infants the message that women's behavior is good behavior. Male babies then get the message that any ways in which their behavior differs from women's, their behavior is bad. This occurs even while male babies are being taught the expectation that their behavior *will be different* because they are male. This message is well learned by male infants before age three because males are already into over-achievement, a shame response, by that age. Because girls' feelings of achievement inferiority become dramatically evident around puberty, boys' inferiority feelings may be learned much earlier in life than are girls' inferiority feelings.

In summary, few men will willingly expose themselves for any extended period to a counseling environment where they are shamed or where their legitimate concerns and needs are ignored or even discredited. Therefore, the most important way to get men involved and to keep them involved in seeking help for their emotional problems is for the process to become conscious of and sensitive to and, thus, to address men's concerns honestly and without shaming.

Chapter 8
On Men, Guilt, and Shame'

FRANCIS BAUMLI

It was while working as a therapist that I first became aware of the necessity of distinguishing guilt from shame. This awareness came about during a time when I was working with a fairly large number of male clients who came in unaccompanied by wives or female lovers. Seeing a man in therapy when he is accompanied by a woman who is significant in his life is usually a very difficult experience. She quite often presents herself as the "emotional expert" in the relationship; she knows what is "wrong" with the man, and wants to solicit the therapist as her ally in getting the man to do as she wants. Dealing with a male client in this situation presents a host of problems, which I will not here go into. But I mention this type of man because he contrasts so much with the man who comes in by himself.

The unaccompanied man presents problems for the therapist, too, but they are problems of a very different sort. For example, he is often very difficult to get moving. He says he wants help, but he does not talk very much. When asked what his problem is, he presents it as a general malaise: he is depressed, although he isn't sure why; he says he isn't feeling good, but he can't really say what feeling good would mean for him; he may try to define his problem summarily by saying, "I just don't communicate well with others," but as a therapist I cannot get very far with this revelation because he is not communicating very well with me.

Seeing all those unaccompanied male clients was quite a burden for me during this time. I was nearly at my wits' end, trying to pry some of these men loose, when I began noticing that over and over the men were using the word "guilt." The term came up in contexts so various I certainly could not draw parallels between the men, but I was curious about the frequent mention of this emotional state. I began pushing at this guilt. "What do you feel guilty about?" I would ask. The men couldn't really say. "When do you feel it? Are there specific times it comes in?" They would answer that it might come in at any time, or that, in one way or another, it was always present. "Do you remember ever feeling this in earlier years? Perhaps during your childhood?" Yes, they remembered feeling this way in earlier years. In fact, they had always felt this way. But now they were tired of it, and wanted to do something about it.

"Well, what *is* this guilt?" I persisted. They could not talk about it. It was there, it was painful, they wanted to do something about it, but they felt helpless.

I was more than challenged by all of this; I was mystified. Here were several men, all referring to a similar feeling, but none of them able to articulate it.

It might have been easy to have dismissed this impasse with the general judgment that men have trouble discussing their feelings, and have left it at that. But such a judgment would have been inappropriate. Some of these men were very articulate about feelings, and, however sparse they might be with words, they were not at all afraid to open up – at least in therapy. I knew that something besides inhibitions or masculine armor was blocking these men.

A breakthrough came. I do not now remember what brought about the realization, but one day I saw something. These men were using the word, "guilt," but maybe they were actually talking about something else. If so, what was this "something else"?

I was taking a stab in the dark the day I interrupted a client, who was talking lamely about feeling guilty, and asked him, "What are you *ashamed* of?" My question stopped him cold. He wasn't sure, but it was obvious that we had found an important key. Later that same day, I asked another male client about shame. Again, it was obvious that something important was being probed. Neither of these men could answer my question. They gave halting answers like, "Just ashamed of *myself*," or "I don't like myself," or "I feel bad because I *exist*."

Curiously, these men could not talk about *what* they were ashamed of. Nor could two other men I saw later that week.

The following week I was chafing at this mystery. At one point, I angrily interrupted both myself and a client by saying, "I don't *want* to know *what* you're ashamed of! I want to know *why* you're ashamed!" The man looked at me in surprise, started to say something, and suddenly began sobbing.

For some reason, changing that "what?" to a "why?" opened the lock, not only for this man, but for every one of the other three men I was seeing that week! These previously inarticulate men could now speak! They talked about their mothers, their wives, their former wives, early dating experiences, female coworkers, early elementary school teachers, and on and on! And *always* these men talked about shame in relation to *women*.

It was from working with these men in therapy that I first was struck by and gained some insight into the need to distinguish shame from guilt. But insight does not make for understanding, much less for theory. I knew that if I were going to be a responsible theoretician and figure this thing out, then I would have to probe it as a social psychologist, and not as a therapist only. Furthermore, I would have to do some reading about this matter, dialogue with other psychologists, and also do some careful, personal reflecting about it.[2]

I first began looking within myself. Yes, I had some guilt in me, but I had already pretty much dealt with that. But shame – it was everywhere! In fact, the very memory of certain select experiences caused a lancing shame to pierce through my entire body.

Allow me to recount just one such experience:

I was 18 years old, and it was my first semester in college. I was dating a girl who was slightly younger than I. Our habit for the past several weeks had been to go to a movie or some such thing, and then drive about 10 miles out of town to an old rock quarry and park. We did a lot of kissing, necking, and such, but she put up a strong resistance to my doing anything else – like touching her breasts, or going for the "down-there zone." But then the night came when something was different. This girl was squirming and moaning beneath me, and I was tired of holding back. She let me open her blouse; she let me fondle her breasts; she had a hand pushed under my jeans and was gripping my ass; she let me kiss her breasts. So I raised myself up and reached a hand down to her inner thigh, and... Quite suddenly she tensed, her body went rigid, and as she pushed my hand away, she said in the most accusing voice, "Don't you have any *respect* for me?"

A burning, nauseating shame filled my groin. My whole body went numb, and quite unexpectedly – I say "unexpectedly," given that, at this point, even though my penis was erect, I felt no sense of sexual arousal at all – I ejaculated. It was a long ejaculation, with many a throb, and at the end I was totally drained of both semen and desire. Even amidst the shame, I felt amazed at that ejaculation – a hard erection, a very *protracted* ejaculation, but with no pleasure at all, no orgasm, just a mechanical, far-away pumping. (Yes, this experience should surely lend credence to Herb Goldberg's assertion that a "premature ejaculation" is simply a man's way of saying, "I don't want to have anything to do with this sexual experience." But this is another topic, and I will not belabor it here.)

I felt horrible. I still feel horrible, right now, 20 years later, writing about it. What do I mean when I say that I feel horrible? I do not feel guilt. How could I feel guilt, when there was nothing specifiable to feel guilty about? If I had felt guilty, then I could have gotten angry, or I could have apologized, or I could have asked for clarification. But as it was, I wasn't even sure what I had done that was wrong. She had put her hand under my jeans, and she was, if anything, being more aggressive than I was, and... But you see? The very attempt to explain it only mirrors the confusion. No, it was not guilt I was feeling. When it's guilt, you know *what* you are guilty of. This was shame. I wasn't sure *what* I was ashamed of, because I wasn't really ashamed of *anything* I had done.

But I did know *why* I felt ashamed. I felt ashamed because at the moment when I was feeling accepted, welcomed, and desired, a woman had rejected *me.* And she had done it by putting herself above me, i.e., while nothing was said about her respecting me, *I* was supposed to respect *her,* which meant that she was somehow superior to me. Moreover, since I *should* respect her, but was not even moral enough to *show* this respect, she was even *more* superior to me! How very, very shameful of me! I felt awful. I still feel awful. Yes – awful, horrible, ashamed. Not a very articulate way of putting it, is it? But then, that's the way shame is: inarticulate, inchoate, bewildering, seemingly irresolvable.

Allow me to give a few more examples:

How many times have you heard a woman say of a man, "He's a total *jerk?"*

"Why?" someone asks.

"He just *is!* He's *a jerk!"*

Okay, he's a jerk. So what has he been accused of? Nothing in particular, of course, just everything in general. And how is a man going to defend himself against an accusation like that?

"He's a *loser.*" (Same consequences as above.)

"He's a wimp with women!" (Same as above.)

"I hope you feel *embarrassed* when you realize what you did!" (Same as above.)

"That just *isn't done!*" (Same as above.)

"He's starting to make some changes. Maybe he's finally starting to grow up." *"Finally,"* she says. In other words, he has a long history of something to be ashamed of. *Maybe* he will change from that detestable state he was in before. He is indeed making progress, but since he is just *starting,* he can continue to feel ashamed until he does finally succeed in *growing up,* whatever this means. It evidently means something a man never quite attains, as long as a woman can continue to shame him by telling him he hasn't attained it. But as to *what* it means, he will probably never figure this out.

"You should be *ashamed* of yourself." (This is the big one!!) Yes, she comes right out and says it. She may be his mother, his high school date, his lover, his wife, his female coworker – all of them women – feeling a little uncomfortable with something he is doing, or just wanting to exercise a little more power over him. So she tells him he should feel ashamed, and he is so accustomed to this judgment that, however much he may bluster and try to appear otherwise, he reflexively grovels inside.

I clearly remember an instance when four men (me among them) and a woman, all senior members of a large counseling center, realized that if we were going to get our project finished for the next day, we all would have to stay late after work. Once everyone accepted this, the mood became light, people were talking of ordering food, and the charts were being brought out. "Too bad the secretaries (not all female) have gone home," one of the men said. "They could have helped."

The woman, her briefcase still closed, turned to the man who had spoken and said sharply, "You *men* should be *ashamed* of yourselves," and with her nose in the air, she left the room and went home.

The men's egos toppled like bowling pins. They were all too embarrassed to say anything even to each other about what had just transpired. Instead, with all levity gone, they proceeded to the task at hand, each aware that what had been said could indeed have been construed as something lewd, even though it wasn't. But if a woman could take it that way, then maybe it should never have been said in the first place, which makes it difficult to know what you can say without getting into trouble and feeling this way – vaguely guilty, very vaguely guilty. Feeling so vaguely guilty that it really isn't guilt, but rather it is shame that paralyzes a man into inarticulate acceptance of a woman's judgment that he is somehow morally inferior to her. When, really, if these men could just *say* what they feel, or, more accurately, quit feeling what they feel so they could speak the truth (you see how quickly shame fosters confusion –

verbal and otherwise!), then they might point out that it was not "men" who made the remark, but one man. So, if anyone is to be ashamed, it is that one man only, and, moreover, that one man meant exactly what he said, with nothing underhanded implied, because he was fully aware that without the secretaries, this job was going to take about twice as long as it would otherwise. But then... Yes, the female co-worker has gone home while the men must stay late to do the work.

The next day none of the men brought up the issue with the woman. Each of them felt that he should apologize, but no one was sure what to apologize for. Each of them would have liked to protest her leaving, feeling that if she was that upset, then she should have confronted the man and dealt with it instead. Besides, when she left, she took some of the files with her, which made the men's work that much harder. But the men were too ashamed to protest. It was not until a couple of years later that these men finally discussed the matter. All agreed that she had acted inappropriately. But it is also obvious that they still felt somewhat ashamed . . . of something . . . they were not quite sure what.

Enough with examples. It should be obvious by now that shame, although an elusive concept, is a very present and dangerous feeling. Can this feeling be better understood? Let me try to better expose the feeling for what it is by here entering upon a brief analysis.

I am convinced that guilt and shame are two terms that, from a phenomenological point of view, are decidedly different feeling states. Is it possible, then, that shame can better be understood by looking at it alongside guilt, while being very careful not to confuse it with guilt? Let us see what a comparison reveals. I here list six observations, or speculations, about certain aspects that I believe are salient, even defining, qualities of the two terms:

1. *Guilt* is often referred to as a burden. A guilty person complains of feeling oppressed, weighed down, crushed, smothered. Guilt is often accompanied by a bodily sensation of something weighty that is spoken of as a burden on one's back, or a lead weight in one's belly. Note that the Zen Buddhists speak of guilt as "a corpse you carry on your back."

   Shame is often referred to as a void. A person who is ashamed feels empty inside, without ballast, lacking a sense of self-centeredness or emotional certainty. Shame is often accompanied by a bodily sensation of tactile fear, i.e., a fear that seems to be actually crawling over one's skin, or writhing in one's belly. It often results in an actual physical nausea.

2. *Guilt* is something quite determinate, i.e., specifiable. One has a pretty clear idea of *what* one is guilty of.

   Shame is something indeterminate and non-specific. The feeling is so ubiquitous that one can only begin to grasp it, i.e., give it a determinate boundary, by attaching the shame to something all encompassing – usually one's entire self.

3. *Guilt* is felt in terms of something one has *done,* e.g., one will say, "I feel guilty because I spoke sharply to my son this morning."

   Shame is felt in terms of something one *is,* e.g., one might say "I feel ashamed when I don't spend time with my mother."

4. It seems that *guilt* is largely learned early in life from one's father, whose masculinity is oriented toward the performance of, or failure to perform, specifiable tasks; it also seems that guilt is learned from other men whose masculine conditioning orients them toward competition, fear of failure, and success-oriented values that one never quite succeeds in measuring up to.

   It seems that *shame* is more often learned early in life from the mother, whose approval causes us to feel pride in our entire being, or whose disapproval causes us to feel ashamed of ourselves. Shame is also learned from other women whose values instill in us a sense that morality is something feminine, teach us to fear women's disapproving of us, and give us the sense that we never quite measure up to their expectations of good, moral behavior.

5. I suspect that in our culture a woman feels more *guilt* than shame. Conversely, I rather suspect that in our culture a man feels more *shame* than guilt.

   Guilt is a difficult emotion to grapple with, but once one has the courage to face it, it can either be quite spontaneously discharged via an angry assertion that one has reformed what one was previously guilty of, or it can slowly be cast off as one takes on a new state of awareness – exercising different choices or actions – thus rendering the old guilt irrelevant to one's current intent and values, and perhaps also remedying any harm to others that one has previously done.

   Shame is equally difficult, but it can never quite be grappled with because it has no specific form. Attempts to deal with it tend to leave one feeling helpless. Attempts at being angry have no clear avenues of expression. And shame, therefore, is much more likely than guilt to persist as a toxic, crippling feeling which engenders an anger that, turned inwardly, becomes self-destructive.

Such is my analysis, which, if true, leaves men, the primary victims of shame, in a rather sorry state. Women's justifiable anger over the burden of guilt our culture has heaped upon them has, for the last 30 years, been finding expression. I do not at all believe that such expression has always been healthy. Too often, women's anger, via a feminist ideology, has taken the easier route of hatred and blaming of men. Hence, their ways of ridding themselves of guilt have scarcely been kind; still, I believe they have quite effectively cast off most of the burden of guilt they have carried for too long.

But men? Well, we have scarcely begun. A few of us are beginning to articulate the problem, but perhaps our most valuable insight thus far has been to observe that the very nature of shame is such that it can scarcely be articulated. A sorry beginning, no?

In dealing with shame, we are not entirely without resources. We do have anger. The problem with that is, of course, that our anger too quickly feels ineffectual, impotent, and... . Already ashamed of ourselves, we are also ashamed that we can do nothing about our shame.

Anger, however, is a bipolar process. It sets up boundaries that say "no" to the encroachment of others. It also – and this aspect of anger is too often minimized – is a fierce affirmation of the self. As such, it can strengthen a person to the point that a new independence, a newly created self, begins to emerge. In this emerging process, shame cannot be cast off in the same way guilt can. But it can be dealt with in a different way: it can be eclipsed by the newly emerging self, and thus become irrelevant to one's being and actions. When we men experience this new self, we can feel pride and excitement at who we are, and experience a sense of indefatigable joy as we discover new dimensions within ourselves – exhilaration at our new-found emotional power. It must be noted here that this new-found power is pride based, not upon our *approval* of ourselves, but upon our ability to fully *be* ourselves. Moreover, this pride hurls anger at anyone who reproves us, or who expresses displeasure with us by condemning our entire personhood.

But I deal with this process of self-creation so abstractly. How does it become concrete?

Well, this is what we are doing. Contrary to what I may have implied above, we actually have begun the process. This self-creativity is, to a great extent, what *The Coalition of Free Men* is all about. It happens every time we join a consciousness-raising group and, instead of spending all our time complaining about the women in our lives, talk about who we have been, who we are, what we want to *be,* and how we are moving toward becoming happy, i.e., accepting ourselves. *We discover that we men can only leave our shame behind when we break our addiction to women!!* Only when we are free of this addiction can we learn to enjoy ourselves, and subsequently (perhaps not so paradoxically) learn to truly enjoy women too.

But to enjoy women is to run a risk. In this culture, women are the primary promulgators of male shame. They often feel very threatened by any man who is clearly enjoying himself, celebrating himself. They will try to smother his joy. At the very moment he is laughing and relaxing, they will say something like, "Are you *drunk* or something?" "Can't you *behave* yourself?" "When are you going to *grow up?*" "*Now* look at what you're doing!"

How can a man defeat these attempts to shame him into self-abnegation? The fact is, he can *not* defeat them! It is impossible, because the moment he consents to do battle – to argue or get angry or fight it out – he has given a woman's feminized scheme of values too much validity. He has acknowledged the threat, which means he has acknowledged her power and his own tendency to diminish himself.

Although a man cannot defeat a woman's attempts at shaming him, he can transcend them. He can transcend them by refusing to give up his self-enjoyment. By refusing to forsake joy for battle.

Does this mean he ignores a woman's attempts to shame him? Perhaps. But if he wishes, he can still interact with her, not by battling with her moralistic judgment, but by setting himself over against it in a way that diminishes her judgment. How? Simply by projecting his self-enjoyment through humor. A humor that is directed, not *against the woman,* but *from himself* and *for the sake of his own self-enjoyment!*

To give but one example, a true one:

A woman said to me, "You know, last night at the party you really weren't acting like your usual self."

"Oh really?" I replied.

"Yes. You should be *ashamed* of yourself!"

"*Shame* on you," I said, angry and yet laughing, that is, enjoying myself, "for trying to make me feel ashamed of myself. Shamey shame, *shame* on *you!"*

It worked. Not, I believe, because I clearly reflected to this woman what she was doing, but because I demonstrated quite clearly that, at least for that moment, *I was not at all ashamed!*

For her, this was quite disconcerting, because much of her self-image, her sense of power, was based on a sense of moral superiority – the same sense of superiority which is used by many women, and which nourishes itself by occasionally heaping shame, i.e., a sense of inferiority, on men.

Perhaps – and this is very important – when confronted by the kind of response I gave, a women may feel so disconcerted that she will get angry. And out of such anger, she then may begin making accusations – letting a man know what she is upset about. This is all well and fine. We men can then deal with *what* she is upset about. In this way, the conflict then becomes something that can likely be resolved. As long as it is dealt with in this way, i.e., as long as we can deal with a *what,* we do not have to feel ashamed of our*selves.*

Of course, I have given here but a brief account, along with a few examples, of my initial conceptual reckoning with the shame I myself have experienced most of my life. And I have proffered a rather brief, even cursory, analysis of shame and guilt. And my prescription – my view about what men can do to overcome their shame – is obviously rather abstract, i.e., I must confess that my attempts to incorporate this prescription into my own personality are only sporadically successful.

But we must not be timid about paltry beginnings!

As we begin to escape shame, each escape will nourish what well may become a continuum, not only of *escape* from shame, but also of *freedom* from shame. Above, I listed just one example of how I have dealt with one woman's attempt to make me feel ashamed. In this example, humor was the key. Realizing this, I have used humor several times in similar ways when dealing with women who have tried to shame me. For example, one comeback I have used on occasion (it has become part of my instant repertoire) is, "Maybe you're right. Excuse me for a couple of minutes while I try to grovel." (Of course, I smile while I say this, and along with the smile, there is a bit of a smirk.) The woman then knows – she knows fully well – that she did not succeed in her attempt. Also, I have learned to vary this response somewhat. "Pardon me while I grovel" works well, and so does, "Oh God! Now I feel so ashamed of myself I'll probably sob into my pillow all night long!" Or, just as effective, "I guess I'll have to spend all day tomorrow whimpering in a corner somewhere." Always, of course, there is laughter with the comeback. And, sometimes, this laughter by itself is enough.

Humor, then, is my way of escaping shame – at least, at the particular moment the shame is inflicted. I am sure other men have their own, individually tailored ways of escaping it. As for ridding myself of old shame – shame that is several decades old – that is a different process, and I have not been very successful at it.

But, as I said, we should not be timid about paltry beginnings. Humor is a beginning, and I am slowly learning other approaches. Meanwhile, there are other men escaping the yoke of shame. We must seek their advice on this matter too.

NOTES:

[1] Modified from the original article published in *Transitions*, 7(6), 5-6 (1987), entitled: On Men, Guilt, and Shame: An Open Letter to Roy Schenk."

[2] I did not discover that shame was the crucial problem of all my male clients, nor, for that matter, the crucial problem plaguing *any* of my male clients at that particular time. However, my experience as a therapist had for many years shown me that, when counseling a male client, certain important variables, i.e., aspects of the man's personality must *always* be taken into consideration, regardless of what the basic problem is. These aspects include the man's relationship with his parents, his sexuality (both identity and satisfaction), his relationship with his current family, if he has one, and how his job affects him. I realized, since Dr. Schenk's visit and discussion in September, 1986, that an equally important variable to be explored, which must always be explored when counseling any man, is the extent to which he has experienced or experiences shame as a male.

Chapter 9
Basic Male Shame

JOHN GAGNON

Listen   Brothers   Listen
The alarms are too late
This is the hour for
amorous revolt
Dare to take hold
Dare to take over
Be heroes of harmony
in bedfellow bliss
Man must love man
or war is forever
Outnumber the hawks
Outdistance the angels
Love one another
or die

—*James Broughton, 1990*

In the two decades I have worked as a psychotherapist, I have met men and women with many different psychological diagnoses, and I have traced their disorders to a variety of sources. While many of my clients suffered from low self-esteem, I wouldn't have called their conditions 'shame-based." It wasn't until I gave a great deal of thought to the concept of shame that I began to see its hand in so many psychological maladies.

I came to understand that shame was a component in many personality disorders. In the sanctuary of my consultation room, many clients struggled through the indignity and devastation of shame on their way to healthier living. As I watched them work through their shame, I developed an interest in treating people who suffered from shame-based maladies. I started to keep track of the many subtle, emotional variants that this self-consciousness or self-loathing takes. Out of my observations emerged a system for classifying different kinds of shame.

One classification that emerged from my experiences—not only as a clinician, but as a friend and fellow male—was what I call *"basic male shame":* a feeling of shame and self-loathing for the existential fact of *being a man.*

As the concept became apparent to me, I was amazed at how widespread this fundamental disorder was in the male gender. Deep male shame appeared not only in men who came to see me for psychotherapy, but in men who were my friends, in members of the men's movement gatherings I attended, and in participants of workshops for men. I even encountered it within the day-to-day behaviors, thoughts, and feelings of my own being.

Understanding this basic male shame is important because it often keeps men who could benefit from therapy, peer counseling, or the consciousness raising of the men's movement from seeking the help they need. In men who do find their way to therapy, male shame seems to lie beneath other forms of low self-worth that are more readily apparent. When I developed a clearer picture of this gender-specific disease, I became more successful in treating the men I met in my practice.

Therefore, I want to address the insidious disease of basic male shame. I also wish to suggest a therapeutic approach for treating this disorder of Self. As you will see, my exploration of basic male shame has been a long one. This exploration unfolded over a period of 20 years and touched every important aspect of my life: my work as a psychotherapist, my relationships with other men and, most important, my relationship to the core of my own thinking and feelings as a male child, and ultimately as a man.

BEGINNINGS OF SHAME

Basic male shame results when a boy sees the intrinsically male part of himself humiliated or denigrated within the familial or social context. For example, it can result when a boy is unloved or even rejected and abandoned by the most significant man in his life: his father. If a boy never receives love, protection and nurturing from the man who raises him, the boy never develops a sense that he is worthy of care and nurturing by other males. What results is male abandonment, a feeling that to be a man is to be—and consequently feel—fundamentally unimportant and of little or no worth to other men. This is one starting point for basic male shame. There can be others.

From birth, male children experience different developmental influences from those that female children experience. Boy children are held less, breast-fed less, spanked more, and desired less by mothers (as demonstrated by "reaching out" and "cuddling" behaviors). Boys receive numerous messages that males are worth less during their early life development (Jesser, 1987). This pattern of gender-distinctive treatment occurs all through the male child's development, and culture and society strongly support it.

The pink and blue we use to differentiate our babies have less impact on the male psyche than the nonverbal communications—the looks and tones of voice—that little boys receive. These messages are often tougher, louder, more demanding, and harsher than those given to girls. Even the violent, work-oriented toys we give to boys reinforce the early messages that men must learn to be rough and tumble, fight, and even destroy one another. Men are supposed to eschew more tender and nurturing feelings. The preceding verbal and nonverbal directives that shape one's view of oneself as a particular gender or role are known as *stereotyping events.*

Stereotyping events include, therefore, persistent and long-term cultural attitudes that give to males less physical and emotional worth than females. These messages are repeated so many times in childhood that a man's negative self-view is well established long before he attempts to engage in adult relationships.

WHAT SHAME DOES TO MEN

Long before I learned about the causes of male shame and arrived at my theory, I encountered, first hand, the results of the destructive way we raise male children. In the mid-1970s, I joined a local chapter of a famous male liberation group. The group began with approximately 30 men, ranging in age from the late teens to the early 70's. For the first time, I heard men talking openly about male anger at women, the devastating effects of the macho stereotype, the inequality men experience in divorce court, and other topics. Many of the men shared their personal pain and some even cried openly, expressing how important it was to "have the support of other men."

But, when these same men began to feel better, they started to skip meetings and eventually dropped out. This kept occurring until the group dwindled to three members, one of whom was the president and one of whom was myself. Throughout this decaying process I searched for what had gone wrong. Weren't these men getting what they had come for? Didn't the group satisfy them? I asked these questions of several ex-members and most of them merely replied, "I got what I needed from the group, so I just decided to leave."

At this same time I was also examining my relationship with my own father. During my childhood, my father, a hard-working man who had been orphaned at the age of 8, had done everything he could to keep me at an emotional distance. He did it by simply ignoring me, or by telling me aimless stories, playing solitaire whenever he was in the house, or with partial deafness caused by his job and his refusal to use a hearing aid.

Mostly, my father used pet projects in his workshop to keep me away. For a while, I tried to be his apprentice, but he found ways to reject me there. I was forever holding the light *wrong*, or handing him the *wrong* screwdriver, or holding a piece of wood for him the *wrong* way. He also rejected me outside of the workshop during his favorite pastime, fishing.

The single time he took me fishing, I managed to hook something, but it pulled me off the slippery rocks and into the river. I didn't know how to swim and began to drown. I can vividly remember seeing my father, calmly unaware of me, facing in another direction while I choked on the muddy water. After I slid to the bottom of the river bed and managed to crawl up on shore, my father came running up to me and said, "How dare you fall in and lose my favorite pole, you stumblebum. I will never take you fishing again." He never did. Although it took more than this single event to make me feel worthless in the eyes of my father, the story is a powerful metaphor for his persistent rejection of me.

Over the years I ached for my father's love and acceptance. I yearned for, but never saw, a change in his feelings. So I chose to reject manual labor—I would be bookish, an intellectual, a *wunderkind*. My father and I grew steadily apart. In the mid-1970s, when my father was 83 years old, he was diagnosed with stomach cancer. During those last 2 1/2 years of his life, I visited him more than I had in any previous period of our lives. I talked with him, and I tried to share feelings with him in ways we never had when I was growing up. I made every effort to have him understand that I loved him and that I needed to hear affection from him. Finally one day, when he sat wrapped in a blanket like an old Indian, he looked up at me with his sunken eyes and said, "You know, Johnny-boy, I love you and your brother Ernie, and I've always been so proud of you." Despite my 30 years, I ran from the room and screamed in pain. We opened the door to a hole in my core that existed since my childhood, but that hole could not be filled by a single statement.

I don't know how many times I tried to capture that lasting sense of love and acceptance with my bosses. I put on all kinds of shows for them: I achieved great things, won awards and even lied about the things I had accomplished to get their loving approval. But I never got satisfaction, and that is how it should have been. These bosses were not my father, nor were they the right men to help me find self-love (Osherson, 1986). I slowly began to realize my need for connection with other men, males who could and would love me as a man.

A SEARCH FOR THE RIGHT OUTLET

I decided to gather my closest male friends and develop some kind of men's group through my local church. My hope was that we would talk over liberation topics, and become close and loving with one another. The first meeting would be a potluck dinner at my house. The men arrived one at a time. Almost every one of them looked genuinely uncomfortable at having to make a dish of food and bring it to a meeting of only men. One man joked, "So when do the dancing girls arrive?" Another asked, "We gonna see some porno flicks later?"

When I responded that we would have neither dancing girls nor porno flicks, the tension grew palpably. As the evening wore on, these men, who were my dearest friends, felt increasingly uneasy without an agenda to relieve their anxiety at being in one another's company At first, I chalked this up to homophobia, and shared this concern with them openly. They denied that they were homophobic. Most of these guys could hug one another and myself freely and they didn't feel uncomfortable with men on a one-to-one basis. But somehow, this men-only meeting disturbed them. There was no fishing, no baseball, no television, no porno flicks, no poker hands to play. What the hell was a group of men supposed to do? Talk? About *feelings?*

Some admitted that they were unaccustomed to talk about how they felt with other men and that to identify with their feelings seemed somehow . . . unmanly. In other words, male shame kept them from admitting their vulnerability (Astrachan, 1988).

After a fashion, we did talk, and what came out was a fundamental malaise that these men felt about being male: Men simply could not offer each other safety, nurturing, acceptance and love; they expected these things only from women. The idea that another male could be as important to them as the significant women in their lives was totally foreign. When we talked about going to singles bars with male friends, many men admitted dumping their companions to go home with some "foxy chick." Men who had been abandoned in these situations accepted this as "natural," or "the way things are." Any suggestion that a bond between men might be more important than meeting a sexual partner was agreed with intellectually but shunned in practice. As a matter of fact, not far into the evening several men left to go home to their wives or lovers.

The men agreed, in principal, to meet like this on a regular basis, but unless I consistently prodded them, the meetings never happened. Finally I gave up and decided to join a different group of men. My church was holding a program for men on women's *thealogy,*[1] the study of female goddesses and how women think, spiritually. Here was a men's group with an agenda. We had exercises and a format to follow. But what emerged from our weekly meetings was a hunger for something more. Many of the men admitted that they had no personal relationship with a male God or even to their own fathers. Others mentioned male friends but regretted how seldom they got together since they were out of school, where occasions for meeting had more easily presented themselves. Several of us decided to start a men's group as soon as the women's spirituality program was over.

This all-male group met once a week for 2 years. We talked over many issues in our meetings, but it was our discussion of male nurturing that revealed the most to me. Most men reported that they could, and did, nurture one another when the occasion presented itself, but none of them felt that nurturing was an important part of being male. Feelings of nurturing and loving applied to men simply weren't that appealing; their custom was to avoid these feelings toward other men, and consequently with themselves.

Even though we could explore this topic on an intellectual level, it didn't stop members from arriving late, skipping meetings without first notifying the group, or complaining that they "had better things to do with the family on a Sunday night." After 2 years and many changes in membership, the group dwindled to a few men and disbanded.

A THEORY EMERGES

By the end of this latter group, I had developed a theory of basic male shame. I believed that men, raised by women and loved by women, had learned not to look to other men for love. In other words, "If my father did not spend time with me, empathizing with me, holding and loving me, then why should any other man?" The corollary is, "If I am a man, then I am basically unimportant to other men" (Diamond, 1985). At its worst, it becomes, "If I am a man and men only love women, then I can mistreat another man any way I like."

I guessed that men dropped out of male support and consciousness-raising groups because of basic male shame: They believed that they simply were not that important to the other men in the group. They could experience the novelty of accepting love, empathy and caring from other men, but they did not realize that other men needed them to return the gift. Once their own needs had been met, they were ready to move on.

This theory frightened me. If it was true, then the men's movement was doomed. No matter how many men sought out one another, they would not build lasting relationships because they hadn't learned to love maleness. In Jungian terms, it was as if men had no loving animus. The animus might be cruel or intellectual or a good rule maker, but it did not love other men. Worst of all, it did not love the male in the self. As a man, I myself found that several hours with an attractive and admiring woman fulfilled me more than a whole evening with a group of caring and nurturing men. Other men admitted feeling the same way What was going on in us? Did it mean that every time we felt our own "male energy" that we had to deny it to keep from losing the love of women, the only gender we felt was a source of love? (Moyers & Bly, 1990)

I felt trapped. I wanted to make men more important to me. My friends felt the same way But we lacked a deep feeling that men are important to other men as nurturing figures. We might work on feeling empathy and caring, but we couldn't love or desire another man, nor could we believe that he truly loved or desired us back. I'm not talking about homosexuality but about heartfelt love. And I believe that gay men suffer from this lack of male love as much as straight men do.

Basic male shame prevents men both from loving other men and from ever really loving themselves. If I don't love myself then I will fall prey to a whole host of other problems: low self esteem, self-degradation, stress, guilt for any imagined wrongs done to women (my only source of love), and a compulsive need to undo feelings of worthlessness when the woman I love leaves me. I may feel so mortified that I self-destruct when I cannot support myself after a woman rejects me. Like the men on television commercials who can't cook, clean, or find the medicine when their wives are sick in bed, I may play the role of the "male fool."

When I do encounter truly male thinking and feeling, I will probably reject them as antisocial, and feel misplaced guilt or shame for having them. For example, If I blow the whistle on a corrupt aspect of established order—a true act of male assertion— I may feel like I've done something wrong, that I've violated my mother's wish that I "shut up and keep the complaints to myself."

Basic male shame gives rise to a lack of commitment between men, male competition for virtually everything, and a desire to "dethrone" men who have already established themselves (Bly remembers "shooting arrows at the older poets" when he was young). Basic male shame leads us to the societal view of men as the disposable sex, expendable in times of war, or when the ship is sinking and men are told "women and children first," presumably because men cannot take care of children (Farrell, 1990). Basic male shame denies everything else that is male: noble behavior, love, beauty feelings of tenderness, grace, integrity, morality, living healthfully, and identity with maleness.

WITNESSING SHAME IN THERAPY

While I encountered the effects of male shame in my own life and in the men's groups I joined, I also witnessed how shame worked in the men I saw for therapy. Ted was a hard-working man, raised in an Irish-Catholic family in the Boston area. When Ted was growing up, his father and mother favored his three sisters and made it very clear that he was less in need of their attention because he was a boy Ted was always blamed for any argument he had with his sisters, and he was even beaten by his father on several occasions. Ted took this treatment for granted; he thought it was normal.

Ted came to me with his wife, Jennifer, for therapy. Over the course of our 3 years together, I learned that Ted felt totally responsible for everything that made his wife unhappy. If she wasn't comfortable with something he said, it was his fault for not saying it in a way his wife desired on a particular night. She complained he was insensitive to her needs. He always felt like he was accountable for her feelings, especially if she felt anger, sadness, or displeasure.

In the sessions, Ted became increasingly aware of the shame he felt for being a man. He thought that he was morally inferior to his wife. After a few months of recognizing these feelings of worthlessness, Ted decided to change his behavior. He would treat his wife as he always did, but would no longer take responsibility for what she did not ask of him directly. He also decided he no longer wanted to give her everything she asked of him. Ted's wife did not like this decision.

At home, she became more manipulative. She concluded that Ted's interest in his own needs was due to selfishness alone. Ted eventually saw that he would no longer be happy in a relationship that contributed to his own sense of shame and worthlessness. He divorced Jennifer and continued to work out the sense of basic male shame that he had been taught as a child.

To help Ted resolve his feelings of shame, I employed several Gestalt experiments allowing him to express feelings toward his mother and father about the lack of support he felt for being a man. He became very angry in several sessions, and he cried a lot at the thought that neither of his parents wanted him for his maleness. In time, he resolved these unfinished experiences with his parents. Ted moved on to find more ways to love himself and care for other men. He eventually left his job in a large industrial corporation and became the director of a nature museum. Years later, he reports that these changes bring joy to his life.

Another client heard different messages from his parents but still grew up feeling male shame. Alex was a 38 year-old electrical engineer and very capable in his work. His intellectual parents always prized his ability to think well, but they gave him absolutely no support for playing sports, being with other males, feeling sexual, or loving his own father. In fact, his father was particularly cool toward him and, like many working fathers, spent a great deal of time away from home at the job.

Alex presented himself to others, as a very rigid, easily frightened man. He spoke with deliberate hesitation and often reworked his sentences until he had them "correct." He constantly monitored himself in front of me and others and felt basically ashamed of himself for being male. Alex had ulcers and other gastrointestinal problems, and was mildly anorectic.

Timid around both men and women, Alex told me that when he attempted to develop a relationship with a woman, he felt inferior to her and immediately tried to impress her with his intellectual prowess. This failed to engage most women either in or out of the work arena, and Alex had never been in a romantic relationship. Before therapy, he had no male friends, although he was highly regarded by several male colleagues. They might socialize with Alex around job-related projects, but they never discussed or showed their feelings to him. Alex reported feeling immensely isolated and in a "great deal of emotional pain."

When I began working with Alex, I had him make a list of "the messages you would have liked to have heard from your parents." He followed my instructions compulsively and listed, among other things: "that I can feel my feelings and show them to others," "that my body is O.K. and deserves exercise and sex," and "that I can have meaningful, contactful relationships with other men and nonintellectual relationships with women."

With time, Alex learned that he did, indeed, have a body. He became proud of his body and wanted to take better care of it through jogging and a healthier diet. He even started several friendships with other men and a relationship with a woman with whom he could relate in a more feeling way.

OUTSIDE THE OFFICE

My clients aren't the only men who suffer from basic male shame. It also affects men I know and care about. My friend Jim is a police officer. His middle-class parents taught him to respect others and to have a high regard for ethical principles, but they also sent him another message. As he grew up, they made it clear to him that to earn their acceptance, he had to prove himself as a disposable man. To do this, Jim joined the Army during the Vietnam conflict and even reenlisted when his tour was over. He was often scared in combat, but true to his ideal of the macho man, he never showed his fear and always acted as if his life was totally unimportant. Jim never questioned the self-destructive messages his parents had instilled in him.

Jim has many macho buddies but no close male friends except me. He values our friendship and intimacy and he often comes over to my house to talk about his feelings. Yet, while he shares his feelings with me, he admits shame over having fears and insecurities, doubts, and confusions. Jim still believes that he does not have a right to these feelings, and that he should avoid them to please his mom and dad. Jim's father died of a heart attack last year and Jim, himself, has suffered from angina for several years now. I am trying to help my friend take better care of himself, especially his "heart."

Three other friends have had heart attacks in the past 5 years. One of them needed a triple bypass operation. I worry about them and am often aware of the driven and stressful lives they all lead. Even my father was driven and self-destructive. He never complained of pain and eventually died of the cancer that developed from the stomach ulcers he never told his doctor about. Even though I wanted to be different from my father, I too felt embarrassed and sometimes ashamed of my physical pain, fears, and sickness.

MY SEARCH CONTINUES

In the late 1980s I was still trying to unlearn the lessons my father had taught me. I wanted to take my life into my own hands, but it was seldom as easy as I had hoped. Once again, I went looking for a healthy group of men, a place where I could give and receive love, somewhere I could share the complete range of my feelings. But where—in this age of absent fathers and forgotten male initiation rites—would I find a group of healed, loving men? Where were the role models who would teach me to love and accept the man in myself?

I found some of what I was seeking in the work of Robert Bly. I attended several of his lectures but that wasn't enough. I wanted a complete, loving, and self-giving initiation experience, and I couldn't make it to one of Bly's weekend retreats. Instead, a friend and I organized a group of a dozen men to explore the possibility of initiating one another. We built our meetings around Francis Baumli's (1985) excellent book, *Men Freeing Men.* We gathered regularly to discuss and receive acceptance for the experience of our male sexuality, work, and daily stress, our male bodies and our male feelings.

At one session we conducted an initiation rite. The ceremony opened with a meditation on passage into manhood. Then we began drumming and chanting. We explored a complex ritual we had designed and one by one each male was initiated by the group. Each man had written his own "words of initiation" and had brought a personally meaningful item—a pocket knife, a fishing rod, a cooking pot—that for him symbolized passage into manhood. Another man chosen by him would say the words back to him and present him with the gift he had brought. We who attended got a lot and gave a lot during the ceremony. Several of us felt great sadness and wept openly in grief for the acceptance we had never felt before. Others laughed from the belly with great joy.

Several members of the group, however, missed this event and did not call ahead of time to say they would be unable to come. By now, I recognized this pattern from the other men's groups. I decided to raise my theory of basic male shame with the initiates. I found them generally accepting of the theory but several men said they could not identify with it at all.

PUTTING MY THEORY TO WORK

In my work as a psychotherapist, I found myself more aware of basic male shame and helping many men undo the shame that they had received in early development. The result? More of these men worked through numerous other issues more quickly and easily. I was amazed, and so were my clients and colleagues.

Here is an example: During a session with a group of musicians, Bill, a master cellist, told the group about an intermittent difficulty he was having with his performance. I asked Bill to play for us and he settled himself in front of the group, looked at us, then averted his eyes and began to play. His phrasing was precise and sensitive, his rapport with his instrument perfect, until the last few measures, when he looked up at someone in the group and faltered. I guessed that this eye contact was significant to Bill in some way and I immediately stopped his playing.

I asked Bill what had happened at the time when he erred in his bowing, and he told me that he had looked directly at John, another musician in the group. At first he did not understand why this made him falter, so I asked him to try playing again while looking at John. He quickly realized that he felt "competitive and scared . . . of physically being hurt" by John—by any man.

> *Bill:* "When I was a kid, my mother refused to let me play sports with the other boys. She frightened me . . . told me I would hurt my hands and then I would never be able to play cello again."

> *Therapist:* "So now you frighten yourself with mama's warnings and when you feel like making playful contact with some man, you do become momentarily unable to play cello.

> *Bill:* "Wow! I never thought of it that way, but it's absolutely true."

Bill's mother had shamed him out of aggressive male contact. I suggested a playful "wrestling match" between them on a soft rug. John agreed. Bill was reluctant but was willing to try as long as I acted as referee.

The two musicians grappled, first tentatively then with more and more energy. Each tried to get the other onto his back. John seemed to have the advantage of youth and almost pinned Bill to the rug. Others in the group cheered for one of the wrestlers. Both Bill and John were grunting loudly as they tried to turn the other over. Finally Bill's superior strength won out, and he held John's shoulders down as I counted John "out" and declared Bill the winner. The group cheered joyously. Bill was flushed and sweating but grinning broadly. Finally he and John caught their breath, rose to their knees, and spontaneously hugged each other. The love hidden beneath Bill's fear of being hurt had emerged.

Bill readily admitted that he no longer feared assertiveness in himself or other men. When he was ready he took up his cello again and rendered the sonata beautifully. Several times while he played, Bill looked up at one of the other men and smiled. And this time he didn't miss a note. Later, Bill wrote to me:

> It was a great relief. from those long standing and generally hidden fears . . .
> You were most helpful in bringing these skeletons out of my closet . . .. We
> [John and Bill] found out we could wrestle and that we would not be hurt or
> hurt the other person . . .
>
> The musical accomplishment [during the session] was indeed profound for
> me. It was the musical expression of my state of ease: emotional connected-
> ness to my male playfulness with John.

Bill was one of the many men in therapy who eventually benefited from a recognition of basic male shame as an underlying issue leading to other problems. Many of my clients realized that their poor health and reluctance to get a yearly physical examination was the result of their basic male shame.

MALE SHAME IN THE MEDIA

The message that a man's well-being is not important, that being a man is a shameful exer-cise at best, comes to us from many quarters. Take the movie, *Glory,* for example. It was a deeply moving film about a Union Army regiment comprised of freed black slaves. During their long and rigorous training together, these men developed a profound amount of love and respect for one another. They didn't recognize this wealth of feelings until the night before they would lose their lives in a hopeless attack against a well-armed fort. In their prebattle celebration, one soldier says, "Tomorrow, we will be MEN!" There was a resounding shout of agreement, and much caring for one another. Watching that scene, I felt so sad for these men who could only revel in their maleness when they were about to give up their lives for some cause. This is not glory, but stupidity. Because we learn this stupidity first at the knees of our parents, we men desperately need to reparent ourselves, and especially to refather our inner child.

BECOMING THE FATHER WE NEVER HAD

What can men do to reparent themselves in the face of so much negative familial and cultural programming? While I believe there are several ways men can undo the societal and parental inculcation of basic male shame, I will offer one that I have used with myself and others. It is called "creating a fantasy father," and it involves imagining a new father in one's mind. I learned it in 1979 from Stuart Alpert and George Rogers at Hartford Family Institute, but did not apply it for a few years.

When called on, this "father" always gives good advice and never asks the son to do anything self-destructive. He might say things like, "I love you, son, not for what you do or become in your life but just because you are you. I love you as you are, and if you never change anything, not even in your therapy, I shall always love you." A man can bring this fantasy father wherever he wants and can "talk" to him in his mind whenever he likes. He might not be able to picture his fantasy father's face, or visualize his physique or imagine his particular tone of voice, but that doesn't matter. The important part of the technique is that the man *feels the fantasy father's presence and loving support* when he needs it most.

If a man summons his fantasy father and hears a shaming voice, then he either has the wrong fantasy going, or he is listening to destructive voices from his childhood father or some other adult who injured him as a child. The goal is to dismiss these people as harmful and wait patiently until he can hear the fantasy father once again.

For men who have tried this, the results have been marvelous. They have experienced a new relatedness to the positive animus within themselves. They reparented themselves with the father they would have liked to have had when they were boys. At the same time, they experienced that to be male is to love the self as male and thus to love other men as well.

Like prayer and meditation in other systems, this therapeutic intervention must be practiced faithfully, for some time, before the effect is felt. But eventually a man learns to summon his fantasy father whenever he has a question that needs answering, and this is reinforced when the man learns that the "father" will give him a useful answer. The fantasy father never encourages selfishness, only self-love, so the man who calls on his fantasy father will also experience real humility in daily life and remorse whenever he hurts another.

After several months or years, the fantasy father becomes a very real substitute for what a man missed as a child. This "father" eventually recedes into the background, unless he is called forth for help with a particular question. In fact, the man who develops a fantasy father may not be sure his fantasy father ever really "existed." Nevertheless, the effect of this form of imaging seems to be quite powerful. One internalizes the ability to love oneself as a male. One learns to trust oneself and to develop lasting, committed bonds with other men.

There are other ways to internalize self love. Robert Bly, Ed Tick, and Joseph Jastrab are but a few of the loving men who run frequent experiential workshops in which male bonding, affirmation, and love abound. In these workshops one gets the experience of being loved as a male from the other men in the group. One weekend, however, does not change the brain patterns of a lifetime. It takes many such exposures to loving men before this message can replace the basic male shame of childhood.

Whatever method you choose to follow to overcome male shame, remember to test the effectiveness of your personal change by getting together with men on a regular basis. Experience how important these men are to you and feel how important you are to them. This is not the clinging dependency of a child, but the ability of grown men to give and take adult love (Gottlieb, 1987). You should be willing to pursue this bonding; you must realize that despite their liberated attitudes, your closest friends may be struggling with their own basic male shame. You can't save them. But you can be an example. You *can* teach them with your own love that love between men is nothing to fear. On the contrary love between men is deeply fulfilling and something every man needs to overcome the destructive effects of basic male shame, to stay nourished for a lifetime and to nurture others.

NOTE:

¹ Thealogy is a feminine form of theology.

Chapter 10
Male Initiation:
Filling a Gap in Therapy*

CHRISTOPHER MILLER

Men are less likely than women to enter psychotherapy. And when they do, it is often difficulty with women that, directly or indirectly, brings them to the consulting room. As a pastoral psychotherapist, I have noticed that my male clients are often poorly prepared to function in heterosexual dynamics.

Emotional awareness, expression of feelings, and the empathy often desired by females are poorly developed skills in many men. Moreover, men seem to think they are more rational and objective than they really are, misunderstanding the emotional systems that influence their perceptions and behavior. This puts them at a disadvantage with women, who are likely to be emotionally aware and expressive in negotiating for their personal needs.

TWO MALE STYLES

Generally, men in my practice seem to adopt one of two interpersonal styles. The more stereotypically "macho" men endure or deny emotional pain, concealing their reactions behind a cool poker face or Marine toughness. Anger is usually the most acceptable form of emotional expression. Their aggressive energy is channeled into competition, dominance, and hierarchical structure. Although women may admire or respect these men for their power, they may also experience them as controlling, uncooperative, and demeaning.

In contrast, the stereotypically "soft" males will directly acknowledge pain in themselves and others but may have trouble expressing anger. Such men may channel their aggressive energy into niceness and cooperation, sometimes resulting in low self-esteem or a sense of inadequacy from compromising self. Women find them affectionate, understanding, and more compliant, but may also find them son-like and difficult to respect.

Neither type of man is adequately prepared to negotiate a satisfying relationship with a woman. Disregarding their spouses' positions or automatically adapting to them, both types miss emotional cues in themselves and their partners, thereby failing to establish interpersonal boundaries through clear and direct communication. Unable to readily say, "I need," "I want," "I can't," or "I won't," they become overly dependent on women to interpret their feelings and positions for them, often inaccurately.

Culturally trained to disregard their own feelings, men may not know how to empathize with a woman's perspective and needs without losing themselves. They may experience women's expressed wants and needs as demands, criticisms, or orders requiring an immediate solution. Our biological programming to protect the nest manifests in a "fix-it" syndrome—an automatic tendency to respond to female distress with problem solving. The male alarm system makes it difficult to tolerate conflict with female partners long enough to generate win-win solutions. By abdicating to what she wants, or by dominating or oppressing women to control the situation, many men are ineffective in their attempt to resolve conflict. Women who would prefer empathy rather than a solution will be frustrated and disappointed by a compliant or controlling response to their distress.

Neither the macho nor the soft style enables men to establish satisfying long-term relationships with women. Furthermore, the tendency to focus emotional needs only on their female partner and not into a variety of relationships—as women tend to do—adds to the problem. These men not only lack skill in negotiating with women, but they also need something that cannot be provided by a woman's love.

As a son must turn to his mother for all his emotional resources when the father is unavailable, so these male clients were looking to women. But the need for a father and the unexpressed grief about this father deficit cannot be met or resolved in the mother-son, heterosexual relationship. So my clients have been vaguely discontented or openly hostile toward their female partners, experiencing them as somehow inadequate or withholding. The unfulfilled or underdeveloped father-son relationship was damaging marriages.

A boy needs to bond with a strong, nurturing male. The experience of closeness with his own kind positively mirrors his own maleness and alleviates over-dependency on the female. For a boy to develop a shame-free sense of himself as male, he needs to experience *cellular contact* with the male, resulting from physical proximity to a strong male figure who models and teaches the boy life skills. From this he learns how to handle himself successfully with females. Ideally, the boy learns a way of relating that allows an exchange of physical and emotional nurturing without violating the integrity of either person.

The man who never experiences such male contact longs for a true soul protector with whom he can discover and fulfill his true self. He feels the "hole" in the self, and may be driven to compensate for the loss in any way he can. He may settle for substitutes, attaching dependently to a woman. Or he may be drawn to the exploitative boss, the competitive coach, or the drill sergeant. Such people rarely function as adequate soul protectors.

THE BENEFITS OF INITIATION

It has been difficult for men to find true soul protectors to satisfy our father hunger. Hope came when one of my clients attended the New Warrior Adventure Training. This male initiation weekend shows men how to meet their needs with other men and begins to fill the gaps left by our culture in male development. My client and his wife were getting a divorce. He was angry and frustrated because he couldn't communicate with her. The New Warrior training helped him develop a remarkable new ability to be emotionally present and communicate with his wife, even though they continued to divorce. I made plans to attend New Warrior weekend for myself.

My experience there was profound personally and enlightening to me as a therapist. The leaders redefined the standards for what a man is. These standards were clearly mandated in stereotypical Western male style, which circumvented our automatic resistance to female styles. We were directed to be present for each other and to give focus to each other. We were told that a real man does the hard work of finding, naming and owning his own feelings. We were challenged to be men who act with integrity among other men, directed from within by our own sense of mission. We saw that a man needs men to love, and needs to be loved by other men. We discovered new possibilities for being good sons and fathers.

This training allowed me to address my own personal issues in ways not possible in individual or family therapy. I entered into the emotional, physical and spiritual experience of being present and intentional with other men, and emerged deeply touched, excited and somehow changed.

As a psychotherapist, I can see how such an initiation experience facilitates discovery of the true self. It promotes awareness, objectivity and a respect for the feeling system that directs our behavior more powerfully than the thinking system. Initiation grounds a man in honest acceptance and responsibility for himself. From this new viewpoint, he can pursue his goals by taking action that is response-able rather than reactive to others. He can acknowledge the unique experience of the other person. He becomes receptive, rather than reactive, to the stranger, especially to the female stranger.

When men are good to each other, when we function as soul protectors instead of adversaries, we create a positive approach to the world. When we say, "I need," "I hurt," and "I can't" to ourselves and others instead of hiding behind a "macho" or a "nice guy" stereotype, then we can reach out to our environments rather than exploit them.

Such men aren't codependent or adaptive to dysfunction, and they don't blame. They communicate clearly and directly about themselves and are good advocates for their own needs. They are neither the oppressor nor the oppressed.

IMPLICATIONS FOR MEN IN THERAPY

Many men sense that something is wrong but haven't been able to name it. Many of us secretly concluded that something was wrong with *us*. We achieve goals that parents or culture establish for us, but then we hide in hierarchy to protect ourselves from the shame of being out of integrity with our true selves. If we are intelligent or otherwise talented, we usually master a false personality that is rewarded by our parents, wives and children. Or we can defy society's conventions, maintaining ourselves by avoiding commitment and keeping others at a distance. Either way, in the long run we lose our souls.

Psychotherapy is difficult for many men because it contradicts a male code that mandates denial of feelings and personal needs, and supports a silent, do-it-on-your-own achievement orientation. Therapy may appear humiliating, shaming, and wrongheaded. Seen from a perspective that glorifies hierarchy and dominance, it looks like submission—the all-knowing therapist will fix a man only if he surrenders control of his life.

Beyond this, many therapeutic styles do indeed emphasize pathology and treat the client as someone who needs to be "fixed." Therapists who practice these methods devalue men and reinforce the secret sense of inadequacy and shame that many men carry.

Therapy often subtly expects men to compromise themselves by adopting feminine modes of being and feeling. Male styles are often perceived as wrong by women and by men who have mastered feminine styles of communication. Men usually talk without facing each other or making much eye contact, and we generally don't match up feelings with language as easily as women do. Yet many therapeutic styles require us to face the therapist, sustain eye contact, and name our emotions with precision.

Men have a unique mode of feeling and communicating, achieving closeness in ways different than females (See Dougherty, 1995). Men in therapy have a fundamental need for their maleness and male styles to be understood, mirrored positively, and affirmed. Perhaps a woman therapist can do this, but the basic need for admiration by an older man suggests that many men need a male therapist. Father-hunger in male clients must be addressed.

Because men are often at a disadvantage in female-style relational skills, therapists need to teach men how to negotiate for themselves in relationships with women. Men need to learn how to handle themselves when women are emotionally intense or expressive in ways that men can find overwhelming or threatening. Men need to learn aggressive empathy—listening without reacting, then reflecting back what they hear—as an alternative to feeling hurt, manipulated and enraged. Working with other men on identifying feelings is excellent preparation for male-female dynamics. We learn to understand the male mode of feeling and become advocates for our own emotions. When a man does not know what he feels, he probably doesn't know what he wants, so he can't tell his partner what he needs. This leaves him disabled in relationships. He then must choose to take whatever she gives him, or move on.

My experience with the men's movement confirms that men need to have a mission, and therapy should not overlook this. Personal change is much less difficult when it serves a personal mission. Therapy must consider the authenticity of a man's career choice in light of his sense of a larger purpose or mission, and help him identify subtle and obvious ways he may be compromising himself and thereby eroding his self-esteem. A man must learn to consider whether his life is consistent with his own ideals.

Therapy needs to challenge the usual style of male-male relationships and teach men how to connect securely with other men. Male clients should learn how much they need other men, and be coached in developing relationships with them. And they also need to know what can and cannot be expected from relationships with women.

A man needs a therapist who is a soul protector. Such a therapist will help him rediscover his soul, and guide him in the art of being authentic—true to what he is meant to be, and graceful in his respect for himself and others. The therapeutic process should look beyond a client's defects and the issues he needs to resolve. A man deserves a therapeutic process that consistently serves to mirror his personal worth, bless his manhood, reveal his mission in life, and teach him to relate to others in ways that bring joy to his existence.

NOTE:

---

* Based on a presentation to the national conference on "The Men's Movement and the Churches," convened at Chicago Theological Seminary by Robert Moore, October 1991.

Chapter 11
A Shame-Based Model for Recovery from Addiction

GEORGE LINDALL

From my private practice of psychotherapy, I developed a therapeutic model that is effective for people addicted to a variety of self-destructive behaviors.

THE ADDICTION MODEL

Concentrating on adult behavior and adult shame is likely to put a Band-Aid on the proble— and create a dry drunk or a straight junkie. Adult compulsive behavior (acting Out) tends to obscure underlying issues, so it needs to be stabilized before the major childhood issues are treated. But this concern with obvious adult behavior is only a beginning; when it becomes the major focus of therapy, relapse is much more likely to occur.

The model clarifies the forces involved in the perpetuation of addiction (see Figure 11.1). The addiction cycle begins when a child experiences victimization and learns to insulate himself

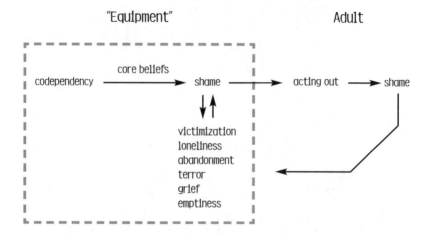

Figure 11.1   Addiction Model

from painful feelings and memories by developing layers of shame and later codependency. The child aspect of the model is called the *equipment* because it's a given (i.e., the person carries it with him from his family of origin). The *adult* aspect of the model includes acting out (compulsive behavior) and the shame the person associates with acting out.

Our traditional method for treating addiction places too much emphasis on the adult side of the model. I propose an "80/20 rule" for addiction: 80% of the feelings that drive addiction come from the childhood equipment, whereas only 20% of the feelings come from the adult shame an addict feels. The crucial issues are the childhood issues.

ASSUMPTIONS

This therapy for addiction starts with a set of assumptions about all people, whether or not they see themselves as addicts or are actively seeking treatment for addiction.

1. All human beings are addicts. All of us look for some form of distraction to protect ourselves from our existential predicament. We are each alone with God, as we understand him. Each of us entered this world alone and will leave alone. We are all fearful, to some degree, about this predicament. Recovery is about learning to face this fear.

2. All addicts are shame-based. Shame is the first distraction we turn to when faced with the pain in our lives.

3. All human beings are victims. When we were children, we all had needs that were not met. In that sense, we were all abused in childhood. Whenever this happened, our emotional development was interrupted. So, every one of us has feelings of loneliness, abandonment, terror, grief, and emptiness. These painful feelings propel us to seek distraction from our existential predicament.

4. All human beings are codependent. We all engage in caretaking, pleasing, and achieving behavior in the hope that *it* will make us feel better about ourselves. We look outside of ourselves, instead of inside, for our self-esteem.

5. Each of us has dysfunctional core beliefs that reinforce our addictive cycle. Subtly but powerfully, we tell ourselves things like, "It's not okay to be angry" or "Sex is my most important need."

METHOD OF TREATING ADDICTION

A method for treating sexual addicts arose from this addiction model and these five assumptions. Although each addict has his own unique reality and situation, the method covers issues each must face in order to recover successfully Are these issues best taken up in linear order, one after the other, or interwoven like threads in a piece of fine fabric? I see recovering people use both approaches. Although a client might be involved with two or three stages simultaneously there is usually an identifiable progression from mostly stage 1 to mostly stage 2, and so forth. What follows is a kind of check list of typical issues that addicts encounter in their therapeutic journey.

1. Because acting out anesthetizes an addict's feelings, he must cut back his addictive behavior in order to start feeling again. Whether he's using alcohol, sex, food, or gambling to numb his emotions, he needs to reduce his coping behavior until it isn't as profound and powerful as it once was. Only then can he get closer to his feelings and begin productive work on his childhood issues.

2. The addict must let himself feel shameful without medicating his shame with distractions. I believe that all compulsive behavior comes from trying to avoid shame. The cycle begins when we are children. We're victimized when our parents weren't there for us emotionally or when they abused us in some way. We felt shame as children, and we decided that shame hurts too much. We learned to avoid feeling it at all costs.

As adults, we still look outside ourselves to relationships, work, food, or sex to make us feel better. Sooner or later, we'll fail when we try to get our self-esteem from our environment. This triggers shame—that emotion we learned to avoid as children—and we try to escape it through compulsive behavior, which only leads to more shame.

We simply can't manage to avoid shame in our lives, nor do we want to. A turning point in treatment occurs when the client decides that his shame is to be honored, rather than avoided. Shamefulness is part of our personalities, and I want clients to learn that they can live through it without the anesthesia of compulsive behavior to distract them from feeling this emotion.

3. The addict must allow himself to make mistakes without condemning himself. During early recovery, I ask my clients to focus less on avoiding their compulsive behavior and codependency, and more on allowing themselves to engage in this behavior without beating themselves up. I'm certainly not encouraging people to get drunk, take drugs, overeat, or break the law. But I do encourage clients to be gentle with themselves and give themselves permission to be just the way they are. When addicts condemn their own compulsive behavior, all they do is reinforce their shame and the cycle of addiction.

4. The addict must hold his abusers accountable for his childhood victimization. He must learn that 80% of his feelings—80% of the power behind his compulsive behavior—arises from childhood issues.

    We all suffered at the hands of our parents or the people who raised us. Each of us started life as a unique person with unique desires, beliefs, opinions—all of us had our own unique reality. And to some degree, each of us had parents who didn't allow us to be our own unique selves. They tried to force their own feelings, beliefs, and values on us. I call this abuse.

    As recovering adults, we have to realize that although we are responsible for our adult behavior, we are not responsible for the "equipment" our parents provided us. This childhood equipment is part of us; it will always affect how we respond to life. But we did not create it ourselves. Recovering addicts must acknowledge the abuse they experienced as children and learn to hold their abusers accountable for it. It's really useful to stand up and say out loud, "It was not my fault. I didn't deserve this. I'm an adult now—no longer the child who didn't have enough power to stand up to you and your beliefs."

5. Once he learns to hold his abusers accountable, the addict must learn to express his anger about the abuse. Standard methods (yelling at surrogates, pounding pillows, etc.) are usually effective.

6. The addict must reach back to his unresolved victim feelings and be able to cry over them. This marks his safe arrival through an important series of emotional transitions. We have many layers of feeling, and shame is only the outermost layer, the one that lies closest to the addict's acting-out behavior. As his compulsive behavior wanes, the recovering addict comes to the realization that he has lived

continually—24 hours a day, for years on end—in shame, depression, and repressed anger. Then he learns to feel his shame instead of medicating it. In time, the shame recedes, and he's left with his innermost feelings of abandonment, loneliness, grief, and terror. When a client cries, I know he has reached these victim feelings.

7. The addict must recognize his tendency to depend on others to make him feel good about himself, and begin to change. Now that he's in touch with his victim feelings, he starts to notice how his adult environment triggers these feelings, especially his fear of abandonment. He begins to see how he gives up his own power to others and that he can start taking his power back.

8. The addict must learn which of his core beliefs reinforce his addiction. For example, as a little boy he may have been taught that he wasn't okay unless he pleased everybody else. When he fails at this—and he's bound to fail—his shameful feelings will beckon him back into compulsive acting out. As he learns to counteract the belief, he gains strength to avoid active addiction.

9. The addict must make amends for past behavior that has harmed others. Making amends is step 9 in the AA program of recovery. Such action teaches the addict that he can survive feeling intensely guilty and ashamed, and that he can act responsibly while experiencing these emotions. Amends often restore broken interpersonal bonds, to the benefit of both parties, and reduce long-standing shame.

FIVE STAGES OF RECOVERY

Elisabeth Kubler-Ross (1969) developed a model of five stages for working through grief. I've adapted and modified her model to describe the stages of recovery from addiction, because I think these are similar processes. Inside the adult addict is a child who didn't get his needs met. He's grieving the loss of his childhood; grieving the loss of protection when he was vulnerable; grieving the absence of blessing from his parents; grieving especially that he was not allowed to develop in ways that are necessary for healthy adulthood.

These stages are slightly different from Kubler-Ross's, and are listed in Figure 11.2 with behavior typical of each stage.

To summarize the stages and the internal dynamic in each stage: In stage *1—Acting Out*, the addict engages in various behaviors in order to escape painful realities in his life. In stage *2—Denial*, he perceives that he must protect his addiction and the lifestyle he has created around it—in order to survive. In stage *3—Anger*, the addict sees that he has been a victim and learns to express his anger toward those who victimized him. In stage *4—Grief*, he grieves, and allows himself to feel his terror, abandonment, and emptiness. In stage *5—Acceptance*, he accepts the equipment he carries from childhood and learns how to live with his childhood feelings without acting out his addictive behavior.

Stage 1—Acting Out

Caretaking, Overeating, Flirting, Fantasizing, Having lunch with a woman, Bragging about my sexual history, Going out with the old gang, Watching TV, Working out, Achieving, Performing, Telling sexual jokes.

Stage 2—Denial

Rationalizing, Controlling, Minimizing, Blaming, Depression, Using anger to control, Not listening.

Stage 3—Anger

Holding abusers accountable, Feeling shame, Doing anger work, Asserting myself, Standing up for myself, Naming the abuse.

Stage 4—Grief

Crying, Feeling empty, Feeling terrified, Feeling abandoned, Feeling a loss, Shaking.

Stage 5—Acceptance

Accepting responsibility, Making amends, Experiencing intimacy, Being good to myself, Getting excited about a sunrise, Feeling affirmed, Surrounding myself with recovering people, Exploring, Taking risks.

Figure 11.2 Behavior During the Five Stages of Recovery from Addiction

Recovery from addiction involves moving through these stages. There are specific experiences, practices, and behavior that may help addicts make the transition from one stage to the next. Useful books for each transition are listed in Figure 11.3.

From Acting Out to Denial

First the addict has to identify the things he does to escape from reality. When he engages in such behavior, he is abandoning himself. His task is to learn how to stay with himself. Part of being present for himself is setting goals for reducing his acting-out behavior and noticing how long it takes him to realize that he has entered an episode of acting out. But he doesn't need to do this alone. He can ask others to give him feedback when they see him acting out.

From Denial to Anger

At this stage, he starts talking about his acting-out behavior. He goes back over his personal history and tells others how he acts out and how he abuses others. He starts to be honest with others and with himself. Group therapy provides a good opportunity to do this, and it also gives him a safe place to share his secrets. Keeping secrets reinforces the shame he feels and perpetuates the cycle of addiction. If he's going to work through his shame, he has to start sharing his secrets, even if this means compensating those he has harmed or serving time for illegal acts in his past. In this stage, staying with himself involves taking responsibility for his actions and for their effects on others.

From Acting Out to Denial

Carnes, Patrick. (1992). *Out of the Shadows* Minneapolis: CompCare Publications. An overview of sexual addiction.

Woititz, Janet G. (1990). *Adult Children of Alcoholics.* Deerfield Beach, FL: Health Communications. Outlines the core beliefs and childhood origins of addiction.

From Denial to Anger

Viscott, David. (1976). *The Language of Feelings.* New York: Arbor House. Helps clients to recognize and label their emotions, and find permission to own their anger.

Millman, Dan. (1984). *The Way of the Peaceful Warrior.* Tiburon, CA: H. J. Karmer, Inc. A guide to being one's own person.

Andrews, Lynn V. (1983). *Medicine Woman.* San Francisco: Harper. Tips for being quiet and reclaiming one's identity.

From Anger to Grief

Schaef, Anne W. (1985). *Codependency; Misunderstood and Mistreated.* San Francisco. Harper. *Understanding codependency.*

McNaron, Toni A. H., & Morgan Yarrow, eds. (1982). *Voices in the Night: Women Speaking About Incest.* Pittsburgh, PA: Cleis Press. *Personal stories useful for sexual abuse victims both male and female.*

From Grief to Recovery

Kubler-Ross, Elisabeth. (1969). *On Death and Dying.* New York: Macmillan. An exploration of how people work through grief.

Recovery

Woititz, Janet G. (1985). *The Struggle for Intimacy.* Deerfield Beach, FL: Health Communications. The work of recovery can become an obsession. This book helps clients to stop focusing on recovery and start focusing on living.

Figure 11.3 Readings to Facilitate a Client's Recovery

He also needs to start identifying his own feelings. It's absolutely crucial that a recovering addict learn some basic labels for his feelings, learn to recognize his feelings and listen to them, and then learn to connect his feelings with the labels. I teach addicts eight basic feelings: mad, sad, joyful, scared, lonely, empty, abandoned, and shameful. I encourage them to use these labels because they're especially descriptive and specific. Words like "depressed," "addictive," or "confused" are dead ends—they tend to keep an addict stuck in the idea that he's diseased, and probably incurable.

My goal is to get clients closer to their own inner voices, to their own inner selves. Out of the true inner self, a real identity and personal integrity can emerge, along with behavior that's consistent with this real identity. This is a time to slow down and look inward. Sometimes it requires him to work less, give up television, or call a moratorium on family contact—whatever it takes to allow him the time and space to discover his own reality.

From Anger to Grief

After the addict has learned what his shame feels like, and is able to stay with the shame without doing something to medicate it, he has to face his huge reservoir of shame from childhood. He needs to know deep down that it's not about his flaws but about what was done to him. When he was a child, he learned to abandon himself to please his parents. This was not something he chose freely, but was necessary for survival. It was perpetrated on him. Anger work—hitting pillows and yelling at his abusers—will help him experience his victim feelings of abandonment and emptiness and shame.

Presenting his victimization history is also helpful. He can talk about all the ways he was abused—most importantly how he was not allowed to be himself but forced to be what his parents wanted him to be. When he does this, he sets the record straight for himself: He makes a subtle shift from saying, "I was sexual with . . ." to "I was sexually abused by . . ." Instead of telling himself that he was responsible for what happened to him, or that he participated in it willingly, he sees that it wasn't his fault. Sexual addicts begin naming the covert sexual abuse they suffered. Many of these men had fathers who were absent, and mothers who were invasive and intrusive. The mothers turned their sons into surrogate spouses, and the sons now learn that Mom's sharing and touching was inappropriate behavior and constituted covert sexual abuse.

From Grief to Acceptance

The addict needs to learn how to cry and be able to get in touch with his victim feelings (e.g., emptiness, loss, abandonment) whenever he wants to. When an addict has a compulsive urge, he's less likely to act it out if he sees that it arises from childhood feelings, not from what's happening right now. In this stage, it helps to present his history of caretaking and codependency, both past and present. Going back to childhood, he talks about all the ways his parents forced him to be codependent with them. And as an adult, he needs to examine how he still gives his power away and allows himself to be a victim. He must see clearly how he continues to control, manipulate, and lie in order to please others. Although the pattern began in childhood, he needs to see himself perpetuating it in adult relationships with his mate, his kids, his boss, and others. When they decide to break up their lifelong patterns of codependency, I often ask clients to make the decision more concrete by writing good-bye letters and visiting graves.

From Acceptance to Recovery

Eventually the addict is ready to focus on the here and now, and prepare to move on with his life. He can look at the subtler ways he loses and abandons himself, and start to tighten up contracts he has made and boundaries he has set. His emphasis turns to the present moment, the present reality, his current relationships. He makes amends and leaves therapy.

Clients often stay in therapy too long. It's important to get out and take risks, one of which might be leaving therapy too soon. It's good to take that risk, and return to therapy if necessary.

MOVING ON

What does a recovering person look like? How does he behave in order to keep on recovering? First of all, he sees himself engaged in a process (recovering) which he can handle "good enough," rather than as one who has finished a task (recovered).

My clients work hard to get in touch with their childhood victimization feelings. Instead of abandoning themselves, these recovering addicts stay with their feelings and follow them back as far as they go—whether that be the present moment or a painful childhood scene from long ago. That work doesn't end when their therapy ends. Staying healthy means using the 80/20 rule whenever the need arises, and that requires continuing access to childhood emotions.

But recovering addicts get beyond spending most of their energy doing this emotional processing. They learn to enjoy the sun's warmth and the light of love in another's eye. Perhaps they'll spend an hour a week remembering and taking an emotional inventory, but mostly they find excitement and joy in other aspects of their lives. Recovering addicts no longer see themselves as diseased, but feel some acceptance of themselves as they are, and tend to regard their histories of abuse, shame, and addiction as things that normal people may experience.

NOTE:

[1] A sexual addict is defined here as a person who *compulsively* masturbates, has affairs, uses pornography, patronizes prostitutes, thinks and fantasizes about sex, exposes himself in public, etc. The repetitive and compulsive nature of these practices causes these people to feel intense shame and other emotional distress, and significantly harms their relationships, work, finances, and enjoyment of life. Most of these addicts are *not* sexual offenders or criminals, who rape, molest children, or commit similar offenses.

ANNOTATED GENERAL BIBLIOGRAPHY:

For therapists and other professionals. These books were the most influential in developing my therapeutic practice.

Bandler, Richard, and Grinder, John. (1979). *Frogs into princes.* Moab, UT: Real People Press.

Bandler, Richard, and Grinder, John. (1981). *Retraining: Neuro-Linguistic programming and the Transformation of Meaning.* Moab, UT: Real People Press. *Two books on effective and pragmatic technique, based upon trust of the body and its primary role in communication.*

Carnes, Patrick. (1988). *Contrary to love.* Minneapolis: CompCare Publications. *For professionals who treat sexual addiction.*

Ferguson, Marilyn. (1987). *The aquarian conspiracy.* Los Angeles: Tarcher. *A detailed discussion of the cultural transformation which we call recovery.*

Fossum, Merle A., and Mason, Marilyn J. (1986). *Facing shame: Families in recovery.* New York : Norton. *Understanding shame and its relationship to addiction.*

Grinder, John, and Bandler, Richard. (1981). *Trance formation: Neuro-linguistic programming and the structure of hypnosis.* Moab, UT: Real People Press. *The genius of Milton Erickson needs interpretation before ordinary folks can understand and use it.*

Hackbarth, Judy, and Lindall, George. (1989). *Against the tide: Why addicts aren't recovering in today 's world. Unpublished manuscript, available from author.*

Haley, Jay (1993). *Uncommon therapy,* 3rd ed. New York: Norton. *Introduction to the non-rational techniques of Milton Erickson.*

Schaef, Anne W. (1985). *Women's reality.* San Francisco: Harper. *Affirms clients' experience of never fitting in.*

Schaef, Anne W. (1988). *When society becomes an addict.* San Francisco: Harper. *Addiction is embedded in the culture, not just in the individual or the family.*

Yalom, Irvin. (1980). *Existential psychotherapy.* New York: Basic Books. *Everything you ever wanted to know about right-hemisphere psychotherapy.*

Chapter 12
Grandiosity:
The Shadow of Shame

DAVID L. LINDGREN

"... if we now consider the fact that, as a result of psychic compensation, great humility stands very close to pride, and that 'pride goeth before a fall,' we can easily discover behind the haughtiness certain traits of an anxious sense of inferiority. In fact, we shall see clearly how his uncertainty forces the enthusiast to puff up his truths, of which he feels none too sure, and to win proselytes to his side in order that his followers may prove to himself the value and trustworthiness of his own convictions."

—*Jung, 1928, ¶ 225*

THE FALL

For the past six years, as director of a men's organization, I have facilitated hundreds of men who have attended our initiation trainings. The major focus of these trainings is to empower men to take responsibility for their lives. We emphasize in this work that a man examine the shadow side of his psyche. The challenge is in confronting the shadow and the natural resistance to revealing these deeper underlying feelings which men so frequently bury.

The strategy of our trainings is to confront the various defenses men construct to avoid the shame of revealing to a group of men that they have indeed "fallen"—fallen into a pit of self-doubt and uncertainty. Becoming a man of real emotions and integrity tends to make superfluous the wrappings and armor[1] that we men have acquired. The urgency and necessity to expose our real selves is at once the most terrifying and the most exhilarating experience.

This circumstance appears universal, in that every man has taken a "fall." At some point in childhood, every little boy has a "fall from grace" and chooses to let go of his uniqueness or decides to become something other than who he is intended to be. A series of ego splitting experiences occurs. The child "decides,"[2] at this point, that he cannot please his primary caretakers with a certain set of behaviors. He adapts by betraying his ego to receive the reinforcement he needs to proceed to the next step in his development.

There are necessary but painful losses at each step in the process. Manifestations of the "fall" may appear in different forms. Each child selects strategies to protect himself from further harm. Later in life, these strategies become armor which prevents him from developing in a healthy way. During an initiation training, the internal experiencing of this process is accelerated in time (Greenwald, 1995). Initiatory experiences heighten the drama of a man's life and expose it to an intensive mirroring. Shame has little chance to escape exposure.

CONFRONTING SHAME

SHAME is a common feeling expressed by men who have reflected honestly on their lives. When men can acknowledge their shame, we repeatedly hear the phrase: "I am afraid of making a mistake ... of not being good enough." An extreme but stereotypical pattern is that of a man who is frozen in a shame-bound state.

Many men are aware of the importance of shame (Bradshaw, 1988), and the desirability of examining the "little boy" inside. Some men appear to be the type of man who is "life-sustaining" and not "life-giving" (Bly, 1990). That is, instead of being generative and supporting of others, they themselves need nurturing. These men had mothers who were typically more dominant in the relationship in comparison to the fathers who are described as being too weak or absent.

These men are waiting to project their father-need on the leaders who are idealized for having personal qualities which they aspire to. Leaders are not always aware of this hunger and the propensity to project "father hunger" on to them. The holding of this idealizing projection by the leader is essential to a man's process in initiation. Leaders need to reflect this father hunger back to the man and then stimulate the idealization into healthy grandiosity.

While these men's stories may range from the horrific to the pathetic, some of these men appear to have made a decision to stay in a position of shame. They reason that the world expects too much of them, and they are convinced that their resources are too limited. These men, in effect, seemingly choose shame over looking at the myriad of other possibilities available to them.

The frequency of men holding their shame-bound position seems to be on the rise. By "holding," I mean that given a choice to express deeper emotions, they stay with shame as the emotion of choice. In their shame-bound state, they resist standing up as a man and "hold on" to a posture of being a scared little boy.

Most of these men did not take the rebellious route as children. They adopted strategies to please "dear old Mom."[3] These men have learned to sell out to the needs of women in a heartbeat (Bly, 1990). With the absence of masculine spiritual energy in their lives, they lose the will to resist. None of us actually are immune to this temptation. Given the possibility that Mom might leave us, most of us would do virtually anything to "hold on" to her love.

Such men hold their shame in their bodies. For example, we confront men with sloped shoulders and distended bellies with the necessity of standing up and grounding themselves. To enlist a man's pride or his inner beauty requires an assault on the enemy named shame.

When these men drop their disguise of shame, they first reveal the absence of father energy in their lives. They are ashamed that they were not "good enough" to be loved and respected by their father. Ultimately, what is revealed is hunger for the masculine spirit.

MODEL OF GRANDIOSITY AND SHAME

Moore and Gillette (1990) have proposed the bipolar nature of the shadow of the major male archetypes. In their model, the particular energy of the archetype is split in the shadow realm. The more active, extroverted side of the split chooses a more exhibitionist, grandiose path. The more passive, introverted side of the split involves more shame and fear of exposure. Together they form two poles like two ends of a teeter-totter. If you push/confront one pole of the shadow, up pops the opposite energy. *Shame and grandiosity are opposite ends of the same continuum of self development,* much like introversion and extroversion.

Moore and Gillette (1990) present a developmental scheme wherein each archetype has opportunities for expression. If these energies are blocked, the child "decides"[2] basically on a strategy to disguise the "gold" of these archetypes. The strategy itself unfortunately creates a diminishment of the self and either an under- or over-adequate view of the self. Parents and adults take on a size in the person's mind that is disproportionately larger than reality.

We have observed in this process that "pride" and "fall" exist side by side. Pride and grandiosity are always a dynamic with men who present themselves as shameful.

If we start from the passive side of the split in a man's presentation, we find that he may be stuck in his shame, exhibiting some hopeless/helpless anxiety. He claims that his issue is shame. However, upon confronting the shame, with a question such as, "what is keeping you from your goal?" the hidden nature of the grandiosity is revealed.

The man typically resorts to defending and protecting his strategy of withholding from view the opposite side of the split. And the challenge reveals the split in its paradoxical form. Yes, "pride goeth before a fall," and we also know that "pride" will resurface upon challenging a man's defenses. The direction of his process resembles more the "fall" preceding the "pride."

The active side is usually some manifestation of anger/rage or disappointment/grief. In either case, the basic energy of grandiosity is at play. When a man's shame is challenged, particularly the "holding" of the shame, he faces a choice (usually unconsciously). He can choose to recycle his shameful feelings, as he has for most of his life. Or if he accepts the challenge to be a warrior of his own heart, he can then open himself to a profound transformation. He can stand tall, touch deep breathing and powerful sounds which resonate in his soul, defend his internal and external boundaries and enjoy the revengeful fantasies he has previously suppressed with shame.

Having experienced his grandiosity in its fullest, a shame-bound man begins the transformative process to being an erect warrior. Men can then accept their ancestral heritage of waging battle against "evil," that is, the admonitions given and learned that "I am bad/no good." This is the spiritual battle of authentic warriorship and "won" only by those willing to first risk feeling the grandiosity next to the shame. And those who "win" must first risk being seen as something other than how they presented themselves.

Self Psychology as presented by Kohut (1971; 1977) and more recently by Lee and Martins (1991) illustrates the developmental course of "infantile grandiosity" in children. By "grandiose self," Kohut (1971, p. 106) refers to "that aspect of a developmental phase in which the child attempts to save the originally all-embracing narcissism by concentrating perfection and power upon the self." The parents may react to this primitive bravery by shaming these initial excursions of the child away from the safety net of the family comfort zone.

Under favorable circumstances, the child is able to acquire, through various maturational stages, the capacity to recognize and to accept his limitations in a realistic manner. The grandiose fantasies can be consolidated as ambitions through empathic mirroring principally from mother and father.

However, if the ego gets too attached to the deep self structures within the unconscious (the archetypes), "inflation" of the ego occurs and potentially we can kiss the humility of the self good-bye. Manic-Depressive psychosis awaits the "winner" of the "where did my humility go" award.

Conversely, Kohut points out, the greatest achievements of our civilization did not come from men shrinking from ambition by de-flating/de-pressing themselves into curious, shame-bound onlookers. A poorly modulated grandiose self is the risk for men encountering this aspect of their shadow (Kohut, 1977).

To paraphrase Moore and Gillette (1990), grandiosity is a temporary but false energy state which can be self-stimulated to compensate for feelings of inadequacy and shame. It is a risk inherent in any challenge or ambition for the future. Continued exertion of the self in a grandiose state will deplete the self.

From my personal and "analyzed" experience, I can recognize the fusion of shame/grandiosity when someone asks me what I am feeling. My internal reflection is something like, "Dah, I feel nothing . . . (next) I feel empty . . . (next) what is wrong with me?" I know at that point that I have been hanging out over the cliff of self denial by defending my shame with grandiosity. Rather than state my feelings of shame to a friend or my significant other, I have chosen to deplete myself through ambitious efforts which create a false energy state. I stimulate my active side of grandiosity for fear that I will be seen as inadequate

Passive Side

Gary W., who attended one of our trainings, was 36 years old and had decided to marry for the first time. He felt ashamed of the fact that he had never married. He presented himself as emotionally shut down with feelings of inadequacy and a sense of hopelessness. Making the decision to marry had caused him to be uncertain and paralyzed in making future decisions. His fiancée, Julie, had provoked his uncertainty by hedging on her commitments—saying "maybe" or "I will have to wait" or "just let me think about It." Gary was overwhelmed with anxiety that Julie would not marry him, fearing that he would be deeply ashamed for again not succeeding in a relationship.

Gary's parents had frequently kept him waiting and parceled out their love in a "maybe" manner. As he became aware of this pattern, Gary released great physical spasms of hopelessness. Falling into grief, he cried out questioning how could he ever get married to a woman who would "maybe" love him. Severe shaming from the "aristocratic" family seemed right around the proverbial corner. Then he discovered the desperate requirements he had for a "perfect" girl/woman as his bride. Julie would spoil his plans of having a perfect marriage by not fitting in with the "aristocratic" family. He became infuriated with Julie. "How dare she spoil my perfect plan." As he held on to his rage, he sounded like a spoiled little boy.

The fusion of shame and grandiosity is apparent in Gary's case. The rambunctious little boy appeared occasionally, but mostly he had taken the passive, shameful route. His world was a "maybe," tempering and controlling his every move.

If his parents had given in and pandered to Gary's demands, his infantile grandiosity might have been stimulated. Then he would probably have moved to the active side of the split—demanding special recognition rather than repressing his needs.

Gary was able to break through and work out his relationship with Julie when he understood how his repressed sense of grandiosity could be activated in a healthy manner. He learned to take responsibility for fulfilling his needs rather than projecting them onto Julie. He began organizing his goals and ambitions around more realistic expectations without resorting to false modesty or being overwhelmed with temporary disappointment.

Active Side

Bruce M. was a flamboyant entrepreneur who perpetually was either on the verge of making millions or filing for bankruptcy. I asked Bruce to colead a group with me because of his extraordinary skill in group facilitation and because of his ability to help others to experience a sense of awe and magic in their transformative process. As long as his perceived successes were recognized and acknowledged, we had an acceptable working relationship. When his work was not acknowledged, Bruce would pout and dramatically ask for praise, or set up scenarios whereby he would make a dramatic, all-encompassing intervention to draw attention to himself.

"I can't handle any criticism right now" was his standard answer to critical comments, challenges of his emotional outbursts, or requests to be on time for the group. There never was a time to review our work, because he would always have the same answer. In effect, he was protecting his shame with grandiosity.

Bruce could speak the word "shame" only while grimacing and grinding his teeth. He found it difficult to accept my criticism because he seemed to project me as his "good father." During his childhood, Bruce's father had let Bruce know that his performance was not good enough and that he had to be ultraspecial to earn his father's love.

When this pattern was pointed out to Bruce, he finally made the connection between his fear of being a failure in life and not being loved by his parents. He collapsed into deep shame, sadly requesting that he just needed a little attention. "Is this so much to ask?" As Gary could not handle grandiosity, Bruce was immobilized by shame.

As we explored his sense of shame, Bruce's grandiosity and the resultant rage became tempered. It became possible to be more ordinary in a way that others could see his humility and sense of caring. Bruce began to receive feedback from others that he was open and available to be loved. Experiencing shame unlocked the door away from debilitating and dysfunctional grandiosity.

The transformations of Gary and Bruce illustrate how using the opposite poles of shame and grandiosity can bring balance and wholeness to the healing process. The way out of shame leads through the passageway of grandiosity. Integrity of the self depends on resolving this tension of opposites.

SOCIAL IMPLICATIONS

Shame can be seen as an introverted feeling and a defense to protect oneself from becoming inflated. Introverts typically prefer defenses that focus on the past, rather than projecting into the future and considering ambitions to be pursued.

Present theoretical positions overemphasize the passive receptiveness of shame. Individuals tend to see themselves as passive victims of abuse, humiliation and neglect. They resist exploring the grandiose side which lurks in their shadow. When men are confronted with their holding on to shame as a defense, their "repressed" grandiosity is awakened. The process of rebuilding a unified self (Individuation) can then be enhanced by owning one's defenses and strategies to protect the shadow.

Grandiosity conversely appears to be an extroverted feeling and a defense to protect one from feeling humiliated or ashamed. Extroverts avoid introspection about their past by projecting externally and into the future. Men who exhibit grandiosity run into the same wall of self-denial as shame-bound men. Grandiose men seek external answers to internal dilemmas. This kind of man runs as fast as he can to avoid feeling the depth of despair that is required to embrace his shadow of shame and become a whole man.

Why is shame such a predominate emotional reaction? Why are we so indulgent with shame-bound men? Why are we so inhibited in pressing forward and risking internal inflation?

When we are individuating and moving forward, we have a sense of anxiety about how our life will unfold or our world will change. We seem to be living in a shame-based culture that restricts us from projecting into the future. Perhaps we cling to our shame because otherwise our world projections would be out of control. There is a part of us that does not want to identify with outrageousness in the world—with violence, pollution of our environment, or warring between genders, races, and nations.

We are reminded constantly of the shamefulness of our world. Public media have picked up the shaming where religion left off. Our hyperinflated commercial, materialistic world exploits our shame by bombarding our senses with messages to suggest that we are not good enough unless we purchase and consume a certain product or experience some romantic vacation. In the extreme sense, we need shame as a defense mechanism to avoid the fear of a world out of control, that is, personal inflation, ultimate disappointment, and identification with the enemy.

In our shame-based culture, we are especially ashamed of our grandiosity. As children, we were punished for wanting too much, so that grandiosity never served us well. I have yet to meet a shame-bound person without an accompanying grandiose shadow. However, admitting how special and important one is can also activate shame.

Social critics of psychotherapy and of "introverted" men's work (Hillman, 1989) are wary of the possibilities of creating an improved social order with "little boys needing permission rather then taking the initiative to act." Psychotherapy itself in its classical style is a passive encounter that often requires long-term "sitting" on the horns of a personal dilemmas before action is taken in the world. While Rome is burning, we therapists, are fiddling with a one-sided approach that denies the "active pole" of decision making and purposive behavior.

In one way or another, we are all in a stage of recovery. We wouldn't feel alive if we weren't dealing with something. For some the battle with shame becomes a perpetual bout with an invisible shadow opponent. Shame gets recycled in a variety of guises. The struggle for recovery may become a "Sisyphus" drama, in which pushing the heavy stone to the hilltop is always followed by the fall. If only a man could glimpse how great he really is, grandiosity and shame would not be necessary.

Somehow an *ordinary* battlefield must exist where the ego and Self can reside without shame or grandiosity. Presently, these two co-exist with "eternal boys" (von Franz, 1970) with their accompanying need to be special. Ordinariness is an antidote to this specialness. To be "good enough" requires an ordinary, down-to-earth reality testing, transcending our old ways and letting the specialness die.

NOTES:

[1] Some refer to this armor as "ego." Although the ego eventually needs to be shed, at this point, the ego in relationship to self is necessary to understand one's internal holding of opposites.

[2] The word "decides" is used intentionally to challenge the passive mode of victimization. Certainly children *are* victimized, but consciously or unconsciously, they still choose their path or their poison, subsequent to being victimized.

[3] I suspect that the frequency of rebellious, "hyperactive" boys has decreased. "Nice" boys have taken their place—boys who know how to please women by being "good".

Chapter 13
The Rescue Triangle: Shame Update

JOHN EVERINGHAM

The Rescue triangle – also known as the Karpman (1968) or drama triangle – has been used for a quarter-century to untangle dysfunctional relationships and expose ulterior motives. The early authors practiced Transactional Analysis, with its emphasis on social psychology and interpersonal "transactions," and were mostly unaware of the modern understanding of shame. The continuing utility of the Rescue triangle may be enhanced by exploring some of the shame-based motives involved.

Three fundamental positions or roles dominate both literary drama and dysfunctional relationships. Figure 13.1 diagrams these basic positions and their synonyms.[1,2] The interaction of these roles in the triangle may be illustrated by a *type scenario*: an eager Boy Scout (EBS) takes a little old lady (LOL) in hand to help her across the street, unaware that she doesn't *want* to cross here. Halfway across, LOL thinks to herself, "He's such a nice young man. I won't tell him that my bus is coming." On the other side, her bus missed, LOL clouts EBS over the head with her umbrella.

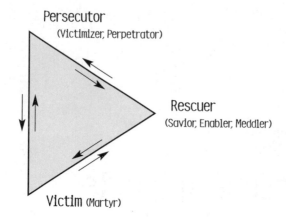

Persecutor
(Victimizer, Perpetrator)

Rescuer
(Savior, Enabler, Meddler)

Victim (Martyr)

Signs of a Rescue

A. I'm doing something for you that you haven't asked me to do.

B. I'm doing something for you that you can do for yourself.

C. I'm putting more energy into *your* problem than you are.

D. I realize that I don't really want to do what I'm doing for you, and come to resent you.

Figure 13.1 The Rescue Triangle

An essential feature of the drama triangle is that all the players shift positions: EBS from Rescuer to Persecutor to Victim, and LOL from Victim to Rescuer to Persecutor. Note that the positions shift quickly, easily, almost automatically, and that each position feels uneasy and ungrounded. People running around the Rescue triangle tend to keep doing it over and over again. There's often a feeling of "Here we go again, round and round."

If I continue to *Rescue*, I'll soon find myself playing *Victim* or *Persecutor*. Recognizing the triangle (or one of the roles: Victim, Rescuer, and Persecutor) often clarifies enmeshed relationships and makes me aware of ulterior motives, games, and disowned parts of myself (my Shadow).

Staying in the Rescue triangle reinforces codependency and internalized shame, and stepping out of it usually brings a great sense of relief (sometimes followed by a desire to grieve). But let's avoid perfectionism and blame about this. We all find ourselves in the triangle from time to time; the trick is to get out early, and to learn to play the drama (trauma) *lightly* (Berne, 1964, p. 64; James & Jongeward, 1971, p. 34).

Why I Rescue (or Play Victim)	How I Can Stop Rescuing
1. I'm not aware of doing it.	1. Read the signs, check out my feelings, and become aware. Then stop it.
2. I'm taking responsibility for *your* problem (Gordon, 1974, pp. 38-42, 118-122).[3]	2. Let *you* own *your* problem.
3. Somebody (maybe you, society, my Critical Parent, or an unnamed fear) is telling me I *should* own *your* problem.	3. Let my Adult reject the *should,* or just consider the probable consequences. Then let go of owning *your* problem.
4. You are insisting, shaming, or seductively inviting me to Rescue you.	4. Make an I-statement (Gordon, 1974, pp. 125-155). Or simply stop whatever I'm doing "for" you. *Step out of the triangle!*
5. I'm afraid of hurting your feelings, or that you'll be lost without me, or that I'll be ashamed if you find out that I...	5. Get in touch with *my* hurt, *my* pain, *my* shame, *my* fear of abandonment or rejection.
6. I want to build up credit with you, so that maybe you'll offer me something that I'm afraid – ashamed – to ask for directly, for my own sake.	6. Ask clearly for what I want. If you say "No," allow myself to feel hurt and ashamed for asking. Then ask someone else.
7. I'm involved in *your* problem because this allows me get "righteously" angry and contemptuous of those who are oppressing or abusing you.	7. Get angry with those who are oppressing or abusing *me* (or used to do so). Risk the shameful possibility that someone may think that I'm being selfish.
8. I'm focusing on *your* problem to avoid facing *my* shame.	8. Face the true source of my discomfort and dysfunction (Kaufman, 1989).
9. The Victim in me responds to the Victim in you. I'm trying to ease my pain by easing yours.[4]	9. Feel my own pain and shame, and let you experience yours. Let go of Victim.
10. I was a true victim as a child, and I identify deeply with another's pain and shame.	10. This is a gateway to healing. I need to cross the threshold into my own shame and pain, rather than continuing to creep up to it, and then veering off into the triangle again.
11. I seek the moral comfort of the Victim position, which provides justification for me to play the Persecutor role "righteously."	11. Befriend my anger, jealousy, contempt, and self-righteousness. Acknowledge my Shadow (Bly, 1988).

NOTES:

[1] James and Jongeward (1971, p. 86) explain the convention of capitalizing the *manipulative roles* that constitute the triangle. They also describe *true* (non-manipulative, legitimate, lowercase) victims, rescuers, and persecutors, who usually *stay out* of the triangle. I was a true rescuer when I entered Lake Michigan to aid an exhausted swimmer, and as I approached him, asked if he wanted help.

[2] The triangle may be entered from any of the three positions. Referring to it as the Rescue triangle seems to have arisen as many therapists and clients became aware of how the unbalanced ideal of "helping" led them to enter the triangle primarily from the Rescuer position. In recent years, entering the triangle from the Victim position has become more socially acceptable and even almost expected for one to be considered politically correct. Only time will tell if we shall one day refer to the Victim triangle, but the basic pattern of interaction remains unaltered.

[3] It sometimes happens that both of us legitimately "own" a part of the same problem, and some thoughtfulness and discussion may be required to clarify each person's piece.

[4] Thanks to David Lindgren for this insight.

Chapter 14
Forgiving the Unforgivable:
Overcoming Abusive Parents*†

JOHN GILES

Silence is my shield. It crushes.
Silence is my cloak. It smothers.
Silence is my sword. It cuts both ways.
Silence is the deadliest weapon.

What legacy is to be found in silence?
How many lives lost?
So seductive its grip… this silence.

Break it! Our silence!
Loosen the tongue.
Testify.
Let's end the silence together, baby.
Together.
Now.

— *Marlon Riggs*, Tongues Untied

I love holidays. For most of my adult life, I have loved the parades, the Sousa marches, and the fireworks on the Fourth of July. But on June 30, 1986, the Supreme Court ruled in *Bowers v. Hardwick* that the U.S. Constitution afforded gay men and lesbians no legal rights to sexual privacy, and that state governments could do anything they wished with us.

Four days later, waiting for the fireworks to begin in Chicago's Grant Park, I felt completely alone, although I was surrounded by 600,000 people. When Mayor Harold Washington stepped to the platform, I had a surge of hope. Surely this liberal mayor, a man whose political career was built on championing the downtrodden, would condemn the Court for its bigotry.

Yes, he gave a speech praising the Fourth of July as a holiday all Americans could embrace. blacks, Hispanics, Poles, the handicapped, feminists, Croatians, and a hundred other constituencies were named. Yet he never mentioned the gay and lesbian people who had provided his razor-thin electoral majority. The Mayor's silence spoke volumes to me. And suddenly the flag, the marches, the patriotism all seemed shallow, and I wept.

I did not realize at the time that this situation uncannily mirrored my childhood: injustice surrounded by silence. Big, strong people hurt little, weak ones. And all the while, others stood silently by, silently doing nothing to intervene.

A RITUAL OF FORGIVENESS

Five years later, I spent my Fourth of July in a very different way. I celebrated the holiday by declaring my own independence from my abusive mother. At my mother's grave in southern Illinois, I enacted a ceremony of forgiveness culminating four years of recovery from physical and sexual abuse. No flowers or other signs of special care marked the grave, and I realized that I was probably the first person to visit since her funeral 22 years before.

The ceremony began. I read passages from her letters and other documents, all the while interjecting my own comments, expressing feelings I wanted to voice as a child but had been too afraid to utter. I shouted, I whimpered, I showered sarcasm. Sentence by sentence, phrase by phrase, I exposed my mother for the fraud she was. And the whole time, I took notes for my declaration of independence and my own bill of indictment. After 45 minutes, I read my bill of particulars aloud, adding the phrase, "I forgive you" to each sentence:

> For tying me up to a chair, binding my legs so tightly that they became numb… I forgive you.

> For leaving me in the chair, for hours at a time, time after time… I forgive you.

For partially undressing while I was tied up in the chair and saying that I wasn't "man enough" for you… I forgive you.

For forcing me to help put on your undergarments, and for slapping me if I accidentally touched you while doing so… I forgive you.

For ruining the only birthday party I ever had by getting drunk… I forgive you.

For embarrassing me in front of the neighbors so many times that I was ashamed to have friends over to our house… I forgive you.

For encouraging and forcing me to watch you while you used the bathroom or took a bath, and for never giving me any privacy, in the bathroom or elsewhere… I forgive you.

For turning me into your substitute husband, and for perceiving me and treating me as a sexual object… I forgive you.

For teaching me that sex is dirty, yet fun; for never holding me or hugging me… I forgive you.

Following this reading, I placed my indictment on the grave and burned it. As the flames died away, I sang my own setting of Psalm 32, a psalm of forgiveness and the transcendence of shame. I had composed the music for just this occasion. At last we departed, and I left behind much more than the ashes of my indictment.

CHILD ABUSE

I am a human being who endured a childhood of repeated, serious abuse at the hands of my parents and older sister. I used to be an abuse victim; then I became an abuse survivor. Now I am walking the slow path of forgiveness to overcome my past. I spent several years in therapy. I have read almost every book in print on adult children of alcoholics, process addictions, child abuse, male rape, and incest. I still attend meetings of Adult Children of Alcoholics, Incest Survivors Anonymous, and Sex Compulsives Anonymous. And I live a program of recovery designed to help me become a fully healthy, completely functional, joyfully serene man. This state of being is my birthright. But for a long time, the actions of my family denied it to me.

People have asked me why I bother with this now. I was abused a long time ago. Decades have passed since I left my small home town in southern Illinois. I've achieved many successes; I have many friends and a new life. Why revisit so painful a past?

DANGERS OF REMAINING A VICTIM

Here is my reason: the past has consequences. If you are raised by toxic parents, you may well become a toxic adult. Simply stated, untreated abused children will become either victims, victimizers, or rescuers when they grow up. All of these options have serious consequences (Everingham, 1995c).

I did not become a victimizer, although many who are abused as children do abuse their own children. I *did* occasionally flirt with rescuing others, but would abandon them when my rescuing efforts became too difficult, as I played out a process that only now do I understand. Instead, I became a victim.

I chose to be a victim by overeating, and then by losing weight inappropriately. I married a woman even though I was gay, and then gave her everything in the divorce settlement. I chose to be a victim by pursuing a PhD in a field where there were few prospects for employment when I graduated. But my self-victimization became most toxic when I passionately embraced the seductive gay-liberation beliefs that sexual license equals sexual freedom, and that promiscuity could overcome homophobia. I became sexually compulsive, just as my mother had been.

Unfortunately, I engaged in sexual activities that were not only unwise, but with the advent of AIDS, proved unsafe. I found myself in a doctor's office on December 17, 1987, faced with a diagnosis of chronic hepatitis and advanced HIV infection. My doctor gave me a life expectancy of six months to two years. Pursuing victimhood had proved the most toxic choice of all.

THE MOST DIFFICULT CHOICE: TO FORGIVE

At this point, what were my choices? Rescuing others? Victimizing others? I had reached bottom: I had no resources to rescue someone else. I didn't have the physical energy to abuse another, even if I had wanted to. The answer had to be outside my previous experience; so I cast my eye upon the water.

And what did I see? I saw that men with "advanced HIV infection" who confronted and resolved childhood issues lived longer and coped better. I saw that even if they died, they died in the arms of a lover or surrounded by friends and family. Those who did not face the past died quickly, died hard, and died alone. Facing the past became a matter of survival: I did not want to die from AIDS.

Thus I began walking the path to health. Had I known what dangers and difficulties lay before me, I might never have begun the journey. But after following the road less traveled for four years, I finally reached a safe place where I could truly forgive my parents.

Forgiveness Is Not Forgetting

I'll say it again: Forgiveness is *not* forgetting. Shame leads to denial, denial leads to forgetting, and forgetting breeds silence. Abuse thrives in an environment of denial, shame, and silence.

It's difficult to believe that when I began the healing process, I did not remember any of the abuse described. I had painted a rosy picture of my childhood: My parents were eccentric but championed rational education in the midst of their conservative fundamentalist community. They bought me a piano and encouraged me to become a musician. They supported liberal causes. I *liked these* pretend parents.

It had been too easy for me to forget a family vacation in Montana when my parents came back to the motel dead drunk and vomited all over the beds. It was so easy to forget my sister, too young for a driver's license, driving us home from St. Louis because both Mom and Dad were too drunk to drive. I didn't realize that I had lost all memory of first and second grades, when the incest and abuse was worst. As these painful memories surfaced, at first I denied that my mother had actually tied me to a chair for hours at a time, so that she could drink the day away.

As the memories resurfaced, I was grateful for my training in graduate school, where we learned how to gather documentation, even from unwilling sources, and to search out the truth behind the facade by taking a hard look at the data. As my sister and I looked through parents' and grandparents' letters, photos, diaries and newspaper clippings, the truth gradually emerged. My family, on both sides, was toxic. Compared to other abuse victims, I was unusually fortunate. We found notes written by my mother as she lay dying. Safely hidden in a false-bottomed drawer, where my father would never find and destroy them, they were her deathbed confession – the "smoking gun" that most incest survivors never find. I will let my mother's words speak for themselves:

> When my children ran away from home, I would tie their feet, sit them on a chair, and make them stay there for a few hours. After that punishment, they didn't think running away was worth it.

> The last time my son noticed my sexual charisma was in New Orleans, when the taxi driver escorted us to the door of Brennen's. Both the taxi driver and my son knew they were in the presence of one voluptuous woman.

> I once told my son: "Be moral, be clean, be abstinent, but isn't sex fun and dirty?"

My son has always remembered me as smelling opulently, being well groomed, and wearing the newest, sexiest fashions. Men of 70 and boys of 17 both respond to me. Even my son admits that I enchant people, and by people I don't mean men, for that is basic. I have the charm and wit to entrap even women.

These words are etched on my heart. Never again will I worship my mother and father with pretense and denial. Only by remembering them as they really were, both their positives and negatives, can I honor them. Only by honoring them in truth, not forgetting the abuse, can I ensure that "my days will be long in the land which God has given me." (Exodus 20:12)

Forgiveness Is Not Condoning

In her award-winning book, *For Your Own Good: Hidden Cruelty in Child Rearing and the Roots of Violence,* Alice Miller shows that our society will accept almost any argument, no matter how transparent, to condone child abuse and incest. The aphorisms, "Father knows best," "What goes on in my house is none of your business," and "Shut up, or I'll really give you something to cry about," are only a few of the phrases we use to discount the needs of children. Even worse is the biblical injunction, "He who spares the rod hates his son." I constantly heard the corollary "spare the rod and spoil the child" as I grew up. And I silently watched as aunts, uncles, teachers, ministers, neighbors, and policemen committed acts of violence against me and other children, all in the name of discipline.

At the same time, not everyone who quotes the Bible uses it to justify cruelty. The babysitter who confronted my mother about her behavior and helped end the most obvious forms of abuse was a devout member of the same fundamentalist church that preached, "Honor your father and your mother."

Calling violence against children "discipline" makes no more sense to me than pretending rape is "sex education." When my mother tied me to that ugly white chair, she would say "I'm doing this for your own good, so you can learn to come right away when Mommy calls." As she forced me to watch her disrobe, she said, "I'm doing this so you can learn what a woman's body looks like." Abuse done in the name of discipline or sex education is neither. Abuse is abuse, and cannot be condoned.

Another insidious form of discounting abuse occurs in the name of feminism. Some militant feminists will quickly believe that fathers sexually abuse their daughters, but admit only reluctantly that some mothers abuse their sons. One woman called me a liar point blank – my memories of my mother were "patriarchal fantasies," and the "smoking gun" in her deathbed confession was either a dying woman's delusions or my own forgery.

Feminists sometimes forget that even when a woman counts for nothing in society, that same society invests her with unlimited power over her small child. The powerlessness that all too many women experience – which is correctly addressed by feminists – often sets the stage for child abuse. A woman who feels trapped, a woman whose husband offers no support, a woman who feels older than her years may act out her rage and frustration by abusing the only person weaker than she is: her child.

My own mother grew up in university communities and had lived in large cities as a young adult. Her mother was a teacher, and together they enjoyed the amenities and artistic activities that cities and university towns provide. When my father returned from World War II, he decided to take the "little lady" to his home town in the Bible Belt, so that he could work in his father's factory. My mother hated that small town almost as much as she hated my father for making so important a decision without consulting her. And she took out her rage on my sister and me. Abuse performed in the name of a woman's rage, however justified, is not feminism. Abuse is abuse, and cannot be condoned.

Forgiveness Heals Lingering Effects

The effects of abuse cannot survive once the abuse has been forgiven. One would think that my abuse must have ceased more than two decades ago, at my mother's death. But the effects of abuse often linger for years after the perpetrator has died.

Touch was not allowed in my family. My parents did not sleep in the same bedroom. They did not hold hands, sit together on the couch while they watched television, hug, or kiss hello or good-bye. They ridiculed couples who did touch, hug, or kiss. After I was four years old, my parents did not cuddle me, hold me when I skinned my knee, or comfort me when I was stung by a bee. After all, "big boys don't cry." My sister and I never dreamed of hugging. Our grandmother lived next door, but saw her grandchildren only on holidays and never allowed us to touch her, lest we muss her hairdo or wrinkle her dress.

The only times I was touched as a child were when my mother tied me up or erotically touched me, when my older sister beat me, or when my father "tickled" me even after I begged him to stop. Is it any wonder that I learned to associate touch only with sexual arousal or physical abuse? No wonder I used to say, "Don't touch me unless you mean business," meaning "have sex with me."

At 38, I learned about touch—friendly, comforting, therapeutic, playful, and sensual touch– from a book! Today I say, "Never turn down a hug from somebody you trust." Forgiveness has opened me to new and healthier ways to live. I no longer allow my mother's abusive behavior to control me.

Forgiveness Is Saying "NO" to Continued Abuse

Learning to stop my father's abusive behavior is more difficult because he is still alive. He can no longer abuse me physically, but his abuse has gone underground and can still affect me if I allow it.

Stopping my father's abuse means setting new boundaries between us. I no longer accept his monetary gifts at Christmas. Money may be the only way he can show love, but important as it is, money does not equal love. If he insists on sending me cash, I donate it to the AIDS Alternative Health Project. I am repaying his loans, money I used to support my addictive behavior. I no longer allow my father to play "let's show John how stupid he is" by asking me trivia questions I cannot possibly answer. No longer do I follow his practice of discounting the opinions of others by correcting their grammar. Forgiving my father has meant learning new behavior. I will not allow his abuse to live on in me.

FINDING A PROCESS THAT WORKS

When the memories of my childhood abuse and incest first surfaced, the last thing on my mind was forgiveness. When I heard phrases like "learn to open yourself to love and forgiveness," I could only tremble with rage. I vowed that I would never forgive them for what they did. It took a long time for me to see that forgiveness is not a gift I owe my parents, but a gift long overdue to me.

In time, my rational side surfaced and asked, "What are my options besides forgiveness?" I could see only two: seeking revenge or holding a grudge. Revenge... the word sounded so sweet. But how could I exact revenge on my mother and sister? Dig up their graves and smash their bones? And my father? No matter how hard I tried, I could not conceive of a retribution I could wreak on my father – physical, emotional, financial, or legal – that would not hurt me as much as it hurt him. I learned there are reasons why St. Paul wrote, "Vengeance is mine; I will repay, says the Lord." (Romans 12:19)

Holding a grudge looked even less attractive. Even as I raged, I could see how addicted to anger my sister had become. I saw how anger ate away at her until she died of breast cancer at age 47. I noticed how many people in my 12-step groups simply traded one addiction for another as long as they did not face their anger and release their grudges. I saw person after person with AIDS die while nursing grudges and harboring hatred. I was left with only one option: forgiveness.

I came to realize that revenge and grudge holding only strengthen the twisted bond that joins both perpetrator and victim like ill-formed Siamese twins. My reading taught me that only a process carefully crafted to face anger and fear (without being possessed by them) can break this bond between perpetrator and victim.

LIVING THE PROCESS - STEP BY STEP

My first step was education. I learned that any sexual behavior between an adult and a child constitutes incest. I had to learn that simply because my abuse wasn't as bad as someone else's, it was still abuse. I learned that emotional incest is as real and harmful as physical incest. I had to learn my own history, my true history.

And I learned that neither the abuse nor the incest made me gay. Although they shaped the kind of gay man I became – undoubtedly encouraged my sexual compulsion – I was gay long before the abuse started. Incest tends to confuse children on *all* sexual issues, not only sexual orientation. I finally understood why I did not discover my gay identity until I was age 29 and had been married to a woman for several years. Abuse got in the way of discovering my true sexual identity.

The second step was finding my anger. Finding it was easy enough; the trick was not letting myself take out my wrath on friends, colleagues, or lover. What worked for me was to come to church long before others arrived and descend to a basement room, where I would pound at pillows and bang a wiffle bat on the floor. At first, I could only scream. Eventually I could shout, "I hate you Mommy" or "I'm scared of you Daddy." When my words changed to "I hate it when you… " or "I'm scared when you…" I knew I was beginning to heal. One day, after a particularly draining anger session, I became too exhausted to continue. With tears in my eyes, I plopped to the floor and thought, "I guess I'm too tuckered out to be mad anymore." I was ready to move on to the next stage of healing.

The third step was finding my sorrow. This was harder, because I couldn't summon my grief as easily as I could raise my rage. Tears came to me at the most unexpected times, and I had to learn to accept my sadness whenever it appeared. I was in a restaurant reading *Don't Hurt Lauriel* (a young adult novel by Willo Davis Roberts). Although Lauriel's story has many differences from mine, the feelings were the same, and I was transported emotionally back to my childhood. I burst into tears and fled to the bathroom, where I had a good 10-minute cry. Today, I let myself grieve for my lost childhood, even when it's inconvenient.

The fourth step was designing my own rituals for forgiveness. With my sister, forgiveness consisted of holding hands and forgiving each other for all past wrongs as she lay dying. For my mother, it meant the ceremony at her grave. With my father, it required several letters in which I simultaneously set new boundaries and made amends in accordance with my 12-step programs.

Along the way, I had the help of many people – in my meetings, at my church, among my circle of friends – who showed their care for me in so many ways. I also had the help of a Higher Power, whose total love and forgiveness remain beyond my comprehension.

The final step is absorbing the lessons of the past and moving on. Now I believe the old maxim, "The best revenge is living well!" My great-grandfather abused his son, who abused his daughter, who abused me. I cannot change the past, but I can learn from it. The chain of abuse that once looked endless will end with me. I will neither forget the abuse, nor condone it, nor perpetuate it. I am ready to live.

I believe this is what Jesus meant when he said, "No one who puts the hand to the plow and looks back is ready to enter the Kingdom of God." (Luke 9:62) I have put my hand to the plow of life, and am ready to sow the seeds of serenity. To paraphrase 12-step literature, I stand ready to carry this message to others and to practice the principle [of forgiveness] in all my affairs. I have learned to love life more than I loved my biological mother; I no longer confuse my earthly father with a god-of-my-misunderstanding.

And when all else fails, I remember one of my own rules of life: "Everybody does the best they can with what they've got, but sometimes what they've got is *toxic*." The first half of this little saying helps me to forgive; the second half reminds me to set appropriate boundaries.

FRUITS OF RECOVERY

And the payoff for all this work? When my mother used to tie me up, she bound my feet and legs extra tight, so I could not run away. Perhaps she had abandonment issues, but all she accomplished was to make me ashamed of my legs and feet. Once I understood this relation-ship and worked through my feelings about it, I could comfortably wear sandals and shorts for the first time in my life. I no longer have the debilitating foot cramps that awakened me at least once every night.

But the clearest sign of healing came on the Fifth of July, the day after the graveside ceremo-ny. I went swimming for the first time in nine years, and after I had paddled around a bit, I suddenly realized that I was kicking my feet! How many lifeguards have tried to teach me to kick? A swimming coach in high school exclaimed, "Giles, do you have invisible chains on your legs?" Neither of us realized how close he came to the truth. I have finally broken my invisible chains.

Next Fourth of July I plan to join the rest of America: enjoy the fireworks, wave the flag (although I may wave the rainbow coalition flag of gay liberation), and listen with gusto to the marches of John Philip Sousa. I will remember that on Independence Day I found the courage to forgive my mother. And the truth of that forgiveness set my feet free, set my legs free, and set free both the scared little boy within and the brave, authentic adult gay man I am today.

If you have been wronged, I invite you to work a miracle.
    A very special miracle: forgiveness.

We perform it alone. Others can help us, but when we finally do it,
    we perform the miracle in the private places of our inner lives.

We do it silently. No one can record our miracle on tape.

We do it invisibly. No one can record our miracle on film.

We do it freely. No one can ever pressure or trick us into forgiving someone.

It is *outrageous:* When we do it, we commit an outrage against a strict morality that
    will not be satisfied with anything short of an even score.

It is *creative:* When we forgive, we come as close as any human being can to the
    essentially divine act of creation. For we create a new beginning out of old pain
    that never had the right to exist in the first place. We create healing in the future
    by changing a past that allowed no possibilities but sickness and death.

When we forgive we ride the crest of love's cosmic wave; we walk in stride with
    God.

And we heal the hurt we never deserved.   Amen.   Shalom.

NOTES:

* John Giles died August 22, 1996.

† Based on a sermon given August 18, 1991, at the Unitarian Church of Evanston, IL, where the author was Lay Minister of Music

Chapter 15
Inadvertent Shaming: Family Rules and Shaming Habits

JOHN EVERINGHAM

Sometimes things go sour in men's organizations and support groups or between individual men. We're floundering and feeling edgy about each other. It's especially hard to bear because we share such strong bonds of brotherhood, affection, and respect. Maybe we're shaming each other without realizing it. This chapter explores how to recognize and stop unintended shaming.

Most of us have a shaming habit. As boys, we learned to obey certain unwritten family "rules." Today we understand how obeying these rules generates internalized shame and keeps it going from generation to generation. To kick the shaming habit, we consciously *break the rules!*

Two recent books, Fossum and Mason (1986) and Bradshaw (1988), list nine of these rules and discuss their power to maintain family shame and dysfunction. Here we combine these lists and add another rule, Moral Intimidation.

We can't break invisible rules. So for starters, we "call 'em out," like gunfighters in the mythical Old West. Here come 10 bad shaming rules, called out of the dimness of the saloon – into the street at high noon. Maybe you recognize some of these desperadoes.

SHAMING RULES[1]

Control. Be in control of all behavior, interactions and feelings. Control is basic to these rules.

Blame. If something goes wrong, blame somebody, even yourself. Don't blame the shame-generating system or these rules.

Perfectionism. Always be, do, and feel "right." Don't try if you might make a mistake. Justify everything.

Incompleteness. Don't resolve disagreements or complete transactions. Keep feuds and resentments going. Don't confront.

Denial. Deny feelings, needs, and desires – your own and others', especially "inappropriate" ones. Deny – even the obvious.

No Talk. Hide secrets with a strict code of silence among ourselves and others. Hold your breath, look away, and shut up.

Disqualification. Deny by disguising. Spin the shameful episode around; call it something else; distort it. Look away from the shameful part and focus on the positive or truthful part.

Unreliability. Don't be reliable or trustworthy or act in a predictable way. Keep 'em guessing. Expect the same from others.

Not Allowing The Five Freedoms (Satir, 1974). Don't let folks perceive, think and interpret, feel, desire, or imagine *in their own way.* Especially not children, clients, subordinates, or yourself.

Moral Intimidation. Assume the right to decide what – and, therefore, who – is right, appropriate, humane, enlightened, professional, mature, or politically correct. Enforce moral authority with shaming threats, rhetorical questions, and subtle or overt name-calling.

These...rules for interaction would serve as effective guidelines for developing a dehumanizing, shame-bound regime in any human system, whether a nuclear family, a staff work group, a corporation, a medical school, or an elementary classroom. The interaction flowing from these rules insidiously nullifies or voids one's experience as a person. Relationships in the system...inhibit the growth of a self-accepting outlook. (Fossum and Mason, 1986, p. 87)

This eloquent passage summarizes the dysfunction which habitual shaming imposes upon any human group. Disobeying the rules that maintain dysfunction may look simple, but it's not always easy to do. Let's first look at the general nature of these rules.

Rules Written in Stone?

"Rules" is used ironically and metaphorically. These are not regulations enacted by some congress or king, but rather, habitual patterns of human interaction that have taken on the force of unwritten law. We act like they're written in stone and accept them like the law of gravity. Much of their potency comes from rarely being questioned.

Our response to shaming rules is entirely natural. If I suddenly slapped you in the face, you would naturally feel surprised, hurt, and angry. You'd react with voice and maybe fist. Nobody's surprised when a blow generates emotional consequences; it's equally predictable for a man to feel ashamed when he's been hit with a shaming rule.

But the natural consequences of shaming acts are usually ignored or made fun of (shamed). Books, movies, and television display and decry physical violence *ad nauseam*, but say very little about shaming. Anyone but a saint is allowed to feel angry if he's punched, but the ordinary man is expected to be "mature" and rise above shame when he's being controlled, left incomplete, or morally intimidated. To *expect* to feel ashamed when hit by a shaming act – this is a giant step toward liberation.

Shame is felt and expressed in silence, so it may be difficult to recognize at first. It takes practice to learn to feel primary shame for even a fraction of a second. Most of us move double-time to anger or internalized shame (frozen and dull-eyed, pretending to feel okay), and this leads to trouble (violence, addiction, etc.). But when you see the rules being applied, the shame reaction is happening somewhere, even if masked. Recognizing patterns of shaming interaction—spotting the rules being acted out, however unintentionally—may help a man become conscious of feeling the emotion.

All of these rules involve some form of hiding and trying to disguise the true self. Incompleteness and Disqualification use particularly subtle forms of disguise, misdirection and mystification. Subtlety bestows extra power to confound us, so extra space is devoted to these two rules.

Shame breaks, or strains, the bond between men. It may start as only a tiny tear, but the wound tends to enlarge if not repaired. If I swallow my feelings and don't admit any problem (Denial), it's tough to fix the rupturing bond (Incompleteness). We may sense that something has come between us, but not know what, and we may start relating in unauthentic ways, generating more shame. Finally we move away, sour in the throat. But there may be a silver lining to this scenario: When we finally break the rules and start telling it like it is, the restored bond tends to become stronger than before.

The cumulative effect of living by these rules is to embed toxic shame in families, men's support groups and organizations, and between individual men. If nobody sees or challenges the rules, nothing changes. Toxic internalized shame, barely noticed, accumulates its deadening effects. Many men think it's just normal to feel ashamed and alienated.

But now we know that Shame – the Invisible Dragon—has an Achilles' heel. He can't handle being seen as he really is. When we take away his invisibility, call him by name, broadcast his description, expose his hideouts (obvious and subtle)—then his fire cools, and his awesome power begins to drain away.

Control

If I keep a tight rein on the situation, maybe I won't fall into a sea of treacherous self-doubt, and feel vulnerable or acutely ashamed. I often choose the short-term 'fix' of control, despite knowing about long-term consequences. Fossum and Mason (1986) cover this rule well, and have an additional chapter on "The Interaction of Shame and Control."

Sometimes we get into power struggles and compete for attention. A man may interrupt a lot, shut others out with longwinded or forceful talk, or crack jokes that impede the flow. 'Heart talk' suffers.

Group procedure can trigger control issues. One man or faction may assume the role of lawgiver or enforcer without group consent, or may presume agreement (often based on "principles") that doesn't exist. Those who disagree feel resentful and carry internalized shame. My group often sets a time limit on the initial check-in; we're careful to *rotate* the job of timekeeper, calling him the "Asshole" for the evening.

Having no single leader, we often struggle for control over who, and how, to facilitate a man's emotional work. It's good that we know a variety of styles, but it's rarely clear at first which approach will work best for this man tonight. Sometimes it can be a real zoo. We find it essential to air our disagreements about facilitating. Usually it's best to do this after the work is done, or maybe the following week, but occasionally it's necessary to interrupt the work in order for men to confront each other about how we're competing to control "helping" another man.

Let's not demonize power struggles or attempts to control men. Both are essential for vitality and are part of our inbred masculine style. But our forceful ways carry the risk of hidden shaming, and we need to appreciate and counterbalance this risk. We may feel ashamed of competing for control, but it won't harm us if we're honest and confrontational about it.

Blame

Blaming involves a maldistribution of responsibility. Taking on too much gives us the obvious sense of violation and shame. And the man who avoids his proper share may find himself with a pocketful of "innocence," which must be defended against exposure. The blamer may feel frustrated; it's not his fault, so he's powerless to fix it. Fossum and Mason (1986, pp. 94-96) discuss cogently other aspects of the Blame rule: how it's used to avoid surprise and vulnerability, to project one's own shame onto another man, and as a backstop for any temporary breakdown of the Control rule.

Overt blaming doesn't seem to be a big problem in men's support groups today. But a man may blame himself for his sexual, angry, or competitive feelings, often calling them "macho" or "sexist." Men's socialization is a handy scapegoat. Some men take most of the blame for war, crime, "patriarchy," or troubles with women (Bilgere, 1997). When a man assumes too much responsibility, I advocate calling him on it. Unwarranted self-blaming is not a virtue, but a risk factor for chronic infection with toxic shame.

Sometimes one man becomes the group "goat" or "screw-up," often with his own complicity. Humor may abound, and it's rarely noticed that the other men are projecting much of their own immaturity and irresponsibility onto him. Or the group may be using him to deny the seriousness of an issue.

A good tool for breaking the Blame rule is the language of responsibility. When speaking it, I take explicit responsibility for my own feelings, values and opinions. Concretely, this means using lots of "I-messages" and few "You-messages" (Gordon, 1974, 1976).

Perfectionism

Internalized shame whispers, "I don't really belong here. I'm a defective alien in disguise, who'll be banished when they find me out. My only hope is to look so good that they don't examine me carefully. Maybe–maybe–I can 'pass.'" Or perhaps a man is a touch grandiose (Lindgren, 1995) and secretly believes that the world will end if he doesn't do it all perfectly. The pretense and denial generated by such reasoning continues to reinforce shame.

Perfectionism may come in with some code of masculine honor. It ruined King Arthur's court, and it still plagues men today. In a group called the New Warriors, men sometimes ask whether the Warrior "way" is being followed. In moderation, this is useful, but it escalate into Perfectionism. We sometimes forget that the Warrior archetype needs to be balanced by King, Lover, and Magician (Moore & Gillette, 1990). Let's remember also that "injured reserve" is both honorable and necessary among warriors (Bly & Meade, n.d.). Perfectionism and shame denied will wreck any code of honor among flesh-and-blood men.

Fossum and Mason (1986, p. 91) say that "this rule imposes a requirement and a tension on people to comply with a perfect external image, which is sometimes vaguely defined and shifting." This tension is quite different from "a morally congruent life [or]...pleasure in knowledge." These authors describe also "a competitive or comparative aspect to this rule... Being right never means 'right in terms of what fits for me.' There is a better-than-others aspect to it..., a more-right-than-others aspect." Men may exhibit this perfectionist tension in cautiously "correct" talk, exaggerated politeness, or "walking on eggs." For more on perfectionism, see Hendlin (1992, 1993).

Perfectionism is strong in men who use withdrawal as their main defensive strategy against shame. Compaan (1997, p. 85) writes that these men "continue to believe that they should be able to be without inadequacy. Their ideal is perfectionism, not some combination of adequacy and inadequacy." Such men are usually quite aware of feeling ashamed, but have difficulty sorting out the shame that is projected onto them by others. So they tend to take on "the shame of the whole world," and it's too much for them.

Obeying this rule may lead to withholding honest feedback because it might be wrong. This is a serious loss among good friends and in intimate men's groups, for it increases emotional distance. A man may hesitate because "maybe I'm projecting." *Of course* he is. All feedback contains projection. Let's relax and give ourselves a break. A rough measure of group intimacy is willingness to risk being wrong. Usually the feedback giver has an opportunity later to own his projections. Here's a motto for giving feedback: I don't have to be right; I just have to be honest.

Incompleteness

Type Scenario. A man leaves his group with no warning or good-bye, and can't or won't be contacted. He's too ashamed to show up again, perhaps because he fears boundary violations. Those who remain feel a mixture of hurt, anger, mystification, shame, and concern for the absent man. They may feel abandoned or vaguely sense that "we must have done something to drive him away, but what?" Some may speak rationally of him, but with a hard edge in their voices, denying their feelings of hurt and shame, or perhaps relief.

In one group, the men remaining felt almost as if there had been a death among them. So they had a group good-bye ritual (like a memorial service), expressed themselves, and then felt more accepting and less mystified or ashamed.

Fossum and Mason (1986, pp. 100-102) explain that this rule masks unresolved disputes, which may reappear in unrelated issues. An unresolved dispute between adults may be projected onto a child.[2]

Incompleteness prevents interpersonal bonds from being repaired (Kaufman, 1989). There's no opportunity for amends or a makeup. Decisions are left up in the air. Resentments fester. We often don't realize how many interactions we leave incomplete, so relationships deaden, or men may drift away from each other in pained silence.[3]

If there's a lot of fighting but no resolution, Incompleteness feels like guerrilla warfare, dragging out endlessly and sapping our strength. Men may wrangle over superficial matters, avoiding awareness of the real issues. But let's keep on wrangling if we're capable of honesty; the deeper issues may appear in time.

This is the rule I obey most when practicing my personal addiction to shame. Self-doubt, procrastination, and passive-aggressive bullshit can be pretty thick at times, and I become fearful of exposure and ashamed to face *anybody*. Incompleteness tends to feed upon itself and snowball.

"Do I have to give up me, to be loved by you?" (Paul and Paul, 1983). Incompleteness whispers "yes" in my ear, but deep down I want to shout, "Hell no!" Completion of our transactions affirms that I'm basically okay, even when I displease or anger you. The true self is strengthened, and toxic shame recedes.

Examples Of Incompleteness In Action:

1. In a small men's group, the guys aren't directly sharing their feelings about *each other*, especially resentment, impatience, anger, boredom, or disappointment. There's a surly, strained, low-energy atmosphere, with grumbling and put-down jokes about absent members. Yet most of the men keep coming to the group because it's so unique to be able to talk about their feelings with guys.

2. To minimize Incompleteness, vital men's groups give high priority to members confronting each other, often having a time for "clearing" or "coming clean" in each meeting. We need to air out the inevitable conflicts and irritations that arise between us, and the sooner the better. To begin the process, one man tells another of his feelings toward him, based on the other's words, actions, inaction, body language, tone of voice, etc. The two men address each other directly. Perhaps they move into the center of the room, so that others can surround them with support and containment, honoring the sacredness of their difficult work and its importance to the group. A man's anger or distrust is treated as a simple fact, with minimal explanation, justification, or judgment.

   Sometimes other activities are interrupted in order to deal with what's "hot." If avoided, emotions simmer in Incompleteness, and toxic shame begins to cover the group like a wet blanket. More about confrontation on the next page.

A father and son agree that the son will rake leaves this morning; the father returns from his golf game to find leaves unraked and his son off to play soccer. He rakes the leaves himself, his anger growing. When the son returns, father conveys his low opinion of him, using rhetorical questions, dirty looks, yelling, interpretations, or blows. The son tries excuses (which don't work), and may leave with head hanging, or stay feeling frozen and resentful. His internalized shame is even worse if the father does *not* confront him, both pretending that nothing is amiss. The eyes transmit the curse, more powerful than words. And if the eyes cannot meet, the shame is deeper still.

The son has lost integrity with both his father and himself, and needs to do a makeup (make amends) in order to repair the interpersonal bridge. Usually a makeup can be negotiated, but if it cannot, I'd advise father to impose it unilaterally. Better an authoritarian power play than lingering toxic shame generated by the Incompleteness rule.

3. In a men's organization, some leaders interact with other men in an intrusive, prodding, provocative way. They profess to be open to confrontation and certainly are at times, but they're Busy Men Doing Important Work. Time for confrontation and coming to completion is limited at best. Incompleteness abounds, with attendant intimidation, gossip, and swallowed shame.

   The leaders need to be more aware of the shame generated by their hit-and-run way of operating, and resolve not to start things they don't have time to finish. But time isn't the only factor; some of the men are just plain intimidated. They need to be more aware of what's happening, and speak up sooner.

Confrontation: Pros And Cons

Vital relationships require confrontation. Here's a man whom I've learned to love, respect, and rely on. I feel hurt by something he's said or contemptuous of some action he's taking. It's never easy to confront him, but I must, or our respect and intimacy will suffer.

"Low tolerance for bullshit; high tolerance for imperfection" is the motto of one group. Men's organizations and support groups function much better when they give active blessing to confrontation, and provide and priority for it. A periodic group inventory may help. Are there men who never confront others? Is there someone whom nobody confronts? Leaders heavily into Control, Incompleteness, or Disqualification need especially to be confronted, or deposed, or abandoned.

Confrontation is often loud and angry, and sometimes physical, but need not be so. A neutral adult tone of voice can be perfectly effective, as can sadness or humor. Whatever the emotional component, it needs to be genuine. For best results, match the intensity of the emotion expressed to the confronter's feelings at the moment, with minimal under- or over-shooting (Gordon, 1976, pp. 133-135). Avoid sarcasm and rhetorical questions. Some kind of "I-statement" is best. ("I feel bored and irritated when you take 30 minutes to check in.") Direct and genuine talk improves the odds for resolution and completion.

Confrontation is not control. Please don't deem it a failure if the other man refuses to change, for it is a basic expression of your true self. To be sure, the man confronted *is* often affected, but the benefit does not depend upon controlling him.

We come to regard confrontation, scary and embarrassing as it may be, as a *gift*. One facet of this gift is that my friend sees the real me, not some caricature. We learn that love and respect survive episodes of blunt, caustic opposition. Confrontation can be educational, by revealing an unrecognized part of my Shadow. And best of all, something in our male soul craves conflict with a worthy adversary.

Deep down in our genes, we men remember how to fight vigorously without inflicting permanent damage. As with males of many species, we know that we may hurt a brother, but need not injure him. Our bonding deepens as we exchange the gift of energized authenticity. When we show love and appreciation, it has a ring of truth tempered by the fire of conflict. We learn in our bodies that anger and love may coexist.

I've come to realize that many of the men I feel closest to are those at whom I've been able to explode with all-out anger, and they at me.

Pain, physical and mental, is normal and necessary to life and growth (Peck, 1978, p. 15). We become willing to inflict hurt and to receive it, to wound and be wounded (Bly and Meade n.d.). If we're stuck in our fear of hurting, the Denial and Incompleteness rules create shameful conditions that rip off those nearest and dearest to us (Mason & Fossum, 1987). "Nice guys ruin lives" (Bach & Goldberg, 1974).

These are the pros. What about the cons? Confrontation and anger may be overdone, or be used to avoid scarier feelings of hurt, shame, vulnerability or tenderness. In support groups, this usually works itself out in a few months. There's a more serious problem when one or two angry men are confronting all over the place, but nobody confronts *them*. Bad news! Equality is required for confrontation to be of lasting value. The entire group should support the most timid (or intimidated) member in confronting the most overbearing. A role-reversal exercise may work wonders.

We discern a dance of bonding and confrontation. Bond a little, confront a bit, share and trust. Bond more deeply, confront with more spontaneity and on scarier subjects, bond even more deeply… and the beat goes on.

Bonding and confrontation work best when equally balanced. How far can an imbalance go before it becomes troublesome? That's an intuitive call, but please don't wait for near perfection. And confrontation may trigger shame, so there needs to be a rough balance between the depth of the shame and the group's time and ability to deal with it.

Denial

Denial of our emotions is almost a generic plague among American men. Fossum and Mason (1986, p. 96) show how denial of feelings can produce "a very cold system of relationships," and suggest relationships that allow us to "practice" so that we'll become more comfortable expressing our feelings honestly. This is a major theme in men's liberation, and most of our groups do good work in this area.

But there are some hitches. Some groups are safe for certain feelings–perhaps anger, sadness, or fear, but don't welcome others–often shame, competitiveness, or impatience. Feelings of dependency, hopelessness, self-pity, or self-hatred are especially likely to be denied. Once one or two men start sharing their "incorrect" feelings, others may discover the same feelings in themselves.

Denial, along with Disqualification and No Talk, is often supported by dismissive or machismo humor, or by changing the subject. Men may issue shaming threats using code words and warning looks, or suppressive nonverbal messages via rigid bodies, holding the breath, or averted eyes. Rational analysis may talk a man out of trusting his intuition. Soon an undercurrent of internalized shame undermines group intimacy, gathering force as denial builds.

No Talk

Shame builds if men keep silent about personal secrets, taboo subjects, or resentments. When these are withheld even from close friends or the support group, barriers rise as anxiety about exposure drives men apart. Subjects often taboo among men include:

Money: who has how much; jealousy about it; resentment if some men are paid by a men's organization and others aren't.

Feelings about penis size, unusual bends, warts, etc. Lots of good humor when this taboo is broken.

Anger at women, racial prejudice, feelings of fear or contempt for other groups of "approved" Victims (Everingham, 1995c).

Feeling superior to others, grandiose fantasies, suicidal feelings, feeling ashamed.

Feeling intimidated by another man, especially one in the group.

Obesity, alcohol abuse, toxic relationships, gambling, or the seriousness of these.

Disappointment or bad feelings about the group. It's helpful sometimes to consider the Shadow of the group as a whole.

When one man finally breaks the No Talk rule on any subject, there's usually a flood of discussion, with similar feelings being acknowledged by others. A collective sigh of relief may ensue.

Breaking the No Talk rule should not be confused with invading a man's privacy or bulldozing through his boundaries (Schneider, 1977; Fossum & Mason, 1986, p. 103). Sometimes a group member will want to impose his own time/priority schedule on another man's work. At first we may not discern the fine line between between a conspiracy of silence and disrespecting a man's emotional rhythms. Of course, breaching an agreement of confidentiality is not to be seen as breaking the No Talk rule, but as a serious betrayal of trust. Occasionally someone forgets this.

Disqualification

Type Scenario. Mother is consoling her 12-year old daughter, who has been sexually molested by father. "Don't be upset, dear," she says. "That's just Daddy's way of showing his love for you." Focusing on this small part obfuscates a mountain of other truth: confusion, violated trust, pain, self-doubt, humiliation, lack of protection, and collaboration by mother.

The scenario is both extreme and stereotypic. I chose it to counterbalance the silent massiveness of Disqualification in its ability to "sanitize" serious shaming and abuse.

Disqualification is denial by disguise and distraction. Distorting, applying false labels, and reframing add to the disguise. Fossum and Mason (1986, pp. 103-104) pack a lot into two paragraphs on Disqualification, but this potent and confusing rule deserves fuller treatment here.

A common form of Disqualification is to focus truthfully on one part of the picture, while not acknowledging another important part. The elephant in the living room is ignored (despite olfactory evidence), while everyone admires the colorful lights of the swinging chandelier. The type scenario illustrates how abuse (and neglect) can be "dressed up" in a clever disguise. By directing attention away from the essential part, the abuse is not denied directly, but recast as something quite different. A common distraction is the shift to a charge of impropriety ("How dare you say that!" or "Such language is inappropriate.") to focus attention away from the shameful content.

This technique of denial-by-distraction is widespread. It's the stock-in-trade of most advertisers, politicians, lawyers, "spin" artists, and bureaucrats. Because Disqualification is so common, we tend to think of it as normal, and so lose sight of the part(s) being disguised.

When encountering this rule in any form, I usually feel a vague sense of shame in my body, sensing that "something's wrong here." But at first my mind doesn't recognize the part(s) disguised. I may mistrust my intuition, suspecting that I'm at fault for not buying the "line." I want to swallow my perception, but I still can't digest it. Confusion seems to intensify the shame and hasten its internalization, because there seems to be no way to speak my truth, even to myself. Self-doubt is magnified.

Disqualification may serve to maintain the status quo when neither party wishes to face the discomfort of confrontation. Or a man may sense that he can be out-dueled on a verbal, rational level. Maybe this works when the relationship is not highly prized, but there's a price to be paid whenever I collaborate to obey this rule: The extra shame creates emotional distance between us. Moderate Disqualification may not break the interpersonal bond, but it certainly strains it. Our interactions become more stylized, less real, less intimate.

Examples of Disqualification in Action

1. Joe is furious at Pat. They get into the center of their group. Joe looks Pat in the eye and starts telling him off. Before he really gets into it, somebody asks Joe who Pat reminds him of. Premature question! If Joe interrupts his anger to answer, he's been deflected by Disqualification, adding shame.

    It's probably true that Joe's anger is intensified because Pat or his actions remind Joe of someone else. George Lindall (1995) writes of the 80/20 rule, which estimates that 20 percent of my emotional intensity is truly directed at the person in front of me now, whereas 80 percent belongs to people in my past, often parents. But the 20 percent needs to be dealt with *first*. The Disqualification here comes from bad timing. The reality and validity of Joe's anger *at Pat* has been denied. Joe and Pat need to deal with what's in front of them, to restore their bond and avoid residual shame.

    Even worse, there's a risk that Joe may get the idea that his anger is "inappropriate" or an "overreaction." I favor banishing these two words forever from men's support groups. Joe is likely to feel ashamed of his anger now, and may be slow to confront the next time, adding Incompleteness to Disqualification.

    Later on in their work this evening, when both Joe and Pat have allowed their true selves out for exercise, the time will come to ask Joe to connect his feelings toward Pat to someone in his past. Then he'll be more able to learn something valuable from the question. How does one recognize this magic moment? Mostly by intuition and experience, and sometimes by noticing a certain calmness and deep breathing that comes over Joe when he's expressed himself with full integrity. Joe has within him the best sense of when the moment arrives, and may decline to be distracted when the time is wrong. But let's avoid Perfectionism about hitting it exactly right. Part of Pat's gift to Joe is that he's willing to take on (temporarily) the 80 percent of Joe's anger that is really directed at someone else.

2. In a similar group, or at an initiation weekend, Pete is working on a heavy emotional issue, and getting bogged down. A man suggests that Pete express his anger, so he starts yelling or pounding pillows with a tennis racket. But his anger doesn't ring true, and he soon loses energy. Several men begin to insult or mock him to try to *really* get him angry. Sometimes this technique works readily and is useful.

   But when prodding to anger isn't working, to continue it adds shame from Disqualification and can be downright abusive. Pete is undoubtedly suppressing some anger, but right now he's feeling much more of some other emotion, perhaps sadness or shame, hurt or fear (Fossum, 1989, pp. 77-79). Pete may be ashamed of himself because he's not performing the way many in the group wish he would. Or he may be deeply frustrated and in pain because he's not being encouraged to perceive, think, feel, desire, or imagine *in his own way*. Whatever it may be, Disqualification denies this more-important feeling, and may soon generate so much shame that Pete freezes up emotionally.

3. When they are confronted, some leaders of men's groups deflect other men's feelings about them by using Disqualification. The muttering or angry men are said to be projecting their father issues onto the leaders, or acting out of a shadow part of the King archetype, which seeks to depose the King without being willing to take up his responsibilities.

   Again, all this is probably true to a certain extent, but "explaining" the situation in this way denies the role of the provocative actions of the leaders. The use of Disqualification in this situation just makes matters worse; the "explanations" do not heal. Interaction of this kind is almost always a reciprocal dance. For the bond to be restored, each man needs to own up fully to his part in the problem.

Denial, No Talk, and Disqualification form a continuum of suppression. Why have three rules instead of one? It's easy to underestimate the shame generated by these rules. So it seems useful to distinguish between not being aware of feelings or other matters (Denial), being aware but not saying anything (No Talk), and the distraction and misdirection which are the foundation of Disqualification.

"Shadow naming" is an exercise that has power to break all three rules, because it tends to bring out what's being hidden or ignored. As a ritual, it's described in greater detail in Chapter 6. Otherwise, when a man takes the talking stick, or at the beginning of the meeting, or when he feels superficial or inauthentic, the man names that part of his Shadow of which he's most aware. The effects can be felt immediately–a clean, fresh wind circulates among us–diminishing our shame and bringing calm, honesty, and new respect.

Unreliability

When a man is erratic in keeping agreements, being on time, or attending a group, other men are likely to feel irritated, and that will convert to shame if unexpressed. There may be a sub-liminal complaint of "How come he can get away with it, and I can't?" or identification with the elder brother in the biblical parable of the Prodigal Son. Evidently this dynamic has been with us for millennia.

More serious are situations where a man never knows when his boss will be severely critical. Or a friend will be supportive and gentle on one occasion, but harsh and pugnacious the next, without any apparent reason. Men around this friend learn to think twice before opening up in his presence. For many years, my family never knew whether to expect me to arrive home cheerful and loving, or withdrawn, angry, and filled with internalized shame.

Unreliability derives most of its potency from a violation of the atmosphere of trust. Trust is fundamental to healthy functioning. Erikson's (1963) first crisis is Trust vs. Mistrust (Autonomy vs. Shame and Doubt comes in second in his scheme of human emotional devel-opment.) Similarly, in Maslow's (1954) hierarchy of motivation, safety is second only to physiological needs. Part of this universal need for safety is described as the desire for "a pre-dictable, orderly world" (Maslow, 1954, p. 86). In recent years, we've noted how many chil-dren and adults seem to cling to abusive relationships that are predictable, if not always order-ly. Unpredictable behavior by those who matter to us tends to upset our emotional founda-tions and erode trust.

We do well to be respectful of "exaggerated" responses by adult men to unreliable behavior. They may irritate us and lead to feelings of mild contempt, but they offer unusual opportuni-ties to heal deep wounds. Strong feelings coming from childhood may be triggered. Children often blame themselves for mistreatment by parents or other caretakers. Betrayal of trust tends to engender deep shame in the one betrayed. Unreliability deepens the wound, because a boy has no clue about "what he's doing wrong," and thus no hope of correcting his "fatal flaw." But he tries and tries to discover and correct it anyway, deepening his internalized shame and self-distrust.

A man may come to realize that he has been an unreliable best friend *to himself*. The rule may be so deeply internalized that he can no longer trust himself to act consistently and reliably in his own behalf. If he can't count on his own friendship, he needs to give this matter high priority in his own work, for it adds major difficulties to his other efforts to learn and grow. Fossum (1989, p. 80) advises making "a solemn vow…no longer [to] give your energy to hos-tility against yourself… Make a conscious decision to be on your own side…" Few of us do this perfectly, and hopefully we forgive ourselves for occasional lapses. I personally feel more connected and calm when I become aware of the need to become more reliable to myself, and it pleases me to set aside quality time to practice this 'skill' for greater proficiency. Probably we have more to learn about this aspect of unreliability.

On a surface level, avoiding ongoing shame from unreliable behavior by others is relatively simple: confront the behavior and negotiate a makeup. Confrontation is worthwhile whenever feelings are evoked, even if the matter seems trivial. We're no longer dependent little boys, and are much more free to choose our associates. Speaking up–man to man and eye to eye–removes a great deal of the shame, and may lead to an adult reassessment of the trustworthiness of the other man.

A variety of responses is possible from the man being confronted. He may trivialize my feelings, argue and justify, or say, "Fuck you, buddy. Get out of my face!" Shame is compounded whenever a man silently accepts the idea that his feelings are childish or trivial. Emotions never require justification. Getting caught up in argument and justifying can be frustrating and emotionally tiring, but may be seen as both men's efforts to maintain their boundaries (Fossum & Mason, 1986, pp. 59-85). Personally, I much prefer the more direct and vulgar style of boundary maintenance.

In a different vein, the man being confronted may be willing to move deeper into his trust or shame issues, or he may simply apologize and offer an amend. I'm not doing my friend a favor when I silently allow him to be unreliable with me. On some level, he probably knows that he's being provocative and acting out old unresolved issues. He may even be yearning for someone to take him seriously and call him on his Unreliability. The other man's response to such confrontation is usually more positive than I had feared. It's worth the risk.

Not Allowing The Five Freedoms

John Bradshaw adds this shaming rule, "Denial of the Five Freedoms," to those previously reported. "The five freedoms, first enunciated by Virginia Satir, describe full personal functionality. Each freedom has to do with a basic human power... the power to perceive; to think and interpret; to feel; to want and choose; and the power to imagine. In shame-based families, the perfectionist rule prohibits the full expression of these powers. It says you shouldn't perceive, think, feel, desire, or imagine *the way you do*. You should do these the way the perfectionist ideal demands" (Bradshaw, 1988, p. 40, emphasis added).

I expand this valuable concept in three additional ways. Shamefulness may arise from doubt that I'm in adequate contact with my own reality. Whether from shaming tactics (often some form of the Moral Intimidation rule) or my own uncertainty, I fear that others know me better than I do myself. I'm afraid that they can see right into me and that their penetrating eyes have the power to take command. I want to run away and hide, or fight like hell. Abrogating the Five Freedoms teaches that personal autonomy is suspect or downright sinful, and magnifies self-doubt.

Whenever a man's desires and needs are not being met, shame is likely to be part of his reaction. There may be a quick, barely conscious monologue blaming himself for wanting what he "can't have," even though "others can." This may arise from the original activation of shame in infancy. Kaufman (1989, pp. 30-35) describes the infant's need to establish an interpersonal bond via face-to-face gazing and body contact. This bond not only makes the child feel loved, wanted, and "okay to be," it lessens the shame of wants being denied. When bonding is weak or inconsistent, I think the infant's first awareness is that "something is amiss" (distress), which later becomes "something is wrong *with me*" (shame), and then "maybe they'll tolerate my being defective if I don't complain." In time, unmet needs feel shameful, neediness becomes anathema, and both needs and neediness are denied with stubborn fervor. Men especially are ensnared in this sequence.

Restricting the Five Freedoms is a form of spiritual abuse, which may be defined as being shamed or punished for one's myths, rituals, dreams, fantasies, values, heroes and heroines, opinions, preferences, style of expression or appearance, sexual symbolism, interpretation of reality, concept of the Divine or denial thereof, form of spiritual practice, paradigm of epistemology, etc. This kind of abuse denigrates a person for the *things that (s)he values most*. It attacks that vital sense of who I am, deep down. Spiritual growth involves strengthening this vital sense, and learning to enjoy being authentic in new areas of life. The true self needs to be blessed and validated, not cursed with shame.

Not Allowing the Five Freedoms may be broken by personal confrontation, independent of control. Group rituals or other dramatization of important values are helpful. On the social and political level, an unfortunate byproduct of regulations enforcing "political correctness" is to justify shaming with this rule. Any action or rule that denies *the freedom to be me* is to be exposed and actively disobeyed.

Moral Intimidation

Roy Schenk and I have discussed for several years the need to recognize another shaming rule. We didn't want to clutter the concept unnecessarily, and we're aware that the original rules were never meant to be exhaustive, but rather "a working list of recognizable patterns" (Fossum & Mason, 1986, p. 87). After much deliberation, we propose a tenth shaming rule, called Moral Intimidation.

This rule comes into play when one man *assumes* himself to be an authority on matters of right or righteousness. It's good old-fashioned moral superiority redone in modern makeup.

As before, tones of voice and body language are employed as powerful triggers of toxic shame. But the epithets and code words have changed to keep up with today's demonology. Most "- ist" words, when used as put-downs, carry messages of moral superiority by the user, as well as threats to shame any who dare to challenge or disagree.

Expert practitioners of Moral Intimidation use lots of rhetorical questions. "You *still* don't get it, do you?" Rhetorical questions are not questions at all, but statements recast to evade taking responsibility for one's values and prejudices. Displaced responsibility usually generates shame, as well as confusion and resentment.

We may extend the Five Freedoms to include *valuing in my own way*. Moral Intimidation judges a man's values and opinions as inferior, and implies that he himself is pretty depraved. Recantation is of little help, even with much groveling. As with Disqualification, the shameful feelings are magnified because the shamed man rarely realizes how he's been set up. Knowing that I've been manipulated into being ashamed is better than feeling (again) that somehow I'm inherently flawed.

Silence and defensiveness mark the man well 'trained' to obey this rule. An early challenge to the posture of moral authority is helpful. "I don't agree," "Bullshit," or "Says who?" confronts the original topdog assumption. Refuse to answer rhetorical questions and insist they be reframed as statements. Say, "I'm feeling defensive, for no valid reason," or "I refuse to be addressed in that tone of voice." Mimicking the intimidator's voice or body language usually stops it, but you may take a parting shot as (s)he heads out the door.

Be prepared for some anger. Moral intimidators use this shaming rule on men whom they expect to be cooperative and "take it." When you don't, they tend to get panicky about losing control and furious at you for refusing to "play by the rules." The ire of an unsuccessful moral intimidator feels better than a big gob of nauseating shame, silently swallowed.

Shaming Rules: Afterwords This concludes our survey of the ten shaming rules. Disobeying them can do much to relieve dissension among us and will support our work and friendship. But we all follow them at times, especially when we're under stress, so let's not get into Perfectionism or Blame about it. As with the Rescue triangle (Everingham , 1995c), the trick is to use them infrequently and lightly.

Shaming doesn't invalidate a group. Although the rules perpetuate shame in any system, much that is healthy and valuable may reside in the same system (Mason & Fossum, 1987). Men's Lib isn't perfect, but that's no reason to condemn or trivialize it.

Inadvertent shaming among men is an unnecessary burden. Restoring a broken bond is likely to involve confrontation, mutual sharing of feelings, and some kind of mutual amend or makeup. A simple, honest statement that "I value our friendship and want it to be better" is a good start.

SHAMING THREATS

Sometimes the shaming isn't direct, but takes the form of a threat. Moral Intimidation is often policed by threats, and probably other rules are, too. The threat is usually delivered in code, but the message is quite clear: "If you…, I *will shame* you." Among adults, shaming threats today are as common as direct shaming, yet often more subtle and thereby more powerful.

Shaming threats are harmful because they activate and reinforce our internalized shame, which can freeze us in our tracks, suppressing anything that might lead to more primary shame. We may 'require' only occasional reinforcement from without, because we have become our own oppressors. A big part of our task is to learn how to get out from under.

Shaming threats can result from expressing our feelings honestly (Kaufman, 1995). Friendships based in emotional dishonesty are indeed threatened, so a counterthreat shouldn't be a surprise. The other man probably isn't ready for a change. And the *enormity* of his feelings may constitute a threat that comes from inside.

There's fear of being 'tarred' with a shameful reputation: "pervert," "stuck up," "off his rocker," "wimp." Code words and gestures are often more damning than the names themselves. See Baumli (1995) for shaming one-liners, which threaten more to come if a man doesn't cringe back to his "proper attitude."

Among straight men, shaming threats that imply homosexuality often inhibit open expression of genuine affection. If there's a code of honor (favoring such virtues as honesty and integrity, sensitivity, or activity over passivity), a man may fear being shamed for those times when his true feelings run counter to the code, and the threat may tempt him to "fake it."

To deal with shaming threats, personal and group awareness is a first step. One might try naming it ("Hey, that's a shaming threat!"), but I would use this sparingly, because the Blame rule can be activated easily. Humorously saying, "Oh, oh, here comes the threat of shame" may work wonders.

Primary shame can be shared by saying, "I'm concerned that you'll shame me," or "I want a blessing right now, not a shaming." Things may change rapidly, the shamer feeling ashamed himself or quickly changing the subject. I see both the shamer and the man being shamed are doing a kind of dance in which each bears equal responsibility. This viewpoint will minimize further shaming and blaming among honest men who care about each other.

You might try, "I don't think I'll carry your projected shame today. Carry it yourself!" (Thanks to Robert Bly for this one.) Or maybe, "I'm not buying any of your shame threats today. Go find some other sucker." If shaming intent is denied, suggest that he go to a shrink to learn emotional honesty. If he suggests that you deserve to be shamed, tell him about pro-jection. As long as the threatener remains undeterred, I don't see any reason to let up my own shaming tactics. But when he turns toward honesty and humanity, I'd be quick to shift to empathy and respect. We're all in this together; shaming and threats may be a manifestation of our deep longing to confront and heal our own shame.

These last tactics carry a risk that I may overlook my own feelings of shame, which are pres-ent whenever I absorb a shaming threat or act, or whenever I see someone else being cruelly shamed. Sometimes I remember to take a deep breath and say a silent, "I'm feeling ashamed," for *unacknowledged* shameful feelings are risky business for a "shamenik" like me. A man may be harmed more by internal denial than by the external shaming threat.[4]

Combinations of these tactics are compatible. I'm sure you can develop some of your own, and maybe you'll tell us of your discoveries. Here's a helpful attitude toward shaming threats and acts: "Your thrust has hurt me, but I am not injured; I am not deterred; I have not quit the field. Your maneuver has wounded me, but it has failed to drive me off."

SHAMING TACTICS AND POLITICAL CORRECTNESS

This and the following section examine how a combination of shaming rules and threats set up a shame-laden atmosphere that pollutes our lives today. Ironically, one goal of political correctness is to reduce overt shaming and restrictions of freedom and opportunity. Sanctions, counter-shaming, and threats thereof are instituted against speech and other symbology judged to deny equal rights of citizenship by class discrimination. My major objection to PC is that its tactics work powerfully *against* its stated goals.

But there's moral irony as well. By assigning special status to a wide variety of Victims, political correctness *de facto* directs the lion's share of its shaming attack against a single class: Able-bodied white men who aren't poor. A professor at my university, who for some time had been calling male students "rapists" because of their opinions, was "busted" when a black man complained.

For several decades, we have offered members of some groups a modicum of preferential opportunity to partially compensate for past discrimination and to increase the critical supply of mentors for each group. I support this policy. In parallel development, a new moral double standard has arisen—one which exploits the manipulative Victim position (Everingham, 1995c). Victims now "deserve" to shame and castigate their "oppressors." This seems to come from Karl Marx's concepts of class struggle, and implies that the beneficiaries of past injus-tice carry full responsibility and guilt for it, as well as the obligation to make restitution. ("Correct" is almost a lexical diagnostic for American Marxism of the 1950s and 1960s.) Epithets, heavy with the threat of shame, are waved in our faces to induce us to remain silent and in our "place" of moral inferiority. Disqualification disguises the shift from a reasonable social policy to an atmosphere of institutionalized shaming. The witch hunt for "oppressors" is in full cry today, complete with severe shaming threats and a lot of Moral Intimidation.

The Defender of The Correct has mastered a certain body language and superior tone of voice. He will speak of this or that "-ism" in a knowing tone, which implies that he has a hot-line to the throne of true knowledge and Divine justice. He'll fight to maintain his position as moral "king of the hill." His weapons are an imperious demeanor or fierce readiness for verbal battle, a handy arsenal of factoids, and demonstrable prowess at being "sensitive" to the plight of victims.

Although the external consequences are much less serious, the shaming tone today reminds me of mainland China during the Cultural Revolution, and of America in the days of McCarthyism. The epithets of that era ("comsymp," "pinko," "fellow traveler") were code words for "traitor;" they had added power because their users could not be held directly accountable for charging loyal Americans with treason. Today's shamers also seek to hide behind innuendo and code words, as a kind of street fortification to shield their malice from public view and attack. Other commonalties include suppression of dissent by shaming threats, guilt by association, accusation interpreted as conviction, and widening the net of supposed oppressors to include those who call for honesty, fairness and equality.

Such tactics stockpile internalized shame and buried rage. Shadow—individual and societal—is projected *en masse* onto others. Resentment toward the shamers festers, inhibiting social healing. We risk an explosion when the unknown critical mass is attained. Public shaming can no longer be dismissed as an amusing game, for we now see how deadly its political effects can be (Kaufman, 1992).

SHAMING MEN FOR BEING MEN

There is a prevalent posture today which, subtly or blatantly, blames men ("patriarchy") for most of society's troubles. Broad hints suggest that testosterone is an evil drug, rendering men morally suspect, and requiring ever stronger legal and moral restraints for the "protection" of us all. Men's liberation operates under constant shaming threats to conduct itself in ways that women (and men enthralled with political correctness) will not find offensive.

Women may use the "rights" of Victimhood to shame us as a routine matter of course, perhaps because we "deserve it." Some even appear to believe it their *duty* to shame men. Shaming threats compound the Moral Intimidation. "Patriarchal," "sexist," "macho," "deadbeat," etc., are paraded like tanks and cannon on Lenin's birthday, ready to blow away anyone who voices disagreement or demands equal treatment.

Such name-calling may be indirect, and is often nonverbal—an exaggerated sigh of exasperation or a rolling of the eyes to imply that I'm hopelessly debauched or deficient in understanding. But if the threat is not heeded, the shaming may get more direct, although still in code. I objected when a nationally respected psychoanalyst equated "patriarchy" with dysfunctional families, and in the ensuing discussion she advised me to join a men's group! I suppose she thought that a group might convince me that family dysfunction is mostly men's fault (some "men's" group!), and the comment certainly implied moral retardation.

Why do we put up with this shit? Disqualification may blind us to the true picture. For example: Women wield much more decision-making power about sexual activity. When I first wrote that sentence, I imagined a storm of angry rebuttal focusing on men's power during rape. Despite the long-overdue emergence of male/female rape from the closet, it constitutes a small fraction of the decision-making concerning sex. The intensity of (long pent-up) emotions about rape tempt us to believe lies which cast blame and shame upon us just because we're men (see Bilgere, 1997).

We're not yet accustomed to the idea that feeling ashamed in response to shaming tactics has an instinctive, biological component. It's natural to respond with shame to a certain tone of voice. And some of us have the idea that it's just not honorable to pick on girls, even when they're picking on us.

Let's not blame women. We men are responsible for learning to break the shaming rules, as an integral part of healing our own shame. Anger is useful, but staying in the Rescue triangle isn't. Initiation and bonding to men is *very* useful (Gagnon, 1995; Greenwald, 1995; Miller, 1995). Good luck!

INTENTIONAL SHAMING

Generally, obedience to these rules is to be avoided. But occasionally there's a situation where I may choose to apply a shaming rule, or choose to use one rule in order to avoid a nastier one. When this happens, it's helpful to make an open acknowledgment to the man concerned. Shame owned and felt is much less destructive than shame hidden and internalized.

During initiation rituals, neophytes are often shamed deliberately or as a byproduct of the destructuring that is a necessary part of the process (Bridges, 1980). I think this is appropriate, *provided that an opportunity for an amend or makeup is clearly offered.* The makeup is best mutually agreed to, as among men of integrity. It can be wonderfully educational to experience this cycle: Lack of integrity and emotional dishonesty are confronted, leading to shame and alienation from the group; then the situation is resolved via honesty and a makeup, so that both personal integrity and broken interpersonal bonds are restored. See! Nobody has to remain alienated and ashamed; there's *always* a way back for those who want to find it.

[1] Rules 1 through 8 are based on Fossum and Mason (1986, pp. 86-104); rule 9 on Bradshaw (1988, pp. 39-41).

[2] I once heard a woman say, "That's why men hate women. They want revenge on their mothers." I thought, "That's why women are so cruel to their sons. They're paying back their husbands." This dynamic of sexualized intergenerational abuse is underestimated even today, and shows how destructive the Incompleteness rule can be.

Maybe we're angry with women because they push our shame buttons so easily. And why shouldn't they? Women installed most of these buttons. But the more basic issue is that our fathers didn't embody the mature masculine, and we missed the experience of initiation to free us from the feminine power orbit (Greenwald, 1995).

[3] Men's relations with women too often have this quality of withdrawal into silence. The sexes typically use different styles of confrontation. Men often face the Hobson's choice of either (a) trying to use the woman's style, which places him at a big disadvantage, or (b) using his own style and risking the shame of being called "crude," "violent," or "insensitive;" or of picking on someone who appears weaker or more vulnerable. It's understandable that many opt for surly silence. However, I recommend against that choice. Stylistic equality can be negotiated with an honest and caring confronter, and perhaps knowledge of these shaming rules may strengthen a man's position (Miller, 1995). Incompleteness can be a potent weapon, but its use is often destructive to both parties (see Bly & Meade, n.d.).

[4] If the response to "I feel ashamed" is "That's your problem," then it's time for serious confrontation *right now*—no changing the subject or pretending it was a joke. Failing that, you may have to kick the bastard right out of your life, for you've offered him the pearls of your honesty and vulnerability, and he's responded by spitting in your face.

Chapter 16
Men and Goodness*

ANDRE HEUER

The harder I tried to explain the more difficult it became. "Please!" I said to John. "Please listen. It's just not that difficult. We just need to be ourselves. That's good enough." John, like so many men I have worked with, wanted to be different from who he was. I often feel the same anxiety. I have often said to myself, "Maybe if I just do this a little bit different then I'll be okay. I'll be happy." I make the change and somehow things feel the same or sometimes, I even feel worse. What's going on with us? What is this discontent? Why are we so filled with self-hate that we spend thousands of dollars on therapy, books and workshops to change ourselves? Even worse, why is it that so many of us medicate ourselves with chemicals, sex, work, or exhaustion to forget the pain of being?

We live in an age of self-contempt. Throughout our lives we are told to be different than what we are. As little children we are made to conform and to meet the expectations of parents and teachers. We are forced to conform to their image of being human or risk being unloved. As adults we are told to dress in the right way, to have the correct political attitudes, and to have the proper psychological demeanor. These expectations and the sense of being unworthy of love fill us with dread and anxiety. We believe that we don't quite measure up. In being told so often that we are wrong or not quite right we no longer have any sense of our own goodness. This sense of not being good enough affects both women and men. In this essay I will explore some of the reasons why men feel this lack of goodness and the effects on men.

We were walking into a small supper club when my father recognized an old acquaintance. My father, reaching out for the man's hand, asked, "Have you been behaving?" The man's reply was quick and to the point, "Yeah, I have to. My wife and daughter keep me in line and my sister is staying with us right now. I have no choice." He then looked my father in the eye and asked, "How about you?" My father's face lit up with a boyish smile. His eyes rolled back looking over his shoulder at my mother. He calmly recited, "Of course, can't upset the good woman here. Right, Maryan?" My mother quickly snapped back "You better not." My gut tightened.

Soon after being with my parents, I was on a walk with a woman friend. As I began to say something, she looked at me and with much indignation snarled through grinding teeth, "Men!" Immediately, I looked over my shoulder at her with a sheepish grin and wondered, "What did I do wrong?" There it was again. My gut tightened. I felt a wave of anxiety come over me. I asked myself, "What is this about? Why do I feel this? Where did this come from?"

When the walk was over, I went home. I sat on the couch and let myself feel the anxiety. Her statement seemed to be such a small thing. Yet, it had created such a reaction in me. As I listened to my insides, memories of being a little boy came to me. I had been out playing and gotten terribly dirty. My mom grabbed me, pointed me towards the stairs and said, "Get washed! Now!" As I walked up the stairs I remembered her saying, "Boys," with a tone that seemed to my ears as disgust.

I later remembered how my older sister taunted me and told me how boys were bad and that girls were good. She would tease me and often would hold me down until I couldn't breathe. When I complained to my mother my sister would say "Mom! He was being mean to me and he's so strong. You know how mean boys are." I would sit there hurt and angry. I couldn't figure out what I had done wrong.

Many memories came to me once I remembered my sister's behavior. My fourth grade woman teacher would give the girls treats at recess. The girls told us that the teacher said "I don't give the boys treats because they're bad." All through school we boys knew that, "Boys were bad, and girls were good." This message was particularly strong around sexuality. Boys were out of control, only interested in one thing, and not to be trusted when sex was involved. Girls on the other hand weren't interested because they were good. This, of course, meant I was bad. As I thought more, another memory came to me. My mother was having a conversation with relatives. A young neighbor man had gotten into some trouble. He was single and a little wild. The consensus was that, "What that boy needs is a good woman. She would straighten him out right away." All these memories meant one thing to me. Boys and men were bad. We needed women to point out what was bad and to straighten us out. We had no natural goodness of our own. We received goodness from women.

It was at this point that I jumped to a conclusion. It was women that made men feel bad. It was women with their sense of righteousness that made me feel not good about myself. It was not long before I realized what I was saying. As in the case of many who write and study gender issues, it was easy to put the entire blame on the other sex. I quickly reconsidered the issue and asked myself, "How do men participate in this process of not feeling good about themselves?" I realized I had been given this message by many of the men in my life. My father by his actions had colluded in the process of helping me believe that women were better. I had heard plenty of men say how a certain woman had straightened them out. The whole culture had made it clear that women were more righteous and good. That was why we didn't hit girls, why they were allowed to go first in line, why they didn't fight in wars, and why they were called innocent victims and boys and men were just casualties. Most of these rules I learned not just from women, but also from men.

In facilitating groups for my clients it became clear that many men had similar experiences. They had the same feeling of moral inferiority to women as I had. Many of them felt rage and often hid their sense of inferiority with a bravado attitude. "No woman tells me what to do." I would hear often. It was a cover. As I worked with these men I found a deep sense of a lack of personal goodness. They often felt extremely fearful of abandonment. If their women left it would prove that they were not good. It would prove that they were not able to control themselves enough to earn the love of a good woman. In the fear of losing their women some men used violence. The thought of losing their women was so devastating that violence was the answer to the inner chaos they felt and a way of creating order. This was not the only way men dealt with their sense of moral deficiency.

For every man that I worked with who was violent or rageful, I found three who were depressed, passive and exhausted. Many of these men seemed burdened by the need to prove that they could do the right thing. Working hard, doing their civic duty keeping the house up, being a good father and husband, and most of all keeping it emotionally together. Many of these men were motivated by fear of not being good enough. They feared that if they didn't do it right they would lose their family, friends, and work. Most felt that if they could not maintain their lifestyle they would not be successful. Most of these men equated being good with being successful. If they weren't, their fear was that they would lose the love of the people in their lives, especially their wife or lover. After I had heard this several times I was reminded of the phrase "Behind every successful man is a good woman." These men felt without success they were worthless. They suspected that without a woman at their side, they could never be quite good enough.

As I began to equate men's feeling's of being good with being successful and having a good woman, I asked "In what ways—besides a woman being behind a man and success—does our culture give the message that men are not quite good enough?" As a boy what I often heard was "That boy needed to join the service. They would whip him into shape." The phrase "whipped into shape" gnawed at me. I remember the spankings I got as a boy. My sister was yelled at but not spanked. In school the boys received the paddle and the girls got sent to the cloak room. In sports the boys were disciplined and even hit sometimes by their coaches. The girls were protected and allowed to enjoy the few games they were allowed to play. What I learned was that the way a boy could "get it" was to receive a beating—whipped into shape.

As I interviewed other men I was consistently reminded of this attitude. Over and over again, I would hear of men as boys receiving a major beating for a minor mistake. The man would then say "I deserved it. I was out of control. You know how guys are? I wasn't ever very well behaved." If this conversation had only happened a few times I would have forgotten it. However, it happened more often than not, especially with men in prison. The example that most exemplified this attitude was described in an article in a local newspaper. The Star Tribune sports editorial piece of January 15, 1992, was about the 1966 Bills kicker Booth Lusteg. He missed a field goal during a regular season game. This was after Buffalo had beaten the same team for the American Football Championship. Buffalo, instead of winning the game, ended tied.

The article reported that Lustig said that some angry young Bills fans followed him through downtown Buffalo and beat him up. "Booth, why didn't you call us?" police later asked. "Because I deserved it," Booth replied.

This type of attitude prevails in our culture. Mistakes are intolerable and deserving of beatings. In schools, boys are more likely to be labeled behavior problems than girls. They are more likely to be medicated to get them under control. Boys may receive a higher rate of encouragement from teachers than girls but they also receive more punishment. Some studies indicate boys get more praise because they are considered more problematic and need praise in order to be controlled. Men receive more time on prison sentences then women for the same crime. All these attitudes arise out of the expectations that boys are out of control and that, "Boys will be boys no matter what." No wonder men have feelings of being morally deficient or lack a sense of their goodness. The culture not only says that men need a woman and success to be good but also that men will probably need a good whipping in order to be good. In other words a man needs a good woman and the Marines to be good enough.

As I came to these insights, I wondered what could have motivated men to continue to participate in this crippling process. It did not take much time to realize the answer. I already had it. It was my fear of not being loved. I felt that I had to continue to be successful and to find the right woman in order to be loved. I really believed that I would need to be whipped into shape so that I would be good enough to love. This fear of not being loved was the theme that was common to most of my clients and men's groups. Men wanted to be loved for who they were not for their success, image, or for the woman at their side. However, they found it difficult and sometimes impossible to let go of these conditions of their lovableness. They often chose to continue to live their lives in these images rather then take the risk of changing and losing love. Once again I saw how men were responsible for colluding in their own wounding.

As I ended my research, I found that men's sense about their personal goodness is affected in three ways. First, many men see women as being the source of their goodness. Second, men believe that they're morally and sexually out of control and the only way to get under control is to get whipped into shape. Finally men have felt unworthy of being loved because of their lack of goodness. The way men find their goodness is through being successful.

The sad aspect is the damage this process has caused men. It has had damaging results not only for men but also for our culture. The drive for success is probably the most damaging to men. This driveness has led to denial of basic emotional and physical needs. Drugs, sex, overwork, and other self-destructive behaviors are used to meet these needs. Some men have created an inflated sense of themselves in order to feel okay about themselves. This tends to emotionally isolate them from others. Other men cannot find their sense of personal goodness and become depressed, passive and isolated. All these behaviors have caused a need for control and for perfection. The greatest effect that I have seen is that, as men, we are isolated from each other. As men we have become dependent upon women to meet needs that they are not capable of meeting. The tragedy is that our sons are denied the role models to help them discover their own goodness. This leads to the perpetuation of this cycle of hurt and pain for all men and our culture. As men, we need to discover our goodness if we are to stop this cycle. We need to be willing to heal our woundedness.

We face many obstacles in trying to heal this woundedness. It is difficult to admit to having wounds in this age of image. "Men need to have it together." we are told. Trying to be perfect causes us to want to cover up our woundedness and flaws. As we have discussed earlier, it is the fear of not being good that causes the wounding. It causes us to look for quick fixes and simple solutions to heal our wounds. It is ironic that many of the ways men try to overcome their woundedness only causes more wounding. Only when men are willing to enter into their woundedness can we hope for healing. When we bring to light our imperfections we also bring to light our goodness. It is our attempt to hide our woundedness and imperfection that cause our energy to be destructive rather than a creative and powerful blessing. It is rather paradoxical that to find their goodness men must decide to bring to light their flaws.

Each man needs to make his own decision to enter into his woundedness to reclaim his goodness. It is a journey that only he can take for himself. He cannot blame others. He must take personal responsibility for his journey. It is not an easy journey. He will experience loneliness, pain, and most of all, grief. However, it is not a journey that a man can take alone.

In reclaiming our goodness other men will be needed. Only other men can give the full compassion that comes from the common experience of struggling with this woundedness. We will have to be willing to allow men to see and hear our struggle. We will have to ask men to accompany us on our journey. We will need to let men nurture and guide us. As men journey together we will experience a deep and abiding love with each other. This love will be the sign of men's goodness. It is then that men's goodness will permeate and change our lives, culture, and world.

NOTE:

* Based on an article by the same name in *Men Talk*, Minneapolis, MN, spring 1992. Also in his PhD. Thesis, "Effects of Family, Society, and the church on Men's Self-image and Their Spirituality: Approaching Ministry to Men." University of Minnesota, St. Paul, MN, 1993. Copyright © 1992, Andre Heuer.

Chapter 17
Men and Intimacy*

PATRICK DOUGHERTY

Men are different from women. We know that the sexes have different bodies, view and experience life differently, and are raised and treated differently. Yet we are often trying to make what works for one gender work for the other.

Alcoholics Anonymous and similar 12-step programs are examples. From the structure and origins of AA, we can see that it is a program developed by men out of an understanding that men often prefer clear rules and guidelines, especially when working with something as vulnerable and elusive as addiction. Psychotherapy offers a contrasting example. The whole process and environment of therapy is much more geared to what women find comfortable and safe.

Gender differences are also being blurred in the area of intimacy, a situation that continues to confuse men and frustrate women.

If asked about the components of intimacy, many of us would list self disclosure, talking face-to-face, expressing feelings, listening empathically, sharing vulnerability, and being direct and honest. But these components fit women's style of intimacy much better than men's.

While many men may feel intimate under these circumstances, others do not, because much of what men understand and experience as intimacy is missing from this list.

Women do not, as is often said, know *more* about intimacy than men. They only know more about what works *for them.*

Many of the current theories of intimacy begin by looking at childhood. We see that girls tend to be concerned with cooperation and fairness in their relationships, while boys focus on rules and competition. We don't find much face-to-face disclosure among boys—just the opposite. Most boys are taught to deny and repress any desire to show vulnerability, and to toughen up because someday they'll "be a man." The conclusion drawn is that intimacy has been socialized out of males by the time they become adults.

These observations and theories certainly point out some of the struggles that boys experience growing up, and have implications for issues which men will wrestle with when trying to be intimate, especially with women. But the conclusion drawn is simply wrong.

A DIFFERENT INTIMACY

Boys learn *different* ways of being intimate. Boys become friends or buddies, hang out together, play sports together, use their imaginations together in play or to fantasize about the future. They joke around together, drive around together, and explore the world together. Recognizing these typical aspects of boyhood, I can not imagine anyone concluding that boys do not have intimacy in their lives.

Theorists often overlook the substantial change in the male world brought on by the industrial revolution. Before the industrial revolution, most boys worked at their father's side, or were apprenticed to another adult male. A boy learned to be a man by spending most of his day in close relationship with a mature and productive male. After the revolution, the father and other adult males went off to factories and offices for most of the day. The men often came home spent and empty. Both at home and at school, a boy's world came to be filled with women and other boys. Boys lost their fathers and male teachers, and fathers began to be alienated from their sons and families.

How boys are initiated into manhood has changed forever. The father often brings home a distant and seemingly uninterested presence, or one of intolerance and domination. More and more, boys came to be born into a masculine void. The void becomes a lifelong wound—a wound of spiritual neglect, which a man must confront to make sense of his life.

Men today are speaking out about their isolation, about feeling like they are living in an empty world, about the lack of meaning in their lives. They speak of their desire for true intimacy to combat the emptiness. These men are drawn to people who are willing to listen to them, willing to let them articulate the pain inside. They are being drawn toward people who *have* a form of intimacy and are willing to teach them how to be intimate. These people are usually women.

So men learned, by default, to imitate what women call intimacy. It has been very helpful, and perhaps the only way in modern society that this search for deeper intimacy could have begun for us. And the face-to-face style of intimacy certainly has an important place in living a full masculine life.

SEARCH FOR MASCULINITY

But most men after a time begin to sense that there is something missing. We now can share our feelings and communicate, and are getting lots of strokes for doing so, but we come away not feeling grounded in our maleness. Today, what often connects us to our maleness is the pain of being deprived of masculine models in childhood.

We have an important need that is rarely talked about. Men need to connect with their memories of the vibrant and creative *boy,* the one that knew plenty about being intimate and close to other boys. This boy is the one who will help us remember what it's like for a man to be intimate.

More and more men are claiming and affirming our style of getting together and interacting with each other as men, enjoying doing things the way men do them. The word "buddy," long derided as implying a superficial relationship, is being used again with pride and affection. We're remembering how to be intimate while competing with other men—playing football with a group of guys, racquetball with a friend or tennis with a business partner. Although task orientation is often derided by those using the limited definition of intimacy, men are rediscovering how good it feels to help a man move his furniture, to paint a house with a group of friends, to lay sod and get dirty together. Doing these masculine things *together* can powerfully affirm our friendships and our sense of grounded masculinity.

Hunting, fishing and other outdoor sports are also typical male modes of affirming masculinity and facilitating intimacy. Many men tell of the pleasure they feel sitting beside a friend for hours in a duck slough. Or of the tenderness a man can feel toward a friend after a cold weekend of ice fishing, staring down their ice holes and hardly saying a word about anything serious.

There is a resurgence of storytelling in the male world. Men for centuries have found pleasure in listening to myths and stories, and reflecting on what they have to say about a man's life. To some, this may seem to be indirect and unclear, lacking the precision of declarative statements and the directness of face-to-face interaction. Yet men take great pleasure in just listening, and in sitting and allowing the story to sink into our consciousness. A man's way of intimacy does not need to be direct and articulate. Sometimes these qualities actually ruin the experience of being together for men.

Making fun of each another and joking around together is also finding its way back into the world of men. After sorting out the shaming and wounding ways of making fun of someone, men are seeing the affection that is often behind a joke. Native Americans have long believed that making fun of a person is an admission of affection and an acknowledgment of friendship. Some may criticize this style as indirect, but many men say that it feels very good to be on the receiving end of this sort of kidding around.

In current media, from television sitcoms to the printed word, these ways of male bonding are often portrayed as primitive or unevolved, and often pathetic. Such portrayals are just attempts to shame men away from masculine intimacy. The message from these sources seems to be that unless men master the feminine style of intimacy they are to be looked down upon and pitied. In reality, until men come to terms and accept who they are, they will always feel shame at their inability to be more authentic and intimate.

To be truly intimate with either men or women, a man must establish the deep foundation of his masculinity. This can be discovered only in the company of other men. It should be obvious that we cannot learn it from women, or from men who practice only a feminine style of intimacy.

As he continues to experience his deep masculinity, a man's capacity for intimacy becomes infinite. Grounded men can choose when to share their feelings, when to joke around, when to listen to stories and grunt, when to compete and when to be gentle.

This journey to intimacy leads men on a long adventure, often painful but usually exciting. It means revisiting childhood to find both the wounded and the vibrant boy; it means learning about sharing feelings and being vulnerable; it means remembering what we already know about being intimate. And it leads men back to being with other men.

NOTE:

* Adapted from *The PHOENIX*, March, 1989 issue. Copyright © Patrick Dougherty, 1989

Chapter 18
Shame, Initiation, and the Culture of Initiated Masculinity

MICHAEL P. GREENWALD

T he mature Masculine must be reclaimed by the modern world. Its virtual absence from technologically advanced societies has, in the author's view, resulted in one of the more serious moral crises ever to face Western civilization. Earth's population has in its grasp the means to create a virtual Utopia. Yet we lack the collective will even to ensure against the annihilation of entire cultures through starvation and disease. In our world, genocide is barely noticed. Rape is used as an instrument of both pathological male self-expression and ethnic war. We are willing to enhance performance chemically (with antidepressants or steroids, for example) at the expense of accepting our human limitations. We tolerate planetary pollution and disgracefully high infant mortality rates. Violence is becoming the preferred solution to interpersonal disputes. In all this, we see evidence that mature Masculinity, in its fullness, has all but been forgotten, and that "Boy Psychology" (Moore & Gillette, 1990) is prevalent.

To reclaim the mature Masculine, we begin where the young men of traditional societies invariably began—by remembering initiation . . .

INITIATION REMEMBERED

A boy lies safe in the arms of his mother. He does not fit quite as comfortably against her body as he used to. But he is perfectly happy to be cuddled by her, bonded to the warm, nourishing sensuality of her body and the light of love in her eyes.

Suddenly, the door of the hut bursts inward. Men, painted and disguised, storm into the room. Mother wails and clutches at him, trying vainly to offer protection from the demons that have invaded their safe and private world. Rough hands seize the boy, and he screams in terror. Reaching for his mother, he is ripped from her grasp and dragged out into the night. Throughout the village, his playmates are being carried off by large, frightening figures. Mothers follow the parade crying, praying, beating their breasts and tearing their hair. The fires of the village now seem wicked and diabolical, no longer warm and familiar. The boy feels the terror of separation from his anchors to comfort and reality.

As the men leave, carrying off the boys, mothers collect in groups to congratulate each other on their fine performances and the grandness of the show they have just presented. They are sad, yes, to lose their little boys. But they are proud and pleased by their work of nurturing another generation of young men to readiness.

The boys, meanwhile, are taken far into the darkness. They are lost, disoriented, perhaps blindfolded. They have no idea how to get back home, to Mother. Terror, fear of a death they cannot yet conceive, perhaps panic—all roil in their bodies. Soon an overwhelming sense of loss will envelop their fright.

They are carried to a place of isolation, used only at sacred times for sacred purposes. No women are allowed into the place—and no woman would care to go there. Masculine energy reigns here, and the very air is pregnant with the memory of ancient ritual. The earth seems to be stained with the afterbirths of earlier labors—labors of initiation, soon to begin again. Here is ritual space, timeless and secluded. It is liminal space, at the threshold where that which was is no more, and that which will be is not yet.

Men have made preparation. They have gathered the sacred materials, the necessary food. They have tested themselves, cleansed themselves, determined their tasks. Individually and as a group, they have reconsecrated themselves to the spirits of the village, or to something or someone greater than all, and of which each is a part.

In this place, for a timeless period, the boys are subjected to physical, spiritual and emotional processes handed down as sacred tradition. Among such ordeals may be scarification, circumcision, the breaking of teeth, the piercing of flesh. The boys may be buried in mock graves, each face-to-face with his own unimagined death. They may be tricked and taunted by their elders. Discipline is strict, and perhaps they are beaten for transgressing the most minute regulation. They soon realize that no Mother is here to comfort them in their pain. They confront the need to care for themselves, lest they perish. They face tasks which bring them to the edge of their own mortality. Sometimes a boy dies.

But they also are trained. Mentors teach them. They learn the essential values, customs and culture of their society. The curriculum includes the skills and burdens, the rights and privileges, the responsibilities and authority of being a man in the life stream of the village. Each boy will emerge knowing deeply that he is unconditionally a member of the tribe of Men. "All for one, and one for all" may be no exaggeration. He comes to know and trust the initiates within his cohort and the men who have acted as his initiators. Each boy learns by experience who is to be entrusted with which responsibilities, who can be relied upon to exercise communal or civic authority, and who is destined to act as priest or shaman. He assimilates the understanding that his individual future is bound up in a masculine collectivity—a masculine interdependence—essential to the survival of the village.

The boys also receive healing: physical healing from the rigors and wounds of their ordeal, and emotional healing for the pain of separation from their mothers. The boys experience at first hand the power of men to heal men's wounds. They realize that their initiators are healers as well as tormentors, who suffered identical wounding and scarring when they endured the same rite of passage. This recognition opens a door deep in the psyche—a door both to the power of self-healing and to a deep bonding with men.

Finally, the boys discover their own evolving spirituality. They experience the healing reintegration inherent in a communal sense of the sacred. They learn songs and myths of origin, explanations of nature, and the mysteries of their own existence in a universe infinitely large. Ritual elders invite them to surrender themselves spiritually to the right order of things. As they learned that they are unconditionally members of the tribe of Men within the village, so now they learn that the village has its place in the natural order of the world, which has its place in the natural order of the cosmos. They begin to know that all life draws on a larger energy, necessary for the universe to survive.

At last the time of separation is ended, and the initiates return home. They are different now. No longer are they tied to their mothers, looking to them for nurturance. Rather, they have become young men growing toward the prime of their physical strength. Not yet mature enough to be entrusted with command, they are nevertheless clearly separated from the world and work of women. Now they are men, and they know who and what men are in the world. These initiated young men hold the future of the hunt and the future of the physical life of the village. They hold also, in their souls, the future of continuing initiation of men into the spiritual life of village, world and cosmos.

THREE ENERGIES OF INITIATION

My thesis is that initiation is essential to a man's cohesive sense of himself as Masculine. Through initiation, the Masculine becomes enlivened and empowered, so that a boy may become a mature man.[1]

Without initiation, Boy Psychology maintains its grip on the boy's self, and he is never fully able to take his place in the world of men.

Three specific energies of initiation can be identified.[2] The first of these is the wounding-testing-separating energy—the energy of the ordeal. From this dark, confrontational, and threatening energy, the boy comes to know and tolerate different kinds of pain: physical pain more intense than he ever imagined; emotional pain at separating from his mother and from reliance on external nurturing; and the deeper psychic pain of uncertainty and fear. This latter pain is not merely that he has been set adrift without a paddle, but the awful realization that he may well die, alone, bereft of all that has been familiar to him—unknown, unseen and unblessed.

Teaching-bonding is the second specific energy of initiation. Here is a lighter energy, although not always less confrontational. The boy comes to discriminate, identify and participate in both the manual skills and cultural rules that mark him as a man of the village. He learns how men are to behave among themselves, with women, and in relation to the world. He bonds to a male cohort—his fellow initiates—and shares its pride, its achievements, its failures, its responsibilities, and its reputation. Now he belongs to a group in which he may continue to test himself and share the learning of life lessons. Now he can experiment, try his wings, experience ungainliness, practice speaking in a deeper voice, share his dreams of himself as a man—all within the protective cover of other initiates who are experiencing a similar adolescence. Bonds formed here are lifelong, supporting his sense of manhood until death. Initiation's third specific energy is the healing-spiritual energy. The surviving initiate enters into the other world, where all things are pure spirit—a world where magic is ordinary, expected, unremarkable; where death is merely the completion of whatever was to be accomplished at this turn of the wheel. This energy welcomes the initiate to a place of surrender, to a place of paradox, to a wonderful place of understanding that he is absolutely *not* in control of the events that shape his life, yet he is entirely responsible for his own being. This energy is the province of the spiritual elder entrusted to embody the divine connectedness of each to all.

The young man who has been shaped by these energies is ready for the tasks of manhood, and equipped to face the further stages of initiation that he will encounter later in life.

THE MATURE MASCULINE

For most men in Western society, exposure to these energies of initiation is, at best, haphazard and chaotic. Lacking a cohesive experience of initiation, we have to ask—because our bodies, culture, and spirits cannot tell us—"What *is* the mature Masculine?"

The Masculine is not the same as either "male" or "man." Confusion on this point easily derails productive exploration of deeper fundamental structures within all men and women. Each living human being is a potential expression of the Masculine—as well as the Feminine. Another roadblock to deeper insight is to be found in the current entrancement with a cramped and confining "political correctness" that heavily shames and attacks politically anyone who states the obvious: Men are fundamentally different from women. Meaningful understanding of our deeper selves requires that both men and women explore honestly the ways in which we differ socially, psychologically and spiritually.

The Masculine is ancient, deep and powerful. Following Moore and Gillette (1990), I view the mature Masculine as a balanced gathering of archetypal energies. These archetypes are the King, the Warrior, the Magician, and the Lover. The King presides over right order, fulfillment, definition of boundaries and values, fertility, communal abundance and prosperity, blessing, sacredness. The Warrior's function is action, strategy, aggression in service of the King, forward leaping or thrusting, loyalty, discipline, and individual prosperity. He is master of the hunt, guardian of the boundaries, and executor of the King's orders. The Magician's domain is transformation, healing and teaching, to which he brings awareness, insight, manipulation, reflection, and judgment. The Magician confronts the King's power and reminds the other Archetypes of their responsibilities. The Lover enjoys play and display, the arts, sensation, delight, aliveness, passion, appetite, and physical and spiritual satisfaction. He embodies an empathic sense of the world, a boundary-less connection to the Universe, aesthetics, mysticism, and spirituality.

The mature Masculine is not without its dark Shadow. Moore and Gillette (1992a, 1992b, 1993a, 1993b) illustrate their important concept that the Shadow of each archetype is bipolar. Thus, the Shadow King may manifest as Tyrant or Weakling Abdicator; Shadow Warrior as Sadist or Masochist; Shadow Magician as Detached Manipulator or Denying Pseudo-innocent; Shadow Lover as Addicted (Don Juan) or Impotent.

It is important to differentiate conceptually between the Shadow of the mature Masculine, on the one hand, and the immature Masculine or Boy Psychology, on the other. A tangible—though admittedly subjective—distinction can be detected between the Tyrant and the Highchair Tyrant and between the Sadist and the Grandstander Bully. My hypothesis is that initiation is integral to the "death" of Boy Psychology, because it emboldens the flesh-and-blood man to face his Shadow. Unless and until initiated, the boy has no competence or reason to confront candidly those parts of himself that he does not wish to know. Facing the Shadow is a job for the *mature* Masculine.

SHAMING THE MASCULINE

Most boys in our society have no access to initiatory process. In the early and middle parts of the 20th century, male teachers and coaches, the clergy, extended family, and even scout leaders were able to fill the role of initiator, at least to some extent. It is important to recognize the singular contribution the military traditionally made in the initiation of young men. It is probably no accident that the military experience tracked traditional models of initiation fairly closely. The separation of young men from their homes, the isolation and ordeal of boot camp, the perceived universality of service, the availability of training and education in technical skills and leadership, the uniquely male identity of the institution, the overwhelming importance of loyalty to one's unit, and the indoctrination of the ethic of service to the nation—in all these we can see the energies of male initiation.

Today all of these initiatory efforts have pretty much disintegrated. Without the availability of conscious initiation, boys age only to act out caricatures of the mature archetypes and their shadow parts. There is danger in the current prevalence of Boy Psychology, which manifests as :

> abusive and violent acting out behaviors against others, both men and women;
> passivity and weakness, the inability to act effectively and creatively in one's own
> life and to engender life and creativity in others (both men and women); and,
> often, an oscillation between the two—abuse/weakness, abuse/weakness. (Moore
> & Gillette, 1990, p. xvi)

We have forgotten that, like all energy, the Masculine demands acknowledgment and integrated expression. Without legitimate avenues of expression, the Masculine becomes regressive, and seeks outlet in destructive ways—acting out in violence, crime, and abuse of self and others. When a society no longer knows how to initiate, nor even how to recognize and acknowledge the mature Masculine, there is no consensual way for Everyman to experience the constructive nature of masculinity in its fullness. Ignorance of the mature Masculine allows all these deep archetypal energies to seek expression in distorted ways.

Thus, it is not surprising that today's world associates "masculinity" with such things as rigidly hierarchical devaluation of both the Feminine and women, sadomasochistic pornography, exaggerated machismo, growing levels of violence, material acquisitiveness, and pseudo-initiatory gang and college rituals. The more the Masculine is shamed, the more shamefully the Masculine shows up. The more shamefully the Masculine shows up, the more ashamed it deserves to be.

When the Masculine is shamed, it is not enough for flesh-and-blood men simply to be human. To be "real" men, we must become something more. We must now metamorphose into super creatures: sports heroes with multimillion dollar contracts, soulless political candidates saying what will get them elected rather than the truth, financial tycoons. These men are the "winners;" our televisions tell us so. The rest of us, losers by definition, are invited to redeem ourselves from this double dose of shame by further burying our true masculine selves in order to emulate the winners. Where such emulation is clearly not possible, we make a profession out of our shame, joining the ranks of those who see the feminization of our society as the answer (see Zubaty, 1993).

Many American men live lives in which their Masculinity is shamed or cursed. It is essentially shaming to impose on anyone a task or role which is beyond his ability to fulfill—to ask a boy to do a man's job in any realm (e.g., emotional, physical, or spiritual). Yet we do it to each other and ourselves all the time. Similarly shaming is exposure to the ridicule and the ignominy of public failure. Listen to the laugh tracks of sitcoms where men are portrayed as silly wimps who have never "gotten it" and will never "get it." Even more deeply shaming is to hear "You are no man" from a woman and to believe that she speaks the truth. Such scorn for that uninitiated part of a man of which he already feels significantly ashamed can be painfully and enduringly emasculating. Yet the airwaves teem with messages suggesting that deep Masculinity is wrong, an anachronism, dangerous, and no longer welcome or even tolerable in modern society.

When the mature Masculine becomes so deeply buried, the available models of masculinity are mere shades, ephemeral and untrustworthy. Some essential element is missing from the fabric of society, from the very life-energy of the culture. Chaos, violence, wantonness, and denial are predictable outcomes.

MALE INITIATION HEALS MASCULINE SHAME

Male initiation operates in many ways as an antidote to masculine shame. One of the functions of initiation is to separate a boy from his mother's way of being and feeling. In the face of the initiatory ordeal, a boy cannot remain passive and retiring, or helplessly long for rescue by Mother. No longer can he continue to be enamored of his own piteous suffering, or hide behind his own immaturity.

Through initiation, a young man discovers that his pain must be—and can be—carried, that it is a part of his growth. Acknowledgment and containment (neither suppression nor expression) of his feelings become his allies. He can feel the grief and rage of his separation, or the joy and relief of his survival, and learn to embrace the power of that emotional energy, and be strengthened by it. He doesn't need to "stuff" his emotion or dissipate it by undirected flailing or an unfocused outburst. Initiation thus awakens a man's mature emotional body, and so provides him a powerful antidote to the deadening impact of internalized shame. Grounded in the Masculine, he can feel honest pride in his masculinity.

The ordeal aspect of initiation also awakens the physical body to an awareness of the great potential of its own physical strength and determination. An initiated man can protect his own integrity against onslaughts from without and within. From confrontation with physical fear, the boy's body discovers—deep inside—that he can go forward "with fear on the tip of his sword." The young man emerges carrying an extraordinary weapon for vanquishing shame.

The bodily experience of discovering his physical boundaries is more than a metaphor. Especially where shame has been derived from physical, sexual, or emotional invasion, or from athletic failures, the newly awakened physical sense of self—of the "I am"—sends an unmistakable message of empowerment to the spirit. Confidence in his ability to define physical boundaries and then to protect them is, in my view, essential to the healing of internalized shame. As the initiate learns to differentiate from the Feminine and to defend against its regressive pull, he becomes empowered against the malignant wounds inflicted by shaming of the Masculine.

A significant manifestation of internalized shame is a certain general confusion, or ignorance, about everything—especially about anything that might be helpful in healing shame. Shame tends to freeze a man in place because he lacks assurance that what he thinks he might want to do is correct, acceptable, productive, or healing. In this respect, the teaching/bonding energy of initiation informs the boy what is *right*. He has learned not only what are the right things for the young man to do, but also become grounded in what is *right* about masculinity.

Archetypally speaking, initiation teaches that part of a man's job, for example, is to protect, to hunt, to provide governance, to love his mate, to participate in ritual, and to pursue a mission in the world. An initiated young man knows not only what he is supposed to do, but knows that his tasks serve his society, and are honored by it. His role *as a man* is defined and supported by culture. There is no question that his activities sustain his people, as well as his own mission and self-esteem. Society blesses his maturing masculinity and his embodiment of the Masculine.

Such knowledge is significantly reinforced by the fact that *all* the young men share the experience of initiation. They have a common sense of doing and being "right" *as a man*. The cohort of former playmates now collectively embodies culturally sanctioned maturing masculinity. Each young man can turn to them for continuing reassurance that he is "okay." The bonded cohort provides psychological space where it is safe to experiment and express his emerging manhood. It has also a socializing influence, imposing appropriate limits on behavior that would pose an unacceptable threat to communal norms.

Initiation thus confronts shame through the provision of mentoring, of cultural guidance and wisdom, and through the bonding of each man to a cohort—all of which enliven a man's sense of the rightness of the Masculine in the world.

Finally, initiation heals shame by its invocation and evocation of the spiritual. A man surrenders first to a higher sense of order as culturally defined—he surrenders to the secular King—and he accepts his position as a man in the culture. Through the spiritual aspect of initiation, a man surrenders to his place in the cosmos: he submits to the Sacred King and accepts his position as merely human, merely a man.

This sense of self-acceptance, of true humility, is the very opposite of toxic internalized shame. I doubt the two can co-exist, for the moment one accepts that he feels ashamed, the shame itself tends to dissolve.

It is critical to recognize that this spiritual surrender is by no means a surrender *to* the wound. It is certainly not a retreat into an embrace of Boy Psychology or childish pre-initiatory helplessness. It is, rather, an acknowledgment of fallibility, an acceptance that life is imperfect, that life both bruises and blesses. The power of paradox, the power of the joke, the sense of wonder—all of these convey the message to the initiated man: "Lighten up!"

We now see how the process of initiation, by invoking specific energies, can provide both healing and antidote for the shaming of the Masculine that infects our modern social and personal environment.[3]

A SUBCULTURE OF INITIATED MASCULINITY[4]

Over the last 18 years, hundreds of men have invested a great deal of energy to provide male initiatory experience through the New Warrior Training Adventure.[5] The New Warrior program demonstrates that it is possible to expose today's men to the energies of initiation, and to continue the process through the development of a bonded cohort. The program is consciously and intentionally initiatory, and provides ongoing group experience to help integrate initiation into daily life.

Such experience, as with other programs of similar intent, is necessarily quite different from traditional tribal initiation. Our society as a whole no longer agrees that initiation is important, so there is little cultural support for the returning initiates. Moreover, we are heterogeneous and mobile, intensely educated in secular matters, and exposed to conflicting values, traditions, and mores. It becomes almost impossible to imagine, much less to define and inculcate, consensus about how boys should be taught. Although some would suggest that

Western consciousness is now expanding to include wider recognition of the validity of spiritual experience (Redfield, 1993), we have lived through a century in which scientific thinking about human education has made little room for transformative processes such as initiation.

At its inception, the New Warrior Training Adventure was neither consciously initiatory nor concerned with having any particular cultural significance. But after nearly two decades of experience, we may begin to discern an emerging subculture. Cultural change is rarely the result of conscious effort, but emerges as a response to human need. One similarity between tribal initiation and the New Warrior program is that both somehow meet a need deeply felt in our culture.

New Warriors and men who are pursuing initiation in other ways appear to be developing a common set of rituals. A common jargon has arisen, as well as an approach to solving problems and resolving disputes. A set of recognized values has emerged about how men of integrity behave, at least towards other men (Kauth, 1992; Everingham, 1995d). Groups actively define what is required of men who would be leaders, and provide an organized leadership training program. Perhaps most important, these men express pride in their manhood, and tend to be unashamedly committed to realizing the potential inherent in the mature Masculine.

These phenomena look like benchmarks for what may be called a subculture. My purpose here is not to stir up debate about nomenclature, so "subculture" is used tentatively to denote the *direction* of cultural change, and to help make the distinction from a cult or movement. It strikes me that we are witnessing the emergence of a transmissible subculture of initiated masculinity.

Men in our society have been starved for something that will somehow connect them to their own deep Masculinity and encourage its expression. This explains the phenomenon known as the "Men's Movement." Great teachers such as Robert Bly, Michael Meade, Robert Moore, Malidoma Somé, Warren Farrell, Joseph Hillman, and Kenneth Druck have awakened many thousands of us to our yearning to know ourselves as men. The author's experience belies the premature obituaries for the Men's Movement that sometimes appear in the popular press. Throughout North America and in Great Britain—and now emerging in continental Europe, South Africa, New Zealand, and Australia—men continue to attend and provide New Warrior training programs. Similarly, men's councils and other men's groups are continuing to explore what it means to be male in this society, and how the Masculine will manifest in the new millennium.

Where men have been consciously and intentionally exposed to initiatory process, and have experienced the empowerment available in an initiated cohort, they are drawn further into unembarrassed exploration and expression of their manhood. Once men have a vision of what they *can* be, and sense that some portion of society welcomes this potential, they continue to broaden and deepen their masculinity. This is not merely an introspective, self-absorbed exercise. The initiated man understands that his life must be of service to his family, community, and world. In such service lies his ultimate self-esteem as a man.

At the moment, a subculture of initiated Masculinity is more a vision than something susceptible to ethnographic measurement. But as we awaken collectively to our social task of initiating young men of all classes and races, I predict that we will see further evidence of the emerging subculture, and will come to view its consolidation as essential to the realization of the mature Masculine. One vital function of the mature Masculine is nothing less than to cohere much of what is now disintegrating in our society.

SUMMARY

Tribal initiation is described. Initiation is viewed as essential to a male's cohesive sense of being a man in the world. This sense develops from the interaction of three separate and synergistic energies: ordeal energy; teaching-bonding energy; and healing-spiritual energy. Initiation involves separation of a boy from the mother's orbit to bond with a male cohort, and integrates his emotional identity as a man with a secure position as a valued member of the community. The lack of a "Culture of Initiated Masculinity" adds to the toxic shame of men in modern society. As the essential process of masculine emotional, social, and spiritual development (i.e., integration with self, community, and cosmos), initiation is both a powerful healer of internalized shame and a defense against its destructive effects.

NOTE:

---

[1] Initiation is best thought of as a process that opens the door to a new stage of further growth, or that marks a change in direction in a man's life. Transformation does not fully manifest overnight. Further initiation must occur as a maturing man individuates. For example, at some point a man must grow beyond his exclusive identification with the male group (Bernstein, 1987).

[2] I acknowledge with honor Larry Hall, Ph.D., for birthing this concept.

[3] For additional examples of the impact of initiation, see Christopher Miller's (1995) report on "Male Initiation, Filling a Gap in Therapy," and John Everingham's (1995b) discussion of the Shadow, masculine archetypes, and the New Warrior training in "Men Facing Shame: A Healing Process."

[4] I thank John Everingham for valuable discussions that helped me to clarify my thinking on this topic.

[5] Other programs, such as Men's Councils, are also notable in the effort to revive initiatory process.

Chapter 19
From Shame to Self-Esteem*

PHILIP M. POWELL

S hame occurs because we have been taught that something about ourselves is deeply flawed. We just don't have the right equipment to be the right kind of human being. The only antidote for shaming yourself and others is a permanent dose of higher self-esteem. Not the usual bubba like braggadocio. I mean real self-esteem. The kind that involves self-forgetting because you know you are all right, because you are both real and good as a human being. As Jewish people say, you're a mensch—a real human being. So, I am going to tell you how to grow into a real human being—one whom you can take to the bank of life with confidence.

To raise your self-esteem permanently, you must be willing to change, really change your approach to life. I'll show you how to do it. First, you need to understand yourself and there are certain tools to use for this. The most basic tool is William James's theory of the self and self-esteem (James, 1910), supplemented by the ideas of folks like Maslow (1955), Mayeroff (1990), and Sullivan (1953).

WILLIAM JAMES'S THEORY OF SELF-ESTEEM

James believed that the self had two basic ways of experiencing the world with two different modes of consciousness. These he called the "I" and the 'me." The "I" refers to thinking which is automatic or spontaneous but which occurs without reflecting on what you are doing. One example of "I" thinking is when you drive down a familiar road that you travel all the time. You just drove home while thinking about a thousand different things, all of which involved topics other than driving. This is the automatic "I" thinking. An example of spontaneous "I" thinking can be shown using the same example. Suppose something happened that was surprising while you were driving home, something like a gargoyle falling off one high building next to the road and landing right in front of you while you were driving. Assuming you survived this, the swerving you did to avoid the accident is an example of the spontaneous "I" thinking. You did not know the exact movements you would make to avoid hitting the falling gargoyle. The movements you made were spontaneous.

Interestingly enough, this also provides an example of the second form of thinking, called the "me." The moment you became conscious of the fact that you were in a situation which required evasive maneuvering to avoid the gargoyle, you were functioning in the "me" mode of thinking. Now let's be careful here. The "I" part of this car driving example includes the spontaneous movements you made to avoid the gargoyle. The "me" part of this involves you becoming aware that the situation of driving home this particular time is radically different from the usual trips home. If you did not become aware of this difference you would have died or been badly hurt. *The "me" then involves all moments of thinking when you are aware of what you are doing in order to modify your actions as needed.* It typically is induced by being surprised. You think you are going to have something happen one way but it happens another.

So being surprised leads to becoming aware that things in life don't have to happen like you expect them to. The result of "me" awareness is that you learn to be flexible, to take things on the fly, to take things with enough openness that you can change in even a familiar situation if something odd happens. Change does not have to involve bad outcomes. It can also involve good ones. How many a man has thought that he was not good looking in the eyes of a woman he was interested in, and one day he discovered that the woman not only liked him, but saw him as good looking too? So you can be very pleasantly surprised by life, and start seeing yourself as better than you thought you were.

Next, James said that the "me" was divided into three parts: material, social, and spiritual. "Material me" refers to your body and all physical objects you identify with, such as your car or favorite suit. "Social me" refers to all the prestige and recognition you receive. "Spiritual me" refers to all the deep, personal thoughts you think, and related actions you perform, as well as all the psychological faculties that allow you to act this way (memory, intelligence, character, morality, ideology, etc.). The catch is that these three me's are developmental, with the material being first, followed by the social and lastly by the spiritual. So we are one of these types of selves, more or less.

Depending on how we are treated, we develop certain feelings about ourselves. We strive to retain the status quo if we like our treatment, or we act to change our situation. Suppose we are ashamed of ourselves because we feel we are too fat. Then we will engage in what James called material self seeking. We might diet or we might continually make jokes to distract others from looking at our terrible bodies. Or we might become shy to avoid being "seen" by others. Suppose again, we are ashamed of ourselves socially—we just don't fit in. We don't have enough money to buy the right clothes, we don't get enough social attention, we never get promoted in our jobs, etc. What we will do, according to James, is seek ways to get social attention. We might dress in ways which dramatize our need for attention, even negative attention.

I once knew a woman who wore long black oversized dresses because she feared sexual attention. Once she started wearing stylish clothes, it became obvious that she was the finest looking woman around. But first she had to be encouraged by her friends, so that she would want the new attention.

Lastly there is spiritual self seeking. This refers to a person who feels that everything he does has to be deep and important. He rarely just has fun or looks at cartoons or stops reading the *New York Times.* He's obsessed with deep thoughts. The overall point of self seeking is that we all try to correct ourselves when we feel we lack something. And this is all right as long as such acts are temporary, but if they are permanent or chronic, they reflect serious self-esteem problems.

I know a man who can only talk about his ideas and *his* problems. He has serious spiritual self seeking behavior and has low self-esteem. He is trapped inside his own crap.

TYPES OF SELF-ESTEEM

James offered the first definition of self-esteem that was accepted in our culture. He defined self-esteem as equal to a high ratio of successes over pretensions (i.e. expectations). This leads to three basic levels of self-esteem: high, medium, and low.

High self-esteem means that you have a wide range of expectations or life goals you want to achieve and that you are achieving or have achieved. High self-esteem people are low in anxiety; they are risk takers. They are confident, popular, able folks who define who can hurt them and are rated as generally successful in what they do (Coopersmith, 1967). Low self-esteem people are anxious, take no risks, have little confidence, are unpopular, and tend to have or show less ability. Anyone can hurt them, and they are relatively unsuccessful.

Persons medium in self-esteem fall in the middle between high and low in these characteristics. Subtly, James' formula suggests some other types of self-esteem. One is defensive high self-esteem. This is a person who maintains a high level of self-esteem by focusing his attention and efforts to being successful in just a few areas of life. This is the so-called big fish in a little pond. We have all seen people who are hot stuff as long as they stay in their home town and work for their rich father or play basketball as the home town star. But if these people tried to move out into the big time they would fail—if they left their town, left their job, left the rich father, left their town to play ball in the pros.

There is a fifth type of self-esteem called the uncertain low. This is a person high in ability, but who is doing the wrong type of work or is associating with the wrong type of people to support him or her and feels bad about himself accordingly. So you see, we have five types of self-esteem categories, which are from highest to lowest: high, defensive high, medium, uncertain low, and low.

Only the first type of high, the true high, needs no self-esteem enhancement. All other self-esteem types need self-esteem improvement. Another thing, if you know your self-esteem is low, truly low, you need the help of a trained psychologist, psychiatrist, pastoral counselor, other mental health professional, or a transformational group process to help you work on your self-esteem. The procedures offered herein will help you and indeed you will have to do these too if you want to raise your self-esteem, but the anxieties and demons you will have to face will be much more difficult to handle alone than would be true for any of the higher self-esteem levels. I call the low just mentioned "true low" to distinguish it from uncertain low.

EIGHT STEPS TO IMPROVE SELF-ESTEEM

Here are eight steps to improve self-esteem. Follow these and self esteem is bound to rise. If any step becomes too difficult for you, seek the help of a counselor to help you examine the issues and feelings involved.

1. *Measure your level of self-esteem.* This can be done two basic ways: cognitively and emotionally. Here is the cognitive approach. First, list all of the important goals you want to achieve in your life. Second, decide honestly whether or not you are achieving these goals. If you are not, your self-esteem is low. If you are achieving some of your personal goals, your self-esteem is medium and if you are achieving all of them, your self-esteem is high. Next, decide if you have few goals or many. If your self-esteem is

high with few goals you are probably a defensive high. If your goals are many and you are achieving them, you are a true high. If you are a true high, you do not need this process at all, although it may interest you. Most likely, you are somewhere between true high and true low.

The emotional approach to measuring self-esteem involves assessing your feeling tone. Are you pessimistic in your attitude toward life? Or are you realistically optimistic, a person who smiles when he can? Is life a glass which is half empty or half full? Are you depressed much of the time like some sad sack or are you generally optimistic? If you tend to be pessimistic, depressed, and non enthusiastic about life, then you have a low(er) self-esteem. If you are realistically optimistic about your life and its many inter-actions and experiences, not denying bad things that occur to us all, but either always expecting the good stuff to happen to you, or at least trying to see the positive even in the negative, then you have higher self-esteem. Higher self-esteem people are more ener-gized and fun to be around. They tend to stimulate others to be excited about life, too.

2. *See yourself clearly.* This is tough. You may need another honest person to help you here. The goal is to see what type of self you are. Are you a material self, a social self, or a spiritual one? To do this we will use a question inspired by a test devised by Kuhn and McPartland (1954) and scored by measures using James' theory. Write down 20 answers to the question, "What kind of person am I?" Rate each of your answers as "material me," "social me," or "spiritual me." An answer is material if it refers to your physical body or to a physical object you own or respect. Examples: I am 6'4" tall and am a homeowner.

   A social answer refers to a role you play I am a father, a lover (yes, lover is a role—you are expected to act a certain way if you are someone's lover) or a friend. An answer is spiritual when it refers to a psychological characteristic that is peculiar to you as a person such as thoughtfulness or high morality. (Note that James said spiritu-al when we would say psychological.)

   If most of your answers are material ones then you are that type; if most are social, you are this type and so on. This gives you a key to the type of self seeking you are likely to be doing. If you rate yourself as social, you can bet that when you self seek it is done in the area of getting social attention. It tells you what you feel you lack in life!!!!

3. *Change your behavior.* There are eight changes you must undergo in a certain spirit.

   a. Stop engaging in *either-or thinking.* Nothing is either-or. Everything in this world is shades of gray. People mired in either-or thinking see life as a grand vaudevillian stage, where someone like God is waiting for them to make a mis-take before He will take a big Broadway hook and pull them off the stage for a bad performance. This just ain't so. We ain't angels or saints down here on earth. But you might get pulled off the stage of life for *not trying,* not doing the best you can, mistakes and all.

Learn from your mistakes. Learn to give a better performance next time by getting feedback now. So many folks hunger for perfection, rather than strive to be excellent. Perfection is not your destiny. Excellence is. Learn to pat yourself on the back when you are on the road to being better, when you take one step towards your goal. It's like learning to pat yourself on the back for playing the game of life at all. It's tough to be alive.

It's hard to be human. It's a thankless job. Guy goes to work every day making a living to support his family. That's good. Guy goes to a school play after working 10 hours to see poor acting from his kid. That's good. Guy goes to the hospital because his wife is sick. That's good. Learn to keep track of your own goodness, which is the greatest good. Your goodness will never be based on the great things you have done, but on the little things you do daily to sustain yourself and others. You can't be an either-or thinker to act this way. You will damn yourself before you even try.

b. Pay attention to how you dress. It is a truism that the lower the self-esteem, the poorer the dress. If you do not think well of yourself, then why dress nicely? When self-esteem rises, dress improves. This is because you honor yourself, so you start treating yourself better. As self-esteem truly rises, a man will start improving in small ways. This may be the only improvement noticeable at first, but it signals a deeper change within.

c. Present yourself like a winner. If you want to be promoted, act like you are promoted already. Act like those who are profitable. Do what they do. People with self-esteem problems act defeated. People "smell" this and use it against them. Sometimes people are like wolves, tracking a weaker wolf. So dress better, smile, work harder, respect yourself, pray and people will think more of you.

d. Change your friends. If you want to improve your self-esteem, move away from your old network of friends who have been supporting your lower self-esteem. Find other friends, positive people, who will support your improvement. Get a new job where you are valued, where you can create a new social history. Old friends and colleagues tried to treat you as you were—not as you are now. Screw them! Let someone new get the benefit of your new self. This is tough language, but our problems are tough. Tell certain people to screw off, because you have better things to do. One of ten first steps in change is to learn to say NO to anyone and everyone who needs you to do stuff that keeps you down.

e. Take feedback about your behavior but *never* about your essence. This is a subtle step. Never let anyone define who you are, but listen when an honest and accurate person tells you about how you are coming across to him. People in low self-esteem let everyone tell them how to be. They try to please even strangers. Forget this. Let people earn your ear by their deeds. Evaluate the source of feedback. Value accurate feedback even if it hurts, but never let someone tell you what you are.

f. Reflect about yourself and others. Learn to think about what you need, and act accordingly. Figure out what others need from you, and why. Then you can decide what you are going to do and whom you are going to please. Establish yourself as the author of your own existence. Become free.

g. Be consistent with who you are. To do this, you must have some idea of who you are and where you are going in life. If you decide to be a good person, this means you will not gossip about people, you will avoid hurting them even if they hurt you sometimes, you will walk an extra mile to do right as you understand it. Being consistent allows you to take responsibility and authority for your actions and decisions in peace.

h. Be genuinely concerned about yourself and others. This teaches you how to know and to care for yourself and for others (Mayeroff 1990). You need to take care of your needs first before you can help anyone else. Without this, you have only narcissistic, misguided meddling in the lives of others. There is nothing more annoying or boring than being the village narcissist. Also, no matter who you are you have got to learn some social skills to care for others. Here are five that are absolutely necessary:

- Learn how to speak to meet others with respect. Make eye contact. Smile more than you frown if the person is halfway interesting. Otherwise avoid them.
- Never talk down to anyone—treat them like they can raise as much hell or heaven as you.
- Follow the law of reciprocity—if someone helps you, repay them.
- Find folks that interest you so you can stop talking about yourself.
- Work hard, be honest and contribute to your family and society in any way you can.

Following these social rules guarantees that you will be a social success with genuine friends. You will die happy and a crowd of folks will attend your funeral.

4. *Show your true self.* This has three parts:

a. Handle pain and view it differently. Pain is always a sign that something is wrong with the way we are living. It is always positive information. So listen to your body. Take a moment now while you are reading this to calm down and notice any pain in your body or your mind. Now promise yourself to take care of whatever the problem is. Notice that this involves correcting your thinking as well as your actions. When you do this, the pain improves, even if it is cancer! I firmly believe that you can heal yourself if you change your thoughts, actions and feelings.

When you change your thoughts and actions, your feelings must change because you are creating different experiences for yourself. Most importantly start to notice that your pain is always connected to your negative thoughts. This is true for bodily pains, but most true for thoughts you have, painful expectations. I often notice soreness in my joints because I have gout. This reminds me to consume less wine and red meat. I can simply modify my diet to lose weight, without putting myself down for being overweight, which never helps. Correct the problem, but never blame the self, because it is the only tool we have for living.

b. Take vacations. Going on a vacation does not mean planning everything like you do at work, accounting for your time. "Vacation" means to leave what you normally do and do something relaxing. Workaholics don't take vacations. They arrange field trips and activities to occupy every waking moment. They even create activities for the whole family and make everyone feel guilty when they don't want to participate. Take a real vacation to gather new perspectives and relax the body to alleviate pent-up stress and prolong life. Stay away from workaholic, type A personalities on vacations. Leave them home.

c. Accept responsibility for yourself. This involves three related aspects: (a) Explore what you want to do in your life and do it, and explore what you want to become; (b) blame your life on no one; and (c) do things for yourself. Exploring what you want to do and become is important as it keeps you on the path of self-actualization. Never con yourself. I once knew a person who always talked about how her life would be different if she had been a painter. So I asked to see her work. Lo and behold, it was good stuff, but she had never tried to market it. So I told her that I knew some artists connected with well known galleries who might be able to help her. She never took me up on this suggestion! Some people are just afraid to change the way they live. You've got to lose this fear. You've got to put up or shut up.

Blame your life on no one. Everybody has had bad things and good things happen to them and theirs. There is always someone with an even worse life. Also, some of the negative—hell all of the negative and all of the positive, experiences created your self in the first place. You can't be you and blame your life too. That's contradictory.

5. *Meet your basic needs first so you can grow.* Maslow's (1955) theory of self actualization tells us that deficiency motivation must be taken care of before growth motivation can begin life. Deficiency motivation refers to a set of needs being met strictly in this order: 1) physical needs (food, clothing, housing); 2) a safe environment; 3) accept-

ance by others; and 4) self-esteem. Deficiency motivation operates differently from growth motivation. Once you get deficiency needs met, you stop needing to think about them. Growth needs always involve you wanting them more and more. There are two growth needs, the need to self-actualize and the need to understand existence fully These needs become evident only as self-esteem problems decrease in your life. This leads to our next big step.

6. *Reconstruct your self-concept.* People with self-esteem problems always have the basic problem of a dysfunctional self-concept. We have already measured self-concept with the "kind of person" test described earlier. You have to take your list and throw away any "I am" statement that does not reflect what you want to do with your life. Junk any component which is what someone else wants, not you.

I learned an important theory when I was drinking one night. My friend, name of Rufus, is rough, tough and very intelligent. He's a decent guy who drove tanks in the war. He calls his theory the "crap" theory of human development, although crap isn't exactly the name he used. When a guy's bag gets too heavy he sidles up to another guy, sort of friendly like, and puts some of his crap in the guy's bag. You've got to watch your bag to see that it contains your crap and no one else's. If you don't you will be living out the implications of someone else's crap and not your own. This sounds funny but it ain't. It's worth remembering.

Pick new roles you want to play in life and play them with all your heart. Personally I discovered quite by accident that I like to talk to men's groups, to the gifted, to kids and to any folks who are trying to grow and figure that I can help them. I don't like real formal meetings because "I ain't much for airs and such." I like Texas because a lot of people here are the same as me—earthy, proud, reasonably hard working, and God fearing. I figure the world is full enough of highfalutin folks so it doesn't need me as an extra one. I got to live the way I know is best for me and I am ruthlessly pursuing my life from this viewpoint.

Learn new work. By new work, I mean that you will find that by being real about who you are, you will naturally do things that feel right. You will place yourself in the best position to discover what God wants you to do with your life. You will start doing it with a zeal that can be scary. And once you live this new way you will find yourself rising in Maslow's hierarchy of needs—your deficiencies will be corrected and folks will know that when they deal with you, they are dealing with the real *megallah*, the real thing. That's rare. It may be totally different work, or the same work with your personal groove in it, your emphasis stamped all over it. Find this one groove and you are home free.

Never derogate yourself. We all have a ton of negative thoughts. Keep a diary of these thoughts and make every attempt to stamp them out. I call this the "killing the roaches" substep of self-concept change. Don't keep putting yourself down. There are plenty of cynics and bastards who will bad-mouth you. You simply can't afford to do it to yourself. As Winston Churchill might have said, "Never, never, never, never, never give up on yourself".

The biggest roach you have to kill is the ideal self—all those fancy goals you have. All you've got is yourself now. Don't wait to live. Live now. Do your best now. Put all that fancy crap in the fireplace where it belongs, if you can stand the stench. God accepts you in heaven if you start right now, so don't postpone living right. What about the negatives that still come into your life after you have purged yourself of the tendency to put yourself down? I've got an answer for this, too. Analyze negatives for useful information. If there is nothing useful being said, blow it off.

Leave all bad environments. A bad environment is any place or social situation which is dangerous to your growth. This includes marriages, family relationships, ideological beliefs, jobs, even towns, where you do not fit. Drop them as soon as you can, but be practical as you go. Finally expect shakeups of energies as you grow and explosions too as you give up unnecessary defenses. What is happening is that all selves have what Harry Stack Sullivan (1953, pp. 158-171), an Irish-American psychiatrist, once called "good me, bad me and not me" experiences in life.

"Good me" experiences are those where somebody told you you were good and you felt good as a result. You remember your "good me" experiences. You can remember "bad me" experiences with anxiety. "Not me" experiences are those where you broke some taboo and were punished or shamed so badly that you actually repressed and denied these experiences. They are unconscious roaches.

Often when you start working on self-esteem, you will remember instances of childhood abuse which lie at the base of your low self-esteem. How could you learn self-esteem when your true self was rejected in such a painful way? How can you trust that anyone could ever truly love you if your family rejected you? You are permanently ashamed. In severe cases, you feel you are better off dead. Once your self-esteem raises though, you release these fears. Fears bind energy. So expect outbursts of energy which will allow you to both work and play harder!

Finally meditate and relax whenever you need to. This clears the mind and body and will prolong your life. I recommend *How to Meditate* by Lawrence LeShan (1975).

7. *Be realistic in trusting yourself and others.* Accurately examine yourself to see where you are trustworthy If you are a blabber-mouth, ask others not to tell you their deeper secrets because you talk too much. I actually heard a person say this once. Or if a friend talks too much you will be careful about what you say around them. You just accept some personal limitations and the limitations of others.

8. *Be honest yet merciful with yourself.* Give yourself credit for your intentions and behavior as long as you are being productive in the way you personally define it. After all, it's your life, not your family's or society's. You have to live and die for yourself. At this point, your self-esteem is permanently on the rise. Shame is not a part of your vocabulary although you will have a new type of guilt. You will feel guilty any time you are not true to yourself.

Life is like a bank. It's filled with money, pleasure, love, grace, opportunity, growth, and a whole host of God-given experiences. Self-esteem is the way out of shame and despair, a way to get your piece of the action, your share of the bank of life. Interested?

NOTE:

* This chapter reflects ideas based on 20 years of teaching and studying self-esteem. Some of these ideas have been presented in workshops at two International Men's Conferences held in Austin, TX (1992), and in New Braunfels, TX (1993).

Chapter 20
Open Sesame:
When Shame Turns to Gold

JOHN S. GUARNASCHELLI

I sign my name to the entry roster at the gym. Unexpectedly, the desk attendant compliments my handwriting. I recoil with a dismissive joke, and quickly change the subject.

A friend offers me the opportunity to participate in an important project and earn a fair amount of money. I delay my response until the opportunity vanishes.

A man I'm fond of speaks to me in a warm, openhearted way. I cannot look him in the eye, or accept what he is offering.

I have come to recognize that my feelings in these situations are dominated by Shame, and that these feelings of Shame have been central to my experience both as a boy and as a man.

Most of the men I meet in the course of my work have also experienced this Shame. In the simple logic of things, there must, in fact, be some men somewhere who have not been shamed. So far, I haven't met any. Not only does the experience seems universal, but I have reached the conclusion that in our society, Shame functions as the normal master-control of men's feelings.

So, overcoming Shame is essential to healing men's hearts – that is, to opening men to a rich, internally truthful relationship with the whole of themselves, and thus with other men, with women, with animals, and with the earth itself. Men's Soul Work, or any work with men, will have to confront Shame as the chief obstacle to accomplishing positive results.

CAUSES OF SHAME

Any hope of healing Shame must begin with an understanding how it is inflicted or caused. It seems obvious that we must first understand Shame's methods in order ultimately to heal its effects. I am convinced that such understanding does not exist today. I have read a good deal of the available popular and professional work on Shame. Most of that literature is quite instructive when it explores Shame's symptoms and how Shame is experienced in everyday life. But I have yet to encounter a convincing explanation of how Shame is generated.

So, how may we approach this feeling that so resolutely resists access? How is Shame created? How, precisely, does it operate? What are its symptoms and consequences?

As a beginning point, I believe that no person is born into the world in a shamed state. Whatever differences of endowment or personality appear among newborn babies, every child is born into the world equipped and ready to be itself. Basically, then, Shame must be taught.

I am convinced that Shame is generated from the shaming behaviors visited upon us – consciously and unconsciously – as we grow from infancy through childhood to adulthood. However invisibly they do it, shamed people pass on their Shame. In a word, Shame begets Shame. And its "educational impact" is especially powerful during the early years. It is then that we encode into our own unconscious the feelings and emotional patterns appropriate to the world we are made to believe we are entering. As children, we learn swiftly and well.

On a recent plane flight, I watched a radiant, blond-crowned girl, not quite two years old. Her father raised her high so she could explore the overhead light switches and fresh air tubes. She was in her glory. Then she lunged for the button that would summon the flight attendant. Her father spoke not a word of reproach. He did not slap her hand or physically punish her in any way, but his own sudden and unexpressed feeling – whatever it was – impelled him to very swiftly grab her hand, blocking her from hitting that button.

Instantly, glory turned to grief. Darkness occluded radiance. Her smile dissolved into a frown and a wail. She propelled herself from her father's now hurtful arms into the clearly more consoling ones of her mother in the neighboring seat. There, her crying continued. For all his previous care, the father now simply broke out his newspaper, and, with his own needs satisfied and embarrassment averted, felt no further concerns or responsibility to deal with the situation being experienced by his child.

In my seat across the aisle, I was meditating on the writing of this article. Even as I felt sad for the little girl, I knew I'd been presented with a perfect example of Shame's origins. Her tears were certainly born out of her feeling that she had suddenly and inexplicably done something very wrong. How had happy play so suddenly become worthy of reproach? Confused, she had no certain idea. But the swiftness of daddy's gesture conveyed all the clarity required – the certainty that she had been wrong. However little the girl understood intellectually of what had happened, she was in no danger whatever of missing the point emotionally.

Almost instantaneously, memories flowered into my mind of an incident I'd experienced when I was about the same age as the little girl. My parents had left me with friends I didn't know well. Their family was large, and many people taller than I filled the kitchen with talk and pre-dinner hurly-burly. I felt alone, shy, and afraid. So I clung to the foot of a radiator at one side of the room. I must have shaken it because a vase on top of it fell over. The vase didn't fall to the ground or break because Belle, one of the family daughters, rushed over and restored the vase to upright. At the same time, while speaking harsh words, now unremembered, she roughly pulled me away from the radiator. I can still remember my feelings of forlorn devastation. I'd clearly done something very, very wrong, and I wished that the floor would open up and swallow me forever. But, from their point of view, as long as good order was being restored atop the radiator, whatever I was feeling obviously didn't matter.

Over subsequent years, my family lost contact with that family. Thirty years later, Belle entered a wedding reception I was attending. At the sound of her voice behind me, I immediately spoke her name and turned. She was astounded that I had recognized her. But my two-year-old feelings, instantly present with the same devastating force as 30 years before, left me not a second's doubt about who she was.

Once learned as a child, such shaming persists unabatedly into adulthood. At a European site, a group of older tourists was visiting a famous ancient temple located on a mountainside. After walking through three areas of the temple, a rather heavy set, middle-aged woman sat down to rest rather than climb the very steep hill to the temple's final area. Returning to the tour bus, a man of similar age and girth entered, exclaiming loudly about how absolutely wonderful that fourth temple area was. Then he smoothly turned to the woman, with whom he had previously had almost no interaction, and equally loudly proclaimed, "Oh, but you can enjoy the pictures." The woman's feelings of shame about her weight and her age were fairly obvious from her expression. But then, so were the man's!

In the above incidents are fair examples of the first major way Shame is inflicted, and how the cycle of Shame perpetuates itself. I was subjected to what might best be called obvious, aggressive Shame. As an infant, I was born into the world endowed with the healthy ability to grow into the full potential of my life. Everything I did and felt operated in the service of realizing this goal of learning how to live well. All I needed was supportive guidance into adulthood. Instead, Shame was inflicted on me. It was inflicted whenever my caregivers or my culture rejected, opposed, or set at naught who I was, what I wanted, or how I wanted it. This was done repeatedly until, as a result, I entered my adult life impaired by Shame… and simply continued to pass it on because it is what I knew.

Shaming, therefore, occurs because our caregivers' own original needs, wants, qualities, or abilities were previously shamed. Whenever my conduct (however unconsciously) aroused their own shame fear of that same need, quality, or ability, because it was implicitly perceived as manifest in my behavior, they rejected who or what I was.

The emotion of fear, then, is the source and active trigger of adult shaming behavior. Such fear acts in one of two general ways. Either I fear that you possess some gift I am not allowed to possess. Or, I fear that you will not obtain for me in my place the gift that I am not allowed to possess. From either motive, I reject or abandon you, your need, what is in you. As a consequence, a shamed person has generally learned Shame in two major ways. First, caregivers model it. We "see" it in their behavior. Second, they inflict it and make it into the reality of their own real, personal experience.*

In the above examples, it is clear the father's personal aptitude for uninhibited play and pleasure has long since been buried beneath his fear of social embarrassment. His daughter must, therefore, be stopped from pushing that button, and her ensuing distress is clearly less important to him than the latest newspaper. Belle's fear of disorder and consequent need for control bury any sensitivity for herself, so how could she possibly feel anything for a "disorderly" two-year old? The middle-aged tourist's fear of his own obesity and advancing years leads him to demean the woman who had manifested care for those things in herself.

As a general rule in everyday life, we usually confront only the surface of other people's behavior. They simply stop our hand. They just restore a vase and gruffly pull us away. They make an offhand humorous remark about climbing the hill. This is particularly true if the people are close or familiar, and their patterns of inflicting Shame are long since accepted as normal. Entirely oblivious of its underlying emotional impact, we take their behavior for granted and at face value. Consequently, the fear-based attacks that create Shame operate much like hostile torpedoes invisibly launched beneath the surface of a deceptively placid sea. The assault being delivered is not ordinarily available for our scrutiny. Yet, beneath the apparently normal surface of everyday behavior, Shame's basic dynamic – a continual, fear-based war motivated by clashing needs and waged in total darkness – operates with lethal effect. Because of what I so urgently (fearfully) need, what you need or feel does not matter and must be disregarded, pushed aside, buried. Ultimately, what you are, whatever you need, simply cannot "exist" here.

The image of repeated confrontation with rigid, rock-solid limits might serve to describe the daily experience of Shame. I am born with the potential for sailing the entire sea of my life. As I grow older, however, the walls of massive, not-quite-visible icebergs continually block my emotional entrance into certain areas of that sea. Slowly but surely, I learn to fear even the thought of hitting against these dangerous barriers. More and more I sail only in the areas that I perceive as "safe," no matter how diminished and contorted they are. Later, as an adult, the threatening prohibitions are actually removed. I am, in fact, free to roam life's entire sea. But emotionally, I can no longer even imagine such freedom. No matter how reduced or distorted, I continue to sail only within the areas – according to the emotional patterns – into which I was earlier constrained.

In sum, Shame is fundamentally a repeated form of rejection…rejection expressed, rejection received. It originates in the Shame and consequent fear-based needs of the person who initiates the attack. And it is experienced as an assault against one or more vital aspects of the self, even when, or perhaps especially when, a person is unaware of it.

SHAME AS VIOLENCE

When Shame's essence as a form of violence is clear, it must be emphasized that its assaults may be quite attractively, subtly, or indirectly packaged. It may be experienced under neutral, or even outwardly supportive, appearances. This version of Shame might best be called passive Shame.

Growing up, Bill's mother's physical, verbal, and emotional blows were rained upon him. His father stood back from all this – a smiling, neutral figure who, to all appearances, took no part in the abuse of his son. Because Bill habitually focused on his mother's violence, he always regarded his father as, at least, not harmful to him. Only recently has Bill begun to realize how his "neutral" father never supported or protected him against the abuse he routinely received from his mother. In the bargain, he now realizes his father never spoke to him, touched him, went anywhere together with him, or made any time for him at all. In fact, Bill is gradually realizing that his "neutral" father provided almost nothing he needed as a young boy, beyond basic food and shelter, and was actually quite hostile toward him.

All through high school, Jason's father, who never completed the fifth grade, enthusiastically stressed how much he wanted his son to earn a college degree. In due course, Jason fulfilled this dream by earning a Ph.D. from a prestigious eastern university. Jason fully expected his father to be proud of his achievement. Instead, he has recently become aware of his father's frequent contemptuous remarks about "overpaid men with degrees" in his business who "don't know what they're doing." It has been extremely difficult for Jason to understand why his father might fear and demean his education after so often exhorting him to pursue it. At the last, Jason has even begun to wonder whose desires he actually fulfilled by earning his advanced degree.

Martin attended a Little League baseball game during a visit to his brother's family. At the field, young fathers, mostly in their middle thirties, stood on the sidelines, continually screaming their "support" for their eight-year-old sons' performances. Looking at the young boys, Martin could see only their fear of not living up to their fathers' expectations. He wonders if and how the boys could possibly preserve any sense of their own desire beneath the fierce load of "support" they were receiving from their fathers.

The fundamentally aggressive nature of Shame can never be forgotten. But it must always be remembered that "kindly" invasiveness or quiet, "unassertive" withdrawal may assault and abandon just as aggressively as overtly abusive language or behavior... perhaps even more so. In cases of passive Shame, the person is shamed either through neglect, lack of support, withholding of recognition, or through emotional co-option and subtle subversion. Silence may be as shaming as shouting. Kindness may be more deadly than cruelty. And, in fact, because of the apparently neutral or positive camouflage under which passive Shame operates, it may be both the more difficult to detect and ultimately the more damaging. It will, nonetheless, have exactly the same ultimate effect as its more aggressive forms. Either way, my needs or your needs are not worthy of respect. We are not allowed to belong to ourselves.

Its foundation in either aggressive or passive violence allows us to grasp several important qualities of Shame that will be crucial for any effort at healing it to be successful. The first is that the act of shaming must not be confused with the tone or manner of an interaction between people... or, indeed, with any one method of inflicting it. Gruff, derisive, or brutal words implying rejection or contempt are usually easy to see as shaming. But, a sweet, kind, or humorous tone may actually inflict Shame in a far more destructive way. Witness how all sorts of "kindly distractions" routinely invalidate the real feelings of small children. The only true measure of Shame is its actual impact upon feelings. If I feel shamed, with a loss of something really mine, then my Shame is real.

So speaking concretely, men who had an obviously abusive father, accompanied by a kinder or long-suffering mother, are often at an incapacitating loss to grasp the nature of their present Shame. Just what did their kindly, long-suffering mother cost them? On the other hand, men who have had an obviously abusive mother may ultimately have a relatively easy time becoming aware of the profound needs or qualities for which their mother shamed them. At the same time, these men are likely to have a difficult time realizing the harmful effects of their distant or silent fathers.

Burt's mother was a refuge of kind understanding in the face of his father's drunken and physically abusive rages. She often held and consoled him while they shared long hours of intimate feeling. Today, his father's abuse is clear to him. But it is nearly impossible for Burt to see that his mother's affectionate intimacy was almost entirely in the service of her own fear-filled needs and very little in his. He was being used for her consolation, which was essentially abuse. Today Burt cannot understand why his own needs and goals feel so shamed and inaccessible to him. Among the major things he cannot understand is why his intense need to have a woman in his life is accompanied by his "fear of commitment." As is the case with so many men who have been used/abused by their mothers in this way, he cannot grasp how any intimacy now would once more place him in familiar emotional danger.

Confusing Shame with tone or manner can lead to seriously mistaken efforts in the healing process. An internationally respected organization that presents weekend workshops for men begins with an invasion of the men's suitcases and frequent seizure of personal property; this is consciously modeled on a recruit's humiliating and depersonalizing entry into boot camp. As in boot camp, the personal items seized are even referred to as "contraband." It has been pointed out to the leadership that this is profoundly shaming. Since the men who offer this workshop are genuinely good-willed, they have responded to this criticism by somewhat softening the tone of the process. Unfortunately, a change in manner does not in the least modify the humiliating Shame potentially inflicted – the deep invasion of personal space, the right to privacy, the sense of one's own possessions, and bodily safety. Whatever the tone of voice, the violation remains.

SHAME AS EMOTIONAL EXPERIENCE

The second important quality that flows from Shame's origin in violence is the realization that it is essentially an emotional experience. It is a learned pattern of deep feeling, habitual energy shaped by repeated encounters with what really lurks beneath the surface of everyday discourse.

With tears welling in his eyes, John tells of playing with his young nephews at his brother's house. For some reason, his brother flew into an explosive rage in the next room. John and his two nephews were not the direct objects of the rage. They had no "logical" connection to it, but their play abruptly terminated, and all three fled upstairs together in terror. When John sat down at an upstairs desk, his two-year-old nephew approached, his body heaving with inexpressible tears. At two, his nephew could not comprehend what had occurred, but the overwhelming intensity of his feelings filled his little body beyond its capacity. Afterward, John realized that he would not be able to heal his own terrified reactions until he understood what those deep feelings triggered by the event were.

Because, even when experienced obliquely as in this case, most shamed feelings flee into the unconscious, I am often not aware I feel any feelings at all, much less that I feel Shame. Consequently, intuition, imagination, and thought may all certainly assist me to understand and heal Shame. But unless what I really feel is directly confronted, I will never truly experience or heal my Shame. In preparation, therefore, I must learn both how to feel and how to identify my emotions in order to enter the place where Shame resides. Thus, in therapy I must necessarily become aware of feelings and aware of Shame in my feelings, because no deep healing can occur without that. There must be a compensating emotional experience.

TARGETS OF SHAME

Third, it is most important to remember that whether aggressive or passive, whether abusive or sugarcoated, Shame's repeated attacks are always triggered against quite specific targets. Specifically, if my intelligence has been shamed, a display of your intelligence will arouse my unconscious fear. Either I'll find ways to discount your intelligence, or I'll invalidate it by driving you to be super-intelligent for my purposes. If my sense of agency has been attacked, any manifestation of your power will provoke my hostility. Or I may somehow seduce you into being powerful for me, in my stead. If my sexuality has been shamed, I will somehow denigrate yours… or stimulate yours to excess for my purposes. If my neediness as a child, my need to be seen, my need to be validated, supported, or heard were all ignored, I will abandon your needs, leaving you unseen, invalidated, unsupported, and unheard. If my joy and laughter… And so on, and on, and on, through the whole range of human needs, qualities, and styles in a continuous series of assaults against specific parts of what we were born with. I cannot bear your having what I specifically fear I do not have and did not get. Somehow I will shut you down… either by frustrating your desires or by demanding you surrender your desires and live out mine in very specific ways that serve my needs.

Shame begins in connection with single, specific targets, for example, my desire to grow into a mature, independent adult by becoming an artist. I have shame related to my lustiness, my curiosity about prehistoric African fauna, my love for rock music, my reading difficulties, my difficulties with women. I also have shame related to all areas of sexuality, with all kinds of issues about having and not having enough money and with wanting to be noticed. And as long as I remain unhealed, I will, of course, continue to feel Shame in connection with these specific aspects of myself. We might call this the first level of Shame.

CHRONIC SHAME

It is crucial to be aware of Shame's individual "gateways" into feelings, because repeated rejection or abandonment of specific, individual qualities very soon expands beyond them into more general consequences. Continuous repetition reinforces the original Shame feeling and causes it to deepen. It then graduates beyond the individual areas where it was initially inflicted and becomes a more complex feeling, a "two-level" experience. At this second level, I can feel Shame in a global way, quite independent of the specific places where I first experienced it. In effect, I feel ashamed of my self. And I can feel ashamed of myself at any and all times. This feeling of Shame has attached itself to every aspect of my being. It is attached even to those parts of me that were not originally attacked. This level of feeling Shame has appropriately been labeled Chronic Shame. When Shame has attained this level of pervasiveness, it acts as the dominant ingredient of my personality.

The heart of Chronic Shame is that it controls what I feel and what I don't feel about what I feel. However unconsciously, it lurks in judgment over all my energies. Chronic Shame condemns my feelings and activities; it condemns my very being, along with everyone and everything else in the world. It indicts nearly everything I think, say, or do. I act out its negation in all my activities and relationships. In its acute stages, feelings of Chronic Shame become a nearly intolerable "weight" pressing down on how I live.

In a nearby bookstore, I watched Chronic Shame being born. A nine-year-old boy pleaded intensely with his father for a G. I. Joe comic book full of machine guns and rat-a-tat-tat. The father was clearly an advocate for peace and non-violence. Though heavily breathing his fear and resistance, he could not refuse his son outright because of his convictions. After all, a clear "no" would have been a kind of violence. Instead, he repeated with increasing insistence that his son wouldn't like that book, wouldn't enjoy it, and didn't really want it – in direct contradiction to everything his son had expressed, thus denying even his right to want something. After a considerable time, the son realized his passionate pleas were in vain. From his intensity, his reddened face, and the near tears in his downcast eyes, it was evident this situation had happened many times before. Obviously frustrated and angry, he had once again not gotten what he had wanted and not even been allowed to want it. And I was left to wonder how this chronically shamed boy might perpetuate the enormous violence taught him every day by his "peace-loving" parent… about ten years from now, and in my neighborhood.

As a consequence of Chronic Shame – especially if the shaming begins in early childhood, as was the case with the boy in the previous paragraph and is usually the case with most of us – we grow ever more wary of our parents and early caregivers. Eventually, any bonds of trust, connection, and love for them will feel irreparably broken or, at the least, seriously damaged. If I feel that my parents don't love me, then it must be my fault. I must not be lovable.

In the logic of a child, he or she thinks that the all-knowing and powerful parents would certainly love their child if he or she were worth loving, because that is what parents do. In response and in defense of the survival of the self, the child then feels that he can't love his parents… or, perhaps more accurately, the child can't trust them or depend on them. The child will gradually expand such mistrust to most other people and to the world around him. The child might then even be labeled or label himself as "having a problem with authority," but will certainly act against his best interest whenever "authority" rears its ugly head.

Contrary to all the "good advice" urging unqualified forgiveness for parents who "did the best they could," such mistrust must at least initially be considered an accurate and entirely justified reaction to actual experience, even when it endures into adulthood. After all, the caregivers were the initiators of rejection and may legitimately be suspected of having lacked connection with the child in the first place. Indeed, what else really explains their utter lack of "connection" with the infant and his growing needs? What other feelings should a child live by, if not those generated in him by actual experience? They must at least serve as the starting point for any genuine contact with one's own feelings, any genuine attempt to first acknowledge and then to heal this Shame.

As a concomitant byproduct of mistrust for caregivers, lack of trust, connection, or affection will also be turned against the self, turned inward against one's own desires. I may then go through life feeling an incomprehensible rage over all my "bad" qualities. I may feel a continual anger against my unforgivable self. I may end up permanently "floating" in a sort of amorphous internal world, a "fog" where nothing is clear, certain, or reliable – especially not anything in my own damned and unworthy feelings. In my experience of the world around me, no person or thing will feel either definite or trustworthy. With no clear sense of my own right to understand or exist in the world, I feel like a "fog," and live in a "fog." I may not have enough coherent energy at my disposal to make any sort of effort on my behalf. No one has ever been "in my corner." It is now impossible for me ever to be in my own. I can never say "I" or "my" with any confidence whatever.

Men in the grip of this sort of Chronic Shame seem to resort to one of two general strategies. They may lose any real awareness of themselves by "forgetting" that they have a physical body or any feelings in it. Unaware of any "data" from those sources, they will get entirely "into their heads." They will deal with almost every aspect of life by intellectualizing. Adrift within themselves, they may become obsessed with clarity and order. Everyone and everything must be subjected to their need for this order.

Or, they may preserve some sense of body and emotions, "forgetting" they have a mind. Too befuddled to understand their feelings or to deal with them effectively, they will turn their lives into disorganized chaos.

In either case, they will have lost major parts of themselves and their ability to understand themselves. They will not know how to direct their lives in an effective or successful manner; neither will they know how to relate to others.

This is also to say that as a shamed person, I react to the assaults visited upon me by increasingly inhibiting, weakening, or invalidating the aspects of myself that are unacceptable. From one point of view, I react "depressively" to protect myself from further insult. From another, I have learned to feel "depressively" toward my own qualities. Either way, I display who or what I am less and less, and, finally, perhaps not at all. I use much or all of my energy in an internal assault against myself, precisely modeled on how I was assaulted, to inhibit or kill my own energies. Controlled by Shame, I fearfully erase my own needs or desires from my life. To a lesser or greater degree, I keep whatever I need, want, or feel out of play. In effect, Shame always tells me, "Be careful. Stop. Don't." And now, angry, and fearful of so much, I am perfectly positioned to continue inflicting the cycle of Shame on others.

SHAME CAUSES GENDER ROLES

At this point, it is not difficult to observe that Chronic Shame, if not the fundamental, is the defining ingredient in what is regarded as typical male gender behavior. Full proof of this idea is clearly beyond the scope of this article. But we may take a moment to explore some of the salient wounds that Chronic Shame, by definition, imposes on men in our culture.

As a starting point, it seems obvious that men's inborn capacity for kindness, gentleness, vulnerability, and feelings in general, has been under the sort of attack we have been describing… perhaps for centuries. Implicit expectations from both mother and father that a boy in childhood should act "like a little man" shame a boy's fear and uncertainty, shame his early needs for holding, cuddling, reassurance, and support. Shaming his tears – "big boys don't cry" – attacks his emotions and sensitivity. In adolescence, the "obvious" requirement is that he be physically tough, competitive, casually indifferent to his appearance, and stoic in the face of pain... nowhere more devastatingly than on the sports field. Any awareness of or appreciation for his male body (and with it, "excessive" care for his health, clothing, or appearance) will normally remain shamed for the rest of his lifetime. In adulthood, similar expectations that he be unfailingly strong, practical, and productive so he can "keep his job and make the grade" routinely stifle emotional sensitivity and creative intelligence.

It is, therefore, legitimate to suspect that Shame is, in fact, the major source of the "typical" male roles in society, and that what passes for "being a man" is the direct consequence of Shame. A football player dad routinely shames his violin-playing son. A lawyer dad routinely shames his mechanic son. An unexpressive, "manly" father shames his expressive, affectionate son. Unsupported himself, a father simply cannot "be there" to validate whoever his son is. And this does not even begin to address mother's very substantial participation in the process of sustaining "true manliness" in her sons.

All of this prepares men only for submission to a lifetime of industrial or corporate "stoicism"… and an early death. But, granted no permission whatever for being their genuine selves, men willingly take refuge in their assigned roles. Thoroughly conditioned Do-ers, and never Be-ers, we will unquestioningly sacrifice body and soul to the demands of work and providing support for our loved ones imposed upon us throughout our lifetimes. Today, expected to surrender this fictitious "dominance" at work, we are, nonetheless, still required to observe "the other half of the bargain" by caring for and catering to all the traditional female needs at home. The oppression of coal miners or assembly line workers is obvious. Far less obviously, even those supposed master dominators, the CEOs of corporations, entirely surrender themselves in thought, word, and deed to the business system's all-devouring requirements.

Rather than shaping men to exercise "domination" or "masculine privilege," then, traditional male upbringing hollows men out and makes them unfeeling automatons without needs, virtual slaves without rights.

Of course, with almost every major need rejected, the very last characteristic men or women will tolerate in "a real man" is "neediness," any impulse to abandon male stoicism and redefine male roles – that, too, is shamed. Feminist mothers and fathers and doctrinaire schoolteachers may contribute to his "privileged" situation by shaming him for even being a male in the first place. And, for about 35 years, much of the enormous self-sacrifice and contribution to human society men have made in the past 9,000 years has been subjected to similar abuse.

Shamed to the core, it is unfortunately also entirely logical that so many men will steadfastly refuse to acknowledge their present state. Most men truculently deny any problem exists at all. These are the men who demand that anyone questioning the system should "stop whining, and act like a man." The basic wound perpetuates itself because it denies itself.

WHO AM I?

Raising any question about realizing who I genuinely am necessarily obliges me to deny what I've been socialized to believe I am: someone who must never be concerned about himself. There is no way out. It should be clear that it is so difficult to establish a "Movement" sympathetic to men precisely because it is so desperately needed. There is very little sympathy for men or the needs of men, even on the part of men. It should, therefore, come as no surprise to any one, that a number of men energetically join extreme feminists in some of the most vicious and unjustified attacks on men.

Against the prevailing vogue of the past three decades, there is a way of assessing the consequences of male "training" in a way friendly to men. By the time most boys have grown into men, Shame has essentially stripped away substantial parts, if not all, of the endowment they're born with. They have been "hollowed out"... basically shamed for being. Now, when each boy is expected to live up to "being a man," he must effectively reject almost all that he truly is. His qualities and his needs must remain permanently unseen and unsupported... kept hidden even from himself. In the final analysis, it should be perfectly clear that most men have been hurt so deeply that they cannot subsequently reveal themselves or be vulnerable or "available" in relationships. When their very being is under constant threat, can it possibly come as a surprise that most – if not all – boys become distant, fearful, angry men? Yet today, even this minimal self-protection is hurtfully labeled "fear of commitment."

In everyday behavior, men react to their Shame by forging lives in two general ways that are quite opposed to one another in outward appearance. The majority of shamed men react by trying to "justify" their right to exist. To do this, they must achieve, racing ever faster to overwhelm and rise above their Shame. If only I try harder, then surely more effort, more work, more money, more women, power, achievement, promotion, position, two cars, a bigger house, prestigious vacations... any or all of these will somehow render me worthy of love and of having life! Of course, by desperately seeking all these things out of the total void and by the essential negation of them inside myself means I can only "get" what I lack for myself by "plundering" others... by competing. Make no mistake, however: modern society will "reward" me for living my life in this fashion... probably with six figures... and an early death.

A second group of men reacts to Shame in precisely the opposite fashion, by succumbing to it. These are the "underachievers" who fail to accomplish "what they're supposed to" as men. Society usually does not reward this behavior. It condemns these men "losers" or "drop outs." Perhaps they don't marry and don't shoulder their responsibilities and are, therefore, suspected of not "really being men" at all.

Difficult as it may appear to reconcile these two strategies, Chronic Shame must be seen as the common root of both. In both, I never perceive myself or allow others to perceive me as genuinely worthy of wanting anything of my own. In both, my only available strategy is either to accept or to reject the role others prescribe for me as a male.

As an obvious implication, the claims that traditional male roles place men in positions of "masculine privilege" where they "dominate" society must clearly be seen as shallow and nearly nonsensical. Trained from infancy to surrender themselves, men might far more accurately be described as being entirely dominated by the system of social obligations. As such, they can only have experienced the social difficulties (to employ an outrageous euphemism) of the past 35 years – shifting gender roles, hostile feminism, unemployment, affirmative action, downsizing, altered job definitions, and all the rest – from a personal center that has already prepared them only to experience life-long Shame. If anything, the enormous mass of men's Shame in modern society can only be growing.

These observations are not meant to imply women in our society are not shamed in their own right and to a similar degree. However, I cannot directly experience women's Shame, especially as an internal experience, and, therefore, do not presume to speak for them on this issue. It should be clear that, allowing for appropriate differences, a similar case can be made for women's Shame.

SHAME'S TWO-LEVEL NATURE

In any case, when Shame has reached Chronic proportions, it also seems logical to suspect that it causes a great deal of behavior unconnected to gender that is not presently recognized as linked to it. As a shamed person, I cannot soothe myself. My fear of permitting myself any satisfaction has become the operative element of my emotional life. Wanting to be soothed, I even become "unsoothed." This must be very close to the source of addictions. Isn't it likely that repeated attempts to medicate "unhealable" Shame are central to the motives for all repetitive compulsions? Isn't any specific addiction – money, sex, power, gambling, sugar, food, excitement – in some sense an attempt to medicate or heal the pain at my center, my Shame for existing? Does addictive behavior accelerate then because "the addicted object progressively loses its savor and demands more and more?" Or is it far more likely that we are compulsively driven further and further into addictive behavior, regardless of the choice of addiction, because, though we repeatedly attempt to do so, Shame will simply not allow us to experience any sort of satisfaction?

Shame must also be suspected as materially contributing to Depression, if, indeed, it is not its entire cause. Shouldn't Shame's role be examined for at least some of the "damping down" of energy that constitutes so much of depression? And aren't "codependent" and "enabling" behaviors instances of another person's feelings (once again) being more important than mine? If even partially true, understanding Shame's role becomes necessary for dealing effectively with quite a broad range of psychological problems.

To return to our central considerations, the "two-level" nature of Chronic Shame points directly at the great error almost universally made in attempting to heal it – whether for an individual or for society in general. Quite usually, I inflict this error on myself individually when trying to cope with "personal problems." Very often, therapists, social workers, workshop leaders, and other "helpers" fall into perpetrating it when dealing with clients. And social reformers fall into it as a matter of course. Simply put, the error is trying to heal personal problems as if they were "one-level" errors, things I do wrong, or just can't get right, as if they were the sole difficulty in need of simple correction.

So, I energetically strive to cure my over-eating, my habitual lateness, my refusal to work, my sexual addiction, my inability to handle money well, my tendency to procrastinate. Or, as a therapist, I provide my patients with helpful alternatives to "cure" the sadness, anger, mistrust, or inability to express or receive affection that troubles their lives. As a social reformer, I assume that altering political or economic structures will automatically "solve" personal difficulties, much as Progressives, Socialists, Communists, New Dealers, the New Right, and most recently, Feminists have.

In such cases, it must be noted the suggested "cures" may, indeed, contain appropriate alternatives for shamed or shaming behavior. The problem, however, lies in the fact they fatally ignore the essential foundation of such behavior. They ignore the underlying global feeling of condemnation I exercise towards myself for having any "problems" in the first place. Thus, "good advice" that is offered to solve a specific "first level" difficulty overlooks and profoundly reinforces the underlying "second level" of Chronic Shame – my assurance that I am essentially "bad" – that now functions as its real source.

In reality, then, striving for a cure or being pushed to one will very likely add to my problem, perhaps in some more acute form. Beneath the surface of apparently benign assistance, it once more rejects what I'm really feeling. The fundamental message received is that what I feel is yet again "wrong." Once again, I am "off base." I must continue to condemn myself, mistrust myself, and drive myself to be different from what I am. My own authority, confidence in myself, and good feeling toward myself, any of which could function to help me genuinely heal my difficulties, remain under attack and are, in fact, further undermined.

The harmful increase of Chronic Shame delivered under the guise of "helpful" advice is nowhere clearer than in the weekend workshops for men offered by the organization I mentioned earlier. The workshop leaders routinely assumed they knew exactly what solution the attending men needed – usually energetic expressions of anger. And they imposed their solution on most of the attendees through a form of manipulated psychodrama.

Before attending, Jason gave an answer to one particular question out of the many on his application. Because of it, during his weekend the leaders drove him to express feelings about his infant son's death, which had occurred many years earlier. Feeling deeply violated, Jason emerged from the workshop extremely upset and confused. He was in no way ready to confront these feelings. Afterwards, in private therapy, he was not able to confront his son's death until many years after the workshop. Moreover, his feelings of Shame had been reinforced by the "solutions" he had seen imposed on his fellow participants in the weekend workshop.

The importance of understanding Shame's two-level nature cannot therefore be overstated. It imposes an indispensable requirement on any and all efforts to heal it, whether in oneself or in someone else, whether on a personal or on a social level. In the attempt to heal any first level feelings of Shame connected with specific difficulties, we must remain acutely careful not to reinforce the second level feelings of Chronic Shame that are now inseparably connected, and which, in fact, originate and control all I feel and do. Chronic Shame's troublesome "two-level" structure, therefore, ties a paradoxical emotional knot around the very heart of healing Shame.

Energetic efforts to heal Shame may, in fact, deepen Shame because in the effort we once again reject or abandon what we truly feel and make ourselves "wrong." This is the real dilemma posed by Shame: How can we possibly heal one set of feelings without automatically sickening the other?

At this point, I am far from believing we have exhausted all that needs to be said about the causes of Shame. But what we've said thus far allows us to understand the essentials of how a man comes to experience and then express Shame, after repeated, invisible violence has finally installed it as Chronic. We may now turn to consider some of the more important details of how Shame operates in daily life. They, too, must be kept in mind as we look toward healing it.

Almost all of the literature that discusses Shame in operation describes it as fear of being exposed, fear of being seen when I don't want to be seen. And there's no question when we experience Shame, we immediately feel great fear, the need to hide, flee, and be covered. Depending on the degree of Shame, our feelings of discomfort at being seen may vary all the way from a vague, barely perceptible embarrassment to a twisting agony sufficient to make us "squirm out of our skin." As one common expression of this fear, we lower my eyes or look away whenever we're aware of another's gaze. And very often, shamed men consistently hide everything they feel or do. Fear of being seen is indeed undeniable and always present as a usual first symptom whenever we're feeling ashamed.

WHY SHAME CAUSES FEAR

Still, fear of exposure by no means describes the total experience of Shame or Chronic Shame. It does not begin to address *why* we feel such fear. We fear being exposed to anyone's view – or, indeed, to our own – *because* having been repeatedly attacked or unsupported for what we want, we have finally ingested our lesson. "Wrong" again and again for wanting certain specific things, we are at last "always wrong," both for wanting any one thing and for the act of wanting at all. We must not be caught in the act of wanting anything. We only fear being seen by others because we ourselves feel a much deeper fear of the "wrongness" others will see in us. As commonly expressed, "if you really got to know me, you really wouldn't like me." The crucial addition, that I don't like me at all, is just as commonly left unexpressed.

We, therefore, fear exposure *because* when we want anything, we feel profoundly "wrong" – that is, evil, bad, off base, strange, defective, abnormal, weird, weak, unallowable, egotistical, selfish (the permutations of this feeling must be understood as endless for each shamed man invents his own version of it). Our desires to eat, sleep, have sex, enjoy success, make money, feel powerful, determine our own goals, express or receive affection, friendship, intimacy, or almost everything else, feel profoundly "wrong." We experience no inner permission whatever to allow ourselves fulfillment of our wishes. We can ask for nothing. We may feel guilty. We may even feel completely crazy, insane for wanting what we want.

Bill is a man in his forties, obviously in fine physical condition. His tone is wistful as he recounts the golden opportunity he had in his twenties to play baseball professionally. He actually got as far as playing for a major league farm team, but did not succeed. With downcast eyes, he describes how he could never seem to get his heart into practice or play. "It always seemed as though I worked to defeat myself, much as I thought I wanted this career," he says, almost guiltily. "The fact is, I always felt I was wrong to want it. Because I wanted it, it was something I shouldn't have."

At a men's retreat, the participants were asked to express what their Shame felt like. One by one, a surprising number rose to speak. One of them said, "My Shame feels like an endless fall down the bottomless well of home's broken promises. It feels like having to dig out through the dirt and mud at the bottom, though I have no hands, no tools, and no hope. It feels like a demand that I walk my long road, though I have no feet. Like being asked to sing, though I have no voice. Like being required to pray, though there is no god."

Chronic Shame's incapacitating destruction of any sovereign authority to be myself – to stand in my own feelings, define my own truth, possess my own energy or power, confidently pursue my own needs and goals – could not have been more clearly stated. Out of its origins in rejection or abandonment, I ultimately implement Chronic Shame's impairment of my "be-ing" in two senses. It has become a crippling of my actions and a crippling of my existence. I feel guilty for acting. I also feel guilty for being.

Whether I'm aware of it or not, therefore, Chronic Shame often culminates in a feeling of threatened annihilation, obliteration, and death. I simply should not "be." Shame is then often triggered as a felt reaction to a death threat – to my personality, if not to my physical existence. And this often produces defensive rage, the rage so often characterized as "masculine." Under threat of immediate annihilation, I react with violent feeling and, perhaps, violent action as well.

ASHAMED OF FEELING SHAME

Finally and inevitably, because Shame makes all my feelings "wrong" and drives me to hide them, I am, also, too ashamed to feel my Shame. Thus, Shame's crowning achievement is that I usually don't know I am shamed. My Shame becomes, quite literally, invisible. Instead, I more commonly become conscious of a host of other deficiencies: Weakness. Profound hopelessness. Vagueness. Chronic confusion. Blocking resistance. Persistent tardiness or procrastination. Painful emptiness. Complete absence of feelings. Physical pain in the shoulders, chest, stomach, or back. Constant anxiety. Nervousness. Uncontrollable anger. The absence of what I need to do to get the job done. Complete lack of confidence. Needy dependence. Inescapable addiction. Feelings of not being enough or being less than. An inability to sleep restfully. Feelings of deep depression. Insatiable hunger for all I must possess within myself or in the world.

Whichever form it takes, it usually goes unrecognized as a symptom of Shame. I might know only that my life or some part of my life feels blocked. Why can't I write? Paint? Find a lover or a wife? A good job? A good place to live? Function effectively?

To complete the circle, when Shame has become Chronic and has installed itself as the master control of all my feelings, it feels entirely normal for me to mete out Shame to others through habitually rejecting their feelings and desires. Or it feels perfectly normal for me to continue in Shame by arranging to have others systematically reject my feelings and desires. Or both. Shame becomes as constant, necessary, and normal – and as invisible – as the air I breathe. And now we are at the starting point of the cycle with whose description we began this article.

Such behavior is quite evident in the men who attend that weekend workshop mentioned earlier. They usually leave it delighted by their experience. Afterwards, its leaders proudly display photographs of the men's smiling faces as proofs of their methods. Of course, the coercion implicit in the weekend remains unseen. The Shame imposed and received goes entirely unrealized. After all, it feels like a perfectly normal male environment for the leaders imposing it, just as it does for the men receiving it. It's a fine male experience!

As a common expression of Chronic Shame, I may habitually berate myself for my many faults, real and imagined, measured against a standard of unattainable perfection. For a single slight mistake, I may obsess over my defects for hours. Because of such an error, the strength may actually drain from my legs and leave me physically unable to stand. I may continuously criticize myself with lacerating severity. For years on end, I may read books, attend workshops, or consult therapists whose "good advice" consistently delivers the by-now-reassuring message that what I feel is wrong and needs correcting. Over and over, I may conceive of projects I never begin, or whose failure I unfailingly bring about. Or I may repeatedly enter personal or work relationships that systematically reject my needs, confirming my negative vision of myself.

In his euphoria over finding the perfect wife, Will could not contain his happiness. As time passed, he even worked two jobs to provide a fine house and good education for their children. He did "everything a man was supposed to do" to make his wife happy and make his marriage a success. Soon, however, he realized that she seemed to withdraw and increasingly criticize more and more of how he behaved. He was thunderstruck one day when his wife declared "out of the blue" that she wanted a divorce. She wanted it because he did not love her the way she wanted to be loved. His feelings of love were "wrong." Will was devastated and could not leave his bed for days. To be sure, though he had paid for it and their house was jointly owned, both he and his wife assumed he was the one who would have to move out.

I may persistently inflict my Shame on my family, friends, and acquaintances through coldness, belittling humor, eruptive anger, or dismissive behavior, thereby discounting or invalidating who they are or what they achieve. I may become one of those workers brimming with "helpful criticism" and "good advice" for my co-workers. I may become a boss who is satisfied by nothing. Or I may act out Chronic Shame by becoming a workshop leader or therapist whose "helpful advice" routinely "encourages" my clients to feel something other than what they truly feel. Then again, I may become the energetic social activist curing everyone else's problems. When push (literally) comes to shove, better to inflict Shame than to feel it!

At his graduation ceremony from a major eastern university, Peter was awarded his hard-earned degree *magna cum laude*. While a surrounding group of friends congratulated him, his father silently studied the degree. Finally he muttered, "I don't know, Peter. It seems to me they're giving out an awful lot of these *magna cum laude* awards." As a witness, I could hardly imagine how Peter felt. I know I wished I could vanish into the earth.

Finally and above all, when Chronic Shame functions as my master control, I feel hopeless, forever frozen into an inescapable pattern. After all, the shamed cell into which I'm now locked has served through many years to steel me against all those repeated assaults on my needs and wants. By rendering me unaware of possessing whatever parts of me were being rejected, my Shame has, in a sense, successfully shielded both them and me. Finally, unaware of Shame itself, I am certainly not now going to place myself once more in harm's way by tearing down the walls that protect me. I refuse to reexperience the pain that caused me to erect them in the first place. In addition, I may cling loyally to the pattern in the (vain) hope "they will finally love me" for behaving as they wanted me to. Again, there is no way out; I don't get any love where I am. I won't get any love if I depart from where I am.

In sum, I am shamed. I feel unworthy, uncertain, powerless, and blocked. I am paralyzed. I trust no one, including myself. I'm profoundly afraid, though I probably won't admit it, even to myself. My own shamed energy works against me to keep most of my qualities, and my Shame itself, hidden, unknown even to myself. Aware of little or none if it, my Shame therefore denies and protects its own existence.

I have every reason to cling to the shamed reaction that, however unfortunately, has saved me in the face of rejection and betrayal – and that by this time in my life defines the only roles I believe I must assume to truly be a man. I will feel guilty, selfish, or egotistical about trying to do anything to change this situation. And only by ensnaring myself in the literal dilemma of shaming myself further do I usually approach healing it at all.

ALI BABA'S STORY

How ever can we hope to untie a knot so hopelessly snarled? How can we find peace in a war we unconsciously wage against ourselves? The solution, I believe, is symbolized in the story of Ali Baba and the Forty Thieves – in many ways a wonderful collection of details dramatizing how a man may heal his Shame. A fairy tale…but no fiction!

The story itself is quickly told. Ali Baba, a poor man, is gathering wood in the forest. Fearful when he hears many horsemen approaching, he hides. From his hiding place, he overhears the Captain of 40 thieves cry "Open Sesame!" at the blank wall of the nearby mountainside. A door to a cave magically opens where Ali Baba had previously seen none, and the thieves disappear into it. Fearing their reemergence, he remains in hiding.

After their departure, Ali Baba dares to repeat the Captain's exact words, "Open Sesame!" He enters the cave, and where he had expected darkness, he unexpectedly finds bright light, as well as jewels, silver, gold, fine silk, and much other wealth. He returns home from the cave with only a few sacks of gold and the intention of returning for more. However, his rich but greedy brother, Hassim, spies out Ali Baba's new wealth and cajoles him into revealing his secret.

Out of kindness, Ali Baba is willing to share his treasure and reveals to Hassim both the cave's location and the password. Early in the morning, Hassim hurries to the cave, intending to hoard the treasure for himself. Excited by the wealth and dreams of wealth he gathers in the cave, Hassim cannot remember the password to exit. Increasingly frightened at his danger, he forgets "Open Sesame" as if he had never heard it. Sure enough, the thieves discover him trapped in their cave with his bags loaded. Determined to sell his life dearly, Hassim attacks them, but the thieves slay him and cut him into four pieces, which they nail up inside the cave.

Ali Baba returns to the cave, finds his dead brother, and comes home with the four pieces of the corpse, whose honorable burial he arranges – and more gold. When the forty thieves and their Captain find Hassim's body gone, they conclude that two men must have known the secret of their wealth. They have killed one, and must now discover and slay the other.

Soon enough, the thieves discover Ali Baba. But his loyal slave girl, Morgiana, cleverly frustrates every effort they make to kill him. Twice they mark his house with a cross, first white, then red. Each time, Morgiana draws similarly colored crosses on houses to the left and right so that the thieves cannot identify Ali Baba's. Both times, the Captain slays the thief who fails to kill Ali Baba.

On the third try, the Captain himself poses as a traveling oil merchant. He imposes on Ali Baba's hospitable nature in order to stay the night, and is thus able to smuggle into his house the remaining 37 thieves hidden inside giant oil jars. However, Morgiana discovers the thieves inside their jars and kills them all. Ali Baba buries the 37 dead thieves in his garden, sells their mules in the market, and grants Morgiana her freedom for saving his life.

Having lost his entire band of thieves, the Captain is now furiously determined on revenge. He hatches an elaborate plan to kill Ali Baba. Carrying many fine goods from the cave, the Captain of thieves sets himself up as a cultured merchant across from Ali Baba's house. Because he is so cordial, he becomes friendly with Ali Baba's son, and then with Ali Baba himself. Ali Baba judges him a good friend and invites him to dinner. The Captain demurs and begs off, but Ali Baba insists. Finally, the Captain says he demurs because he eats no salt. Ali Baba responds this is no problem whatever, and instructs Morgiana and his other servants to prepare a fine banquet without salt for the "merchant," his own son, and himself.

The fact that the merchant would eat no salt with her master arouses Morgiana's suspicions. She contrives to get a close look at their guest and immediately sees he is none other than the Captain of thieves and is carrying a dagger hidden in his garments in order to kill her master. After the meal, she dons a dancing girl's headdress and offers to dance for her master's guest. As part of her dance, Morgiana brings out her own dagger. In turn, she points it at herself, her master, his son, and their guest as though doing so were part of her dance. At the appropriate moment, she catches the Captain off guard and plunges her dagger into his heart.

Ali Baba's dismay turns to profound gratitude when Morgiana reveals the slain guest as the Captain of thieves. Saying, "See what an enemy you have entertained," she uncovers his hidden dagger, making plain the Captain's plan to slay Ali Baba and his son. In gratitude, Ali Baba offers to wed Morgiana to his son, who readily accepts. Their wedding is celebrated in great splendor. When sufficient time has passed, and no more thieves appear, Ali Baba returns to the cave and brings back as much gold as he can carry. He then reveals the secret of the cave to his son, who also hands it on so that "the children and grandchildren of Ali Baba were rich to the end of their lives."

Ali Baba's story beautifully illustrates most aspects of what needs to be done to heal Shame. Surely the most important is how to deal with the paradox we have already noted at the heart of the problem – how may I heal Shame without shaming myself further?

Let's begin by noticing that though Ali Baba's brother is rich, for some reason Ali Baba himself is poor. This was the clue which led me to suspect the tale might be understood as an exploration of Shame. Ali Baba's poverty reflects how shamed men commonly feel "poorer," less gifted, somehow defective, in comparison to other men. As in the story, the causes for this "poorer state" seem unclear. Because there's something wrong with me, other men always and obviously "have their act together," while I myself just as obviously do not. Such a feeling is a reliable indicator of Shame's presence, an infallible signal that the problem is there to be dealt with.

The 40 thieves and their well-hidden cave were a second indication of Shame's presence in the story. Forty thieves have hidden stolen treasures in their cave. In some traditions, the number 40 stands for totality or completeness – as in the 40 days and nights of rain in Genesis. So we may say the treasures in the cave have been totally and completely stolen, replicating Shame's feelings of total loss. Moreover, as he wanders in the woods "earning his living," the cave of hidden treasures is invisible, not even suspected by Ali Baba, though it is quite nearby. As he ekes out his familiar, poor livelihood, Ali Baba is unaware of the enormous treasure nearby – just as a shamed man often feels little more than the utter absence of abilities, rights, or goals. Never suspecting the existence of his own treasures, he feels only the poverty of his guilt, self-doubt, and uncertainty. Indeed, the theft of myself may be so complete that I may not even suspect I have been robbed of anything.

When he hears the thieves approach, Ali Baba hides, fearing for his life. And after the thieves have entered their cave, he remains in hiding, fearing their imminent return. This suggests a beginning in the process of healing. It is a good description of the feelings I may have when I first begin to suspect I have been shamed. I will fear – fear even the slightest approach toward the dark cave of my Shame and what my Shame has stolen from me. My gifts and talents have repeatedly been attacked, and ultimately, my life itself threatened. Any attempt now to reclaim my feelings and recognize my Shame will plunge me once more into the same terror of annihilation and death experienced during my initial experiences of Shame. I will resist and actually prefer to remain frozen in fear, hidden and unmoving, just as Ali Baba does – because doing so will "save my life."

But because he remains so still, Ali Baba can clearly hear the magic words the Captain uses to open the unseen cave. He hears "Open Sesame!" just as I may hear an opening to my own feelings if I remain still and listen. Fearful as ever but curious, he uses the thieves' very words after they are gone. The cave and all its riches open to him. As he enters it, Ali Baba is apprehensive. But where he had expected darkness, he unexpectedly finds light. And in that light, he discovers treasures beyond his imagining.

We, too, discover "the mother lode" when it comes to healing Shame, for several of the most important components of the process are symbolized by this part of the story. Of necessity, I must discuss them now as single topics in linear fashion, one after another. But, it must be remembered, the life experiences I will now describe happen simultaneously and overlap one another. They may also happen over time, in partial bits and pieces, with a cumulative effect on the new ways I may feel and subsequently live.

Concretely, healing Shame is almost never a one-time, overnight experience. Requiring time, happening gradually, and usually composed of many parts, healing is, in fact, a reversed mirror image of the process whereby Shame was inflicted in the first place.

We observe that once he becomes aware of the cave's existence, Ali Baba steals into it by using the Captain's own words, "Open Sesame!" For healing, this is the first and most valuable clue. Like Ali Baba, I must discover I have a cave of Shame to enter. I must somehow "say the word" and take the risk of recognizing Shame itself. Perhaps, if I'm not directly aware of Shame, I might begin with a sense that something isn't quite right. I may vaguely feel that something always gets in the way of how I wish to live, what I wish to do. Maybe, after the first pages of this article, a reader might speak his own "Open Sesame" by identifying with a feeling or behavior described as "actually the way I do things." However it happens, recognizing myself as shamed represents the indispensable first step into the cave, the first step toward healing. I courageously use Shame itself to "notice myself" and enter my own experience.

In this crucial detail, Ali Baba's story reveals how we may solve the paradox of healing Shame without inflicting further Shame. Ali Baba succeeds because he stands Shame on its head. Normally, I will not "say the word." I wish to get rid of shamed feelings. I desperately desire to change them. I strive to be "cured." I urge myself to "let go of them." I may spend years trying to forget them as though they never happened, and replace feelings I judge to be "bad" with feelings I judge to be "good." I condemn my Shame. But by whatever means I do this, Ali Baba shows us that doing it is quite literally counterproductive, because it actually increases Shame; I am "wrong" once again.

OPEN SESAME!

Ali Baba before the cave reveals that I need to embrace the feeling of Shame itself. I need to say aloud bravely and clearly "Open Sesame! I am shamed!" By doing that, I begin the process of accepting and trusting *whatever* I feel as the utterly reliable, factual foundation of my own authority to feel. I really feel my Shame. By implication, all my feelings are real. And, contrary to Shame's every message, I may observe I am now the one who has both the ability and the right to feel them.

Brian speaks quietly, as though to himself, as he addresses his men's group. "All my spiritual remedies haven't worked," he says, eyes lowered. "I've tried to substitute them for what I really feel. They haven't helped at all. They end up being a kind of emotional bypass, once again burying what I feel. I've finally decided I need to stop avoiding my real feelings. I spoke to my mother recently, describing my experiences growing up with her – the violence, the way she beat me. My anger. She denied everything – said I exaggerated. I feel really sad. I realize now that I'm never going to have the tender, loving mother I've always wanted. And these are the feelings I'm going to live with and work with for the rest of my life."

Once he is inside the cave, Ali Baba expects darkness. As we have seen, Shame strips away awareness of feelings, of gifts, of even a sense of existence. So I almost certainly approach healing Shame hopelessly, expecting darkness. There's nothing for me there but more pain and deficiency. My certainty that I am endowed with nothing of my own leads me to cling needily to women, sex, work, money, power, masculine roles, or any other "external savior." The very last thing I expect is to save or "enrich" my life by exploring my Shame, my self.

But saying "Open Sesame" produces a most important first benefit. Shame leaves me feeling entirely stripped of my right to feel anything. But I have the power to feel that very feeling. From that observation, I set an "unvicious circle" into operation. I may gradually perceive feelings of Shame about specific issues in my life, such as work, money, sex, or relationships, and thereby proceed to feel my larger Shame. On the other hand, by directly feeling my Chronic Shame, I may gradually learn to perceive shamed feelings about individual issues that trouble me. Either way, the important benefit of "accepting" my feelings is that I find the treasure of my own authority.

The process that effectively reverses Shame is in motion. I gradually perceive that I have power that I may ever more accept as mine. I absorb my right to take charge of the process of healing. And, every feeling I accept (regardless of its content or how painful it is) contributes to reaffirming both my power and my authority to do what I need to do for myself.

At a class in psychodrama, Bruce puts forward his confusion about an exercise just completed. Most people in the class, including the leader, urge him to deal with his confusion in the next exercise. Bruce is reluctant, however. Something in the suggestion makes him uneasy. He muses aloud that perhaps it has something to do with the way he was always put down at home for what he felt. Both leader and class continue to urge him. But one member of the class supports Bruce in whatever he wants to do. If Bruce does not want to do the exercise, then his reluctance in itself is the right starting point for him. He is fully entitled to respect his own authority. Bruce exclaims that such recognition makes him feel wonderful. He loves being able to trust and rely on his own feeling instead of being "pushed" by the class.

So, "Open Sesame" is first of all an attitude of acceptance toward the full authority of my own experience. My first reaction is not the usual one of correcting or mending myself. Even in moments of my worst and most painful feelings, I regard myself with kindness and dare to say "Open Sesame" to myself in the depths of my cave. I might even relax and look around a little. By doing so, I undo the attack on my authority perpetrated by the rejection or abandonment that defeated me in the first place.

It all begins with standing still in the cave. Nothing is more important for healing Shame than learning to accept whatever I feel right now.

But even here, the deadly paradox is at work. I must be careful not to jeopardize my feeling authority by "advising" or "pushing" myself to accept my Shame, to be kind to myself – crucial as that is to the process – if, in fact, I feel otherwise! I must learn never to surrender my own truth by trying to "conform myself" to my own ideal, much less anyone else's, about what should happen. Not even to what is being said in this article! It is *never* helpful to "drive away" what I really feel (though, of course I needn't act on it, however real it is). So much, then, for all too many self-help books, workshops, and unfortunately, a fair number of therapists. It goes without saying that the professional who adopts a negative stance – especially in the form of "good advice" – toward a client's shamed behavior is merely avoiding and exporting some form of his or her own.

Speaking "Open Sesame" before the cave yields a second benefit. As Ali Baba speaks aloud in front of the cave, so directly uttering the words of my Shame is an acknowledgement of my existence. However bad it feels, my Shame contains a sense of my own reality. I am here to say the words, feel the feelings. I exist and am present like a boulder, a massive tree, or a chunk of gold. No matter how much "they" used to beat on me and tell me to stop existing, nonetheless I am. I am my own subject. As I say the words, as I walk into the cave, I exist at the center of the process. In this manner, acknowledging Shame helps heal the feeling that I shouldn't exist – the feeling that I'm constantly threatened with annihilation or death – which is so often Chronic Shame's ultimate message.

Recognizing the pain of Shame turns out to be an act of loving-kindness for myself. Paradoxically, my negative experience, bad as it feels, is tangible, positive assurance that I have survived every assault. I am affirmed by it. In a perfect reverse of how I was shamed, my bad feeling itself is proof that I exist, feel, act, even when it tells me I don't exist and have no right to. Thus, whenever I feel empty, needy, depressed, angry, rageful, or suicidal, I may "look directly" and observe that *"I"* preexist. The feeling is in me; I can hold it. No matter how bad or terrible it is, it is mine, in my body. *"I"* am here feeling it. I am here, saying "Open Sesame."

In a paragraph that needs to be read slowly, the process of "Open Sesame" may be summarized in words that stand directly in the paradox of healing Shame. In my young years, I was aggressively rejected or passively abandoned and made to feel wrong. Today, as a shamed man, I continue to feel wrong and act accordingly. However, I now perceive that my feelings during my young years corresponded to reality. I was perfectly right to feel wrong! That was indeed my caregivers' messages. Hence, if today I try to "correct or banish my bad feelings," I simply make myself wrong once again. I reshame myself. But the very act of accepting my "wrong" feelings as right – painful as they are – is kindness to myself. With it, I begin to heal my Shame. I begin to feel both my authority and the underlying sense of my own reality.

This renewed confidence may be expressed by realizing that "I have never been wrong." My adult feelings or reactions may now seem confused, despairing. And perhaps they tempt me to act in ways opposed to my real interests. However, at one time during my growing years, my feelings were an absolutely accurate response to what I was experiencing, and were entirely justified.

Exploring my emotional past now opens the way to looking back through those experiences in order to understand the specifics of how I became shamed – how I came to feel what I now feel. How was my need for affection handled? Was I seen or supported as I needed to be? Could I express my point of view?… my anger?… my pleasure?… my sexuality?… my hopes and goals?… my love? Was I attacked? The precise places I feel Shame will necessarily differ from any other man's in precise correspondence with the unique ways I was attacked while growing up. But exploring Shame will always yield an understanding of how exactly right my reading of the emotional situation was during my young years, and why I feel and act (or react) as I do now. At one time, my rage was justified… my hatred, right on the money… my silence, a lifesaver.

Quietly, almost secretively, Mitchell reveals that he has been feeling suicidal, that he wants to do away with himself once and for all. He looks down as he speaks. He obviously expects to be contradicted and corrected for such a "shameful" feeling. But it is accepted without criticism. Instead, he is gently asked who exactly feels his dark feelings. He looks up with surprise. It is evident a new perception has just dawned on him. "I do," he murmurs, nodding, "I do." Asked to rub his thumb and forefinger together and to notice the act, he looks up again, startled. He sees himself perform this simple gesture over which he has power. "I'm here," he whispers, "I'm here. I feel all these things." And he finds the anchor in himself from which he can more confidently begin to trust, explore, and sort out the real experiences of his life, past and present, including why he feels suicidal.

At a men's weekend, Ben takes part in an exercise that places him before a mirror. The leader asks Ben what he sees in himself. He is clearly stymied. He stares but is obviously not allowed to see anything in himself. Finally, a leader whispers, "Who's looking, Ben?" Ben turns, wide eyed, and begins to repeat ever more emphatically, "I am. I'm looking. I am. I am." As he speaks, he peers intently at himself in the mirror, and the words come with great difficulty. As Ben repeats them, tears well up in his eyes. Allowing himself a kind and accepting feeling while he looks at himself is obviously an unexpected miracle, perhaps never experienced before.

When such men admit their dark feelings of hurt and hopeless Shame, they clearly feel considerable pain. If they stay "inside" their feelings, hearing only what they say – if, in a sense, the feelings stop them in their tracks – they will, of course, feel overwhelmed and humiliated by them. They will continue to feel Shame's destructive condemnations. But if they suddenly glimpse instead that they are present to their feelings – destructive and uncomfortable as the feelings are – they may accept these feelings as only one of the many realities present. They may realize that *they* are bigger than the feelings are. As the containers and hosts of the feelings, the men are in charge. Painful as their feelings continue to be, accepting them actually becomes an act of kindness toward themselves, perhaps the very first act of kindness or tenderness they have ever experienced. It may become the first of many. And they administer it to themselves. "This is my experience, mine. And, no matter what it is, I respect and cherish myself because I'm having it."

Ali Baba now enters the cave and finds the third valuable element necessary for healing. When I accept my feelings and whatever information they contain, they will inform me, perhaps for the first time, that my cave is full of treasure. Contrary to my usual belief, Shame has not in fact annihilated my abilities and talents. I may feel empty, numb, and entirely without feelings, but that is not reality. Gradually I perceive that my feelings of numbness, of desperation, of emptiness, of dire need for some magic person or thing from outside myself to "finally save" me, are really intense expressions of Shame. And, unexpectedly, they contain treasure. My shamed longings, in and of themselves, reveal that something of my own, something inside me, has always remained alive, has always been perfectly aware of what I needed, and has been seeking it intensely, perhaps for quite a long time. Both treasure and light are in the cave.

So, Shame has merely buried and camouflaged my treasures while they were dangerous. Although they feel gone, they are not. I am not empty and lost. I have not been annihilated. My treasure has merely been "robbed" by 40 thieves and buried in a cave. None of my inborn qualities or abilities has disappeared permanently. Lo and behold, within Shame's cave I still possess all my talents! My job as a shamed man is, thus, not at all to conform myself to an ideal or to a "cure" that someone else prescribes. I will not find myself by adhering to some solution, some magic pattern, defined by an authority outside myself. My sole task (difficult and dangerous as it truly is) is to rediscover who and what I am, my authentic self. I am the treasure in my own cave. I am the sole answer to my own questions. All I have to do is "see through" my Shame to "learn" what my riches are – and then start practicing the everyday use of what has remained so long buried.

Just before his 30th birthday, Kevin is attending his first men's retreat. He tells his small group that he has adhered to New Age beliefs since his early teens. Right now, he has never felt worse or more confused. He feels depressed, hopeless. He confesses he is attending the retreat hoping to begin discovering whatever is really inside him. He wants his real feelings to provide him with guidance he can genuinely follow. "Every time I adopted another resolution about the light," he says, "it left me feeling further away from myself, and even more confused. It was just another way for me to abandon myself. From now on, I want to be faithful to myself, whatever that means." He looks contented as the men around him nod in understanding.

From his initial foray into the cave, Ali Baba returns with a few sacks of gold and the intention to return for more. The degree of doubt about himself that Shame imposes on each man varies according to the intensity and frequency of the attacks that inflicted it. Not every man will need the same degree of reassurance. So whatever degree of self-doubt and recrimination my Shame inflicts on my "defective" self, my initial foray into the cave yields whatever first quantity of gold I need.

Assuming a benign attitude toward whatever I feel, assured of my own being, and certain again of my own treasures, I am increasingly allowed to experience what truly heals Shame. Contrary to the message implicit in every act that shamed me, I may now own, trust, and rely on *all* my own feelings, my own reactions, my own needs, whatever they are, however "evil" or "selfish" they may seem – at least for starters. From now on, I will act as my own guide.

THE PROCESS OF UNSHAMING

If Chronic Shame is a "two-level" experience, "Open Sesame" and Ali Baba's cave of treasure imply that it can be healed on two levels. I am unshamed on the first level because the implied act of kindness felt toward myself gradually undoes the unkind acts of rejection or abandonment that initially greeted my individual needs, wants, abilities, and hopes.

I am unshamed on the second level by similar kindness toward myself in recognizing my fundamental authority and the goodness of my being, thereby undoing Chronic Shame's unkind condemnation of my whole person. In other words, I simultaneously heal my Shame about such individual issues as money, sex, or achievement, and my underlying sense of Chronic Shame about almost everything. Above all, if at last I greet it with kindness, it is my Shame itself that teaches me to affirm myself in this way.

In the process of healing Shame, it is crucial, however, to remember the enmity of the 40 thieves and how many times they try to kill Ali Baba. The 40 thieves tell us it is entirely counterproductive (that is, reshaming) for me to assume a stance of hostility toward myself that replicates and reinflicts my childhood experiences – to once again make myself "wrong." Such attacks may assume unlikely disguises. Good advice or "affirmations" are the subtlest forms of this kind of attack. "I ought to stop" these horrible feelings. "I should have" much better ones. It is counterproductive to scold myself, criticize myself, lecture myself, belabor myself with "healing" resolutions, to hurry myself, or to shame my darkness with the "light."

And it is entirely counterproductive for me to allow anyone else to assume that stance. Any such "helpful advice" merely means what I am really doing is fundamentally imperfect. And, of course, I "should" do something different than what I'm doing or feeling. Once again, I shame and reject my own real energy.

Ali Baba's brother, Hassim, illustrates this point to perfection. Ali Baba has been kind to him, has taken care of himself, by entering the cave and returning with gold. No longer "deprived" or poor, Ali Baba has something to share. He can therefore extend his kindness to Hassim by sharing the treasure. He tells Hassim both the location of the cave and the secret password. But Hassim is greedy and in a hurry. Still "poor" (shamed), he intends to hoard the treasure for himself. He rushes to the cave before Ali Baba. Feverish as he is to gather treasure, he forgets the self-kindness of "Open Sesame" as if he had never heard it, and becomes trapped in Shame's cave. Discovered by the 40 thieves, he attacks them and by them is killed.

Hassim symbolizes almost perfectly how I might sabotage healing my Shame if I scold myself or am scolded, however "helpfully." If I hurry the process, if I "grab" at the treasure in a renewed process of shaming, or, above all, if I "attack" myself (my Shame) in my effort to heal the problem, like Hassim I will forget "Open Sesame's" fundamental self kindness. I will once again end up dead in the cave of my Shame. And of course, there will be no kindness to share with anyone else.

Paradoxically, when I say "Open Sesame" to the dark cave of my Shame, it opens the treasure of fundamental kindness toward myself. There are as many ways to feel such kindness as there are individual men. I may feel it as mercy, love, softness, self-acceptance, self-esteem, peace, quietness, strength, confidence, divine grace, joy, or Buddha's smile. Whatever words are used to describe it, the important point is my bodily feeling of allowance, of reception, of gentle opening without fearfully tensing up, whenever I am aware of some inner reality, no matter how bright, no matter how dark or negative. I exist. I'm a good thing. And – however slowly I learn it – whatever I feel is just fine (though I may need a bit more work here or there).

This view of healing Shame may also be described from the perspective of the past. It's certain that my Shame began because my adult caregivers somehow rejected or abandoned my early needs. I still yearn for those needs to be met. But, having been shamed for them once, it now feels wrong (i.e., selfish, egotistical) or hopeless for me to take action that would do so. So, today, in my adult-sized body, I remain in the pattern that was truly appropriate for childhood. I go through life passively aching for someone or something "big" outside of me to take care of me. Once past childhood, however, outside saviors cannot work. Even if anyone does grant me what I achingly yearn for, I feel unworthy and unable (i.e., too ashamed) to receive it. I cannot take in what I deeply believe I'm not allowed to have. Besides, I must remain loyal to my caregivers in the hope they will finally love me for continuing to behave as they desired – this even when they are long dead. So, "nothing seems to work" for me. Constantly yearning, I go through life, feeling hopeless and unchanged.

As an adult man, the only way out of the emotional dilemma is to take charge of both sides of the process – provider and provided for. With firm yet gentle kindness, I gradually realize I am the one who has real power (provider) to care for my needs, qualities, and hopes (provided for). Providing for myself, I learn to consistently align with and support my own power. I learn to discern my own needs. I learn to take care of them. As an advisor for others, all I need do is encourage the same attitude in others. As a writer, therapist, workshop leader, or helper of any kind, I must invariably align with others so they may relearn their own power. Advice, criticism, or any other stance that – however implicitly – attacks them for being "wrong," reinflicts Shame by once again undermining that power.

Therefore, Ali Baba's entry into the cave symbolizes the psychological attitude absolutely required for any genuine healing of Shame, my own or someone else's. More and more, I act as my own father, my own guide, my own friend, my own adult, gradually affirming my authority, power, and right to know my own treasures. I thereby reestablish *within myself* the bond of trust and love that was broken in childhood.

With that loving authority, I am more and more honest about myself, more and more able to trust and nurture my feelings. Slowly but surely I gather them to assess what treasures they contain. No matter what they look like, I may explore them as treasures and mine the riches they yield for my own life and that of others. No matter how Shame presently locks up my genuine energy into self-defeating patterns, I accept those patterns in order to release and reclaim my energy for my productive use. By intimately revealing my own true energies to myself, I allow them to flow into the world once more – for only I can do the job.

KINDNESS THAT HEALS SHAME

We arrive at the final lesson the story teaches, the all-important significance of Morgiana. We notice she begins as Hassim's slave-girl, and comes into Ali Baba's possession after his brother's death in the cave. As Ali Baba's slave, she twice diverts the thieves when they try to kill him by marking his house. He frees her, making her his servant. As Ali Baba's servant, she saves him from death by undoing the Captain's most elaborate schemes, first as a traveling oil merchant, then as a cultured friend. In gratitude, Ali Baba finally grants his son to her in marriage. And, after Ali Baba reveals the treasure to them, it is their children and grandchildren who "were rich to the end of their days."

We might say Morgiana represents the enslaved kindness for themselves that men cannot ordinarily feel after caregivers and society have so thoroughly shamed them. In that sense, she appears as the absolute ally of the "Open Sesame" that gets Ali Baba into trouble with the thieves, with his Shame, in the first place. Her persistent care and concern for Ali Baba save him, even when he is so naïve (unaware) as to believe the Captain of thieves is a cultured friend whom he may invite to dinner. As she becomes the newly freed loyal servant, and finally the bride of Ali Baba's son, Morgiana stands for the care-filled and persistent hard work our own spirit must perform to own its gold. The story tells us that ultimately, I need to marry Morgiana to myself.

She recognizes the Captain of thieves when Ali Baba doesn't. Significantly, because he will eat no salt with his host, she recognizes Shame's unrelenting desire to kill. She honors Ali Baba's guest with her dance, just as each of us must. But while dancing, she points her sharp dagger at herself, then at Ali Baba and his son, and finally at the Captain, whom she stabs to death.

Here is the pattern of kindness that heals Shame: attention first to myself, then to those I love, finally to my real enemies. As always, when dealing with Shame, these are "dark" deeds. But Ali Baba's horror of them turns to joy when he realizes Morgiana has finally killed his hidden enemy. Each step in healing my Shame will horrify me. But in the end, my hidden enemy will truly be dead.

After Morgiana succeeds in killing the Captain, Ali Baba waits until he feels sure no more thieves are about. Then he returns to the cave for all the treasure. The treasures found in Shame's cave are quite real. This is gold I may spend in the practical pursuits of my everyday life. It may require multiple visits for me to bring the gold and jewels home. But in time, the Shame does turn to gold.

The process of healing is no longer a story in a book, but really produces changes in how I live. This happens when, with Morgiana's persistence, I carefully pick up and scrutinize the gold present in every one of my previously shamed feelings – and smelt it into treasure for daily life. I abandon no feeling by "letting go of it" or "leaving it behind." Instead, as I am able, I gather each feeling, each reaction – no matter how dark – with kindness, and scrutinize it carefully in order to see what instruction it holds for me. Relying on these instructions, I increasingly learn to guide my own life, because I may specifically ask each jewel to show me precisely what it wants.

What does this feeling really want? When I ask that question, I come full circle on the path of healing Shame. That is because my feelings contain my reactions to all the specific qualities and abilities that were shamed during my young years, as we have seen in the first part of this chapter. By carefully examining each feeling for what it wants, I can recover all those specific assets. And, little by little, I can bring them to full expression in my adult life.

As he has done before, Philip explodes angrily when another man in his men's group makes a clear request for something he wishes the group to do. A good man with good manners, Philip is embarrassed by (i.e., ashamed of) his reaction. Though he clearly wishes he could, he cannot deny it – it is, in fact, what he feels. Without attacking Philip's anger, another man in the group gently asks him what he is feeling. After a time, Philip blurts out that he is jealous and angry. He's jealous because he hardly ever knows what he wants, hardly knows that he can want.

Philip is also angry with himself for not knowing. But he expresses it with anger against the man who seems to know what he wants so clearly.

After a few moments, Philip is gently asked whether he knows what his jealous feeling wants. Now he is close to tears. He says he can hardly believe he hasn't been criticized and attacked for his anger. He takes a long moment, during which he clearly struggles to stay with his feelings. After a time, with a tone of revelation, he says his feeling makes it plain he really wants to sort out and be clear about his own needs – to know what he wants. It wants him to realize his own right to want things for himself. And it wants him to become clear about what he specifically wants.

Philip would not have been able to see these treasures if he hadn't accepted his own jealous and angry reaction against the first speaker, "ugly" as that was. He also sees that his attack on the other man does not at all gain for him what he really does want. But the clarity his own feelings have given him provides him with some knowledge about how he might more effectively gain his ends.

With great difficulty, Andy shares his terror of homosexuality. A man with a long-term girl friend, he has never acted on his feelings. He has always wondered why any such thoughts would occur to him. Ashamed of his own thoughts, he's astounded that the man he's talking to hasn't simply run away and left him. After some quiet assurance that he would not be rejected for his thoughts, Andy wonders what they might mean for him. After awhile, he says, "You know, it all feels like I need a man." A light dawns in his eyes. His silent, distant father neglected him for long hours of work in his business. As a boy, Andy had no attention from his father or any older men. He had no models, and no support from a man who might have recognized who he was. He smiles sadly as he makes the connection. It's clear he's "looking through" his frightening thoughts. "I did need a man!" he exclaims, "and I still do! Not sexually, but emotionally, from the heart, intimately. I need to know a man so I can know my own heart, know what a man's like on the inside, recognize myself in what I see. Hey, I can do that!"

No matter how "tarnished" it may be, each of my feelings is a gold piece that contains a precious message. I have only to learn that it is OK, whatever it is, and that it contains treasure. By asking what it wants, I may see that I am seeking some "right thing" in a self-defeating way. But I also get to see what I want. And now, I am able to seek it in a manner that attains it successfully.

Brad is often furious with one or another of his friends. He finds himself angrily stalking away from offense after offense. He wants his friends to "talk profoundly" with him, but they always seem to dodge, putting him off. His resulting anger often leaves him feeling isolated, friendless, and lonely. Exasperated after repeated bouts with such anger, he expresses frustration with his own conduct. He is gently asked what his anger wants. He slowly admits that he is lonely and wants to share the affection and friendship he never felt as a child. Does his anger tell him that? It does, if he really listens to it. Does his anger get him that? Obviously not. So his anger has clarified what he wants, and now he may learn more effective ways to provide it.

The experience of healing Shame will often be painful and unpleasant. This is difficult to understand – never mind accept – if I have embarked on the road of self-discovery with the hope of feeling better than I do or with the need to "cure" my ills. Yet, if the necessary first stage of healing Shame is realizing and accepting it, then I inevitably confront what I felt when I was originally shamed. And that is always painful in the extreme. This is the sole door into myself, and it is no wonder that Hassim wants to hurry past the process. Morgiana, however, is wise and clever. She dances with Shame until her dagger puts an end to it.

When Ali Baba has brought home the gold from his cave, he shares the wealth with his son and daughter-in-law, and they and their descendants are rich to the end of their days. Here we arrive at our final observation. Thus far, we have spoken of healing Shame almost entirely as an individual, internal process. This was necessary because whatever the source – personal, social, or environmental – of my Shame, I will invariably need to heal it personally, within myself. But Ali Baba shows us once more that healing Shame cannot be understood as a purely self-regarding internal process, a kind of narcissistic navel gazing.

As I reclaim all of my feelings and accept their guidance toward what I genuinely need – as I reconnect with myself – I discover my very real need for love and contact with others in my life. I also discover my need for connection with society, other people in a more general way, and with the world. Thus, I always heal my Shame by myself, but I never heal it absolutely alone. Yet, heal it I truly may. My authentic self is not an isolate. My rediscovered, healthy, and genuine selfishness will find that it is truly connected with men, women, children, the earth itself, and will see them as connected to me. I care about others, not from a sense of external obligation, a moralistic "should," or any belief system detached from my real experience.

I care for others as a felt expression of care for my own being. Kind to myself once again, I may be kind to others. This is the vast "social" importance of Men healing their Shame. As we do, our emotional wealth will flow down through generations to the end of days.

NOTE:

*Because I am writing this article with the hope of reaching a wider audience, it will remain on a descriptive, phenomenological level. I will not directly address myself to the underlying etiological theory. To be briefly candid on that score, what I suggest about the origins of Shame throughout this article clearly rests on the conviction that it is a phenomenon of the psyche, and is predominately unconscious...at least initially. It does not, however, assume that Shame originates out of any internal system of preordained drives, resultant fantasies, or ironclad relation to sexual wishes. On the contrary, Shame originates intersubjectively from real experiences of competing "wants"...some, but by no means all, of them indeed sexual...that are experienced as multiple blows against the "self" and give rise to real reactions. Of course, the reactions vary infinitely according to the "born personality" of the individual reacting, but a basic dynamic of assault is invariably operative. I hope to address these questions at greater length in a partner article.

Chapter 21
Shame: The Mother Wound†

DAVID SHACKLETON

$\mathbf{I}$t feels like a regular evening as I walk into the Glebe Community Centre for the monthly meeting of the Ottawa/Hull Men's Forum. I have no inkling of what is about to happen.

It is February 1990, and I am eighteen months into men's work. Two and a half years since my first wife left me, to my huge surprise. No, it wasn't that I thought we had a great marriage, just that I was completely unconscious of her truth or mine. But I am awake now, and feeling strong. I have started a men's group and done a lot of work on myself in its first year. With the wonder of a small child, I have begun to see that the world is very different than I had thought, and that most men are still lost in the labyrinth of the male role. I am starting to see myself as a potential leader in this new men's movement. And I have begun attending regular meetings of the Ottawa/Hull Men's Forum, described as a male-positive, safe space for men growing out of stereotypes of masculinity.

The organizing group of the OHMF has arranged for this meeting to be about male violence against women. Three women from the Ottawa Rape Crisis Centre have been invited to lead the group in an exploration of the issue. I arrive early; only a few men and the three women are present, sitting on chairs arranged in a circle. It is unusual to have women present at the men's forum, and so I ask them, "Are you leading the discussion tonight?" In a sign of things to come, the women sigh and exchange despairing glances, and one of them turns to me and says scornfully "Hierarchy already! No, we're not going to lead, we're going to facilitate!"

Rebuked, I sit quietly. More men arrive, we introduce ourselves, and the women are invited to begin their facilitation. They say that violence against women is a part of male behaviour that men must help to eliminate. I certainly agree with that. Then they propose a debate; "Although not all men commit violence against women, all men benefit from it." At first, we are divided arbitrarily into two groups, for and against the contention. After a while we are permitted to "cross the floor" if we wish, in order to take the position on the issue that feels right for us. The debate is orderly, and also passionate. I do not need to cross the floor, as I am already in the group that I feel has the right of the matter.

I think about how men's violence against women has affected my life. I remember that when my wife left me, she did so secretly, saying that she was taking our dog to the vet. When I asked her later why she did it that way, she said, "I was afraid you would be violent." I couldn't understand that. I could scarcely believe it. I had never hit her, raised my hand or threatened her, or even imagined myself doing it. In fact, I haven't hit anyone in my entire adult life. I felt sure that she had been poisoned by the general perception that men are violent. I felt like I had lost a great deal through men's violence against women, if even after nine years of living together, my wife could not feel safe with me. How many years would it have taken, I wondered, for her to see me and not the prejudice? How much had that fear, never expressed, kept her from really trusting me, kept us from coming close? I think of the two or three times when I lost my temper and shouted at her. Was she thinking that I could begin using my fists at any moment?

I imagine a world in which men are never violent against women. It seems to me that, comparing that world to this, there is not a man in it that would not be better off. More trusted, more loved, more respected, more honoured, more rewarded, more happy, more seen and understood. Less feared, less ashamed, less defensive, less insecure. I know which world I would want to live in. There is no question that I feel diminished rather than benefited by the violence of men against women.

Some men have begun crossing the floor. To my surprise, they are crossing in both directions. Some are actually choosing the group that is arguing that they benefit from men's violence against women. I begin listening more carefully, more seriously to what they are saying. I had thought that this issue was obvious.

They are saying that they benefit from having their partner afraid of them. That someone in fear is like a slave, willing to obey them and reluctant to take a stand against them. That they get to have their way much more often than is fair, because she is afraid to offend. I wonder what these men want from their relationships with women. Are they actually attracted to a relationship of fear? What about intimacy? What about happiness? Have they said these things to their wives? I cannot imagine that men in recovery, in the men's movement, should feel that they would benefit from the fear of others. Yet it is so. For the first time, I sense a profound divide within the Ottawa men's movement.

The debate is over. It has been a really valuable experience for me. I have much to think about.

But wait. The women have something else to say. To my group, to the men who do not believe they benefit from men's violence against women, they say this: "You men are worse than the men who beat their wives, the guys in the strip clubs and using the prostitutes. You are pretending to be deconstructing masculinity, you are pretending to be growing into new and more whole, more conscious and responsible men, yet you are denying the very benefits you get from the violent, patriarchal system that you are a part of. You are hypocrites. You should be ashamed."

My God! I am reeling from this. I didn't see it coming. My heart is pounding and I can't think. What can I say? What can I do?

A man talks about his pain, about the way that he is also injured by the patriarchal system. The women interrupt him. "Don't tell us about your pain. Your pain is insignificant. You are the oppressor."

Another man speaks of his experience with his ex-wife. "She accused me of sexually abusing my three-year-old daughter. How could I prove my innocence?" he asks, with tears in his eyes. "I haven't been allowed to see my children for three years." "A woman would never lie about such an issue," he is told.

We seem helpless in the face of the anger of these women. I have recently read Warren Farrell's *Why Men Are the Way They Are*, and I speak of how women have more subtle powers that fully balance those of men. Even as I speak, however, I feel guilty about the anger that I am feeling and that is probably in my voice, and I am ignored by the women.

Another man speaks more eloquently. "Your pain is real and needs to be heard," he says to the women, "and so is our pain. We do not deny your pain as women, please do not deny us ours as men." He too is shamed in response.

The situation is incredibly charged. The women are feeling unheard and angry, their worst fears about the men's movement confirmed before their eyes. The men are feeling shamed and devalued, accused again by women who will not listen. We close the meeting in great awkwardness, with stiff thank yous for the facilitation. The women leave in silence, obviously hugely offended. Some men huddle and talk in low tones, others leave quickly. I feel abandoned, alone again in the playground, the naughty boy standing in the corner, sent to bed without my supper, punished and feeling guilty for not being how I "should" be. I compliment those men that I think spoke well, and leave.

I know that something pivotal has happened for me. I see that I am far from healed, far from secure and strong in my manhood. I don't know the nature of the wound I am carrying, but I know that it disqualifies me from leadership. I am not ready. I must withdraw from a public role in men's issues while I heal myself.

The Forum was never able to heal the divide that was exposed that evening. The drama played itself out over the next weeks and years. The women sent a letter to the Forum, protesting the way that they were "abused." The organizers responded with a formal apology, promising that they would make sure that it never happened again. They renamed the Forum "The Ottawa/Hull Men's Forum Against Sexism" and declared it actively pro-feminist. Men not of that persuasion were subtly (or not so subtly) unwelcome. The Forum continued for another three years, never again attracting the numbers it once had, before ceasing to operate from lack of attendance and lack of energy among the organizers in early 1994. An offer from a new group to restart it on an unaligned, non-ideological basis was rejected by the holders of the name and the mailing list, who felt that they could not allow it to continue as other than specifically pro-feminist. Today it lies dormant, if not dead.

I am either blessed or cursed with a passion to get to the bottom of things. Most days I think it is a blessing. For years I struggled to understand what happened that day. It seemed pivotal to the gender debate, as if the vast forces that move us had risen for a moment to the surface, like a great sea monster from the depths.

Gradually, some things became clear. First was that the women in that room were anything but powerless. In that encounter, they were both the formal leaders of the evening and also the emotional and moral centre of the experience. They felt to me like unshakable rocks against which I and the other men battered ourselves in vain. Yet, as I replayed it over and over in my mind, I realized that they were sincere in the belief that they were victims. They felt themselves to be victims, being abused even as they were defining the terms of the debate and overpowering the protests of the men. They did not experience their power over us as a feeling of power. I knew this was important. They were incredibly powerful to us, yet they felt powerless and abused even as they exercised that power. How could this be, I wondered.

Slowly, I realized that I was the same. As I listened to women talk about men's power, about the oppression of women and the patriarchal advantages I had as a man, I saw that I didn't experience them as power. Indeed, my position that evening had been the denial that men's violence gave them any benefits at all. Yet clearly, the fear of violence seemed to dominate a lot of women's lives. I began to get an inkling that power, between the genders at least, is very much in the eye of the beholder. And that this is very contrary to the way it feels. But I still didn't have an explanation for these differences. Nor did I have any sense of why this issue carried so much energy for me, why I experienced the accusation of those women as so powerful, even devastating in my life.

In 1991, at a ten-day experiential workshop, I found a piece of the answer. It was my first experience with people dedicated to discovering the truth about themselves, undistracted, over several days. For the first few days I risked little, but watched very carefully. I learned that when people dropped their guard and confessed their fears and failings, they were not shamed, but rather supported and held through the experience. What's more, they seemed to emerge stronger and with more self respect, not less.

On about the sixth day, we did an exercise involving shadow fighting with opponents from the group. We chose partners and mimed fighting, with or without imaginary weapons, and then changed partners and did it again. After several changes, I noticed a pattern. When my opponent was a man, I would fight energetically and aggressively, striving to win. When I was in conflict with a woman, however, I would be more anxious and more restrained, and try strenuously to ensure a draw. I remember a moment of astonishment when I discovered myself fighting with a sword in my left hand. I am right handed, but I had taken an imaginary sword in my left hand, because my female opponent had done so. What is going on? I wondered. Why am I allowing her to choose the weapons and the rules? I had never before had any awareness that my behaviour was so different with women than with men.

On about the eighth day, the leaders hauled three mattresses into the middle of the room and said "OK, each of us is going to have a tantrum." "Right," I thought, "you've got to be kidding." I couldn't imagine myself doing such a thing at thirty-eight years old. I made sure I was toward the back of the line that formed around the wall. But, as I watched, I saw that people were really getting into it. One by one, they opened a door into their rage, and kicked and screamed and cried. I decided that when it came to my turn, I would give it a try and see what happened. I had no notion of any anger in me that needed to come out, but I had moved myself into a willingness to discover what might be there instead of a denial and a fear of there being anything in me that I didn't already know of.

As I ran out to the mattresses, I felt sure that I would end up feeling foolish. But, almost immediately, I found myself starting to kick and pound the mattress, and words began to pour out of me. Over and over, I cried, "It's not fair, It's not fair." There was huge emotion in the words, and a great sense of release. "It's not fair." They still carry energy for me. I knew that what I was shouting was my outrage from childhood, when I would argue with my mother, and not once over many years (and still to this day) did she acknowledge being responsibly wrong about anything. Instead, whenever the argument began to go against her, she would end it with an unanswerable phrase like "You'll see when you grow up, you'll find out you're wrong." Or, "You can't understand because you're not a woman." Or worse, "You're always completely unreasonable, there's no sense arguing with you!" At one level, I was dreadfully afraid that she was right, that what seemed right to me was totally wrong, that I was self-centred and arrogant and unworthy, as she claimed. At another level, I knew that this was her defense because she knew that she was on shaky ground. And her unwillingness to ever admit it drove me crazy. I was incensed at her dishonesty. And, for twenty years, I had carried that anger inside me, not suspecting its existence, but unable to really trust a woman because I expected her to turn against me, and to deny all responsibility for her words or her actions.

The next day brought a new exercise. A rolled up blanket, tied with cord, was brought into the room. One by one, we were invited to have the blanket be whomever we wished, and to say and do whatever we needed to. Each person's session was contained within a formal ritual designed by the leaders, to identify the action as sacred space, as symbolic and not something that could or should occur in the real world, with the real person. This was spiritual work.

My heart was pounding with fear as I contemplated what I wanted to do. I knew, now, that I had a great deal of rage at my mother. I knew also that I had never really expressed it to her, because of the power she had over me, the fear that she would abandon me and throw me out of our home. (When I was four, because I refused to run for a bus with her, she got onto the bus alone and left me crying in fear at the bus stop. She got off at the next stop and waited until she thought I had learned my lesson before coming back to reclaim me. I always ran after that!) And so I had never allowed myself to win a fight with her, but contained my anger and held back my rage, as I had shown myself so eloquently in the shadow fighting exercise. Could I give myself permission to say and do what was in my heart? Was I ready to go past my fear of abandonment, still real in me twenty years after leaving home?

I still didn't know as I walked out to begin my work. For a while I just walked around the blanket, looking at it lying on the floor, trying to find the courage to speak my truth and un-shame my anger. I started talking to it, asking questions like "What did you think you were doing to me? Why did you never hug me or kiss me? Why couldn't you tell me you loved me?" Gradually, I began to feel my anger. I began to shout. "Don't you know how much that hurt me? Couldn't you see how afraid I was?" I began kicking the blanket and screaming, "I hate you! I hate you!" I kicked it across the room, picked it up and slammed it down on the floor. I kicked it so high it lifted one of the ceiling tiles. With tears rolling down my cheeks, I stomped my mother's head into the floor. For the first time in my life, I experienced my anger without shame. At thirty eight years old, after spending my life till then unconsciously circling around her, I killed my mother, and began the process of setting myself free and growing myself up.

This process of discovering the mother wound and recovering from it is not trivial. It involves looking deep into one's soul and learning to love what one finds there. It is fearful because what one expects to find is guilt, is unworthiness, is everything shameful. It can only be accelerated, it seems to me, through intensity, through the passion with which we pursue it. Sometimes, if we are willing, life brings us to moments when we are able to go very deep, and return richly blessed. Here is how it happened for me.

Throughout my childhood, my mother had used shame to manipulate me into doing what she wished, into being a 'good boy.' A result of this was that, as an adult, I still needed a woman to affirm me in order to feel that I was worthy as a man. Having married my first wife because she was unlike my mother, I now began to live with a woman who was exactly like my mother (though I certainly didn't see it at the time). She alternately shamed me and affirmed me, and I was addicted to the pleasure I felt in the moments when she acknowledged that I was right, and worthy, and she forgave me or embraced and validated me again. I was dependent on her for this sense of personal worth as a man, but I didn't recognize the reality of this dependence, nor did I see how I was a co-creator of the pattern of rejection and reunion that we danced again and again.

Things came to a head during a vacation. We were traveling in my truck, and she accused and shamed me relentlessly, for hours. I would argue, but eventually I would break down in tears and could not drive any more. I would get out and sit on the side of the road and cry until I recovered, then get back in and drive some more, and the pattern would repeat. It culminated in a night in a motor camp when neither of us slept at all. She spent the whole night analyzing my every behaviour since we had met, and showing me how I had been totally unworthy in every way, while she had been entirely the innocent victim of my abuse. That evening, I chose to surrender totally, to cease to argue at all, and to look for every bit of truth that I could find in her words. I decided to try to see myself through her eyes and to convict myself in every case where it could be done. Again, I don't know why I made that choice, but it was, in hindsight, the most powerful thing I have ever done. In my total humility, I became utterly and completely safe for her, and she shared her most intimate judgments and fears of me. And I used none of it to judge her, but only to see myself more clearly. In that place and at that time, I surrendered totally to the feminine, to my mother, to her power to convict me and shame me and judge me unworthy, and I ceased trying to defend myself from her judgments. I believe that I have never been so spiritually pure—or suffered worse psychic pain—before or since, as I was and did that night. In my humility, I accepted my guilt as accused, and apologized and asked for her forgiveness. I think that if she could have met me in that place at all, could have owned any of her projections, we might have begun to build a real relationship. But she did not, and instead continued to see me as entirely guilty and herself as blameless. And within a month, the distortions and one-sidedness of her perceptions (that I had accepted) became apparent to me, and I returned to balance, to the truth that we both were guilty, and both innocent.

The effect of that ordeal was to heal the deepest part of my mother wound. By surrendering totally to the shadow feminine, by ceasing to defend myself at all, I allowed myself to really look at what it said about me. And I discovered (to my surprise) that it is wrong about me, that my essential unworthiness does not survive the light of day, the test of truth. In my own, personal psychic world, I took *WOMAN* off the pedestal. What a gift that was! My ability to affirm and nurture and validate and bless myself had been tested in a total shame attack from my intimate partner, and I had survived. It was an initiation into adulthood for my feminine side, unchoreographed in any formal sense, and unguided except by my own internal, largely unconscious wisdom. It launched me, within a few months, into a series of new insights into the nature of female power in our society and the codependent relationship between the genders that is described below.

I learned so much from that experience. I learned that no one, not even my intimate partner, can prevent or inhibit my growth. I am profoundly free. If I am willing to look at myself, if I want the truth rather than a reassuring lie, then all the things that she accuses me of become food for my soul. I examine them, work on myself wherever I find some truth in the criticism, and discard what does not fit. Whether she looks at what I raise to her attention is her business, and limits me not at all. What a wonderful power and freedom I found in that discovery.

Further understanding came when I found the field of addiction recovery. I began to recognize my codependency, and the denial patterns with which I had concealed myself from myself. Over the course of a year, in 1992, I read voraciously about addictive behaviours, attended a twelve step self-help group called adult children anonymous, and intensively studied my own behaviour in my current relationship. I began to see the patterns, the ways that my partner, her family and I were all codependently intertwined and interlocked, and the layers of rationalizations with which we hid the real nature of our relationships from ourselves and each other. And as I did so, I stopped my part of the deception. I confess that although all the literature had warned me, still I thought that I would be able to reach them, to help them see the truth that I had discovered. What happened instead was that I was rejected. But, for the first time, I had the strength not to take it personally.

In the spring of 1994, the final piece fell into place for me, at a three day workshop on community building. The workshop invited us to explore what blocked us from experiencing community, what kept us from appreciating and treating each other with respect and equality. On the second day, during the lunch break, a woman approached me privately and said that she had admired my ability to speak clearly in the group, and she wanted my opinion on why people seemed to have trouble accepting what she said in the group. She said that it seemed to her that people often criticised her after she had spoken.

I did have an opinion about this, so I shared it with her. I had been thinking a lot about victimhood, and I told her that, as I saw it, her sharings in the group were frequently coming from a victim place, expressing or implying how others were responsible for how she felt and what she did, and arguing against her having any power or responsibility. I explained that I thought that this was a trap in terms of personal growth, a stuck place, as we can grow only by taking responsibility for our own feelings and actions. Based on the dynamic I had seen in the group, I suggested that those whom she perceived as criticising her might actually be trying to broaden her perspective by suggesting the limitations of her victim worldview, by pointing out ways that she could take responsibility. She thanked me for my thoughts and we ended the conversation on good terms.

After lunch, when the group met for the afternoon session, this woman told the group that she had just had one of the worst experiences of her life. She had asked me for support, she said, and instead I had told her everything that was wrong with her. Between tears, she said that she felt abused and violated, and she didn't think she could stay at the workshop any longer. I was astonished, but even more astonished by what happened next. One after another, all of the twenty or so men in the group (and one or two women) spoke up, apologised on my behalf and pleaded with her to stay, promising her that they would make sure that it didn't happen again. The uniformity of their responses was amazing. As with the experience at the Ottawa/Hull men's forum, I knew I was seeing something important. Not one person appeared to consider the possibility that her perception of what happened might be skewed. No one asked me for my own perception: it seemed that my guilt was assumed. I felt like a woman had cried 'rape,' and all the men were trying to feel and heal her pain. And again I saw how powerful she was in fact, in her ability to draw empathy and to have her version of what happened carry the day, be accepted as fact — even while she felt and expressed her vic-timhood, her total lack of power. And I saw that it was primarily the men who were in her power in this way.

Because, I believe, of the work I had already begun in healing my mother wound, I was able to tolerate everyone's assumption of my guilt and watch the dynamic play out. The woman ended up thanking the men for their support and deciding to stay: the relief in the room was palpable. I spoke at the end about the group dynamic I thought I had seen, and noted that no one had wondered whether the woman had described what happened accurately. I told my own version of our interaction to the group, and commented that I thought that something very important to understand about the power relationships between men and women had happened in that room. I spoke pretty strongly, and I think I described the device of threaten-ing to leave the group as "emotional blackmail." My heart was pounding and I felt the nega-tive judgements of just about everyone there.

I worried over what had happened, and what it might mean, for the rest of the day. And that night, at four in the morning after a restless night of crazy dreams, I received the full answer about what was going on that evening back in 1990 at the Ottawa/Hull Men's Forum, what had been going on between me and my wife and my woman friends since then, and what is

	Reward	Punish
MEN'S POWER (External) · Physical · Economic · Political	Protect Provide Represent	Attack Abandon Oppress
WOMEN'S POWER (Internal) · Moral · Emotional · Sexual	Validate Nurture Favour	Shame Reject Refuse

Figure 21.1 Gender Codependent Power-Over Matrix

going on at the deepest level between men and women in our society. I received what I call the "gender codependent power-over matrix," a model which identifies women's power as equal to that of men, but less visible because of its very different form. Key to understanding this model is the notion of codependency. We are codependently engaged with someone when we transact with them to get our needs met, but hide the truth about our transactions from ourselves and each other with rationalizations, stories that preserve our false opinion of ourselves. A trivial example might be a husband who "has a shell around him" and a wife who "nags." The wife will explain her behaviour by saying "It's because he has a shell around him that I have to repeat and emphasize everything in order to get through to him." The husband will report "I wouldn't have a shell around me if I didn't need it to cope with her nagging." Each is sincere at a conscious level, but the mutual dependence can be seen in the fact that each makes the other responsible for their behaviour. At a deeper level, we can speculate that perhaps the structure provides a kind of stability, and a defense against the vulnerability of real intimacy. The pathology lies in the fact that both parties are (unconsciously) lying to themselves and each other, and each feels powerless, determined by the other.

In the larger gender dynamic in North America, I believe that the codependent exchange of responsibilities has occurred as follows. In general, men have had what we can call external power, i.e. physical (greater personal strength and military might), economic and political. Women have had internal power: moral, emotional and sexual. We are in the strange situation today in which men's power has been well-articulated by the women's movement, while women's equivalent and balancing power remains unrecognized. It is because of the denial structures of our codependency that most of society sees power as unilaterally possessed by men.

The areas of physical, economic and political power held mainly by men are familiar to us. However, women's power areas have not been articulated by either women or men, and so merit discussion.

Women have moral power over men. It has been recognized throughout history that women are the protectors of morals. Alexis de Tocqueville observed this in his 1834 tome *Democracy in America,*[1] and it was specifically noted by the conference that arguably launched the women's liberation movement, in Seneca Falls[2] a hundred and fifty years ago. But what is moral power? This is the power to say whether an action or a person is OK, is worthy, is right or wrong. As I see it, this power balances men's superior physical strength and military might. It is the honour code by which society has traditionally tried to ensure that the violence of the warrior is used only against the enemy, and never against the women and children he is supposed to protect.

Some of this is men honouring or shaming men, of course. However, the root moral authority lies with women. This situation is similar to the fact that while men earn more than half of the income in North America, three quarters of the consumer dollar are spent by women. What matters is the source of the power, not whose hands it passes through, as women have rightly pointed out.

I believe that shaming, a psychological attack on a person's honour or worth, is just as devastating to a man as is sexual or physical violence to a woman. However, men hide their wounds and deny their pain — even from themselves. Sociopsychologist Howard Schwartz recognizes the power of shame in his *Revolt of the Primitive: An Inquiry into the Roots of Political Correctness.* "How does political correctness get its power over its opposition? The stands taken as politically correct are often quite radical and have a great deal of opposition to them among more traditional elements of the university. These traditional elements are often rapidly and decisively overcome. They often stand quite mute in fact. How does that happen? Much of the answer may be found in an understanding of the way the PC university mobilizes the power of shame through public humiliation. ... [u]nder the aegis of university administration, such practices have become the norm."[3]

Consider as evidence the fact that completely one-sided feminist analyses have become accepted as mainstream thinking. For example, the focus on male violence against women carefully isolates only those cases where men are "guilty" and women are innocent. And yet, *every* scientific study of intergender violence that has asked the same questions of *both* sexes has found either equivalent rates of violence initiation and escalation, or that women are more violent than men.[4] So why have men not defeated the one-sidedness of the feminist propaganda? Feminists point out that men appear to control the legislature, the courts, the media, the police and the universities. Why haven't men exercised their social power so as to broaden and balance the perspective on this issue? It is because we are ashamed, and we are ashamed because women have told us that we should be. This is an exercise of women's moral power to define what is right and what is wrong, what is morally important and what should be overlooked.

The roots of this power lie in infancy, when the mother was the source of moral authority, the one who decided when we were good and when we were bad. Our fathers may have carried out the sentence, but for most of us mother was the judge and the jury. Today most men still give this authority to women. This was why I could not stand up to the women at the Men's Forum, this was why I was devastated by their shaming of me, even though I had only met them that evening. They were WOMEN, and I gave them the power to judge me, and I felt unable to refute their judgment.

What is shame? American psychiatrist James Gilligan, who works with the most violent men in U.S. maximum security prisons, sees shame as "… the absence of a healthy sense of self-esteem, self-respect, and self-love which are necessary to survive the inevitable rejections and humiliations which no one can avoid in life." He continues, "Children who fail to receive sufficient love from others do not build those reserves of self-love. Without feelings of self-love, the self feels numb, empty and dead. It may be paradoxical to refer to shame as a 'feeling,' says Gilligan, for while shame is initially painful, constant shaming leads to a deadening of feeling. Shame is like cold. At first it is intensely painful, but when it reaches an intolerable extreme, it results in complete numbness and in the death of the self. The person whose soul has been killed by shame goes through life with an automatic, unconscious reflex for self-anaesthetization which is self-deadening. How, Gilligan asks, can a person who does not experience any feelings himself know that others have feelings or be moved by the feelings of others?[5]

I need to clarify something here. I have identified shame, the notion that we are not OK, that we are flawed and inferior to others, as the basic psychic wound process that moves us from stage one to stage two. I am not suggesting here that this is done to us by our mothers. As I said at the time, I see this as a universal process that happens to every child and has no inherent connection with parenting, abusive or otherwise. What I am saying here is that because shame is the primary coercive tool in the feminine psychological archetype, i.e., the tool that tends to feel more natural to women, the shame of that early psychic wound gets mapped or projected onto mothers more than onto fathers. *Fear* is the primary coercive tool of the masculine archetype, and abusive fathers tend to use fear — intimidation, threats of consequences or punishment, for instance — to compel behaviour of their children. For in the historical balance of power between men and women, women have experienced fear of the abuses of men (the whole feminist movement has been about addressing women's fears of men's abuses). And so women tend in general to empathize with their children's fear (since it reflects something they also experience), which is why they are so concerned with physical safety, for instance. Mothers' area of insensitivity, of lack of empathy, tends to be in the psychological realm, which is why they use shame to coerce the behaviour of the children. Since this is a power area for women, it is harder for them to empathize with what it is like to feel powerless in this area.

Another example: in 1992, under pressure from feminist groups, the Supreme Court of Canada, in a nine-zero decision, defined obscenity in terms of what harms women! Not what harms people, or what harms society, but what harms women. Our highest court could not see the blatant one-sidedness of this decision (or, seeing it, could not oppose it, for shame). Even the extreme external power and success possessed by supreme court judges does not remove or compensate for their subjection to the moral power over held by women.

In a similar way, women hold emotional power over men. By emotional power, I mean that women have had the role of emotional provider, doing the emotional work for the family in the way that men have done the economic work. Thus, in general, grieving, nurturing, excitement, love and passion have fallen to women to feel and express, while men have been "stoic" and unfeeling, and "held the fort." Because of thirty years of feminist rhetoric, we are liable to see this as yet another cross for women to bear, but it is in fact a power area just as much as is the economic power of men, because men, through social conditioning and stigma, cannot readily do this emotional work. They are, in fact, less emotionally competent as a gender, just as women are still less economically competent (although approaching parity). And since psychological health requires that emotions be expressed, vicariously if not personally, this male incompetence gives women a major power over men. (If it seems that this power is overstated, consider that in the two years after a marriage failure men commit suicide at ten times the rate that women do. What have they lost that is so devastating?)

Finally, let us examine sexual power. I am not saying that men's and women's physiological sex drives are different: the evidence suggests that they are not. And yet, to men, women have the sexual "goods;" men need the sexual favours of women in a way that women do not need from men. At a deeper level, I suggest that what men really need is the approval, the validation of women, expressed most fundamentally and unmistakably through access to women's bodies. After all, a woman doesn't open her body to just anyone. Men know that this is the acid test, the real thing. When a woman shares her body with a man, she is risking pregnancy (or used to be, when these cultural mores evolved). And so she is selective — usually highly selective. And men, hungry for the validation, the approval implicit in being thus selected, strive to 'score' with a woman. (The word 'score' itself is very revealing — as in sports, the motivation for scoring is the adulation, the validation of one's skill, prowess, worth.) Thus sex is a "seller's market," and women, with the ability to accept or reject, possess the power. And so in the dating dynamic the man takes risk after risk as he initiates each increment of sexual intimacy, and at each step the woman can favour him, refuse, or postpone. The sexual power lies all with her.

An aspect of this could be referred to as 'beauty power,' and a number of authors (e.g., Warren Farrell) have explored this dynamic in depth. Robert Bly speaks to this in his *Iron John:*

> "I remember a man telling me of a summer he spent at fifteen working as a busboy in a Catskills resort. He and the other boys were doing all right until one day a tall, blond, beautiful self-contained, high-cheekboned sixteen-year-old girl walked into the dining room. It was all over in a moment. The fifteen-year-old boy sank under the waves, bubbles came up, he was lost.

> "It is interesting that neither he nor his equally moved friends ever talked to her. Instead they spent hours after work discussing who spoke to her today, what she wore at breakfast, whom she walked up with, who sat at her table. Her face and its beauty, which seemed inaccessible, or invulnerable, made them all feel like hicks, inarticulate clods of earth, hopelessly matter-ridden louts. She was above matter.

> "For three weeks the obsession went on; they woke up every morning feverish. Then the summer ended; she left, that was it. There was only one event in the summer, that one. …

> "The girl, on her side, is equally confused. She may in reality be lacking in self-esteem, be insecure, shamed, even victimized, but on the outside, in the radiance from her face, she is queenly, self-possessed, golden and invulnerable."[6]

Do you see, do you feel the codependence here. Remember that codependence, that addiction, is a spiritual disease, one in which we worship the wrong gods. There is indeed an aspect of worship in the boys relationship to the beautiful girl. They put her on a pedestal, make an idol of her. And yet, although she is so immensely powerful in their lives, yet she probably experiences little or none of this power *as* power. In codependence, no one is really powerful. And yet, there is an asymmetry: the power that there is belongs to her. The boys worship her, and not the other way around. And at some unconscious level (remember, this is a dance of unconsciousness), she knows this.

Boys grow out of this inarticulate woman-worship, of course. One way is that, as they begin to *achieve,* to become competent providers or potential providers on the world's terms, they begin to feel a little more equal, that they have something to offer, to trade that might be worth the shining value of a woman's beauty and sexual favours. But the basic dynamic, the power of female beauty and sex to compel men's attention and inflame their desire continues. And so women can and do trade on their beauty power, on their sexual power, to get things that they want. The most upwardly mobile class of people, bar none, in North America, is beautiful women. A beautiful woman almost always marries well above the social class of her origin; this is so common that it is almost an icon, we expect it.

Of course, if a woman is too punishing in the dating dynamic, she risks the man resorting to one of his power areas—physical force, for example, and so she doesn't experience her power over as a feeling of power; instead, she feels anxious rather than secure. This feeling of powerlessness on both sides is a major symptom of codependency, and completely misleading since it seems obvious on each side that the other holds the power that matters. (Recall the observation made earlier of the power wielded by the women in the Ottawa Men's Forum, even as they felt themselves to be powerless and abused.) This false notion of one-sided power and oppression is the complete basis of feminist analysis of male power, and totally overlooks the other side of the pattern, namely men's powerlessness in the face of women's power. And so, for example, women have used their moral power to identify date rape, i.e. women's experience of men's power, as the important dating issue, while most men remain afraid or ashamed to acknowledge (or even to feel) their own powerlessness in the same dating dynamic.

Dissident feminist Camille Paglie writes,

> "When I was young, I thought teenage boys were the most awkward, miserable, antsy, bratty, scuzzy, snickering creatures on God's green earth. Now at midlife and, as it were, *hors de combat,* I see them quite differently. Watching them rampage on the street or at the shopping mall, I find them extraordinarily moving, for they represent the masculine principle struggling to free itself from woman's cosmic dominance.

> "Teenage boys, goaded by their surging hormones (at maximum strength at this time), run in packs like the primal horde. They have only a brief season of exhilarating liberty between control by their mothers and control by their wives. The agony of male identity springs from men's humiliating sense of dependence upon women. It is women who control the emotional and sexual realms, and men know it."[7]

What Paglia describes here is not the whole story of teenage male behaviour, it is just an overlooked piece. It is overlooked today because it is sympathetic in tone. It recognizes male *powerlessness*, and so contradicts the story of our time. Paglia has learned to empathize with those boys, to see deeper than they do into their souls (they do not know in any conscious sense, or course, about their dependence on women), into their issues and their challenges, and to feel for them. It is a rare gift in our present climate, from either men or women, and it is received by this male with thanks.

This understanding of the three areas of female power over men provides new explanations for a lot of gender activities. For example, male sexual deviations such as pornography, use of prostitutes, child sexual abuse, or rape can be seen as displacement activities, in which the deep (unconscious) motivation is an attempt to cope with or escape from the sexual power exercised by women. By introducing into the sexual transaction one of men's power areas such as economic (in the case of pornography or prostitution) or physical force (child abuse, rape), men attempt to remove or reduce the risk of rejection and manipulation which they experience from women's sexual power over. Of course, these strategies cannot ultimately satisfy, since they keep unconscious and thus avoid dealing with men's underlying feelings of powerlessness. This suggests that emphasizing the shamefulness of these activities, as feminism has been doing through the use of women's moral power, will not be effective. Instead, the solution lies in greater empowerment of women (leading to less manipulative use of women's sexual power) and of men (so that they are less needy for women's approval and more able to avoid entanglement in the sexual power game).

Victim feminism is also a displacement activity. By taking the areas in which women have felt powerless and manipulated, and introducing women's power into the transaction, i.e. the moral power to shame men into giving them what they want, women attempt to reduce the sense of powerlessness that they have experienced from men's political, economic and physical power over. And in just the same way, this also fails to satisfy since it does not lead to consciousness raising and genuine empowerment, but confirms the power of the other. And so feminists are clamouring about a backlash, and demanding (and getting) ever more one-sided compensations for women's victimization, as we have seen.

In codependency, denial is used to defend against an accurate owning of responsibility. Either we are avoiding acknowledging our responsibility for our situation and seeing ourselves as victims (the feminist story), or we are avoiding the truth that we are a lot less powerful than we want to believe (men's denial structure). In particular, we have as yet acknowledged only two quadrants of the gender codependent power over matrix: women's positive side of nurturers and emotional caregivers, and men's dark side of violence and abuse. As an illustration of this, consider that the women's movement has given us a female word, feminism, as a vision of an ideal future to work towards, and a male word, patriarchy, to stand for everything that is wrong today and in the past. Our task as a society, and in particular as men, is to expose the other two quadrants (shaded in the diagram to represent their hiddenness): women's dark side of shaming and rejection, and men's positive contributions of physical, economic and political protection and support. Contrary to feminist claims about men's activities in these areas, men have in fact strenuously endeavoured to represent the interests of women, as they understood them. That these interests were not well understood cannot be denied; but that is the nature of codependence. Indeed, I argue here that feminism, sincerely believing itself to represent men's interests as well as women's, is just as mistaken.

Codependency is not bad, or wrong, or sinful. It is simply the most universal form of psychological immaturity in physical adults. However, it is important to realize that it is an addiction. Like the denial which alcoholics use to rationalize their drinking, we are currently in deep denial around the relationship between men and women in our society. Thus feminism has seen women as victims of patriarchy (confirming women's dependence on father to change and rescue women), while the men's movement has either identified with women's victimization in order to please mother (pro-feminist men), argued with mother and taken a victim stance of its own (men's rights) or avoided mother entirely for a retreat to the woods and a focus on the father (mythopoetic men). For each gender, the psychological world continues to revolve around the other.

I do not want to shame these movements, to say that they should have been and done differently. These strategies have been necessary way-stations as we prepare ourselves to confront our deepest addictions and our fear of the other. Through the political gains made by feminism, women have been gaining confidence and competence in men's traditional areas of external power. And in therapy, personal growth workshops, retreats and men's groups, men have been doing emotional work and gaining the strength to claim their own moral power. We will soon begin to step out of these protected spaces and acknowledge our gender truth in the public arena. And when we do, we can expect to be shamed. We will be called backlash, misogynist, the privileged seeking to continue their oppression of others. To stand against such shame attacks, we will need to know, to really know, that they are not true. To know this, we will need to have examined our souls as deeply as we can. This work can be incredibly painful. Sometimes, life leads us to it almost despite ourselves.

The real gender revolution will involve breaking denial and doing this hard recovery work, one man and one woman at a time. This work is painful and fearful, which of course is why we avoid it. It involves acknowledging our wounds from the past and the dysfunctional, codependent ways we have used to avoid feeling and owning them. Most importantly, it involves grieving the loss in order to discover (recover) our intrinsic worthiness. This work takes different forms for men and for women. Women, in general, are in denial of their power, which they fear as guilt. Men, in general, are in denial of their powerlessness, which they fear as failure or weakness. We do not break denial patterns "because we should" (a shame attack) but only when we want to. I believe the time is near for a widespread gender recovery movement to begin.

I want to end by pointing out how subtly shame can operate. Because it is so unacknowledged, it is virtually invisible in many of its forms. A final anecdote will make clear how ubiquitous, how invisible, and how powerful shame is in our society today.

My life as a boy circled around the theme of anxiety. Not a burning fear, but a constant, low-level anxiety that I would be thrust at any moment into a sense of failure and guilt, of feeling unworthy, of shame. And yet, I think I was a lucky child. There was only one level of lies that I had to spin in order to survive. I had to lie to myself about my worthiness, but I didn't have to lie to myself about my feelings of fear and shame and anxiety. I knew that there was something wrong with feeling that way. I didn't have to make myself believe that everything was perfect, that my parents were faultless. That's the reason, I believe, that I was able to wake up at thirty five and start to grow, to discover the truth about myself. Most people in society seem to me to be caught in a much subtler trap: they don't think (more precisely, are afraid to consider) that there's anything to recover from. Today, I bless the fact that, as a boy, I knew that I was unhappy.

But, you ask, how can a person not know that they are unhappy? Perhaps a story will make this clear. A few years ago, on Christmas Eve, I went to a Toronto church with family. At one point in the service, young boys and girls were called up from the congregation into a group at the front and questioned about Christmas by a young woman with a microphone. She began, "How do you feel?" One boy replied, "Fine." On to the next child. "What about you, how do you feel?" "Fine." This wasn't going where the young woman wanted to go. "It's Christmas Eve!" she said. "Isn't anyone excited?" A chorus of "Yes" and "I am" in response. The children are getting the drift now. "What are you excited about?" the woman asked. ... This time there was no response. Silence.

I know what they're excited about, of course. These are children aged four to twelve or so. It's Christmas Eve. What they are excited about is the gifts they are expecting to receive tomorrow morning. But not one of them says so. Why not? Well, they know that, although the questions seem to be asking about their feelings, about their truth, that's not what's really wanted. They know, at some level, that they are expected to perform, to pretend to be other than they are, that our approval of them depends on it. They are waiting for more direction so they can figure out the right answers.

The woman gives them a hint. "What's special about Christmas? What's Christmas about?" An older child thinks she knows the answer to that one. "Compassion," she says. The young woman is visibly relieved. "That's right," she says. "And what is compassion?"

The conversation continues, and I look around the church. I am looking to see if anyone other than me is disturbed by this. Among 200 parishioners, I see only smiles of pleasure; parents and other adults enjoying the cuteness of the children. Perhaps they are telling themselves how wonderful children are, how much they love them. I experience a profound loneliness and despair. For I know that what I am witnessing is child abuse, in church, by good, honest, upright folk. And I fear that I am the only one who sees it.

Let's look carefully at what was really going on. We adults in that church, and I include myself since I did not challenge it, were seeking to have the children say the 'right,' virtuous things about Christmas; that it is about love and giving and compassion and selflessness. Perhaps we wanted to hear these things from the innocent mouths of our children, so that we could be reassured in our pious belief that those are the important virtues. We wanted the children to be 'excited' about those virtues—perhaps because we weren't very excited about them ourselves any more. I don't know. But I do know this. We were using the children as objects for our own selfish purposes. We didn't care to hear their real feelings, but only the ones we expected from them. What's worse, we wanted them to fake it for us, to pretend that what they gave us *were* their real feelings. And the stick with which we coerced these lies was our conditional approval. And, of course, it worked, as it usually works.

I looked at their faces as the children walked back to their seats. Some were excited, presumably at having spoken over the microphone. Some were subdued. Some looked a little disturbed. None looked angry. What had happened was unremarkable: it happens every day, a hundred times a day, to almost every child and to almost every adult. It is our way of life. It's completely and totally normal. And it's utterly abusive. I don't know how to express my horror at the universality and the destructiveness of this subtle form of abuse, and of our almost total blindness to it. We had taught those children to be ashamed of who they really were, and to substitute instead a false self for our approval. This deep, essential shame is what I call the mother wound.

Now don't get me wrong. It wasn't done maliciously, in anger or cruelty. No, it was covert, hidden from our awareness—and theirs as well. It was done unconsciously, under a cover story that it was all for their own good. Nevertheless, the children's behaviour proved that they knew, at some level, that who they really were wasn't valued, wasn't loved. And the fact that they, like we, hid the pain of that knowledge from themselves, doesn't make it less harmful, less abusive. In fact, by forcing a kind of self-deception on top of the manipulation, it makes it worse, more convoluted, more difficult to recognize. We get trapped into the conspiracy of the cover up, all of us pretending that what we are doing is loving. Even our feelings of affection while listening to the children are false: they are simply the pleasure of getting what we want from others, the ego-stroking affirmation of receiving — without caring what the gift costs the giver.

These archetypally feminine (not female) forms of child abuse are hard to recognize. They are covert, indirect, manipulative and deceptive: the cover-up is built into the crime. And, to make it even harder, we have little or no empathy for this form of suffering, because we are all caught up in it ourselves. When it was done to us as children under the guise of righteousness, we hid our pain from ourselves, and now, still hiding and in denial of our pain, we fail to recognize the abusiveness of these forms of manipulation and control of others. And, failing to recognize them, we perpetuate them.

I feel overwhelmed by the size of this issue. It is so massive, so universal, and so invisible. And how does one recover from loss of oneself? Once one has substituted a false self, an image that is more appropriate, more acceptable, more "correct", then the road back to authenticity is so difficult. For, no matter how much approval I gain for my 'act,' for my false self, I can never get enough. Because, of course, approval of my false self, my image, isn't approval of me, but just the opposite. No, filled with fear and trembling, I must risk showing my real self to the world, knowing that when I did that as a child, I was usually punished or shamed. What a task lies before us as we start to untangle this web!

I see this as the last great universal challenge facing us as adults and as parents. The archetypically masculine—overt, direct or physical—abuses are easy to recognize today, and universally known to be harmful. No, it is the indirect, the covert, the deceptive, the shaming, the manipulative abuse that is the great destroyer of our children's souls today. Can we, who were not loved for who we were as children ourselves, yet offer to our children that vital soul-food—respect and valuing of their essence, of their real nature—even as we help them shape their behaviours in ways that will work for them in society? If we can, it will be the greatest gift that can be given, the gift of authentic life itself.

To do that, of course, we have to heal our own mother wound, our own essential shame. And the critical first step on that road is to break the cover story, the denial, and to begin instead to tell the truth about one's inner life, one's wounds and fears. That is an act of pure courage, for most will not understand and will be very threatened by such truth telling. But until we accept responsibility, and the pain of the shame that comes with it, we cannot forgive ourselves, for without responsibility there is nothing to forgive. And the shame, futilely projected out onto others, remains with us. I have lived that way. I don't recommend it to anyone.

The mother wound, our essential shame, keeps a part of us locked away in a kind of cage as long as it remains unhealed and unconscious. Robert Bly, in his book *Iron John* that basically launched the mythopoetic men's movement and that remained on the bestseller list for almost a year, suggests that it is our "Wild Man" that is locked up, the earthy, uncivilized, but radiantly alive part of us, our soul, as it were. "The kind of wildness, or un-niceness, implied by the Wild Man image," writes Bly, "is not the same as macho energy, which men already know enough about. Wild Man energy, by contrast, leads to forceful action undertaken, not with cruelty, but with resolve."[8] (It sounds to me from this description that it is associated with healthy warrior energy, about which I will have more to say later.) The king's son loses his golden ball into the Wild Man's cage, and asks him for it back. The Wild Man says he will give the ball back if the prince sets him free from the cage. The key to the cage containing the Wild Man, it turns out, is under the boy's mother's pillow. Why? Because "when the King locked up the Wild Man, he gave the key into the keeping of the Queen."

This speaks to me of the codependence I have been describing, of the way a man and a woman typically transact to cement their relationship, and of the hidden losses from this transaction: that something essentially masculine is locked up, and this affects the children as well.

Bly says,

"… the key is under our mother's pillow — just where Freud said it would be.

"Getting the key back from under the mother's pillow is a troublesome task. Freud, taking advice from a Greek play, says that a man should not skip over the mutual attraction between himself and his mother if he wants a long life. … Michael Meade, the mythteller, once remarked to me that the pillow is also the place where the mother stores all her expectations for you. She dreams: 'My son the doctor.' 'My son the Jungian analyst.' 'My son the Wall Street genius.' But very few mothers dream: 'My son the Wild Man.'

"On the son's side, he isn't sure he wants to take the key. Simply transferring the key from the mother's to a guru's pillow won't help. Forgetting that the mother possesses it is a bad mistake. A mother's job is, after all, to civilize the boy, and so it is natural for her to keep the key. All families behave alike: on this planet, 'The King gives the key into the keeping of the Queen.'

Attacking the mother, confronting her, shouting at her, which some Freudians are prone to urge on us, probably does not accomplish much — she may just smile and talk to you with her elbow on the pillow. Oedipus' conversations with Jocasta never did much good, nor did Hamlet's shouting.

"A friend mentioned that it's wise to steal the key some day when your mother and father are gone. 'My mother and father are away today' implies a day when the head is free of parental inhibitions. That's the day to steal the key. …

"And the key has to be *stolen*. … No mother worth her salt would give the key any-way. If a son can't steal it, he doesn't deserve it.
'I want to let the Wild Man out!'
'Come over and give Mommy a kiss.'

"Mothers are intuitively aware of what would happen if he got the key: they would lose their boys. The possessiveness that mothers typically exercise on sons … can never be underestimated."[9]

Later in the book, Bly uses a different metaphor:

"We know that more than one American man today needs a sword to cut his adult soul away from his mother-bound soul. Australian aboriginal initiators use that sword precisely to cut that psychic umbilical cord. The sword has the edge that cuts clinging away from love, cuts boyish bravado away from manly firmness, and cuts passive-aggression away from fierceness. The Tibetans refer to such a sharp interior sword as 'the Vajra sword.' Without it, they say, no spiritual life is possible, and no adult life."[10]

I don't know to what extent what Bly is describing here corresponds to the mother wound that I describe. There is some degree of overlap, I am sure. Certainly my own experience of "killing my mother" at that experiential workshop was largely about repudiating my (internalized) mother's expectations about what I 'should' be like, and setting myself free of her power over me.

It is also probably no coincidence that the men's movement that feminists find of greatest concern is the mythopoetic movement. In *Women Respond to the Men's Movement: A Feminist Collection,*[11] virtually none of the contributors can find a good thing to say about the men's movement, (actually, their message throughout the book, in a thousand different forms of words, is almost entirely "Shame on you, men, shame, shame, shame"), and the movement they are criticising is the mythopoetic, as seen through the lens of *Iron John.* What's more, the part that seems to really burn them the most is this bit about the key and the mother's pillow. I interpret this as an accurate fear on their part that if men actually do this mother wound work, if they really do steal the key, then they will become strong and independent men, no longer able to be controlled and silenced through the use of shame.

I think there's something very important there. We each, men and women, must move through the shame piece and out the other side. There is a journey set before us, a journey that calls to us all, but each one of us must take that first step alone, in fear and trembling. And yet, it is the journey of life, and until we begin it, we are not fully alive. I believe that we are on the verge of beginning that journey as a whole society, vast numbers of us moving into recovery, perhaps within a single generation. We will need leaders who have healed their own mother wound, to point the way and welcome the journeyers. You have read this chapter through to the end. Are you ready to take the first step? Or a next step?

I offer you the question with which I challenge myself: "If not me, then who? And if not now, when?"

NOTES:

---

†Based upon Chapter 10 in Shackleton (2005)

* David Shackleton, Editor and Publisher, Everyman; A Men's Journal. The only regular Canadian magazine of men's gender issues and gender justice. P.O. Box 4617, Stn E, Ottawa, ON K1S 5H8, Canada. Web Site: http://www.everyman.org

¹ de Tocqueville, Alexis, *Democracy in America,* 1834. Quoted from reprint, ed. Phillips Bradley, Vintage Books, New York, 1945, vol.1, pp.315-8. Quote taken from Bork, Robert H., *Slouching Towards Gomorrah: Modern Liberalism and American Decline,* HarperCollins, New York, 1996, p.272.

[2] Schneir, Miriam. *Feminism: The Essential Historical Writings*. Vintage, New York, 1972.

[3] Schwartz, Howard S., *The Revolt of the Primitive: An Inquiry into the Roots of Political Correctness*, Praeger, Westport, CT, 2001, p.152.

[4] See Farrell, Warren, Ph.D., *Women Can't Hear What Men Don't Say: Destroying myths, creating love*, Tarcher/Putnam, New York, 1999, p.129, pp.323-329.

[5] Armstrong, Mary, "The Price We Pay for Shaming Little Boys," *The Journal of Psychohistory*, vol. 27, #4, Spring 2000, p.449. Original source: Gilligan, James, *Focusing Oriented Psychotherapy*, The Guildford Press, New York, 1996, pp.47-52.

[6] Bly, Robert, *Iron John: A Book About Men*, Addison-Wesley, Reading, MA, 1990, p.135.

[7] Paglia, Camille, "Homosexuality at the Fin de Siècle," *Sex, Art, and American Culture: Essays*. Random House, New York, 1992, p.24.

[8] Bly, *Iron John*, p.8.

[9] Ibid., pp.11-12.

[10] Ibid., p.165.

[11] Hagan, Kay Leigh, ed. *Women Respond to the Men's Movement: A Feminist Collection*, HarperCollins, New York, NY, 1992.

Chapter 22
Toward Epistemology Functional for the 21st Century

JOHN EVERINGHAM

W hen I was a freshman at U.C.L.A., I over-
heard a sophomore ask, "How do you know, that what you know, is valid knowledge?"[1] Later
I learned that this is the central question of epistemology – the study of how one gathers and
evaluates knowledge.[2]

As a scientist, I'm disturbed that so many of my colleagues seem to pay little attention to the
foundations of our work. Much heated argument and misunderstanding is based upon differing, but unstated, assumptions about epistemology and the methodology derived from it. And
much important knowledge is dismissed or ignored for being based upon unfamiliar or devalued epistemology. This is especially true for the human sciences.

We need to adopt the idea that *all* paradigms of epistemology have both strengths and limitations. One area of limitation frequently left unconsidered is how well the knowledge-gathering methods are suited to the questions being asked. To say it more directly: We have to match the paradigm to the problem.

Recall that there are two equally valid ways to predict the behavior of light. But in designing a camera, we *must* use particulate equations for the light meter, and wave theory for the lens. If the paradigm/problem match is wrong, no functional camera will result.

When we take a global view, it seems clear that the "hard" sciences are well suited to the easy problems, but the "soft" sciences are required for the difficult ones. "Hard" sciences are those that test hypotheses by rigorous adherence to the protocol of control, measure, and reproduce (CMR). This protocol is often called *The* Scientific Method; I consider it to be *a* scientific method, and will refer to it as "CMR Science."

The difficult problems are mostly those involving the behavior of members of our own species, and include those covered in this book, as well as broader aspects of men's liberation, human behavioral/emotional/spiritual healing in general, and most approaches to the preservation of our planet. I judge CMR Science to be thoroughly inadequate for solving these problems, even though it is clearly the epistemology of choice in other areas. There's an urgent need for us to develop the "soft" sciences, and to employ with honor those already developed. The first step is to cease expecting CMR to be the *only* valid scientific method at our disposal, and to restrict its use to appropriate applications.[3]

So – how do we know that 'what we know' is valid knowledge? I've made a start toward improved paradigms of epistemology for the human sciences. Science is broadly defined as ways of being honest about the natural world. If it isn't honest, it isn't science. Testing protocols, such as CMR, have great value in exposing error and bias, but the protocol should not be allowed to substitute for the *sine qua non* of honesty.

Four criteria are proposed for a successful scientific method. It should work well for its specific applications, and also be communicable, rigorously honest, and humane.

Where do we look for better methods to facilitate human behavior change for long-term benefit? One source is the method of exemplars, pioneered by Maslow (1954) and by Bandler and Grinder (1975). Choose the most successful method or practitioner you can find for some reasonably specific problem. Analyze the elements of the total exemplary program, and then try them out, singly or in bunches, on other problems. Gather data about what works well, and where, and how often. A variant is to examine several exemplars, looking for common elements that can be tested first.

There follows a preliminary analysis of the 12-Step program of Alcoholics Anonymous, which appears to me to be the best program overall for the problem of alcoholism. The exemplar chosen is not critical to the method, and readers are invited to choose their own. But I do think it's critical that an exemplar be chosen and followed up, rather than just throwing up one's hands with complaints of "too many variables" or "You can't change human nature."

One important characteristic of the 12-Step program is that the 'investigator' is inside the phenomenon, not allegedly standing outside observing from the sidelines, as in CMR Science. This gives him/her more proximate access to information, and substantially enhances the understanding of what is observed. The ability to be an inside investigator/participant makes information more directly applicable to each individual, not only to a group. Individual change is the focus of the "action." Statistical analysis recedes in importance.

In CMR Science, the assumption that the scientist is an objective observer – disinterested in the outcome – is mostly fictional. To be sure, chemists do not personally enter orbitals to rearrange electrons. By physical necessity, they remain outside and alter variables by changing experimental conditions – influencing trillions of molecules simultaneously, but never touching a single one of them – and by measuring a statistical effect. Yet Kuhn (1970) and Barbour (1974) describe the paradigm-dependency of observations even in physical science, and this effect is greatly magnified in the human sciences.

The advantage of having an 'insider' investigate human change is threefold: the investigator experiences the process directly, individuals are more easily observed, and the pseudo-objective posture of the investigator is no longer upheld, thus facilitating honesty.

In AA epistemology, the alcoholic/investigator takes responsibility for his own recovery. No physician or shaman is assigned his case; if he wants their help, it's his job to seek them out. Beginners are encouraged to start practicing the program in small ways at first, but willingness to begin is an essential ingredient.

Twelve-step groups acquire members by self-selection, so that self-acceptance is enhanced by meeting with people who share common experiences, as well as similar failings and forms of addiction. This "magic of shared experience" is an encouragement to honesty in expressing emotions and recounting personal material. Honesty is further upheld by exemplars within the group, and by the tradition of anonymity, which creates a safe 'container' for practice in breaking Denial, No Talk, and other shaming rules. Honesty blesses the true self.

Anecdotal communication is the norm in 12-Step programs. The major portion of *Alcoholics Anonymous* (1976) is devoted to publishing the "stories" of individual alcoholics. Today, "anecdotal" is usually spoken with a slight sneer or other pejorative intonation; we need to rescue it from its present imprisonment in the lexicon of shaming threats. I view anecdotal communication as the style of choice for human behavioral / emotional learning. The effectiveness of "telling my story" is difficult to overemphasize. (See Everingham, 1995b [Chapter 6 here], under Talk About It.)

Communication is usually face-to-face in AA, or by telephone. 'I-statements' are the norm (Gordon, 1976, pp. 133-134), and members who use other forms are often gently reminded. Intuition and other activities of the nondominant cerebral cortex are not greeted with suspicion.

Alcoholics Anonymous (1976, p. 164) states that "Our book is meant to be suggestive only" and predicts that further inspiration is to be expected. The "suggestive only" point is occasionally infringed upon by some members, but anyone can read the "Big Book" for clarification. "Take what you want, and leave the rest" is the usual position.

Twelve-step programs consciously and explicitly include a "necessary vital spiritual experience" (*Alcoholics Anonymous,* 1976, p. 27 and throughout the book). Surrender to a power "greater than ourselves" is integral to the program. Religious controversy is minimized by having the alcoholic choose his own conception of God, Goddess, Higher Power, or whatever name fits his concept. This device encourages 12-Steppers to make a serious investigation of their *own* values, assumptions, and beliefs, and to rework or discard those that are no longer functional. An entire chapter is devoted to "We Agnostics" (*Alcoholics Anonymous,* 1976, pp. 44-57).

Service to others is part of the twelfth step, and is seen to be primarily for the benefit of the server, not the recipient. This reduces the self-surveillance of shame-bound addicts, and forces them (us) to relax for a while and enjoy attending to others.

Kurtz (1982) analyzed the intellectual and philosophical basis of AA. He concludes that AA works because it comes to terms with the reality of essential human limitation, and incorporates this limitation into an effective therapy for shame. His point about shame is extended by Fossum and Mason (1986) to other addictions.

Taken together, these features constitute an epistemological paradigm in which formal reproducibility is sacrificed, but is offset by gains in immediacy, honesty, individual responsibility and freedom, and direct access to information. However, there is a kind of functional reproducibility, which never yields a perfect copy, and is not in any sense guaranteed. The precision possible in CMR Science cannot even be approached by an AA-based paradigm. The question becomes: What price, precise?

Communicability is excellent, personal, and does not require a college degree. The style of communication is quite different from that of CMR Science, but I submit that it is equally effective. There is a moderate gain in humaneness, because CMR Science always faces a conflict of interest over the immediate benefit of individual subjects being subsidiary to the benefit of a larger group, versus knowledge gained. Twelve-step "subjects" rarely face this conflict.

Is AA effective in healing alcoholism? It's not effective all the time, or for everybody, but it's considered to be the best overall approach yet for alcoholism, especially considering the number of people helped and its record over 60+ years. Assessing generalizability of this paradigm to other problems requires further work.

Readers are encouraged to make their own analysis/synthesis of paradigms of epistemology for the human sciences. Produce your own definition and criteria for valid science, look around for exemplars (or devise an alternative method for finding paradigms), and evaluate them in the light of your criteria. I wish you Godspeed, for this is serious business that we can little afford to postpone.

NOTES:

[1] In an absolute sense, one never *does* know. But personally and as a society, we continually rely on incomplete knowledge to make important decisions. I assume that better functional epistemology leads to better, albeit imperfect, choices.

[2] I use "epistemology" in a broadly inclusive way, certainly *not* limiting it to logic, cognition, certainty, or constraint. Conversely, my position is not to deconstruct Western philosophy or traditional scientific reasoning (see Rabinow, 1986; Rorty, 1979), but to point out areas of knowledge in which I see these disciplines as deficient, and to suggest improvements *for these areas*. I agree with those who point out that acceptable "truth" is often influenced by historical practices and systems of power (Foucault, 1982; Hacking, 1984). Above all, my goal is *functional* epistemology, not that which reinforces perfectionism, control, or moral intimidation.

[3] Gould (1989, pp. 277-285) argues cogently for the value of historical aspects of natural science, and for equal validity and status for the methods and epistemology necessary to historical inquiry.

Chapter 23
Vision for Transforming Our World

ROY U. SCHENK

FROM BREAKING THE SHACKLES, 2003

OUR PRESENT WORLD-VIEW

Many of our authors have made the case for internalized shame being the primary cause of interpersonal violence, mindless pollution, and war. In response to shame-filled feelings of defectiveness, people strike out at the world in differing ways. Shame is so prevalent in our world that it is difficult, perhaps impossible, to visualize what human life will be like when we move beyond shame's domination. We do have some hints, and we will look at those later in this chapter.

In Chapter 2, I presented a visualization of our current plane of existence (Figure 2-1). This visualization is reproduced in a modified form in Figure 23-2. It is an existence created by judging and shaming ourselves and others. Judging divides people on the basis of superiority and inferiority, including the subsets of good and evil, better than and not as good as, victims and perpetrators, angels and beasts, as well as not good enough, not worthy, not deserving, defective — all shame-generating responses that further add to our own shame-induced feelings of inferiority and inadequacy. Running through this plane is a fine line of equality that marks the intersection separating superior from inferior, good from evil, etc. In our current paradigm it is only at this line of equality that shaming ceases.

I believe this is a useful depiction of our present paradigm or world-view and of the precariousness of equality within that world-view. There isn't room on the line for everybody. Even when we stand astride the line, we overlap into one or both of the divided categories. What this says to me is that we cannot remove shame and its damaging effects from our lives, and so cannot achieve equality between human beings, as long as we continue to accept this world-view.

Perhaps we could just shrug this off with a remark that "this is the way things have always been and will always continue to be." This is a defeatist attitude that might have been acceptable in the past. But today we are confronted with the human power to destroy life on earth — either dramatically by nuclear war, or more subtly by mindless pollution. We see an epidemic of water, air, and soil pollution all over the world. We see acid rain destroying both fish and forests.

Several studies have found that human sperm counts have already decreased 50 percent worldwide, evidently as a result of estrogen-like pollutants (Hileman, 1994). In addition, wars continue their deadly toll, and are increasingly deadly and vicious as the US government continues to develop and use more efficient military hardware and supply this hardware to smaller nations. The wars in Yugoslavia are so typical of shame motivating violence and war. Men, taught from birth that their primary reason to exist is to protect their women and children, feel intensely shamed when they are unable to do so. Over time, they then arm themselves and proceed to attack and conquer the formerly triumphant group, raping and pillaging in the way they have been treated in the past.

The social fabric of our country continues to deteriorate as more and more people lose hope and strike out in despair, focusing solely on their own immediate self interests, and as we continue to build and fill more and more prisons with men. The bombing in Oklahoma, the killings by teenage boys in schools, and, I suspect, the recent attacks on New York City and the Pentagon are other responses to shame. The U.S. military now has such awesome firepower that no other country can directly confront this might. Thus, shame drives men to engage in subtler, "sneakier" acts of violence.

It is time for us to recognize that judging and shaming are not our only options. We do not have to continue down the same path. As human beings, *we choose* to judge and divide people. These are shame-based habits learned from childhood; habits that can be unlearned or replaced with different habits. We will examine some of the immense benefits to be gained by developing new ways of relating to each other. First, we need to understand the nature of these new habits. It seems a bit ironic that transforming our lives and our world is about replacing dysfunctional habits with new, more functional habits, but that seems to be how it is.

A NEW WORLD-VIEW

The present world-view divides people into categories (good and evil, inferior and superior, etc.), and these divisions arise and are maintained by our habits of judging ourselves and others. Equality appears only as a fine line separating superior and inferior, good and evil. It is only at this dividing line that we are not judging and shaming others and ourselves. I propose that we envision and create a new plane of existence, a new world-view, based on equality, which passes through our present plane at the line of equality. This requires that we no longer think in terms of judging and dividing people on the basis of superiority and inferiority. When this happens, superior and inferior become irrelevant.

This will happen when we accept a new plane of existence where equality is a given — a plane where equality is present everywhere and is understood to be the norm. This new plane is depicted in Figure 23-1, and its intersection with our current plane is illustrated in Figure 23-2. On this plane, everyone will be treated with respect and caring which is what equality is all about. As a result equality will also become irrelevant because everyone will be treated as equals.

This new plane requires us to develop new ways of relating to each other. Rather than using shame and punishments to control people, it requires that we to develop an environment where people will choose to treat each other with respect and dignity and caring, i.e. with equality. I believe this can happen only in an environment where love and acceptance are the norms, and judging and shaming are aberrations, i.e., are abnormal.

We will need to develop a new vocabulary. Blame and shame, deserving, worthy, good enough, are language of the judging paradigm. I think "justice" may also be left behind. I am unsure of "forgiveness." *A Course in Miracles* (1975) states: "God does not forgive because God has never condemned. And there must be condemnation before forgiveness is necessary. In other words, we need to forgive only when we have judged and condemned someone. So we need forgiveness because of what we do, rather than what the other person has done. When we move to the new plane of existence, we will cease judging and condemning and then forgiveness will be unneeded, but for now, forgiveness is of primary importance.

The point is that as we create the paradigm of love and joy, we will need to examine our language and strive in a loving way to determine the multitudes of words that may convey judging and shaming. This is a task for communities and not for a guru.

LOVE: WHAT IS IT?

I have felt unable to complete the revision of this chapter because, although I have been insisting that love is the key to a transformed world, I could not tell you precisely what love really is. Obviously I did have some notions about it. But I felt I needed to know precisely what we mean by "love" in order to be able to write effectively. In the past I have leaned heavily on the definition of my dear friend, Betty Boardman, who defines love as "tender caring." And I do still believe this is an important part of love. But if we are to "love God" as the scriptures admonish, this is not adequate. I recently was introduced to Gay Hendricks' book, *Learning to Love Yourself* (1982). Hendricks defines love as "the action of being happy in the same space as someone or something else." That seems to include God, but what about people we don't particularly like?

Bell Hooks in her book *All About Love* supports M. Scott Peck's definition of love as "the will to extend one's self for the purpose of nurturing one's own or another's spiritual growth." Again it does not relate to loving God. I read this definition shortly before rubbing ointment on the back of my partner, Kathy. As I finished, I asked her if she felt spiritual growth from my efforts. She seemed doubtful, but then decided she surely could grow spiritually from it if that would encourage me to do it more often.

I scoured the New Testament and found a lot of citations saying that love includes a lot of different things, The most significant statement is that "God is love."(1 John 4:8), if God is love, love must obviously be very broad and inclusive.

In her book, *A Return to Love*, which evaluates *A Course In Miracles*, Marianne Williamson wrote: "Love is the intuitive knowledge of our hearts...We experience love as kindness, giving, mercy, compassion, peace, joy, acceptance, non-judgment, joining, and intimacy... Love casts out fear the way light casts out darkness."

I finally concluded that **"love is the living and sharing of goodness; and all positive interactions are expressions of love."** So to love is to share goodness. I've tried examples to test it out and the definition seems to work. It can apply to God. It can apply to rubbing ointment on Kathy. It can apply to everyone, including people we don't particularly like. For everyone, whether we otherwise interact with them or not, and including people we don't know or don't like, I believe love requires us to support having good happen to them.

As I had suspected, compassion, respect, acceptance, and a lot of other positive ways of relating are ways of expressing love. Often love involves intense feelings of affection such as Kathy and I feel for each other. But we can certainly love without those feelings.

Respect
Compassion
Acceptance
Caring
NO JUDGING OF OURSELVES
OR OTHERS

Respect
Compassion
Acceptance
Caring
NO JUDGING OF OURSELVES
OR OTHERS

Figure 23.1   The Future Plane of Existence

Now I can finish my chapter. Since the topics I explore in this chapter are at the cutting edge of my learning, I need to hasten to finish it and get it off to the producers before some major new idea appears.

GETTING ON TO THE NEW PLANE

How do we get onto that plane? It requires moving from our present thoughts and behavior patterns (our habits of judging ourselves and others) and replacing them with the habits of love, which include respect and acceptance of ourselves and other people. Access to this new plane of existence is through establishing love, including non-judgmental acceptance, as the norm for ourselves and others. Non-judgmental acceptance does not mean "anything goes." I don't believe that we must accept being hurt without challenging the person whose behavior hurts us.

It means we have clear boundaries, and we confront the persons who are doing the injuring and invite or challenge them to transform their lives even as we continue to accept them by treating them with respect and dignity. It seems clear to me that it is only when individuals can know they are accepted in a caring way that they can let down the shields protecting them from being further shamed. Then they can accept responsibility for the injuries which they do to others, and can choose to transform their lives.

I believe Cliff Barry (2002) is right that when people engage in hurtful behaviors, these are also expressions of love, expressions that come out as twisted and distorted by the hurts and

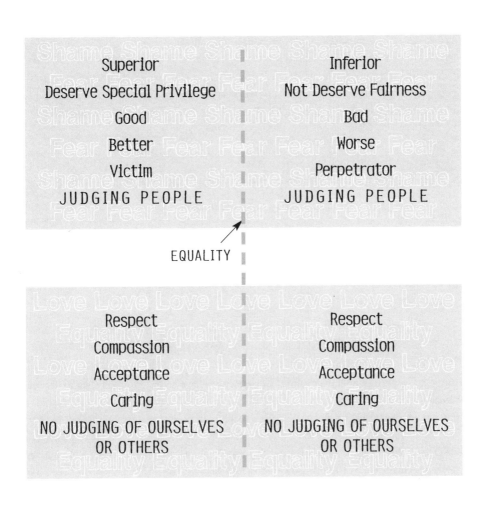

Figure 23.2 Future Plane Intersecting Our Present Plane

injuries that influence how we respond. I know that we live in a world of opposites; but I do not believe there is an opposite of love. But at least for the present I still believe there are things that diminish love, such as shame.

Love and the subsidiary attitudes of acceptance, respect, compassion, equality and caring are terms not unlike those articulated by prophets and spiritual leaders throughout history. Since these ideas have been advocated so often and for so long, it may seem hopeless. It may seem that history teaches us that the goal of creating a world based on love and acceptance being the norm cannot happen now because it has not happened before. That attitude leads to despair.

As the need for this transformation is becoming more critically necessary, we find increasing numbers of people and organizations identifying and pursuing this goal. This does not make the transformation inevitable, but it does offer us a basis for hope. I believe we have over-looked too often in the past the notion that we must abandon or make irrelevant the concepts of superiority and inferiority, good and evil, and all the other ways we judge and divide people. That happens when we create habits based on love as the norm.

I used to think that when we moved beyond shame to self-acceptance and self-love, we would be where we want to be. But now I recognize that this just carries us back to where we were when we were born. I now believe that far more wonderful experiences await us.

If one pulls a helium-filled balloon down into a container of water and then lets it go, the balloon will pop right up to the top. Then the lighter than air property of helium will take over and pull the balloon away from the water surface. And the balloon will continue to rise into the air. That is how I envision human growth as we heal and then expand to open up in ways we may only have hints of now.

THE POWER OF TRANSFORMATION

Today, as we have entered the twenty-first century, we have an increased capacity to destroy human life on earth. At the same time, we are gaining a better understanding of the relationship between love and acceptance, and the possibility of positively transforming our lives.

I became intensely aware of this relationship as a result of participating in transformational weekends conducted by two different groups, the Mankind Project and Landmark Education Corp.. The physical experiences of these weekends were dramatically different. The first was very physical and openly challenging, while the second was very sedentary and intellectually challenging. Yet both experiences created awe-inspiring transformations in many of the participants. Shy wallflowers became outgoing; belligerent bullies became delightful and excited sharers. People broke out from behind protective walls and out of shells built up over decades.

Amazed that experiences so different could produce such similar results, I sought the commonalties in the experiences. I found several. The first is a predominant attitude of non-judgmental acceptance and caring. This does not mean pretending that people are perfect, but rather, that we accept ourselves and each other *as we are*, with all of our limitations.

Because none of us is infallible, we cannot create a milieu of total acceptance, and we don't. But perfection is not necessary. Our present environment is so unaccepting and judgmental that we create a dramatically different one simply by having love and acceptance be the norm.

Perhaps the powerful way that people respond in this environment is a manifestation of the intense desire for wholeness and health that I believe we all share.

A second commonality involves acting together in community. Being in an accepting community facilitates giving ourselves permission to let go of the repressions and inhibitions that have been developed over the years as shields to deflect further shaming.

A third commonality involves challenge and invitation. Each person is challenged and/or invited to take a look at his life and to choose to let go of some of the repressions and inhibitions. Because these shields against shame, these lifelong habits, have been internalized so deeply, it is not feasible to break them down completely in one weekend. This is why both groups incorporate ongoing programs for people to practice and develop their new mind set and necessary new habits.

A fourth commonality is confidentiality. Most people will not expose their shadow parts unless they are confident their revelations will remain within the confines of the group.

These weekends have shown me that we can break out of our old shaming habits and transform our lives. Because of intense wounding in the past, it is unlikely that people of our generations will transform our lives completely. We will continue to have scars from the wounds of the past, just as my knee still bears a scar from a childhood bicycle accident (almost sixty years later). But we can go far. We can create an environment dominated by love and acceptance, a society where love and acceptance are the norms, in which new generations will learn the habits of acceptance and love from birth, and will be supported in maintaining these habits throughout their lives.

ATTAINING EQUALITY

Human beings appear to have an inherent belief in equality. We seem to have "hard-wired" into us a presumption that we are equal to or as good as other human beings. We learn to impose on top of this belief the beliefs about superiority and inferiority and of good and evil.

I have concluded that it is this belief in equality that causes us to react so intensely to inferiority messages. When we accept at some level that an inferiority message is true, including a message that we are bad, we are driven to compensate for this accepted belief in an attempt to regain equality. One of the most powerful ways to compensate is with some other form of superiority in an attempt to balance that inferiority and regain that equality.

The concept of superiority/inferiority functions by our judging people as superior or good or, alternatively, as inferior or evil. So each time we make a judgment about someone, we create a division. This continuing dividing separates us to individuals. Some people even divide themselves further — via schizophrenia or even by dissociation (multiple personalities).

The primary consequence of judging is shame. A judged person responds with shame. This is especially apparent in the person judged as inferior or evil. But a person judged as superior or good also knows that this judgment can be reversed or withdrawn, and so even this supports a milieu of shame.

It is conceivable that this shame-inducing milieu may have been beneficial during the early stages of human development. Shame induces over-achievement. This over-achievement, mostly by males, may have been necessary to create the motivation to produce the knowledge needed to move us from stone-age ignorance to a world where we can live relatively comfortably and share in the wealth of world knowledge.

However, even if over-achievement was beneficial in the past, today it is driving the human race to extinction. If we want the human race to survive, we need to abandon over-achievement, the shame that induces it, and the milieu of judgment that creates the shame.

Inequality is created by the milieu of judgment. To return us to our natural state of equality, we need to abandon this milieu of judgment. But we cannot simply oppose judging. We must replace it with a positive alternative. I am convinced that this alternative is love and acceptance. When we embrace a milieu where love and acceptance are the norms, equality automatically becomes the norm also. So we achieve equality by no longer fighting against inequality. When the judging that divides us and that creates inequalities is replaced with love and acceptance, equality happens.

I suspect that the exemplars whose ideas have produced the world's religions have been striving toward this goal. The failure to recognize the need to abandon judging so that good and evil become irrelevant, may have been the stumbling block that prevented attainment of their vision.

"BEYOND NOTIONS OF RIGHT DOING AND WRONG DOING"

The belief that we need to abandon right and wrong, or make them irrelevant, is not new. Centuries ago, Persian poet Rumi spoke about "Beyond notions of right doing and wrong doing..." More than a hundred years ago, Nietzsche wrote the book *Beyond Good and Evil* (1886). Nietzsche recognized the damage done by dividing people on the basis of good and evil. However, his proposed alternative of Will to Power, without caring for others, seems not much better than good and evil. Increasing numbers of people appear to be recognizing that we need to develop a new belief system. It seems to me that most of them are describing beliefs much like those I am writing about.

In the past, human sacrifice and slavery were perceived as acceptable. Today, human sacrifice and slavery are generally seen as unacceptable ways to treat other human beings. I believe that judging human beings as superior or inferior, as good or evil, as unworthy, undeserving, or not good enough, needs to join slavery and human sacrifice in becoming equally unacceptable. I believe this is what Gandhi, Mother Theresa, Dorothy Day, Martin Luther King, Jr., and other exemplars are striving to teach us. We need to get on with it.

What will this world be like when we no longer judge each other on the basis of superiority or inferiority, good or evil, better or worse, etc.? In an environment where acceptance and love are the norms, we gain control of our lives. No longer can we pass the buck or blame to others. Each of us has responsibility for his or her own life. And when challenged to do so, people can and do take charge of their lives, and as a result live happier and more fulfilling lives.

This is liberating — and scary. It's scary because we have not been trained, nor have we developed the skills we need, to assume control of our lives. But we can learn them. I see men in the New Warrior Network working hard on the process. There is a lot of experimentation and fumbling and error, but we are learning.

I was raised a Christian, and I have a sense that acceptance and unconditional love is the world-view that Christ was talking about. For example, when Christ confronted the woman threatened with stoning for adultery, he refused to pass judgment on her (John 8:11). On several occasions, he stated, "Judge not, that you be not judged." (Matt 7:1, Luke 6:37). "Unless you become like little children..." (Matt 18:3) conveys to me a vision of a world based on acceptance and love and beyond good and evil, as well as a belief that love is the most powerful force on earth. I believe that other religious prophets have brought a similar message. But it seems that they did not recognize that we cannot have a world based on love and acceptance without abandoning our reliance on good and evil.

I have had serious trouble accepting the necessity that we give up "good or evil," or recognize it as irrelevant. What does it mean to say that good and evil become irrelevant, even meaningless? Good and evil seem so real, so absolute, that it is difficult to visualize a world without them as primary determinants. As I began contemplating the idea, a part of my mind protested, "But how will we judge people without good and evil?" Another part of my mind responded, "You've got it! That's the whole idea."

It was while I was fasting, reading and, meditating on an island in the Boundary Waters Canoe Area in northern Minnesota that I found a resolution. I read in a book that good and evil are ideas developed by philosophers about 3,500 years ago as a way to make sense of the world.

MAKING A CHOICE

God cannot judge, love's deminishment.

God loves us, like sunshine on a balmy spring day. Totally!

Ah but we humans, We can live with contradiction.

We can choose to judge and strive to love as well.

Judging creating shame; the black hole of love.

Just like an astronomical black hole sucks

All the surrounding matter into it,

So judging sucks all the love into the shame.

Like pouring a glass of water into a pile of dry, hot sand,

Love's power is dissipated, lost.

Hungering for love, why is it then,

We continue to judge, destroying what we crave?

Superior and inferior, good and evil, righteousness!

All need judging to exist.

Equality achieved when judging ceases,

No other time or way.

What do we wish for more?

Judging, sustaining inequality and shame?

Or love, creating a world of equality and bliss?

Or do we continue insisting on both?

This contradiction creating our conflicted world.

Oh yes, it is we, not God, create the strife.

Particularly, our accepted judgment of men's moral perversity,

And women's moral betterness — human creations both —

Keep judgment's stranglehold alive.

And it's our continued choosing of these judgments,

That will continue the strife,

Or, abandoned, permit us to transform our world,

So we can bask in love and bliss.

Which will we choose?

Roy U. Schenk 7/17/00 #1096

That was a "wow" experience. I recognized that if we humans could develop the concept of good and evil, we could also develop other concepts to organize and make sense out of the world. And it feels exciting to be a part of that development

If we abandon good and evil as ways to judge and control people, on what basis do we confront and challenge people when they do things we think are inappropriate? I believe we need to look to our exemplars to help us understand this. Certainly Gandhi intensely and effectively confronted the British about the harm they were doing to the people of India, even as he was treating the British with respect, dignity and, acceptance, and insisting that his followers do the same. He even stopped one of his major actions when his followers killed some British soldiers.

From this I conclude that exemplars show us that loving acceptance does not mean passively ignoring the individual and structural ways that human beings are harmed or made to suffer needlessly. Instead, abandonment of shame-inducing beliefs results in clarity about boundaries and appears to foster challenges to the systems that hurt human beings. But this is not inevitable.

We must choose, choose to take the risks and encourage others to do the same. I do think there is a great tendency to move us toward that intense joy or bliss that I believe is the natural human condition.

The words "deserving" and "worthy" kept coming up when I was writing about Gandhi confronting the British. But these two words are judgment based and so are nonfunctional in a paradigm based on loving acceptance. We need to accept that we each have a **right** to love, including respect, acceptance and compassion, simply because we are a part of God's creation. And beyond this, will "fairness" and "justice" also become obsolete? I believe many people are experimenting to understand better how the right to respect and dignity and love and acceptance works out in real life, though perhaps not with the clarity I write with here. Other groups have experimented with this in the past (for example, early Christians).

In my experience, a group in our society that presently struggles fairly effectively to live by that message is the Society of Friends, or Quakers. They express this belief with the statement, "There is that of God in every human person." Quakers' centuries long commitment to "gain equality for women" unfortunately became translated as "bettering women's lives." As a result Quakers have supported improvements for women even when women already have the advantage. The U.S. government's Violence Against Women Act is an example of this. Men experience 3.9 million crimes of violence annually while women experience 2.6 million. Yet we work harder to reduce violence to women. The argument is made that men do more of the violence and so working to reduce violence to women is justified. That argument is simply a response to the belief that women deserve special privilege.

That Quakers presently fail to confront our society's and their own demonizing of men, and continue to cling to the belief in women's moral superiority and perceived right to privileged treatment simply reveals the intensity of this belief as well as their own humanness and need for ongoing revelation. The belief in women's moral superiority is so universal that even Gandhi referred to women as "immeasurably man's superior in moral power," "natural messengers of the gospel of non-violence," "special custodians of all that is pure," "the better half of humanity."

I find that in striving to change my habit of judging people, it is helpful to respond to the judging internal voice with the message that the person is "doing the best s/he can." An amazing change of attitude can accompany acceptance of that belief. There is still the temptation to return to the judgmental plane with, "But I am doing better than that person is, so I am better." However, this is not a necessary choice.

There is a part of me that does not *want* to give up judging. Enough residual shame and inferiority feelings remain that I still feel an urge to compensate. These feelings are part of the scars from past wounds, which are unlikely ever to be completely lost by people who reach adulthood in the current paradigm. But that is okay. To be human is to be limited, to make mistakes, to learn by trial and error. We do not need to feel shame for this.

On our present plane, we are judged and shamed for making mistakes. But that is not necessary, and we do not have to accept the shaming messages.

Curiosity is one of our most powerful traits. We often learn by trying and failing. By necessity, we fail or make mistakes often. So failing and making mistakes appear to be an essential human activity. If so, then making mistakes would better be celebrated rather than condemned because it is by making them that we more fully develop our human potential. And how do we respond when a person's mistake hurts other people? Again, we should see how Gandhi and others have responded, but, in any case, we need to continue accepting that person even while we confront the harm.

A VISION OF THE FUTURE

Let's look now at the future. Let us develop a vision of what life can be like when acceptance and love dominate our habitual ways of relating to each other. Prognostication is risky business. One can feel ashamed of being proven wrong by time. But it is equally dangerous to reject such projections without serious reflection. One can look at trends in society and project them into the future with the assumption that the trend will intensify. One can also ask what will happen if some substantial transformation occurs in a significant social attitude.

We will look at the probable effects of an environment dominated by acceptance and love in six areas. These are:

1. The development of our human potential;
2. Our relationship with ourselves;
3. Our relationships with others;
4. Sexuality;
5. Our relations with the spiritual; and
6. The socialization process.

Most of my thinking in these areas is tentative and in flux. But John Everingham tells me, "I don't have to be right; I only have to be honest."

Developing our Human Potential

When we have internalized shame, the experience is so painful that we generally choose to do almost anything that we believe will reduce or avoid further shaming. We tend to inhibit and repress whatever part of ourselves we believe will trigger further shaming. When we remove the shaming messages and learn not to internalize the shame from messages we do receive, we will no longer inhibit and repress these spontaneous and exuberant feelings and actions. Look at the behavior of young children — before they are squelched — to get an idea of unrepressed spontaneity.

We may anticipate that children and adults will develop far more extensive areas in which they are creative. For example, if we are not put down because "You can't sing!" we are more likely to sing. And a lot more people will discover that they can sing well. This is a painful area for me. I love to sing, but when I am around others, I continue to feel fearful that I won't do it "right." Ironically, that fear triggers more mistakes than I might otherwise make.

The same is true for the other creative areas. People will become more creative and will be far more interesting. We will probably be far less sedentary, and far more involved in joyful living.

Play and sports will likely be less competitive, but will still be intensely exciting and challenging, and will involve far more people. Cooperative sports will be developed more than they are today. Alcoholism and drug and other addictions, which appear to be shame-based, will all but vanish. Prisons will mostly become abandoned relics of a barbarous past. Crime will be minimal, and people who commit crimes will be challenged to make amends and lead more positive lives.

Our Relationship with Ourselves

I often remark that as a child I was taught to love my neighbor as myself. And then I was taught to hate myself. And I treated my neighbors as I was taught.

For decades I have struggled to learn to love myself fully. Not that I didn't succeed somewhat; yet I seemed to be unable to do so fully. Recently I was introduced to Gay Hendricks' book, *Learning to Love Yourself* (1998). This was an Ah Hah! experience for me. Hendricks proposes that we enhance our love for ourselves by loving ourselves for whatever we do, think, say, feel, etc. He proposes saying: "I love myself for _____" and fill in the blank with whatever is happening, both positive and negative. I realized that this offered me an answer to my search.

To truly love ourselves we need to love ourselves all the time in everything we are involved in. And why shouldn't we? The Creator sees us totally and loves us, delights in us totally. I believe we have a right, maybe even an obligation to do the same.

I do have one reservation about Hendricks' proposal. I wonder whether loving myself <u>for</u> whatever I am involved in is itself judgmental; and whether it would be better to say "when" I do whatever is identified.

Our Relationships with Others

People will develop much clearer boundaries, and the ability to protect those boundaries, very early on. It is quite normal for us to encroach on other people's boundaries. We are not omniscient. It is important that people be able to identify and protect their own boundaries. This does not have to be an occasion for shame. One can be respectful of the encroaching person and simply make clear what one's boundaries are. In this way, we will have more honest and caring relationships.

I am finding that there are those who are so wounded by past shaming that they perceive an attitude of love and acceptance as weakness, and so strive to take advantage of those who are treating them in that manner. Although they might no longer do so if we were totally able to relate to them with loving acceptance, we do not need to feel shame for our less than perfect attitudes and behaviors. In these situations we may simply have to dissociate ourselves from these persons.

When shame is no longer used to coerce people into conforming, our motivators will change. The standards we live by will move toward integrity, commitment, discretion, caring, compassion, and respect for others. We already know that a self-motivated person is more likely to live up to standards than is a person upon whom standards are forced. This does not mean that we will live in a perfect world. We will still learn by trial and error. But we will honor and respect the trials and errors. As a result, learning will be accelerated, and less wounding will occur. People will be more sensitive and considerate of the needs of others because their own needs are being met more effectively.

Because we will no longer be in a serious deficit of love and acceptance, the urgent drive to find one person who can meet "all of our needs" will no longer be necessary. We will be able to choose our relationships with others on a less needy basis. We will not lack relationships; in fact, we will probably have more relationships. Some of them will be more intense and deeply caring relationships than we are now capable of. We'll be more spontaneous because we'll be less afraid of being shamed. This will, in part, result from a reduced emphasis on achievement, particularly for men, which will free up time for developing relationships. With reduced urgency and neediness for relationships, we can choose more carefully the person(s) we want to be close to, and will feel safer in becoming close to them. Gender will become less important as we reduce the pressure to conform to restrictive gender roles.

I believe that life will become more interesting, more exciting, more delightful, and certainly not dull and boring. It will be a delight to develop our physical, emotional, and spiritual potentials. In fact, I believe the world will become more exciting, delightful, and fascinating than we can now even begin to imagine. I also anticipate that in that future, people will look back on today's world and wonder how we were able to survive all of the rage and hatred, the violence and brutality, and the animosity and shaming that are so prevalent in society today.

I expect that social change will be far easier to achieve. As people become at peace with themselves and are less in pain from extensive wounding, they will be less resistant to reducing the pain of other people.

Sexuality

In our society today, we give immense power to sex. I see several reasons for this. First, the responsibility for initiating sexual relationships is placed squarely on men. Coupled with this is the apparent more intense sexual drive of young men. The result is that every time a man asks a woman for sex and she refuses, he experiences a deficit, and she experiences a surplus of sexual availability (Schenk, 1982).

In addition, as feminist writer Carol Cassell reported in her book *Swept Away (1984)*, "Even today, women find it hard not to see sex as their most valuable commodity." As a result, women are pressured to keep sex in short supply for men, and much of women's "self-worth" is based on their "sexual value." When one adds to this the intense homophobia taught to boys, most males become almost totally dependent on women for their affection, touching, and sex. As a result, when a woman flaunts her "sexual assets" in front of a man, she is doing a kind of severe violence to the man (Schenk, 1982). As Nancy Friday (1980) put it: "How can a man not be in a rage with members of the sex who make him feel dirty and guilty about the very desires they have gone to such pains to provoke in him."

In contrast, men learn that their sexuality has little or no worth and that they must find some other value, such as "economic potential," to gain access to women's most valuable asset, sex. And men also often experience women as using their sexual potential as a way to gain and keep *control over* the men.

So there are powerful reasons for the current intense charge associated with sex. In the future, if the human race is to survive, I believe sex will lose its "market potential" and will be relatively available to each person. As this happens, women will escape from their expectation of controlling men and valuing themselves based on sexuality. And men will learn to turn to each other for more of their affection, touching, and perhaps even sex.

As with other forms of pleasuring, it is important that the pleasuring be mutual as far as possible, and that disease is not transmitted to one's partner(s). I define an unwanted pregnancy as a disease. My partner, Kathy, loves to play cards and sometimes I will join her even when I am not greatly interested because she enjoys it. At other times she joins me in activities from which I get greater pleasure.

It might be interesting to speculate about how sex would be viewed if men controlled morality. It seems likely that sex would be a sacrament and women would be canonized for being daily communicants. In which case, Bill Clinton would likely be blessed for aiding Monica to gain sainthood. But sadly, women control morality and make men's sexual exuberance evil and a terrible sin. Of course, in the new paradigm, morality will be obsolete because people will desire to pursue what is good, not only for themselves but also for others and for the world.

Already many younger people are learning to pleasure each other sexually without coitus, i.e. cock in cunt sex. I think this is a wise development, especially if females can give up seeing sex as a highly valued commodity and can give up using sex to control men.

I realize that I am proposing ideas which conflict with our current societal morals and laws. But I suspect that over the next century, sex will take on a different character, particularly driven by human overpopulation. The present emphasis on sex will continue to shift from re-creation to rec-reation. As this happens, the sexual plumbing of one's partner will become irrelevant except when a couple is committed to making a baby. Sex will move from the current scarcity mode to an experience of plenty. Also, the sexual mutilation of infant boys, called circumcision, will be abandoned.

There will be much more sensual touching and pleasuring of the entire body, and traditional heterosexual vaginal sex may become only a minor part of pleasuring, including sexual pleasuring — perhaps just because there will be so many other forms of pleasuring to be shared and enjoyed. I have read that recent studies show people are less violent when they receive greater pleasuring. This suggests that we need to increase pleasures of all kinds, including sex. It is unfortunate, in my opinion, that lust was defined by Christianity, and maybe by other religions, as a vice rather than as a virtue. I suggest we start now to accept lust as a virtue.

Relation to the Spiritual

Our response to shaming tends to inhibit and repress us, and we become fearful of whatever is different. This may be particularly true of the spiritual, which many regard as foreign, subtle, or mysterious. Also, religious groups and churches tend to claim a monopoly on the spiritual. I propose that spirituality will blossom as we move beyond shame. People will feel freer to talk about their religious experiences, and our understanding of spiritual phenomena will expand dramatically. I do not believe that most earlier prophets and visionaries will be discredited. Instead, I believe that many of their messages will become clearer and will make more sense.

There does appear to be a power that designed, created and sustains the universe, which is often called God. Our knowledge of this power is attained "through a looking glass darkly." Many people, groups, and religions have found ways to access that power — often through some form of prayer or meditation. There are enough differences in the ways this power is approached to suggest that we have not yet learned to access this power in its fullness. More effective access is likely to be achieved in a world where the dominant paradigm is one of acceptance and love.

By whatever name we refer to this power, I believe we will continue to grow in awe of the design of our universe, and we will grow in awe of the designer and creator. I believe this creator holds each of us "in the hollow of his/her hand" (Irish blessing) in an embrace of love and acceptance more intense than we can comprehend. And I believe we will continue learning to joyfully reciprocate that love.

There are faint hints that telecommunication, psychic healing, and other forms of psychic phenomena may become more fully understood and developed. Some alleged psychic phenomena might be found to be fakery. However, I anticipate that we will discover that many of these phenomena are real, and that many of us will learn to use them when we are no longer inhibited by fears of being shamed for being "gullible."

Socialization

Infants and children do need to learn the rules of their society in order to function effectively in it. For example, agreement about which side of the road to drive on is rather important to automobile-dependent societies. For this and other conventions, universal agreement is almost more important than what is agreed to.

If we do not use shame to enforce society's behavioral standards, how do we teach these conventions? We need to look at Montessori schools and other programs designed to reduce shaming in the socialization and education systems. Perhaps the most important thing is being conscious that the goals are to avoid shaming and to create love, respect, and acceptance.

As a part of the socialization process, we need to include the message that as human beings we do make mistakes and we are okay. If we can accept our fallibility as being normal and acceptable, we can learn that it is not something to be ashamed of. We need to teach this important message to members of future generations, while we struggle to learn the same message ourselves.

Our primary schools will need to become places of gentle practicing of better ways to do things instead of places of painful correction and shaming. Learning in general needs to be treated as the joyful and awesome experience it naturally is.

Finally

There are many questions for which I do not have answers. How do we express loving acceptance toward people still operating in the judgmental paradigm in such a way that we are not severely taken advantage of? Are the concepts of "justice" and "fairness" functional only in the judgmental/shaming paradigm? We often speak of a person being worthy or deserving of something. What, if anything, replaces these concepts in the loving acceptance paradigm?

It isn't my responsibility to provide answers to questions like these. As communities of people choose to move into the paradigm of loving acceptance, I believe they will work out the answers by their own experiences.

I am concerned that people may continue to carry some of the myths of the old paradigm into the new. The most intensely accepted and unchallenged myth we are most likely to retain is the myth that women are morally better than men are. This myth needs to be brought into our consciousness along with its causative source — women's control of socialization and their defining of women's behavior as the acceptable norm. We can then lay this myth to rest.

In sum, I believe that by healing our shame and by replacing that shame with self-love and acceptance and love of others, we have the potential to dramatically transform human life on earth. I believe that a valuable test of whether transformation is working is whether we find more joy in our lives. I consider that to be a third aspect of our transformation, to be included with love and acceptance.

I believe that our world has the potential to become the marvelously delightful place the creator designed it to be. It probably will take several generations to fully transform our world. But we can start by creating enclaves, small communities where we can learn to make love, joy, and acceptance normative, and make judging and shaming abnormal. These will be islands of safety from which we will be able to extend our love, joy, and acceptance to those of our brothers and sisters who have not yet learned how to escape their lives of fear.

As we develop small gatherings or communities of people committed to having acceptance, joy, and love be the norms, the old norms of judging, shaming, good and evil, and superior and inferior will become abnormal. We will develop ways to accept each other as we struggle to confront and reduce the ways people hurt us, others, and themselves.

The communities we create will not be "roll over and be walked on" communities. People will know their boundaries far more clearly, and they will strive to maintain those boundaries they feel are needed, even while still loving and caring for those who intrude into those boundaries. And being human beings, with our own marvelous limitations, each of us will at times pass into the boundaries of others.

The transformation, even within ourselves, will not occur instantly or even quickly. It requires learning to practice new habits of love and acceptance, and continuing to love and accept ourselves and others when we revert at times to the old habits of judging and shaming.

We are doing serious work, but let's not get too serious about it. Another test will be that there will be an absolute minimum of coercion in our communities. I believe that as we take charge of our lives and learn to extend our self-interest to include the whole community, and ultimately the whole of earth, we will regularly choose what benefits society without need for coercion.

Finally, making love, joy, and acceptance normative is a powerful challenge for each of us. It cannot be achieved alone or without risks and suffering. We will need to learn how to do it while we live and struggle together.

I personally invite you to recognize the wounds of judging and shaming that have deceived you into forgetting how magnificent you are, and then to join me and others in learning to express your own magnificence with love, joy, and acceptance.

I do believe we are all equal. To me, this means that we each have an equal right to be treated with respect and dignity, caring and compassion, love and acceptance. Also, we each have an equal responsibility/obligation to treat others the same way. This right and responsibility are ours because we are alive and human. We can learn from exemplars, and we can share leadership with others, but we cannot escape this right and responsibility, except by death.

I also believe that we can experience that right and fulfill that responsibility more easily and effectively in a community of people with similar commitment. I encourage you to seek out such people with the goal of creating a committed community. It will require struggle and effort, but it can be fulfilling, joyful, and exhilarating as we succeed.

We will be creating a wondrous new living environment for ourselves and our children, where joy, love, and peace will grow. Intuition tells me that it will also be a world of great excitement.

Still, it won't be easy. We will be seen as heretical and will be attacked, especially by those who benefit from the present belief system. Many will experience our loving acceptance as weakness and will strive to take advantage of us. We will continue to treat them all with loving acceptance even as we struggle to survive the attacks. And many others will be powerfully drawn to the joy, the love, and the acceptance, and they will join us. It will be a life work which will honor each of us. I invite you: Let's make it happen.

My fax number is 608-251-0658. My e-mail (super snail mail) address is ruschenk@aol.com.

REFERENCES

A Course in Miracles. (1975). Tiburon, CA: Foundation for Inner Peace. Anonymous.

Abbott, Franklin. (1987). *New Men, New Minds.* Freedom, CA: Crossing Press.

Alcoholics Anonymous, 3rd ed. (1976). New York: AA World Services.

Ansbacher, Heinz L. & Rowena R. Ansbacher, ed. (1956). *The Individual Psychology of Alfred Adler.* New York: Harper.

Astrachan, Anthony. (1988). *How Men Feel.* New York: Doubleday.

Baber, Asa. (1989). The Little Orphan Girl. *Playboy* 36 (#5, May): 39.

Bach, George R. & Herb Goldberg. (1974). *Creative Aggression.* Garden City, NY: Doubleday.

Baker, Russell. (1987). *About Men.* New York: Poseidon Press.

Bandler, Richard, & John Grinder. (1975). *The Structure of Magic,* Vol. 1. Palo Alto, CA: Science and Behavior Books.

Barbour, Ian G. (1974). *Myths, Models, and Paradigms: A Comparative Study in Science and Religion.* New York: Harper.

Barry, Cliff. (2002, October). Quotation from unpublished *Shadow Work* brochure.

Baumli, Francis. (1985). *Men Freeing Men.* Jersey City, NJ: New Atlantis Press.

Baumli, Francis. (1995). On Men, Guilt, and Shame. Chapter 8 in the present volume.

Benedict, Ruth. (1946/1977). *The Chrysanthemum and the Sword;: Patterns of Japanese Culture.* London: Routledge & Kegan Paul.

Berne, Eric. (1964). *Games People Play.* New York: Grove Press.

Bernstein, Jerome S. (1987). The Decline of Rites of Passage in Our Culture: The Impact on Masculine Individuation. In *Betwixt and Between: Patterns of Masculine and Feminine Initiation*, ed. Louise Carus Mahdi, Steven Foster, and Meredith Little, 135-158. La Salle, IL: Open Court.

Bernstein, Jerome S. (1991). The U.S.-Soviet Mirror. In *Meeting the Shadow,* ed. Jeremiah Abrams and Connie Zweig, 214-218. Los Angeles: Tarcher.

Bertelsen, Kris. (1996). A Positive Approach to Shame. [in part, a review of Jacoby, 1994] *San Francisco Jung Institute Library Journal,* 15 (#2), 5-24

Bianchi, C. (1994). *Elder Wisdom: Crafting Your Own Elderhood.* New York: Crossroad.

Bilgere, Dmitri. (1997). *Beyond the Blame Game: Creating Compassion and Ending the Sex War in Your Life.* Madison, WI: MPC Press.

Bly, Robert. (1985). *Men and the wound* (audiotape). St. Paul, MN. 55107 [524 Orleans St., (612) 291-2652]: Ally Press.

Bly, Robert. (1987). The erosion of male confidence. In *Betwixt and Between,* ed. Louise Carus Mahdi, Steven Foster, and Meredith Little, 189-197. La Salle, IL: Open Court.

Bly, Robert. (1988). *A Little Book on the Human Shadow*. San Francisco: Harper.

Bly, Robert. (1990). *Iron John: A Book About Men.* Reading, MA: Addison-Wesley.

Bly, Robert. (1995a). Seven Sources of Men's Shame. In Roy U. Schenk & John Everingham (Eds.), *Men Healing Shame.* New York: Springer.

Bly, Robert. (1995b). Discussion under the heading, "Shame and Guilt: Several Points of View," in Roy U. Schenk & John Everingham (Eds.), *Men Healing Shame.* New York: Springer.

Bly, Robert & Michael Meade. (N.d.). *The Male Mode of Feeling* (audiotape). Vashon, WA: Limbus

Bradshaw, John. (1988). *Healing the Shame That Binds You.* Deerfield Beach, FL: Health Communications.

Bridges, William. (1980). *Transitions: Making Sense of Life's Changes.* Reading, MA: Addison-Wesley.

Broughton, James. (1990). "Shaman Psalm." In *Special Deliveries,* (p. 170). Seattle: Broken Moon Press.

Campbell, Joseph. (1988). *The Power of Myth.* New York: Doubleday.

Cassell, Carol. (1982). *Swept Away: Why Women Confuse Love and Sex.* New York: Simon & Schuster.

Clark, Thomas. (1975). Institutional and Individual Views of Male Involvement in Family Planning. In *The Male Role in Family Planning Conference Proceedings.* Office of Family Planning, California Department of Health.

Compaan, Arlo. (1997). *The Dynamics of Shame and Shamelessness in Males.* Diploma Thesis. Chicago, IL: C. G. Jung Institute of Chicago.

Coopersmith, Stanley. (1967). *The Antecedents of Self-esteem.* San Francisco: Freeman.

Darwin, Charles. [1872] (1955). *The Expression of the Emotions in Man and Animals.* Reprint, New York: Philosophical Library.

Diamond, Jed. (1985). What Good Are Men? In *Men Freeing Men,* ed. Francis Baumli, 105. Jersey City, NJ: New Atlantis Press.

Dougherty, Patrick. (1988a). Men and Shame (audiotape). St. Paul, MN: Patrick Dougherty.

Dougherty, Patrick. (1988b). Shame: An audio workshop (2 audiocassettes, plus workbook). St. Paul, MN: Patrick Dougherty.

Ehrenreich, Barbara. (2004, May 20). What Abu Ghraib Taught Me. AlterNet via www.google.com >Independent Media Institute 2004.

Ekman, Paul & R. J. Davidson, (eds.) (1994). *The Nature of Emotion.* New York: Oxford University Press.

Eliot, T. S. (1952). "The Love Song of J. Alfred Prufrock." In *Complete Poems and Plays.* New York: Harcourt Brace & Co..

Erikson, Eric H. (1963). *Childhood and Society,* 2nd ed. New York: Norton.

Erikson, Erik H., Joan M. Erikson & Helen Q. Kivnick. (1989). *Vital Involvement in Old Age.* New York: Norton.

Everingham, John. (1995a). Some Basics About Shame. In Roy U. Schenk & John Everingham (Eds.), *Men Healing Shame.* New York: Springer.

Everingham, John. (1995b). Men Facing Shame: A Healing Process. In Roy U. Schenk & John Everingham (Eds.), *Men Healing Shame.* New York: Springer.

Everingham, John. (1995c). The Rescue Triangle: Shame Update. In Roy U. Schenk & John Everingham (Eds.), *Men Healing Shame.* New York: Springer.

Everingham, John. (1995d). Inadvertent Shaming: Family Rules and Shaming Habits. In Roy U. Schenk & John Everingham (Eds.), *Men Healing Shame.* New York: Springer.

Everingham, John. (1995e). Toward Epistemology Functional for the 21st Century. In Roy U. Schenk & John Everingham (Eds.), *Men Healing Shame.* New York: Springer.

Farrell, Warren. (1990). Society's 'Disposable Sex'. *Transitions,* 10(4): 1,4-5,15.

Forward, Susan with Craig Buck. (1989). *Toxic Parents.* New York: Bantam.

Fossum, Merle A. & Marilyn J. Mason. (1986). *Facing Shame: Families in Recovery.* New York: Norton.

Fossum, Merle. (1989). *Catching Fire: Men Coming Alive In Recovery.* San Francisco: Harper.

Foucault, Michel. (1982). The Subject and Power. In Hubert Dreyfuss & Paul Rabinow (Eds.), *Michel Foucault: Beyond Structuralism and Hermeneutics* (pp. 208-228). Chicago: University of Chicago Press.

Frantz, Gilda. (1986). Discussion: [Of Hultberg, 1986]. In Mary Ann Mattoon (Ed.), *The Archetype of Shadow in a Split World* (pp. 174-177). Zurich: Daimon Verlag.

Friday, Nancy. (1980). *Men In Love*. New York: Dell.

Frost, Robert. (1939). "A Servant to Servants." In *Collected Poems*. New York: Halcyon House.

Gagnon, John. (1995). Basic Male Shame. In Roy U. Schenk & John Everingham (Eds.), *Men Healing Shame*. New York: Springer.

Ghandi, Mohandes K. (1982). *All Men are Brothers: Autobiographical Reflections*, ed. K. Kripalani. New York: Continuum.

Gibran, Kahlil. (1923). *The Prophet*. New York: Alfred Knopf.

Giles, John. (1995). Forgiving the Unforgivable: Overcoming Abusive Parents. In Roy U. Schenk & John Everingham (Eds.), *Men Healing Shame*. New York: Springer.

Gilkey, Langdon. (1966). *Shantung Compound*. New York: Harper.

Gilligan, Carol. (1981). *In a Different Voice: Psychological Theory and Women's Development*. Cambridge, MA: Harvard University Press.

Gilligan, James. (1997). *Violence: Reflections On A National Epidemic*. New York: Vintage Books.

Gordon, Thomas. (1974). *T.E.T.: Teacher Effectiveness Training*. New York: Wyden.

Gordon, Thomas. (1976). *P.E.T. in Action*. New York: Bantam.

Gottlieb, Paul. (1987). The Reunion. In *About Men*, ed. Russell Baker, 141-144.

Greenwald, Michael P. (1995). Shame, Initiation, and the Culture of Initiated Masculinity. In Roy U. Schenk & John Everingham (Eds.), *Men Healing Shame*. New York: Springer.

Gutmann, David. (1994). *Reclaimed Powers: Men and Women in Later Life*. Evanston, IL: Northwestern University Press.

Hacking, Ian. (1984). Five Parables. In Richard Rorty, J. B. Sheewind, & Quentin Skinner (Eds.), *Philosophy in History* (pp. 103-124). Cambridge: Cambridge University Press.

Heller, Agnes. (1985). *The Power of Shame: A Rational Perspective*. London: Routledge

Henderson, Joseph L. (1964). Ancient myths and modern man. In *Man and his Symbols,* ed. Carl G. Jung and Marie-Louise von Franz, 104 -157. New York: Anchor.

Hendlin, Steven J. (1992). *When Good Enough Is Never Enough: Escaping the Perfection Trap*. Los Angeles: Tarcher.

Hendlin, Steven J. (1993). Looking God In The Eye: The Religious and Spiritual Roots of Perfectionism. *The Quest* (Spring): 40-48.

Hendricks, Gay. (1982). *Learning to Love Yourself*. Upper Shadow River, NJ: Prentice Hall.

Hetherington, William. (1990). A Warning to All Who Value Justice in the American Judicial System. *Transitions* 10(3): 4 ff.

Hileman, Bette. (1994). Environmental Estrogens Linked to Reproductive Abnormalities, Cancer. *Chemical & Engineering News*: 72[#5]: 19-23.

Hillman, James. (1989). *Blue Fire.* New York: Harper Perennial.

Hooks, Bell. (2001). *All About Love: New Visions*. New York: Harper Collins.

Hovey, Frances. (1989). Five Life Sentences— For Nothing. *Transitions* 9(6): 1-2.

Hultberg, Peer. (1986). Shame, An Overshadowed Emotion. In Mary Ann Mattoon (Ed.), *The Archetype of Shadow in a Split World* (pp. 157-173). Zurich: Daimon Verlag.

Hunter, Mic. (1988). *The Twelve Steps and Shame*. Center City, MN: Hazelden.

Jacoby, Mario. (1990). *Individuation And Narcissism: The Psychology Of Self In Jung And Kohut*. London: Routledge.

Jacoby, Mario. (1994). *Shame and the Origins of Self-esteem.* New York: Routledge.

James, Muriel & Dorothy Jongeward. (1971). *Born to Win: Transactional Analysis with Gestalt Experiments.* Reading, MA: Addison-Wesley.

James, William. (1910). The Self. In *Psychology, The Briefer Course,* ed. William James, New York: Henry Holt.

Jesser, Clinton. (1987). Oh My Loving Brother. In *New Men, New Minds,* ed. Franklin Abbott, 104-106. Freedom, CA: Crossing Press.

Jung, Carl G. (1928). The Relations Between the Ego and the Unconscious. *Collected Works* v. 7. Quoted in Jacoby (1990, 85-86).

Jung, Carl G. (1964). Approaching the Unconscious. In *Man and his Symbols,* ed. Carl G. Jung and Marie-Louise von Franz,, 18-103.

Jung, Carl G. (1983). *The Essential Jung.* Selected and Introduced by Anthony Storr. Princeton, NJ: Princeton University Press.

Karpman, Stephen B. (1968). Fairy Tales and Script Drama Analysis. *Transactional Analysis Bulletin* 7 (#26): 39-43.

Kaufman, Gershen. (1980). *Shame: The Power of Caring.* Cambridge, MA: Schenkman.

Kaufman, Gershen. (1992). *Shame: The Power of Caring,* 3rd ed., revised and expanded. Rochester, VT: Schenkman.

Kaufman, Gershen. (1995). Men's Shame. In Roy U. Schenk & John Everingham (Eds.), *Men Healing Shame.* New York: Springer.

Kaufman, Gershen. (1996, 1989). *The Psychology of Shame: Theory and Treatment of Shame-Based Syndromes.* New York: Springer.

Kaufman, Gershen & Robert Bly. (1995). Healing Internalized Shame. In Roy U. Schenk & John Everingham (Eds.), *Men Healing Shame.* New York: Springer.

Kaufman, Gershen & Lev Raphael. (1991). *Dynamics of Power: Fighting Shame and Building Self-Esteem,* (Rev. ed.). Rochester, VT: Schenkman.

Kaufman, Gershen & Lev Raphael. (1996). *Coming out of Shame: Transforming Gay and Lesbian Lives.* New York: Doubleday.

Kaufman, Gershen, Lev Raphael & Pamela Espeland. (1999). *Stick Up for Yourself! Every Kid's Guide to Personal Power and Positive Self-Esteem.* Minneapolis: Free Spirit.

Kaufman, Gershen, Lev Raphael & Pamela Espeland. (2000). *Teacher's Guide to Stick Up for Yourself.* Minneapolis: Free Spirit.

Kauth, Bill. (1992). *A Circle of Men.* New York: St. Martin's Press.

Keen, Sam. (1991). The Enemy Maker. In *Meeting the Shadow,* ed. Jeremiah Abrams and Connie Zweig, 197-202. Los Angeles: Tarcher.

Kimmel, Michael. & Michael Messner. (1989). *Men's Lives.* New York: MacMillan.

Klein, Lucille. (1990). The Psychology of the Orphan Archetype (audiotapes). Evanston, IL 60201 [1567 Maple, 847-475-4848]: C. G. Jung Center.

Kohut, Heinz. (1971). *The Analysis of the Self.* New York: International Universities Press.

Kohut, Heinz. (1977). *The Restoration of the Self.* New York: International Universities Press.

Kubicki, Tony & Elaine Kubicki. (1999). *Isolation to Intimacy: A Guide for Getting from Hurting to Healing in Relationships.* New Berlin, WI: Relationship Communication Center.

Kubler-Ross, Elisabeth. (1969). *On Death and Dying.* New York: Macmillan.

Kubler-Ross, Elisabeth. (1975). *Death: The Final Stage of Growth.* Englewood Cliffs, NJ: Prentice-Hall.

Kuhn, Manford & Thomas McPartland. (1954). Empirical Investigation of Self Attitudes. *American Sociological Review* 19: 68-76.

Kuhn, Thomas S. (1970). *The Structure of Scientific Revolutions.* 2nd ed., enlarged. Chicago: University of Chicago Press.

Kurtz, Ernest. (1981). *Shame and Guilt: Characteristics of the Dependency Cycle.* Center City, MN: Hazelden.

Kurtz, Ernest. (1982). Why A.A. Works: The Intellectual Significance of Alcoholics Anonymous. *Journal of Studies on Alcohol,* 43: 38-80.

Lee, Ronald R. & J. Colby Martin. (1991). *Psychotherapy After Kohut: A Textbook Of Self Psychology.* Hillsdale, NJ: Analytic Press.

LeShan, Lawrence. (1975). *How to Meditate.* New York: Little, Brown.

Ley, Dorothy C. H., and Inge B. Corless. (1988). Spirituality and Hospice Care. *Death Studies* 12: 101-110.

Lindall, George. (1995). A Shame-based Model for Recovery from Addiction. In Roy U. Schenk & John Everingham (Eds.), *Men Healing Shame.* New York: Springer.

Lindgren, David L. (1995). Grandiosity: The Shadow of Shame. In Roy U. Schenk & John Everingham (Eds.), *Men Healing Shame.* New York: Springer.

Lyman, Peter. (1987). The Fraternal Bond as a Joking Relationship. In *Changing Men*, ed. Michael Kimmel, 148-163. Newbury Park, CA: Sage.

Macchietto, John. (1992). Aspects of Male Victimization and Female Aggression: Implications for Counseling Men. *Journal of Mental Health and Counseling* 14: 375-392.

Machado, Antonio. (1984). *Selected Poems of Antonio Machado.* Chosen and translated by Robert Bly, Wesleyan University Press. Copyright Robert Bly, reprinted with his permission.

Mark, Robert & Buddy Portugal. (1996). *Victories of the Heart*. Rockport, MA: Element

Maslow, Abraham. (1954). *Motivation and Personality.* New York: Harper

Maslow, Abraham. (1955). Deficiency and growth motivation. In *Nebraska Symposium on Motivation*, ed. Marshall R. Jones, Lincoln: University of Nebraska Press.

Maslow, Abraham H. (1968). *Toward a Psychology of Being,* 2nd ed. New York: Van Nostrand.

Mason, Marilyn & Merle Fossum. (1987). Facing the Space Between: Shame, The Invisible Dragon (audiotape). Workshop, AAMFT, Chicago. Highland, IN 46322: Creative Audio.

Masson, Jeffrey M. (1984). *The Assault on Truth: Freud's Suppression of the Seduction Theory.* New York: Farrar, Straus and Giroux.

Mayeroff, Milton. (1990). *On Caring.* New York: Harper.

Mendelson, Eric. (1990). How Relevant an Issue is "Anti-male Sexism? *Standing Committee for Men Newsletter* 9(3): 3-5. [American College Personnel Association, Alexandria, VA]

Mickel, Andy. (1988). Death-in-Living and Twin Cities Men. *Men Talk* 12 (1): 1-9. [The Men's Center, Minneapolis, MN]

Middleton-Moz, Jane. (1990). *Shame and Guilt: The Masters of Disguise.* Deerfield Beech, FL: Health Communications.

Miller, Alice. (1981). *The Drama of the Gifted Child.* New York: Basic Books. [Translated by Ruth Ward from (1979) *Das Drama des begabten Kindes.* Frankfurt am Main: Suhrkamp Verlag. Also published in English as *Prisoners of Childhood.*]

Miller, Alice. (1984). *For Your Own Good: Hidden Cruelty in Child-Rearing and the Roots of Violence,* 2nd Ed. New York: Farrar Straus Giroux. [Translated by H. & H. Hannum from (1980) *Am Anfang war Erziehung.* Frankfurt am Main: Suhrkamp Verlag.]

Miller, Alice. (1986). *Thou Shalt Not Be Aware: Society's Betrayal of the Child.* New York: New American Library/Meridian. [Translated by H. & H. Hannum from (1981) *Du sollst nicht merken.* Frankfurt am Main: Suhrkamp Verlag.]

Miller, Christopher. (1995). Male Initiation: Filling a Gap in Therapy. In Roy U. Schenk & John Everingham (Eds.), *Men Healing Shame.* New York: Springer.

Moore, Robert. (N.d.). Rediscovering Masculine Potentials (audiotapes #232 A-D). Evanston, IL 60201 [1567 Maple, 847-475-4848]: C. G. Jung Center.

Moore, Robert & Douglas Gillette. (1990). *King, Warrior, Magician, Lover: Rediscovering the Archetypes of the Mature Masculine.* San Francisco: Harper.

Moore, Robert & Douglas Gillette. (1992a). *The King Within.* New York: William Morrow.

Moore, Robert & Douglas Gillette. (1992b). *The Warrior Within.* New York: William Morrow.

Moore, Robert & Douglas Gillette. (1993a). *The Magician Within.* New York: William Morrow.

Moore, Robert & Douglas Gillette. (1993b). *The Lover Within.* New York: William Morrow.

Moyers, Bill with Robert Bly. (1990). A Gathering of Men (videotape). New York: Mystic Fire Video.

Nathanson, Donald L. (1987). Shaming Systems in Couples, Families, and Institutions. In *The Many Faces of Shame,* ed. Donald L. Nathanson, 246-270. New York: Guilford..

Nathanson, Donald L. (1992). *Shame and Pride: Affect, Sex, and the Birth of the Self.* New York: Norton.

Nathanson, Donald L. (1994). Shame Transactions. *Tranactional Analysis J.* 24: 121-129.

Nietzsche, Friedrich. (1886). *Beyond Good and Evil.* Various English translations of this classic available from various publishers.

Osherson, Samuel. (1986). *Finding Our Fathers.* New York: Fawcette Columbine.

Paul, Jordan & Margaret Paul. (1983). *Do I Have To Give Up Me To Be Loved By You?* Minneapolis: CompCare Publications.

Pearson, Carol S. (1986). *The Hero Within: Six Archetypes We Live By.* San Francisco: Harper.

Pearson, Carol S. (1991). *Awakening the Heroes Within: Twelve Archetypes to Help Us Find Ourselves and Transform Our World.* San Francisco: Harper.

Peck, M. Scott. (1978). *The Road Less Traveled: A New Psychology of Love, Traditional Values and Spiritual Growth.* New York: Simon and Schuster.

Perls, Frederick S. (1969). *In and Out the Garbage Pail.* New York: Bantam.

Perry, Danaan. (1985). We're Not Ready Yet, But Soon: Exploring the edge of maleness. *In Context* #10: 47-49. [Box 11470, Bainbridge Island, WA 98110, (206) 842-0216]

Potter-Efron, Ronald & Patricia Potter-Efron. (1989). *Letting Go of Shame.* Center City, MN: Hazelden.

Pynchon, Thomas. (1973). *Gravity's Rainbow.* New York: Bantam.

Rabinow, Paul. (1986). Representations Are Social Facts: Modernity and Post-Modernity in Anthroplogy. In James Clifford & George C. Marcus (Eds.), *Writing Culture: The Poetics and Politics of Ethnography* (pp. 234-261). Berkeley: University of California Press.

Redfield, James. (1993). *The Celestine Prophecy.* New York: Warner.

Robertson, John & Louise Fitzgerald. (1990). The (Mis) Treatment of Men: Effects of Client Gender Role and Life-style on Diagnosis and Attribution of Pathology. *Journal of Counseling Psychology* 37(1): 3-9.

Roloff, Lee. (1996). *Facing the Light: The Third Force of Life* [Audiotape, #429]. Evanston. IL: C. G. Jung Center.

Rorty, Richard. (1979). *Philosophy and the Mirror of Nature.* Princeton, NJ: Princeton University Press.

Rosenthal, R. (1966). *Experimenter Effects in Behavioral Research.* New York: Appleton-Century.

Sartre, Jean-Paul. [1943] (1966). *Being and Nothingness.* Reprint, New York: Washington Square Press. Quoted by Schneider (1977, p. 23).

Satir, Virginia. (1974). *Conjoint Family Therapy.* Palo Alto, CA : Science and Behavior Books.

Schachter-Shalomi, Zalman. (1997). *From Age-ing to Sage-ing.* New York: Warner Books.

Schenk, Roy U. (1982). *The Other Side of the Coin: Causes and Consequences of Men's Oppression.* Madison, WI: Bioenergetics Press.

Schenk, Roy U. (1989). *We've Been Had: Writings on Men's Issues.* Madison, WI: Bioenergetics Press.

Schenk, Roy U. (1991). *On Sex and Gender: Thoughts of Dr. Schenk.* Madison, WI: Bioenergetics Press.

Schenk, Roy U. (1995a). Shame in Men's Lives. In Roy U. Schenk & John Everingham (Eds.), *Men Healing Shame.* New York: Springer.

Schenk, Roy U. (1995b). Beyond Shame: Transforming our Lives. In Roy U. Schenk & John Everingham (Eds.), *Men Healing Shame.* New York: Springer.

Schenk, Roy U.& John Everingham (Eds.). (1995). *Men Healing Shame.* New York: Springer.

Schneider, Carl D. (1977). *Shame, Exposure, and Privacy.* Boston: Beacon Press.

Schneider, Carl D. (1987). A Mature Sense of Shame. In *The Many Faces of Shame*, ed. Donald L. Nathanson, 192-213. New York: Guilford.

Schneir, Miriam. (1972). *Feminism: The Essential Historical Writings.* New York: Vintage.

Schoenbeck, Lorilee. (1992). Yoga: On and Off the Mat. *Poor Joe's Metrozine* (now *The Portland Metrozine*) (November):20-21. [Box 42252, Portland, OR 97242]

Shackleton, David. (2005). *The Hand That Rules the World.* In Press.

Singh, Kathleen Dowling. (1998). *The Grace in Dying: How We Are Transformed Spiritually As We Die.* New York: HarperCollins.

Smalley, Gary & John Trent. (1986). *The Blessing.* New York: Pocket Books.

Smith, Cyprian. (1987). *The Way of Paradox: Spiritual Life as taught by Meister Eckhart.* New York: Paulist Press.

Sourcebook of Criminal Justice Statistics. (Published annually). Washington, DC: U. S. Dept. of Justice, Bureau of Justice Statistics.

Stevens, Anthony. (1983). *Archetypes: A Natural History of the Self.* New York: Quill.

Straus, Murray. (1993). Physical Assaults by Wives: A Major Social Problem. In *Current Controversies on Family Violence,* ed. Richard J. Gelles and Donileen R. Loseke, 67-87. Newbury Park, CA: Sage.

Sullivan, Harry Stack. (1953). *The Interpersonal Theory of Psychiatry.* New York: Norton.

The Twelve Steps: A Healing Journey. (1986). Center City, MN: Hazelden. Anonymous.

Tomkins, Silvan S. (1987). Shame. In *The Many Faces of Shame,* ed. Donald L. Nathanson, 133-161. New York: Guilford.

Tornstam, Lars. (1999-2000, Winter). Transcendence in Later Life. *Generations* 23 (4): 10-14.

Twelve Steps and Twelve Traditions. (1950). New York: AA World Services. Anonymous.

Underland-Rosow, Vicki. (1995). *Shame: Spiritual Suicide.* Shorewood, MN: Waterford

von Franz, Marie-Louise. (1964). The process of individuation. In *Man and his Symbols,* ed. Carl G. Jung and Marie-Louise von Franz. New York: Anchor.

von Franz, Marie-Louise. (1980). *Puer Aeternus.* New York: Harcourt Brace Jovanovich.

Williamson, Marianne. (1992). *A Return to Love: Reflections on the Principles of "A Course in Miracles."* New York: Harper Collins.

Zubaty, Rich. (1993). *Surviving the Feminization of America.* Tinley Park, IL: Panther Press.

INDEX

A

Abandonment, fear of, 299
Abridgment of the Five Freedoms, 221-22, 268
Abuse
    child, 197-97, 202, 311-13
    feminism and, 200-01
    and forgiveness, 96, 98
    intrusive, 5
    neglectful, 5, 264
    perpetuated, 312
    spiritual, 221
    See also specific types of abuse
Abusive parents, forgiving, 195-205
Accelerated Behavior Change (ABC) Training,
    114-15
Acceptance
    as goal, 325-26
    transformation process and, 7-8
Accountability, of abusers, 176
Achievement, 21
Acknowledge Wounds, 96
Acknowledgment
    in healing process, 72-73
    Mature Masculine and, 242-43
Addiction
    addiction model, 173-74
    assumptions, 174-75
    codependency as, 309
    emotional processing, 178-81
    recovery from, 301
    as secondary reaction, 33
    shame and, 5, 274
    stages of recovery from, 177-78
    treatment methods, 175-77
Adler, Robert M., 121-23
Adult Children of Alcoholics, 197
Affect
    defined, 32-33
    types of, 81
Affect theory, 33
Affirmation
    alternating with shaming, 300
    by women, perceived need for, 300
Aggression
    lack of, 37-38

    stereotypes and, 168
    verbal, 26
Aging, 106-08
Aidos, 11, 78
Alcoholics Anonymous
    clear guidelines in, 234
    epistemology of, 317-18
    forgiveness technique, 98
    function of, 8
    philosophy of, 9
    power over addiction paradox, 99
    use of Talk About It tool, 90-91
Alcoholism
    gender differences, 131
    human potential and, 335
    maintained shame and, 65-66
    parental, 49-50
Ali Baba and the Forty Thieves, 279ff
Ali Baba, 279-89
    calls "Open Sesame," *see* "Open Sesame"
    enters the cave, symbolizing affirmed self-
        authority, 289
    as poor man, symbolizes shame, 281
    shares his wealth, 292-93
Aloff, Irwin, 123
Amends, *see* Forgiveness
Ammann, Dieter, 114-15
Anecdotal communication, 319-20
Anger, *see also* Confrontation
    blame and, 80
    Disqualification rule and, 217
    expression of, 126
    integration and, 91-92
    sexual abuse and, 203
    shame and, 4
    shame for, 299
    shame-free, 299
    toward women, 126, 215, 299
    withdrawal and, 72
    women's, 149-51, 296
Anima, 14
Animus
    Jungian theory, 159
    reparenting and, 165-66
Annihilation,
    fear of, 284

shame warns about, 11
Archetypes, 99-101, 110, 210
Attitude, change of, 334
Avoidance, 2, 33
Awakening, 8-9
Awareness, shaming threats and, 223

B

Baber, Asa, 114
Balance
    of guilt and innocence, 300
    necessary, 14
Basic male shame
    beginnings of, 155
    guilt and, 161-62
    impact of, 155-56
    in media, 164
    reparenting, 165-66
    support group, impact of, 157-58
    theory of
        application of, 163-64
        emergence of, 158-59
    witnessing, in therapy, 160-61
Battered spouses, 26, 135-36
Batterers Anonymous, 135
Baumli, Francis, 129-33, 143-52
Beauty power, 307-08
Betrayal, false self and, 67
Bilgere, Dmitri, 3, 137-40, 210
Blame
    feminist approach, 140
    guilt and, 34-35
    rule *see* Blame rule
    transfer of, 36
Blame rule
    breaking, 90, 95, 97, 100, 210
    defined, 87, 207
    discussion of, 210
Blessing
    as Elder function, 107
    in healing process, 109
    of the King, 109
    need for, 129
Bly, Robert, 6, 29, 94, 113, 162, 166, 223, 307,
        311-15 and chapters 4 & 5
Bodily feeling, of healing shame, 289
Body image, imperfect body, 61-62
Body language
    eye contact, 4, 43-44
    moral intimidation and, 221-22
    primary shame and, 86
    shaming threats and, 225
    significance of, 4, 33, 185
Body shame, 4

Body shape, inadequacies of, 61-62
Bonding
    confrontation and, 213-214
    male, *see* Male bonding
Boundaries
    establishment and maintenance of, 92
    violations of, 92
Boy Psychology, 238, 241, 242, 246
Bradshaw, John, 87, 106, 206, 220, 230

C

Campbell, Joseph, 23
Captain, of 40 thieves, 279-80, 290
Castration, fear of, 124-25
Catch-22, 17
Challenge, transformation and, 329
Chanting, 162
Child abuse, 197-98, 202, 311-313
Childhood
    abuse, *see* Child abuse
    learning process, 21, 26, 142, 149
    mourning process, 54
    shaming, 196, 260-69
    socialization process, 339
    victimization during, 176
Chronic Shame, 269ff
Clichés, 54
Code of honor, 210
Code words, shaming, 225
Codependency, 92, 170, 180, 192, 300-01, 303,
        307, 309
Codependent Power-Over Matrix, Gender,
        303-05
Cognitive keys, 88
Communication
    anecdotal, 319-20
    inarticulate, from shame, 146-48
    male and female styles, 171-72, 234
Community, accepting, 329
Compaan, Arlo, 11
Competition
    decrease in, 106, 335
    as motivation, 124
Confidentiality
    breach of, 216
    as commonalty, 329
Conflict, living with, 70
Confrontation, and Incompleteness, 207, 212-215
Confront Shaming Behavior, 92-93
Consciousness, raising, 3
Contempt, as shame reduction strategy, 36
Contrasexual, 14
Control
    measure and reproduce (CMR), 318-21

rule, *see* Control rule
Control rule
  breaking, 90-91, 98, 102
  confrontation and, 214
  defined, 87-88, 207
  discussion of, 209
Counseling, mandatory, 136-37, 141
Cowardice, 38
Criminalization, 19-20, 335
Crying
  in healing process, 46, 80, 177-80, 300
  as shameful feeling, 37
  shaming of, 270
Cultural injunctions, types of, 33-34, 41-42, 69
Culture of Initiated Masculinity, 109, 246-48
Custody, 19

D

Dancing the Four Quarters, 100-101
Dating, emotional risk in, 306-07
Darkness, poetry symbolism, 50-53
Death and dying, dealing with, 38
Defender of the Correct, 225
Defensiveness, letting go of, 301
Deficiency motivation, 256-57
Dehumanizing, 20
Denial, in healing process, 55, 72, 177-78
Denial rule
  breaking, 89-91, 93, 95, 97, 102, 109, 310
  defined, 87, 207
  discussion of, 212-13, 218, 303
Denial-by-distraction, 216
Denying Pseudoinnocent, 242
Dependency
  in therapy, 117, 125, 132
  on women, 132-33
Depression, shame and, 6, 273
Detached Manipulator, 242
"The Devil's Sooty Brother," 81
Diggs, Lawrence, 115-17
DiLallo, Frank, 123-26
Discouragement, 34, 42
Disputes, Incompleteness rule and, 210-12
Disqualification rule
  breaking, 93, 95, 97, 100, 103, 108
  defined, 88, 207-08
  discussion of, 214-18
Disrespect, violence and, 2
Distress affect, 33
Distress emotions, 36-38, 98
Distress-shame bind, 38
Divorce, 18
Domestic abuse, 26

Domestic violence, husband as victim, 135-36
Dominance-submission, 43
Double standards, 24, 224-25
Dougherty, Patrick, 5, 96, 98, chapter 17
Drama triangle, *see* Rescue Triangle
The Drama of the Gifted Child (Miller), 66
Drives
  impact of, 232
  physiological drive system, 81
Drug abuse, 232
Drug addiction, human potential and, 335
Drumming, 139, 162
Duluth Domestic Abuse Intervention Project, 135
Dworkin, Andrea, 130
Dying
  grace in, 108
  nearing, *see* Nearing Death Experience

E

Eastern cultures, 42, 69
Eating the Shadow metaphor, 93-95
Ego-splitting, 184, 186
Either-or thinking, 255
Elder, growing the inner, 106-08
Electra complex, 4
Embarrassment, 34, 262, 275
Embrace paradox, 98-100
Emotional
  blackmail, 302
  bypass, 283
  keys, 88
  needs, 132
  power, 306
  treasure, discovery in the cave of shame,
    286-87
Empathy, 6, 23, 159, 167-68, 223
Empowerment, in therapy, 123
Enchantment, shame as, 49
Energy, of initiation, 241
Environment
  self-esteem and, 259
  significance of, 134-35, 329
Epistemology
  of this book, *xi*
  paradigms of, 317-18
Equality, confrontation and, 212
Erikson, Erik, 102, 106-08, 219
Euphemism buries shame, 9
Events, shaming through, 60-61
Everingham, John, 25, 113, 119, and chapters 1,
    6, 13, 15, 22
Exemplars, method of, 318
Exposure, and shame, 275-76

Eye contact
  avoidance of, 4, 8-10, 260
  male bonding and, 95
  power in, 41, 43-44

F

Facing Shame: Families in Recovery
    (Fossum/Mason), 63, 65
Failure
  compensation of, 129
  dealing with, 113
  in poem, 84
False self, 4-7, 66-67, 312-13
Family rules, *see* Shaming rules
Farrall, Warren, 296, 307
Father
  absence of, 29, 162, 184
  as executor of mother's sentence, 305
  failure to embody the mature masculine, 253
  fantasy, 165
  importance of, 44
  influence of, 57-59
  intimidation by, 42-43
  love from, 156
  neglect by, 264
  relationship with, 69-72   *See also* Father-son
    interaction
Father hunger, 185
Father-son interaction
  cowardice, 38
  example of, 187
  and father's expectations, 265
  Incompleteness and, 213
  power in, 39
  reparenting imagery and, 75-76
  significance of, 154-55
  silent response, 57-59
  underdeveloped, 169
Fear
  of abandonment, 299
  as diagnostic for shame, 281
  excessive, 21
  expression of, impact of shame, 37-38
  as masculine coercive tool, 305
  men's benefit from, 296
  secondary to shame, 4
  and shaming, 263
  why shame causes, 275-76
  women's, 296, 305
"Fearful Shame," 110
Feedback
  projection and, 211
  self-esteem and, 254-55
Feelings,

expression of, 89-90, 112-13, 126-28
types of, 36-38
What does this feeling really want? 291
Female mode of feeling, 121
Feminine, Masculine initiation *vs.*, 274
Feminism, victim, 309
Feminists
  denial by, 296
  inferiority and, 17
"Fifty Males Sitting Together," 50-53
Fitzgerald, Louise, 136
Five Freedoms
  abridgment of, 220-21
  Not allowing the five freedoms rule, 87, 207,
    220-21
  restricting, as spiritual abuse, 221
"Five Stages in Exiling, Hunting and Retrieving
    the Shadow," 94
Fix-it syndrome, 168
The Flying Boy, 119-20
Folk tales, 79-81
Forgiveness
  abuse and, 202
  condoning and, 200-01
  example of, 199-200
  and forgetting, 199-200
  healing effect, 98-99, 203
  living the process, 203-04
  makeup or amend in, 98
  recovery and, 204-05
  as ritual, 196-97
Fossum, Merle, 86-87. 106, 206, 211, 216, 218,
    221
Four Quarters, dancing the, 100-01
Freud, Sigmund, 314
Friedan, Betty, 130
Friendship
  male style of, 262-65
  need for, 42
From Age-ing to Sage-ing, 107-08
Frost, Robert, 60

G

Gagnon, John, 117, 153-66
Gender Codependent Power-Over Matrix, 303-05
Gender reconciliation, 13-14
Gender recovery movement, beginning, 305
Gender differences
  in child rearing, 155
  in intimacy, 234-35
  power struggle, 2-3
Gerotranscendence, 107
Giles, John, 96, 98, and chapter 14
Gilligan, James, 2, 24, 305

Gillette, Douglas, 100, 185, 242
God, companionship with, 104
Gold, symbolic of shame healed, 290-93
Goodness/badness, 231-33
The Grace in Dying, 108
Grandiosity
    confronting shame, 184-85
    the fall, 183-84
    infantile, 186
    model of
        active side, 188-89
        overview, 185-87
        passive side, 187-88
    social implications, 189-90
Grandstander Bully, 242
Grief process, 53, 81, 180
Group therapy, denial and, 178
Grudge holding, 202
Guilt
    awareness of, 144-45
    debilitating, 13
    expression of, 35-36
    inarticulateness and, 144
    incidence of, 145
    shame *vs.*, 12, 78-79, 143, 148-49

H

Hamlet, 61, 314
"Hans" (Grimm brothers), 79-80
Hassim [Ali Baba's brother], 279-80, symbolizes
    hurry and hoarding, 288
    sabotage of healing process, 288
Harris, Ian M., 126-27
Healing process
    integration and, 91-92
    internalized shame, *see* Internalized shame,
        healing process
    need for intensity and passion in, 300
    physical contact and, 40, 44
    requires time and persistence, 8, 283
    risk in, 45
Healing-spiritual energy, 241
Healthy shame, 11, 77-78
Helplessness, men's, facing women's anger, 296
Hidden treasure, symbolic of shame, 281
Hiding, symptom of shame, 4, 5, 262, 287
Higgins, John, 113
Hit the Wall, 91
Holding, significance of, 38-40
"Holding" shame, 185
Homophobia, 113
Honesty, 223, 225
Honor
    code of, directing warrior violence, 304

shame and, 2
violence and, 2
Human potential, 335
Humiliation, in relationships, 70-71, 296-97,
    300-02
Humility, 77, 246, 300
Humor
    blame rule and, 210
    in healing process, 72-73, 126, 152
    masculinity and, 237
Hurt feelings, 81, 82-83

I

Identification
    need for, 41
    taboo against, 41-42
Identity, shame-based, 5-6
Imagery, reparenting, 73-76
"Impenetrable Barrier," 30
Inadequacy, feelings of, 21
Incest, 61, 200-02, 214
Incest Survivors Anonymous, 197
Incompleteness rule
    breaking, 93
    defined, 87, 207
    discussion of, 211-14
Independence, 34
Infancy
    sex role expectations, 16
    shame in, 221
    socialization process, 339
Infantile grandiosity, 186
Inferiority
    feelings of, 34
    male/female feelings, 21-22
    in women, 142
Inherited shame, 59-60, 98
Initiated masculinity, 246-48 *See also* Initiation
Initiation
    benefits of, 169-71, 240-41, 243-46
    energies of, three, 241
    healing shame, 244-46
    illustration of, 239-40
    intentional shaming and, 226
    male styles, 168-69
    mature masculine and, 242-44
    subculture of initiated masculinity, 246-48
    therapy implications, 170-72
Integration, in healing process, 91-92
Intensity, need for in healing, 300
Intentional shaming, 56-59, 226
Internalized shame bind, 37
Internalized shame
    characteristics, 5, 33

defined, 5
healing process
   acknowledgment, 73
   denial, 72
   distress response, 81
   in folk tales, 79-81
   guilt, 77-81
   humor, 72-73
   integration in, 91-92
   internal withdrawal, 72
   relationships, redefining, 68-72
   reparenting imagery, 74-75
   primary shame and, 5
   repairing, 212-13
   resolving, 46-47
   and shame-based identity, 5
   shaming rules and, 7
   toxicity of, 5
Interpersonal Bridges, 93
Interpersonal needs, primary, 39-44
Intimacy
   components of, 234-35
   learning, 235-37
   masculinity and, 236-37
Intuition, trusting, 215, 217
Invisible Dragon
   defined, 1
   fearful, now, 110
   invisibility of, 208-09
   metaphor, 5-6, 8, 86
   shaming rules and, 7
Iron John, A Book About Men, 313
Isolation, in intimacy, 232, 236
I-statements, 193, 210
"I" thinking, 250

J

James, William, 249-52
Japanese society, 42
Jastrab, Joseph, 166
Judgments, 22-26, 323-24, 326-34, 340
Jungian psychology, darkness and light, 50

K

Kammer, Jack, 126
Kaplan, Helen Singer, 130
Kaufman, Gershen, 12, 27, 56-57, 76-79, 81-82,
   106, 113, 221 and chapters 3-5.
Kauth, Bill, 126, 139
Kell, Bill, 44-45
Kindness, that heals shame, 288-93
King archetype, 99-101, 109, 210, 242
Klein, Lucille, 95

Kohut, Heinz, 187
Kubicki, Tony, 135
Kübler-Ross, Elisabeth, 108, 177

L

Landmark Education Corporation, 328
Language
   common, 40
   significance of, 3-4, 9, 10-11
Learned shame, 10
Learning
   from mistakes, 254
   from mother, 21, 25, 149, 299-301
Let Go of Victim, 97
Light, poetry symbolism, 50
"Listen Brothers Listen," 153
"Little Boy Hiding," 96
Love
   acceptance of, 159
   definition of, in depth, 325
   lack of, 188
Lover
   as Archetype, 210, 242
   metaphor, 101
"The Love Song of J. Alfred Prufrock (Eliot), 66
Lovestar, Jim, 127-29
"Loving Moose," Michael, 119-20

M

Macchietto, John, 135-36
Machado, Antonio, poem by, 83-84
Macho men, stereotype, 22, 168
Magician (Magus) archetype, 99, 100, 210, 242
Maintained shame
   overview, 62-66
   rules of, 86-87
"Making A Choice," 332
Male bashing, 19
Male bonding *See also* New Warrior Training
   Adventure *and* Victories of the Heart
   by cellular contact, 169
   from confrontation, 214
   from New Warrior weekend, 100
   proscribed, 135
   by Shadow naming, 95
   by various means, 236-37
Male-female dynamics
   communication and, 171, 225-26
   dark side of, 21-22, 295-300
   displacement in, 308-09
   inferiority/morality issues, 17-21, 143, 304-07
Male identity, 133
Male Identity Development, University of

Wisconsin-Milwaukee, 118
Male initiation groups, 31 *See also* Initiation
Male mode of feeling, 113, 119
Male mode therapy, 113
Male styles, types of, 168
Mandatory counseling
   content of, 135-36
   reasons for, 141
Marx, Karl, 225
Masculinity
   deconstructing, 296
   mature, 13-14, 238
   search for, 236-37
Maslow, Abraham, 219, 249, 256
Masochist, 95, 242
Mason, Marilyn, 86-87, 106, 206, 211, 216, 221
Mature Masculine
   defined, 242
   and facing the Shadow, 243
Maturity, shaming rules and, 207-08
McCarthyism, 225
Meade, Michael, 48, 314
Media, male shame in, 164, 208
Meditation, 105, 258
Mediterranean cultures, 42
Men Freeing Men, 117
Men in Therapy: The Challenge of Change, 119
Mendelson, Eric, 146-47
Men's conferences, 115-16
Men's Councils, 247
Men's Forum, Ottawa/Hull, 294-97
Men's Movement
   function of, 247
   healing process and, 138-39
   love and, 159
   media and, 117
   men's rights, 310
   mythopoetic, 310, 315
   Ottawa, divided, 296
   profeminist, 310
"The Men's Room" *see* "Victories of the Heart"
Mental keys, 88
Mentoring, 240, 246
Metaphors, 6, 54, 86, 100
"Me" thinking, 250
Missing twin force, 55
Mission
   initiation and, 169, 245
   need for, 172
Mistakes
   acceptance of, 28
   incidence of, 28
   learning from, 254
   tolerance for, 231

Mistrust
   of caregivers, 269
   turned inward, 269
Modesty, 77
Moore, Robert, 100-01, 185, 187, 242
Moral Intimidation rule
   breaking, 95, 100
   defined, 87, 207
   discussion of, 221-22
   examples of, 295-97, 300-02, 309
Moral power, 303-06, 309
Morality
   feminist approach, 17-18, 308
   honoring, 19
   women's superiority in, 150
Morgiana, 280, symbolizes
   awareness and decisive action, 290
   kindness, enslaved in men, 290
   need to 'marry' a disowned part, 290
Mother, *see also* Mother Wound
   absence of, 64
   dominant, 185
   as emotional resource, 169
   as judge and jury, 305
   learning from, 21, 25, 149, 299-301
   nurturance from, 239
Mother Wound
   deeper part of, 301
   discovery of, 300
   as essential shame, 313
   general discussion of, 294-316
   and perceived disqualification for leadership,
      297
   recovery from, 300ff
Motivation, *see also* Drives
   deficiency, 256-57
   hierarchy of, 219
Music, effect of, 46
Mythopoetic approaches, 9
Myth, power of, 23-24

N

Name It, 88-89, 94, 103
National Coalition of Free Men (NCFM), 137
Nearing Death Experience, 108
Neediness, 271
Needs, denial of men's, 271
Neglect, 5, 264-65
New Warrior Training Adventure, 31, 91, 102,
      139, 169, 210, 246-47, 325
North of Boston (Frost), 60
No Talk rule
   breaking, 96, 103
   defined, 87, 207

discussion of, 215-16, 218
Not Allowing the Five Freedoms rule
   defined, 87, 207
   discussion of, 220-21
Nudity, 61
Numb feeling, from shame, 286, 305
Nurturance, significance of, 39, 158-59

O

Oedipus, 314
"Open Sesame," 279-287, symbolizes
   accepting full authority for true experience,
      284
   confronting fear of annihilation, 284
   opening to shame feelings, 282
   the power to feel, 283
   recognition of shame, 282
   trusting all one's feelings, 283-84
Oppression, male, 139-40
Oppressor, men branded as, 296
Orphan, Experience the, 95, 99
Outreach programs, 133
Overachievement, 20
Overwork, 232-33

P

Paradox
   embracing, 99-100
   in aging, 107
   in healing shame, avoid further shaming,
      284-85
Paralysis, of self, 33
Parents, *see also* Father, Mother
   abusive, 196-202
   influence of, 54-57
Passive therapy, 115
Passivity, 64
The Path of Least Resistance, 121
Patriarchy, 92, 225-26
Pearson, Carol, 95
Pence, Ellen, 135
Penis envy, 4
Perception, 57, 135-36
Perfectionism rule
   breaking, 90, 91, 95, 98, 100, 105
   defined, 87, 207
   discussion of, 210-11
   as shame reduction strategy, 36
Persecutor role, 7, 97, 191-94
Personal goodness, *see* Goodness/badness
Personal growth programs, 118-19
Pessimism, 138-39
Phobias, 39-40
Physical connection, importance of, 44, 169

Physical keys, 88
Physiological drive system, 82
Plane of existence, 25, 322-24, 326-27
Poems, and excerpts therefrom
   by Antonio Machado, 83-84
   by John Giles, 205
   "Fearful Shame," 110
   "Fifty Males Sitting Together," 50-53
   "Impenetrable Barrier," 30
   "Listen, Brothers, Listen," 153
   "Little Boy Hiding," 96
   "The Love Song of J. Alfred Prufrock," 66
   "Making A Choice," 332
   "North of Boston," 60
   "Rowing the Rio," 99
   "Tongues Untied," 195
Poetry, symbolism in, 50-53
Poisonous pedagogy, 7-8
Political correctness, 224-25, 242, 304
Porter, Bob, 118-19
Portugal, Buddy, 117-18
Positive shame, 11, 35
Potent Blessing, 109
Power
   of beauty, 3, 307
   of the breast, 3
   denial of, by women, 310
   from drawing empathy, 302
   female, 301
   gender, perception of, 298
   of the hearth, 3
   miscalculation of, 3, 306-08
   need for, 3, 39
   in psychotherapy process, 135-37
   real, misperceived as absent, 297-98, 307
   of shame, 304
   as shame reduction strategy, 36
   women's
      internal: moral, emotional, sexual, 303-08
      less visible, unrecognized, 303
Powerlessness
   denial of, by men, 310
   false, 297
Power-Over Matrix, Gender Codependent,
      303-05
Preaching, 20
Prejudice, 295
Presence, spirituality and, 104
Primary affects, 4,
Primary shame
   bring it out of the closet, 8
   defined, 4
   manifestations of, 86
   shaming threats and, 223

"Primordial male," 133
Process of Unshaming, 287-90
Procrastination, 212
Projection, 94, 211
Provider and provided for, as male role, 289
Psychic umbilical cord, 314
Psychological inventory, 69
Psychotherapist, choosing a, 8-9, 106
Psychotherapy
  avoidance of, 132
  cost issue, 129, 137
  fear of, 121
  feminist ideology, 131, 135-38
  as healing program, 106
  irrelevance of, 137
  men's difficulty with, 121,123-26, 135-38,
    170-71
  perception of, as male hostile, 129-33
  public acceptance of, 133-34
  reluctance about, 140-41
  resistance to, 170
  setting for, 135
  shame in, 137, 140
  submission and, 171
  threat of, 119
Public shaming and humiliation, 225, 304

R

Rackets, 6
Rage, *see also* Anger
  abuse and, 202
  as shame reduction strategy, 35, 83
Rebirthing, 55, 75
Reciprocity, law of, 255
Recognize Shame, 87-88
Recovery, five stages of
  acceptance, 180
  acting out, 178
  anger, 180
  denial, 178
  grief 180
  overview, 177-80
Recovery movement, 33
Recurrent shame, 113
Reformation, transformation *vs.,* 7-8
Rejection
  false self and, 66-67
  and reunion, alternating, 300
Relationships
  with father, 69-72 *See also* Father-son
    interaction
  in healing process, 68-72
  need for, 39-40
  significance of, 336-37

  vertical, 92
Remedies, spiritual, and emotional bypass, 283
Reparenting
  imagery, 73-76
  purpose of, 165-66
Rescue triangle
  boundaries and, 92
  characteristics, 191-92
  examples of, 23, 191-93
  Victim and, 97
Rescuer role, 7, 97
Respect, significance of, 3, 95, 224
Revenge, 202, 204
*Revolt of the Primitive: An Inquiry into the Roots
  of Political Correctness,* 304
Rhetorical questions, 214, 222
Ridicule, 72
Ring, Al, 113
Rituals
  archetypes and, 101
  of forgiveness, 196-97, 203
  initiation rites, 162, 266-69
  in men's movement, 139
  shadow naming, 94-95, 218
Robertson, John, 136
Role behavior, nontraditional, 136, 138
Role reversal, 92, 214
"Rowing the Rio," 99

S

Sadist, 95, 242
Safety
  defined, 114
  lack of, 16-17
Sages, 107-08
Sarcasm, 72, 214
Sartre's shudder, 4
Satir, Virginia, 220
Schenk, Roy, 14, 112-13, 140-42, 221 and
    chapters 2 and 23
Schneider, Carl, 27, 106
Schultz, LeRoy, 135-37
Schwartz, Howard, 304
The Scientific Method, 318
Secondary reactions, 33
Self-acceptance, 88, 207, 319
Self-actualization theory, 256-57
Self-anaesthetization, 305
Self-awareness, 168, 170
Self-blame, 79, 221
Self-consciousness, 34
Self-contempt, 79, 228-29, 254
Self-creation, 105
Self-destructive behavior, 15-17, 232

Self-doubt, 8, 14, 21, 209, 212, 216
Self-esteem
    defined, 251-52
    erosion of, 171
    improvement steps, 252-59
    low, 154
    theory of, William James's, 250-51
    types of, 251-52
Self-help groups, emotional needs and, 132-33
Self-love, 158-59, 163-66, 305, 336
Self-protection, 129, 131
Self psychology, infantile grandiosity, 186
Self-reflection, 255
Self-seeking, 251
Self-sufficiency, 34,
Self-surveillance, 88
Self-victimization, 198
Seligman, Martin, 138
Seminars, 114
Seneca Falls Declaration of 1848, 18
Sex, as a "sellers market," 306
Sex Compulsives Anonymous, 197
Sex drive, 82
Sexual abuse
    impact of, 61, 197-98, 201, 204
    perpetrator, 65
    sorrow and, 203
    victims of, 65
    by women, 136, 196-97, 199-201
Sexual
    deviations, as displacement, 308-09
    functioning, 82
    harassment, 19-20, 136
Sexual power, 306-08
Sexuality
    damage to, 232
    significance of, 116
    as target of shame, 267-68
Shackleton, David, 294-316
Shadow
    of archetypes, 101
    bipolar, 101
    characteristics, 13
    defined, 13
    eating the, 94-95
    facing, 242-43
    false self and, 66-67
    feminine, 301
    mature masculine and, 243
    naming, 94, 218
Shadow fighting, 298
Shadow Lover, 242
Shadow of the King, 95
Shame, see also Shame of Maleness, Shaming

ashamed of feeling shame, 277-79
attack, 45
awareness of, 276
basic dynamic, 264
begets shame, 261, 278
causes of, 48-67, 261-66
Chronic, 268-70, 274-78, 281
cycles, 63-64
defined, 32-33, 264, 304-05
as early psychic wound, 305
as emotional response, 265-67
as feminine coercive tool, 306
feels like cold, 305
flooding, 6
forms of, 34-35
and gender roles, 270-71
healing without further shaming, 274, 281-82,
    284-85, 288
healthy, 11, 77-78
invisibility of, 310
modeled by caregivers, 263
must be taught, 261
as normal master-control of men's feelings,
    261, 278
passive, 264-65
positive, 35-36
power of, 296-97, 304, 310
reduction strategies, 45-47
strategies against, 45-47
subtlety of, 263-65, 310
targets of, 267
as two-level experience, 268, 273-75
universality of, 261, 305
and violence, 2, 24-27, 264-66
Shame of Maleness
    and Basic Male Shame, 21
    defined, 16-21
    manifestations of, 25-27
    men's movement, 28-31
    violence and, 25-27
Shame-rage, 81
Shaming
    and affirmation, alternating, 300
    by body language, 295
    defined, 304
    expected, as men claim moral power, 310
    inadvertent, 206-09, 222
    intentional, 226
    manipulation by, 300
    men for being men, 225-26
    obvious, aggressive, 263
    rules, see Shaming Rules
    sources of, 17-20
    tactics, political correctness and, 224-25

threats, 223-24, 302
Shaming rules
  breaking, 206-07, 252 [and under each
    specific rule]
  confrontation and, 207, 212-15
  impact of, 10, 207-09
  overview, 10, 206-09, 222
  response to, 207-09
  specific rules
    Blame, 207, 210
    Control, 207, 209
    Denial, 207, 215, 218, 303
    Disqualification, 207-08, 217-18
    Incompleteness, 207-08, 211-15
    Moral Intimidation, 207, 221-22
    No Talk, 207,215-16, 218
    Not Allowing the Five Freedoms, 207,
      220-21
    Perfectionism, 207, 210-11
    Unreliability, 207,219-20
Shuddering, as primary shame, 4, 8
Shyness, 34
Silent response, 57-59, 265-66
Singh, Kathleen, 108
Smith, Cyprean, 99
Social connection, need for, 293
Social importance of healing shame, 2-3, 292-93
Social me, 250-51
Social work, reexamination of, 133-37
Socialization
  female *vs.* male, 133
  impact of, 339
Soft males, stereotype, 168, 170
Solutions, not problems, 116, 139
Sorrow, sexual abuse and, 203
Soul protector, therapist as, 169, 171-72
Spiritual abuse, 3, 221
Spiritual me, 250-51
Spirituality
  abuse and, 221
  description, 103
  God, relationship with, 103-04
  healing and, 14, 240-41
  twelve-step programs, 103-04
  reintegration in, 240
  relation to shame, 338-39
  significance of, 104, 116
Standards, in relationships, 336-37
Steinem, Gloria, 130
Stereotyping events, 155
Stevens, Wallace, 63
Subculture of initiated masculinity, 246-248

Sullivan, Harry Stack, 249, 258
Support groups
  benefits of, 94-95, 103, 106, 214
  disadvantages of, 104, 106, 133
  failures of, 132-33
  function of, 126,
  physical activity, 133

T

Taboos
  crying, 36-37, 81, 270
  eye contact, 41-42
  identification with father, 42-43
  types of, 215
Talk About It, 90-91, 93
Teaching-bonding energy, 241
Tertiary shame, 6
Therapist, function of, 170-72
Therapy, *see* Psychotherapy
Threats, shaming, 223-24
Tick, Ed, 166
Toleration, 57
Tone of voice
  in conversation, 3-4
  response to, 225
  significance of, 3, 90, 222, 226
Tosi, Rich, 114, 141
Touch, significance of, 38-41, 45, 201
Transformation
  power of, 328-29
  reformation and, 7-8
Trust
  betrayal of, 216, 219
  in healing process, 101
  significance of, 139, 219, 258
"Tongues Untied," 195
Twelve-step programs, 8, 103-04, 319-21 *See
    also* Alcoholics Anonymous
Tyrant, 242

U

Unshaming, process of, 287-90
Unreliability rule
  breaking, 93, 100, 207, 219-20
  defined, 87, 207
Unworthiness, 12, 228-29

V

Validation, men's by women, felt strongest by
  sexual contact, 306
Verbal aggression, 26-27
Vertical relationships, 92

Victim
   history of, significance of, 180
   remaining a, 198
   role (manipulative), 7, 89, 93, 97, 99, 301-02
   as stuck place, 302
Victimization, self, 198
Victories of the Heart weekend, 103
Violence
   "dissing" (disrespect) and, 2
   intergender, studies of, 304
   shame and, 2, 24-27, 264-66
   against women, 295
Violence Against Women Act, 23, 233
Vision of the Future, 334ff.
Visualization, reparenting, 73-75
Vulgarity, xi, 3-4
Vulnerabilities
   denial of, 235
   emotional needs and, 132
   gender differences, 3
   maintained by shame, 65
   reactions to, 132
   therapy and, 127

W

Wants, shame suppresses knowing, 291-92
Warrior archetype, 101, 242
Weakling Abdicator, 242
What does this feeling really want? 291

White Knight assumptions, 109
Who am I? 271-73
'Wild Man,' The, 313-14
Williamson, Tom, 133-37, 140
Wilson Schaef, Anne, 49
Withdrawal
   in healing process, 68-69, 72
   as silent response, 57-58
Women, see also Male-female dynamics
   anger toward, 126, 215, 227
   as innocent victims, 300ff
   negotiations with, 170-71
   relationships with, 167-68
   as source of men's shame, 149-152
Women's liberation movement, 131
Work, overvaluation of, 34
World view
   future visions, 334-40
   new, 324
   present, 323-24
   transformation, power of, 328-29
Woundedness, goodness and, 232-33
Wounding-testing-separating energy, 240
Wounds, acknowledgment of, 96

Y

Your problem, 193
You-statements, 210

God cannot judge, love's deminishment.

For many years both editors struggled individually to understand the negative forces and feelings that were harming us and holding us back. We each came to the conclusion that what hurt us most was the embarrassment, fear of exposure, negative messages and inadequacy feelings that are combined under the term: Shame. We discovered that shame is a silent emotion, and one that we usually bypass quickly to land in anger, fear or depression. We learned that — paradoxically — shame loses most of its toxicity when we allow ourselves to feel it, talk about it, and even joke about it and become friendly with it.

We've talked to many other men who also feel 'shackled' by the power of shame. Once we compared notes, we decided to collaborate in writing/editing this book, both to help ourselves and to assist others to 'break the shackles' that inhibit us as men.

Roy U. Schenk and John Everingham